Marquee Series

Office

Microsoft®

2010

Instructor's Guide

Nita Rutkosky

Denise Seguin

Audrey Rutkosky Roggenkamp

Paradigm
PUBLISHING

St. Paul • Indianapolis

Senior Editor: Brenda Owens
Production Editor: Donna Mears
Cover Designer: Leslie Anderson
Production Specialist: Ryan Hamner

Care has been taken to verify the accuracy of information presented in this book. However, the authors, editors, and publisher cannot accept responsibility for Web, email, newsgroup, or chat room subject matter or content, or for consequences from application of the information in this book, and make no warranty, expressed or implied, with respect to its content.

Trademarks: Some of the product names and company names included in this book have been used for identification purposes only and may be trademarks or registered trade names of their respective manufacturers and sellers. The authors, editors, and publisher disclaim any affiliation, association, or connection with, or sponsorship or endorsement by, such owners.

We have made every effort to trace the ownership of all copyrighted material and to secure permission from copyright holders. In the event of any question arising as to the use of any material, we will be pleased to make the necessary corrections in future printings. Thanks are due to the aforementioned authors, publishers, and agents for permission to use the materials indicated.

ISBN 978-0-76383-773-0 (IG & CD)
ISBN 978-0-76383-769-3 (IG)

© Paradigm Publishing, Inc.
875 Montreal Way
St. Paul, MN 55102
Email: educate@emcp.com
Website: www.emcp.com

Printed in the United States of America

19 18 17 16 15 14 13 12   2 3 4 5 6 7 8 9 10

Contents

Note: Lesson Blueprints providing detailed lesson plans for a 16-week course are provided on the Instructor disc and on the Internet Resource Center.

End-of-Section Rubrics

Supplemental Skills Assessments and Rubrics

Supplemental Marquee Challenges and Rubrics

Note: Project Model Answers are provided in the student textbook at the beginning of each section.

Planning the Course

Most educators would agree that the key to teaching a successful course is careful, thorough planning. And, as noted in *Exceptional Teaching: Ideas in Action*, published by Paradigm Publishing, "Instructors assess, plan, implement, and evaluate . . . repeatedly. They do this based on many of the factors that make teaching learner-centered and on several other variables. Before students even think about entering or logging into the classroom, instructors make decisions about the course. These begin with identifying the heart of the course. That is, what, exactly, are the most important outcomes that students should achieve? And what plan of action can the instructor devise that will help ensure those outcomes?" Thinking through a course action plan typically includes four phases:

1. Developing the course outcomes
2. Determining the course delivery mode and structure (dividing the course into parts, each with outcomes)
3. Selecting the course's instructional approach, resources, and activities
4. Developing an assessment strategy

Developing Course Outcomes

In developing course outcomes, some of the key issues to consider are the following:

- When this course is over, in what ways will the learner be permanently changed? Should instruction result in
  - o building knowledge?
  - o developing higher-order thinking?
  - o developing independent learning skills?
  - o developing technical literacy?
- Think about the course content in terms of what types of problems are faced.
  - o What decisions are made?
  - o What must be communicated?
  - o Under what conditions is the work performed on the job?
  - o How will the performer learn the work is satisfactory?
  - o How will the performer receive feedback?

Considering the questions above, a set of end-of-course outcomes for a one-semester class on Microsoft Office 2010 could include the following items, stated as performances. At course conclusion, the student will be able to:

- Use Word 2010 to create and edit a representative range of professional-quality documents common to academic, personal, and workplace environments, including letters, research reports, and newsletters.
- Use Excel 2010 to create and format spreadsheets with a variety of numerical data and then manipulate the data to analyze financial trends and forecast economic outcomes.
- Use Access 2010 to build databases and then perform queries and create reports that provide the foundation for planning and decision making.
- Prepare visually attractive and informative presentations using PowerPoint 2010.
- When presented with a typical workplace scenario, determine what type of informational documents are required and prepare them using the appropriate software, which may include integrating data from two or more programs in the Office suite.

For another, more detailed, version of the course outcomes for a one-semester class in Office 2010 consider the following:

- Analyze, synthesize, and evaluate school, work, or home situations and use application software to complete information-processing tasks efficiently and effectively.
- Access the Internet and use the browse, search, and hyperlink capabilities of Web browsers.
- Learn strategies for merging and integrating source data from different applications.
- Create, design, and produce professional documents using basic word processing software. Topics include design options for formatting and layout, strategies for working with multiple documents, and techniques for using templates and predesigned styles.
- Process, manipulate, and represent numeric data using the basic functions of spreadsheet software. Functions include: using formatting techniques for preparing a spreadsheet, creating and testing formulas, using multiple worksheets, exploring what-if scenarios, and converting to chart formats.
- Plan, structure, and create databases for efficient data access and retrieval using database software. Functions include: search and sort capabilities for extracting data, data retrieval commands, techniques for record specification, and design options for report layout.
- Design and create informational and motivational slides using presentation software and images that contain hyperlinks, tables, clip art, and animation.

Determining the Course Delivery Mode and Structure

Frequently, the course structure has been determined previously by your department. However, if you are in a position to develop a plan or modify an existing structure, consider these questions:

- What topics in each subject area are essential for demonstrating the course outcomes?
- Is this the only course that will address this subject and skill set?
- What do students already know about each subject? What can they learn on their own independent of your direct instruction?
- Where in each subject will the instruction "begin" and "end"?

Your answers to these questions will help you divide the course content into parts and identify the associated learning outcomes (also called performance objectives). Note that course outcomes are marked by higher and more challenging skill sets and typically require the integration of many skills, while unit or part outcomes are more narrowly defined and focused.

Course Delivery: Traditional Classroom, Online (Distance Learning), or Hybrid?

While the core considerations are the same whether you are planning a traditional on-campus course, an online course (also called a distance learning course), or a hybrid of the two courses, the instructional delivery differences create distinct needs you must address in the planning stage. A critical challenge in teaching online courses is the issue of interacting with students. How will you communicate with them? How will they submit assignments and tests? How will you deliver feedback? How will you get to know your students?

Here are some additional questions to consider when planning an online or hybrid course, as suggested in *Exceptional Teaching*:

1. What course management system will be used: Blackboard, WebCT, or some other platform?
2. Will you offer a Web course where everything is done online? Or will you teach a course where students work independently offline and use the course management system to review course outcomes, the syllabus, and assignment due dates; communicate with the instructor; take online quizzes; transmit completed work; and participate in chat sessions?
3. Will you have an on-campus orientation meeting with your students at the beginning of the course? In some situations, because of the distance factor, students will not be able to come to campus. However, if feasible, by all means do so. Many students will likely have the same questions that can be answered at one time, and the face-to-face contact at an orientation will benefit both you and the students.
4. Will the students come to the campus or school to take exams? If not, will students be directed to offsite locations where exams can be administered to verify that the person taking the exam is indeed the person getting credit for the course? It is critical that this step be set up before the online class begins.
5. What PC configuration and/or software requirements must a student have to participate in your online course?

Both the student and instructor resources offered with *Marquee Series Microsoft Office 2010* can be adapted for use in an online learning environment or a hybrid of traditional and online learning contexts. The SNAP Training and Assessment product, in particular, is well-suited for these course delivery modes, and the Blackboard files are expressly designed for a distance learning situation.

The Syllabus

A comprehensive syllabus should help you and your students prepare for each part of the class. Syllabi are useful for both traditional, on-campus courses as well as courses that are delivered online. Generally, the following elements are included in a syllabus:

1. Course identifying data
2. Prerequisites
3. Instructor contact information
4. Course outcomes
5. Required course resources
6. Major assignments
7. Grade composition
8. Class structure
9. Course schedule
10. College/school requirements

Figure 1 is an example of a traditional, on-campus course syllabus designed for a 16-week course that meets three times a week designed to use *Marquee Series Microsoft Office 2010*. Figure 2 is an example of a 16-week online course covering the same material. Lesson plans, called Lesson Blueprints, which correspond to the syllabus in Figure 1 are available on the Instructor Resources disc and on the password-protected instructor resources on the textbook's Internet Resource Center.

Figure 1. Traditional 16-Week Semester Syllabus Example

Course Description

This course prepares students to work with Microsoft Office 2010 in a career setting or for personal use. Using courseware that incorporates an accelerated, step-by-step, project-based approach, students develop an introductory-level competency in Word, Excel, Access, and PowerPoint 2010 and explore the essential features of Windows 7 and Internet Explorer 8.0. Students also develop an understanding of key ethical issues they will face in the context of using information technology.

Prerequisites: None

Instructor Contact Information
- **Name:**
- **Office Phone:**
- **Office Email:**
- **Office Location:**
- **Office Hours:**

Required Course Resources
- Marquee Series Microsoft Office 2010 with Windows 7 and Internet Explorer 8.0, by Rutkosky/Seguin/Rutkosky, © Paradigm Publishing Inc.
- Student Resources CD (provided with textbook)
- Internet Resource Center, www.emcp.net/Marquee10
- USB flash drive

Computer Time

Approximately six to eight hours per week of computer time outside of class is recommended for successful completion of course requirements.

Grading

Final grades will be calculated as follows:

Average of all Knowledge Check assignments	5%
Average of all Skills Review assignments	15%
Average of all Skills Assessment assignments	20%
Average of all Marquee Challenge assignments	20%
Average of all Integrating Skills Review assignments	10%
Average of all supplemental activities and/or tests	30%

College and Course Policy Information
- This college conforms to the provisions of the Americans with Disabilities Act. You are invited to report any special needs to your instructor.
- Your attendance is expected at all class sessions. Excessive unexcused absences may result in withdrawal from the class.
- We subscribe to the college policy on academic honesty found in the school catalog.

Course Schedule

Week	Class	Program, Section	Lesson Plan File*
1	1	Windows 7, Section 1: Exploring Windows 7	Marquee10_Blueprint01_7S1.doc
	2	Windows 7, Section 2: Maintaining Files and Customizing Windows	Marquee10_Blueprint02_7S2.doc
	3	Internet Explorer 8.0, Section 1: Browsing the Internet Using Internet Explorer 8.0	Marquee10_Blueprint03_IE8S1.doc
2	4	Word, Section 1: Creating and Editing a Document	Marquee10_Blueprint04_WordS1.doc
	5	Word, Section 1: Creating and Editing a Document	Marquee10_Blueprint05_WordS1.doc
	6	Word, Section 2: Formatting Characters and Paragraphs	Marquee10_Blueprint06_WordS2.doc
3	7	Word, Section 2: Formatting Characters and Paragraphs	Marquee10_Blueprint07_WordS2.doc
	8	Word, Section 3: Formatting and Enhancing a Document	Marquee10_Blueprint08_WordS3.doc
	9	Word, Section 3: Formatting and Enhancing a Document	Marquee10_Blueprint09_WordS3.doc
4	10	Word, Section 4: Formatting with Special Features	Marquee10_Blueprint10_WordS4.doc
	11	Word, Section 4: Formatting with Special Features	Marquee10_Blueprint11_WordS4.doc
	12	Test	Marqucc10_Blueprint12_Test.doc
5	13	Excel, Section 1: Analyzing Data Using Excel	Marquee10_Blueprint13_ExcelS1.doc
	14	Excel, Section 1: Analyzing Data Using Excel	Marquee10_Blueprint14_ExcelS1.doc
	15	Excel, Section 2: Editing and Formatting Worksheets	Marquee10_Blueprint15_ExcelS2.doc
6	16	Excel, Section 2: Editing and Formatting Worksheets	Marquee10_Blueprint16_ExcelS2.doc
	17	Excel, Section 3: Using Functions, Setting Print Options, and Adding Visual Elements	Marquee10_Blueprint17_ExcelS3.doc
	18	Excel, Section 3: Using Functions, Setting Print Options, and Adding Visual Elements	Marquee10_Blueprint18_ExcelS3.doc
7	19	Excel, Section 4: Working with Multiple Worksheets, Tables, and Other File Formats	Marquee10_Blueprint19_ExcelS4.doc
	20	Excel, Section 4: Working with Multiple Worksheets, Tables, and Other File Formats	Marquee10_Blueprint20_ExcelS4.doc
	21	Integrating Word and Excel	Marquee10_Blueprint21_Integrating1.doc

Week	Class	Program, Section	Lesson Plan File*
8	22	Integrating Word and Excel	Marquee10_Blueprint22_Integrating1.doc
	23	Test	Marquee10_Blueprint23_Test.doc
	24	Access, Section 1: Maintaining Data in Access Tables	Marquee10_Blueprint24_AccesS1.doc
9	25	Access, Section 1: Maintaining Data in Access Tables	Marquee10_Blueprint25_AccesS1.doc
	26	Access, Section 2: Creating Tables and Relationships	Marquee10_Blueprint26_AccessS2.doc
	27	Access, Section 2: Creating Tables and Relationships	Marquee10_Blueprint27_AccessS2.doc
10	28	Access, Section 3: Creating Queries, Forms, and Reports	Marquee10_Blueprint28_AccessS3.doc
	29	Access, Section 3: Creating Queries, Forms, and Reports	Marquee10_Blueprint29_AccessS3.doc
	30	Access, Section 4: Summarizing Data and Calculating in Forms and Reports	Marquee10_Blueprint30_AccessS4.doc
11	31	Access, Section 4: Summarizing Data and Calculating in Forms and Reports	Marquee10_Blueprint31_AccessS4.doc
	32	Integrating Word, Excel, and Access	Marquee10_Blueprint32_Integrating2.doc
	33	Integrating Word, Excel, and Access	Marquee10_Blueprint33_Integrating2.doc
12	34	Test	Marquee10_Blueprint34_Test.doc
	35	PowerPoint, Section 1: Preparing a Presentation	Marquee10_Blueprint35_PowerPointS1.doc
	36	PowerPoint, Section 1: Preparing a Presentation	Marquee10_Blueprint36_PowerPointS1.doc
13	37	PowerPoint, Section 2: Editing and Enhancing Slides	Marquee10_Blueprint37_PowerPointS2.doc
	38	PowerPoint, Section 2: Editing and Enhancing Slides	Marquee10_Blueprint38_PowerPointS2.doc
	39	PowerPoint, Section 2: Editing and Enhancing Slides	Marquee10_Blueprint39_PowerPointS2.doc
14	40	PowerPoint, Section 3: Customizing a Presentation	Marquee10_Blueprint40_PowerPointS3.doc
	41	PowerPoint, Section 3: Customizing a Presentation	Marquee10_Blueprint41_PowerPointS3.doc
	42	Review/Catch-up	Marquee10_Blueprint42_Review.doc
15	43	Integrating Word, Excel, and PowerPoint	Marquee10_Blueprint43_Integrating3.doc
	44	Integrating Word, Excel, and PowerPoint	Marquee10_Blueprint44_Integrating3.doc
	45	Review	Marquee10_Blueprint45_Review.doc
16	46	Test Week	Marquee10_Blueprint46-48_Test.doc
	47		Marquee10_ Blueprint46-48_Test
	48		Marquee10_ Blueprint46-48_Test

*Lesson Plan Blueprint files are located on the Instructor Resources disc and the Internet Resource Center.

Figure 2. Online 16-Week Semester Syllabus Example

Course Description

This course prepares students to work with Microsoft Office 2010 in a career setting or for personal use. Using courseware that incorporates an accelerated, step-by-step, project-based approach, students develop an introductory-level competency in Word, Excel, Access, and PowerPoint 2010 and explore the essential features of Windows 7 and Internet Explorer 8.0. Students also develop an understanding of key ethical issues they will face in the context of using information technology.

Prerequisites: None

Instructor Contact Information
    Name:
    Office Phone:
    Office Email:
    Office Location:
    Office Hours:

Required Course Resources

- *Marquee Series Microsoft Office 2010 with Windows 7 and Internet Explorer 8.0,* by Rutkosky/Seguin/Rutkosky, © Paradigm Publishing Inc.
- Student Resources CD (provided with textbook)
- Internet Resource Center, www.emcp.net/Marquee10
- USB flash drive

Computer Time

Approximately six to eight hours per week of computer time is recommended for successful completion of course requirements.

Grading

Final grades will be calculated as follows:

Average of all Knowledge Check assignments	5%
Average of all Skills Review assignments	15%
Average of all Skills Assessment assignments	20%
Average of all Marquee Challenge assignments	20%
Average of all Integrating Skills Review assignments	10%
Average of all supplemental activities and/or tests	30%

College and Course Policy Information

- This college conforms to the provisions of the Americans with Disabilities Act. You are invited to report any special needs to your instructor.
- We subscribe to the college policy on academic honesty found in the school catalog.

Course Schedule

Week	Program/Section/Additional Activities
1	Windows 7, Section 1: Exploring Windows 7
	Windows 7, Section 2: Maintaining Files and Customizing Windows
	Internet Explorer 8.0, Section 1: Browsing the Internet Using Internet Explorer 8.0
	Word, Section 1: Creating and Editing a Document
2	Word, Section 2: Formatting Characters and Paragraphs
3	Word, Section 3: Formatting and Enhancing a Document
4	Word, Section 4: Formatting with Special Features
	Supplemental Word Activity or Test
5	Excel, Section 1: Analyzing Data Using Excel
6	Excel, Section 2: Editing and Formatting Worksheets
	Excel, Section 3: Using Functions, Setting Print Options, and Adding Visual Elements
7	Excel, Section 4: Working with Multiple Worksheets, Formatting Sheet Tabs
8	Integrating Programs: Word and Excel
	Supplemental Excel Activity or Test
	Access, Section 1: Maintaining Data in Access Tables
9	Access, Section 1: Maintaining Data in Access Tables
	Access, Section 2: Creating Tables and Relationships
10	Access, Section 3: Creating Queries, Forms, and Reports
11	Access, Section 4: Summarizing Data and Calculating in Forms and Reports
12	Integrating Programs: Word, Excel, and Access
	Supplemental Access Activity or Test
13	PowerPoint, Section 1: Preparing a Presentation
14	PowerPoint, Section 2: Editing and Enhancing Slides
15	PowerPoint, Section 3: Customizing a Presentation
	Integrating Programs: Word, Excel, and PowerPoint
16	Supplemental PowerPoint Activity or Test
	Supplemental Integrating Activity or Test

Selecting the Instructional Approach, Resources, and Activities

After the course outcomes and structure are determined, it is important to plan the main content of the course. This includes selecting courseware, identifying resources for English language learners, considering instructional support materials, and reviewing other resources.

Student Courseware

Selecting high-quality student courseware is an important step in the planning process. Learning materials should be engaging and accessible. The Marquee Series offers several valuable learning tools to support course performance objectives.

- *Marquee Series Microsoft Office 2010* textbook with Student Resources CD
- Student Internet Resource Center at www.emcp.net/Marquee10
- SNAP Training and Assessment software
- Blackboard Cartridge platform

Textbook Structure

Marquee Series Microsoft Office 2010 prepares students to work with Microsoft Office 2010 in a business office or for personal use. Incorporating an accelerated, step-by-step, project-based approach, this text builds student competency in Word, Excel, Access, and PowerPoint 2010 and the essential features of Windows 7 and Internet Explorer 8.0. The Marquee Series is made up of the following textbooks:

- *Marquee Series Microsoft Office 2010 with Windows 7 and Internet Explorer 8.0*
  - Information Technology Essentials
  - Windows 7 (Sections 1–2)
  - Internet Explorer 8.0 (Section 1)
  - Word 2010 (Sections 1–4)
  - Excel 2010 (Section 1–4)
  - Integrating Programs: Word and Excel
  - Access 2010 (Sections 1–4)
  - Integrating Programs: Word, Excel, and Access
  - PowerPoint 2010 (Sections 1–3)
  - Integrating Programs: Word, Excel, and PowerPoint
- *Marquee Series Microsoft Office 2010 Brief Edition with Windows 7 and Internet Explorer 8.0*
  - Information Technology Essentials
  - Windows 7 (Sections 1–2)
  - Internet Explorer 8.0 (Section 1)
  - Word 2010 (Sections 1–3)
  - Excel 2010 (Section 1–3)
  - Access 2010 (Sections 1–3)
  - PowerPoint 2010 (Sections 1–2)
  - Integrating Programs: Word, Excel, Access, and PowerPoint
- *Marquee Series Microsoft Word 2010*
  - Windows 7 (Sections 1–2)
  - Internet Explorer 8.0 (Section 1)
  - Word 2010 (Sections 1–4)

- *Marquee Series Microsoft Excel 2010*
  - Windows 7 (Sections 1–2)
  - Internet Explorer 8.0 (Section 1)
  - Excel 2010 (Section 1–4)
  - Integrating Programs: Word and Excel
- *Marquee Series Microsoft Access 2010*
  - Windows 7 (Sections 1–2)
  - Internet Explorer 8.0 (Section 1)
  - Access 2010 (Sections 1–4)
  - Integrating Programs: Word, Excel, and Access
- *Marquee Series Microsoft PowerPoint 2010*
  - Windows 7 (Sections 1–2)
  - Internet Explorer 8.0 (Section 1)
  - PowerPoint 2010 (Sections 1–3)
  - Integrating Programs: Word, Excel, and PowerPoint

All of the textbooks in the Marquee Series introduce each program in the Microsoft Office suite of programs with a program opener that provides an overview of the software's best uses and gives students a preview of the software features and workplace applications. The openers also provide an overview and visual representation of some of the projects that students will complete.

Following the program openers, the first in a series of three or four section openers lists the skills to be taught and provides an overview of the projects that will be completed in the corresponding section. Next, the model answers for the projects that students complete in each section provide a preview of the finished projects before students begin working and allow them to compare their own results with these models to ensure that they have created the materials accurately. Instructors can access live files of the model answers for the section activities on the Instructor disc and on the Instructor Internet Resource Center.

The bulk of the section work is presented in two-page activities, which include the following features:

- A short explanation of the program's features that are taught in the activity introduces the project.
- Streamlined, point-and-click instruction that pares reading to a minimum.
- Screen captures are correlated with exercise steps to provide instant reinforcement.
- Problem boxes provide troubleshooting hints that anticipate common obstacles or missteps and redirect students toward success.
- In Brief—bare-bones summaries of major commands and features. These provide instant review and a quick reference of the steps required to accomplish a task.
- In Addition—sidebars that offer extra information on key features and subfeatures.

Each section ends with the following features:

- Features Summary—Commands taught in the section are listed with button, ribbon tab, Quick Access toolbar, and keyboard actions.
- Knowledge Check—Objective completion exercises allows students to assess their comprehension and recall of program features, terminology, and functions. Answers to these items are found in the Assessment section of this *Instructor's Guide*.
- Skills Review—Exercises provide additional hands-on computer exercises to reinforce learning. These exercises include some guidance, but less than the section activities.

- Skills Assessment—Framed in a workplace project perspective, these less-guided assessments evaluate students' abilities to apply section skills and concepts in solving realistic problems. They require demonstrating program skills as well as decision-making skills and include Help and Internet-based activities.
- Marquee Challenge—Culminating assessments test students' mastery of program features and their problem-solving abilities.

Only instructors have access to the end-of-section model answer files. Both live and PDF files are available, and they are found on the Instructor Resources disc in the End-of-Section Answers folder. For the end-of-section model answers, the file naming of the model answers (both live files and PDFs), reflects the name indicated in the exercise's directions but also includes the Skills Review, Skills Assessment, or Marquee Challenge number at the beginning. So, in Word 2010, Section 1, the answer for the first Skills Review exercise is called WS1-R1-FCTHawaiianSpecials(Review1), the answer for the first Skills Assessment exercise is called WS1-A1-PTMarqueeLtr(Assessment 1), and the answer for the first Marquee Challenge is called WS1-C1-MPLtrtoWB(Challenge1). The PDF and live files are also available on the password-protected instructor's Internet Resource Center.

In addition to the end-of-section exercises provided in the text, two supplemental Skills Assessment exercises (the first to follow Section 3 and the second to follow Section 4) as well as four supplemental Marquee Challenge exercises (one for each section) are available to instructors for evaluation purposes. These exercises are available in the Assessment section of the Instructor's Guide as well as on the Instructor Resources disc.

Grading Rubrics are provided for all End-of-Section exercises and for the Supplemental Skills Assessments and Supplemental Marquee Challenges. The rubrics are included in the Assessment section of this guide, as well as on the Instructor's Resource disc and on the instructor's Internet Resource Center. Instructors should feel free to customize the rubrics to suit your grading standards and/or to adjust the point values.

Integrating Programs sections are included that highlight the benefits of using the Office suite. Projects include copying, exporting, linking, and embedding data. In these sections, students learn how to manage data efficiently in the business office or for personal use.

Student Resources CD

Files that serve as a starting point for completing many of the section activity and end-of-section exercises are included on the CD that accompanies the student text. Typically, students are directed to open one of these files, save the document with a new name, and then edit and print the document. As students begin a section, they should copy the folder of files for the section activities and end-of-section exercises to the storage medium of their choice. This folder name is displayed next to a CD icon on the first page of the section. The instructions also suggest that, with instructor approval, the student delete files from previous section to create storage space for the next section's files. This step may or may not be necessary, depending on the storage medium chosen.

All of the files on the Student Resources CD are also available on the Instructor Resources disc included with this *Instructor's Guide* and on the Internet Resource Center.

Marquee Series 2010 Internet Resource Center

The Marquee Internet Resource Center at www.emcp.net/Marquee10 offers valuable information for both instructors and students. For students, the Internet Resource Center includes quick access to the student data files, PowerPoint presentations, informational Web links, study aids, and special aids for English language learners, including a link to the *Computers: Understanding Technology, Fourth Edition* glossary offering computer concept terms and definitions in English and Spanish.

SNAP Training and Assessment

A web-based program designed to optimize skill-based learning for Word, Excel, Access, and PowerPoint, along with Windows and Internet Explorer, SNAP is comprised of:

- A learning management system that creates a virtual classroom on the Web, allowing the instructor to schedule tutorials, exams, and textbook assignments and to employ an electronic gradebook
- More than 50 interactive, multimedia tutorials, aligned to textbook sections, that can be used for direct instruction or remediation
- A skill item bank of more than a thousand performance skill items that simulate the operation of Microsoft Office 2010 and allow the instructor to assign pre-tests, to administer section post-tests, and to create practice exams
- Over 600 concept items that can be used to monitor student understanding of technical and computer literacy knowledge
- A concept item generator that will allow instructors to create up to ten kinds of new concept items
- A document checker that will download, collect, correct, and score 26 document assessments taken directly from the textbook

SNAP tutorials are available to support learning of programs in the Microsoft Office 2010 suite. Table 1 shows how the SNAP tutorials align with each section in *Marquee Series Microsoft Office 2010*.

Table 1. *Marquee Series Microsoft Office 2010* and SNAP Tutorials Correlation

Marquee Section	Marquee Lesson	SNAP Tutorial	SNAP Tutorial Title
Windows 7			
Windows Section 1	1	1.1	Exploring the Windows 7 Desktop
	2	1.2	Opening and Using Windows
	3	1.3	Exploring the Taskbar
	4	1.4	Getting Help
Windows Section 2	1	2.1	Browsing Devices and Files
	2	2.2	Creating a Folder
	3, 4, 5, 6	2.3	Selecting, Copying, Moving, and Renaming Files
	6, 7	2.4	Using the Recycle Bin
	8	2.5	Exploring the Control Panel
	9	2.6	Searching for a File or a Folder
	10	2.7	Customizing the Desktop

Marquee Section	Marquee Lesson	SNAP Tutorial	SNAP Tutorial Title
Internet Explorer 8			
IE Section	1	1.1	Browsing the Internet
	2	1.2	Searching for Specific Sites
	3	1.3	Researching Information
	4	1.4	Downloading Images, Text, and Web Pages
Word			
Word Section 1	1	1.1	Creating, Saving, and Printing a Document
	2, 3, 4	1.2	Editing a Document
	5	1.3	Using the Spelling and Grammar Feature
	6	1.4	Using the AutoCorrect Feature
	6	1.5	Using the Thesaurus
	7	1.6	Organizing the Document View
	8	1.7	Finding and Replacing Text
	9	1.8	Using the Help Feature
	9	1.9	Previewing and Printing Documents
	10	1.10	Creating Documents Using a Word Template
	11	1.11	Managing Folders
	11	1.12	Managing Documents
Word Section 2	1	2.1	Modifying the Font Using the Font Group
	1	2.2	Formatting with the Mini Toolbar
	2	2.3	Modifying the Font Using the Font Dialog Box
	2	2.4	Using the Format Painter
	3	2.5	Aligning Text in Paragraphs
	3	2.6	Changing Text Indentation
	4	2.7	Setting Line and Paragraph Spacing
	5	2.8	Finding and Replacing Formatting
	6	2.9	Creating Bulleted and Numbered Lists
	7	2.10	Inserting Symbols and Special Characters
	8	2.11	Setting Tabs Using the Ruler
	9	2.12	Setting Tabs Using the Tabs Dialog Box
	10	2.13	Adding a Border and Shading to Selected Text
	11	2.14	Applying Styles and Using the Quick Styles Gallery
	12	2.15	Changing Default Document Formatting

Marquee Section	Marquee Lesson	SNAP Tutorial	SNAP Tutorial Title
Word Section 3	1	3.1	Cutting, Copying, and Pasting Text
	2	3.2	Using the Office Clipboard
	3	3.3	Modifying Page Orientation and Changing Margins
	3	3.4	Applying Themes
	4	3.5	Adding Borders, Shading, and Watermarks to Pages
	5	3.6	Inserting Page Numbers and Page Breaks
	5	3.7	Creating Headers and Footers
	5	3.8	Modifying Headers and Footers
	6	3.9	Inserting and Modifying Sources and Citations
	7	3.10	Inserting and Modifying Bibliographies
	8	3.11	Using Click and Type
	8	3.12	Using Vertical Alignment
	8	3.13	Inserting, Sizing, and Moving Images
	9	3.14	Creating and Printing Envelopes
	10	3.15	Creating and Printing Labels
Word Section 4	1	4.1	Inserting and Modifying WordArt
	2	4.2	Inserting and Formatting a Shape
	3	4.3	Creating SmartArt
	4	4.4	Creating a Table
	5	4.5	Modifying a Table
	6	4.6	Changing the Table Design
	7	4.7	Inserting Section Breaks
	7	4.8	Applying Columns
	8	4.9	Creating and Previewing Web Pages
	8	4.10	Creating and Editing Hyperlinks
	9	4.11	Creating Form Letters Using Mail Merge
Excel			
Excel Section 1	1	1.1	Creating and Saving a Worksheet
	2	1.2	Writing a Formula
	3, 4, 5, 6	1.3	Copying and Testing a Formula
	6,7	1.4	Sorting Data and Using Help
	8	1.5	Formatting and Printing Options
	8	1.6	Previewing and Printing a Workbook

Marquee Section	Marquee Lesson	SNAP Tutorial	SNAP Tutorial Title
Excel Section 2	1	2.1	Editing Data in a Worksheet
	2, 4	2.2	Inserting, Adjusting, and Deleting Rows and Columns
	3	2.3	Moving, Copying, and Pasting Data in a Workbook
	5, 6, 7	2.4	Applying Formatting to Cell Contents; Using Undo and Redo; Changing Alignment
	8	2.5	Adding Borders and Shading to Cells and Using Format Painter
	9	2.6	Formatting a Worksheet Using Table Formatting and Themes
	10	2.7	Finding and Replacing Data and Formatting
	11	2.8	Freezing Panes, Splitting Windows, and Changing the Zoom
	12	2.9	Inserting and Using Clip Art Images and Diagrams
Excel Section 3	1	3.1	Creating Formulas and Absolute Addresses
	2, 3	3.2	Writing Formulas in Excel
	4	3.3	Using Financial Functions
	5	3.4	Naming and Using a Range
	6	3.5	Using the Logical IF Function
	7, 8, 9	3.6	Creating Charts in Excel
	10	3.7	Changing a Chart Type
	11	3.8	Changing Page Margins and Layout Options
	12	3.9	Adding Headers and Footers
Excel Section 4	1, 2	4.1	Inserting, Moving, Renaming, and Hiding a Worksheet
	3, 4	4.2	Linking Data and Using 3-D References
	4	4.3	Setting a Print Area and Printing Multiple Worksheets
	5	4.4	Inserting a Page Break
	6	4.5	Formatting Data as a Table
	6	4.6	Adding Rows to a Table
	7	4.7	Using the Sort Feature in Tables
	8	4.8	Filtering a Table
	9	4.9	Inserting and Editing Comments
	10	4.10	Using Templates
	11	4.11	Converting a Workbook to a Different Format
	12	4.12	Creating a PDF/XPS Copy of a Worksheet

Marquee Section	Marquee Lesson	SNAP Tutorial	SNAP Tutorial Title
Access			
Access Section 1	1, 2, 10	1.1	Opening Access, Navigating and Printing a Table
	3, 8	1.2	Formatting a Datasheet
	4	1.3	Finding and Replacing Specific Data in Records
	5	1.4	Adding Records in Datasheet View
	6	1.5	Adding Records and Navigating in a Form
	7, 8	1.6	Deleting and Sorting Records
	9	1.7	Filtering Records
	11	1.8	Using Help
Access Section 2	1, 2	2.1	Creating a New Database
	3	2.2	Creating a Table and Setting a Primary Key
	4	2.3	Modifying Field Properties
	4, 8	2.4	Modifying Table Fields
	5	2.5	Validating Data in a Table
	6, 7	2.6	Using the Input Mask Wizard and the Lookup Wizard
	9, 10, 11, 12	2.7	Creating a Relationship between Two Tables in a Database
Access Section 3	1	3.1	Creating Queries Using the Simple Query Wizard
	2, 3	3.2	Creating Queries in Design View
	4	3.3	Using Criteria Statements in Queries
	5, 6	3.4	Using And/Or Criteria in Queries
	7	3.5	Performing Calculations in a Query
	8	3.6	Creating a Form
	8, 9	3.7	Modifying a Form
	10	3.8	Adding and Modifying Objects
	11	3.9	Creating a Report
	11, 12	3.10	Modifying a Report
Access Section 4	1	4.1	Using Aggregate Functions
	2, 3, 4	4.2	Using Advanced Queries
	5, 6	4.3	Modifying Forms
	7, 8, 9	4.4	Modifying Reports
	10	4.5	Creating Mailing Labels
	11	4.6	Compacting, Repairing, and Backing Up a Database

Marquee Section	Marquee Lesson	SNAP Tutorial	SNAP Tutorial Title
PowerPoint			
PowerPoint Section 1	1, 2	1.1	Creating and Saving a Presentation
	3, 4, 5	1.2	Opening, Organizing, and Viewing a Presentation
	5	1.3	Editing Text within Slides and Modifying Placeholders
	6	1.4	Organizing Slides
	7	1.5	Using Help
	7	1.6	Using the Spelling and Thesaurus Feature
	8	1.7	Working with Presentations
	9	1.8	Adding Transition Effects and Sound
	10	1.9	Printing a Presentation
	10	1.10	Previewing Slides
PowerPoint Section 2	1	2.1	Editing and Moving Text
	2, 3, 4	2.2	Changing Font Attributes
	5	2.3	Changing Paragraph Formatting
	6	2.4	Customizing Slide Backgrounds
	7, 8	2.5	Working with Clip Art and Bitmap Images
	9, 10	2.6	Inserting and Formatting SmartArt
	11	2.7	Applying Animation to Objects
PowerPoint Section 3	1, 2	3.1	Using the Clipboard and Finding, Replacing, and Moving Text
	3	3.2	Using the WordArt Feature
	4	3.3	Inserting and Modifying Shapes
	5	3.4	Displaying Gridlines and Customizing Text within Shapes
	6	3.5	Creating Tables
	7	3.6	Inserting Action Buttons and Hyperlinks
	8	3.7	Formatting Text Using Masters
	9	3.8	Working with Headers and Footers
	10	3.9	Adding Multimedia Elements
	11	3.10	Setting Timings for Slides

Blackboard Cartridge

This set of files allows instructors to create a personalized Blackboard website for their course and provides course content, tests, and the mechanisms for establishing communication via e-discussions and online group conferences. Available content includes a syllabus, test banks, PowerPoint presentations, and supplementary course materials. Upon request, the files can be available within 24-48 hours. Hosting the site is the responsibility of the educational institution.

Resources for English Language Learners[1]

One of the fastest growing groups of students in higher education is comprised of students whose first language is not English and whose English is not yet equivalent to that of native English speakers in lexicon and syntax. The wide differences in fluency among limited English speakers makes your planning for meeting their needs somewhat more complex—and very important.

Chances are that you already know you will have some students whose language skills are not up to the level we expect or want. What? You're not the ESL instructor? Not your job? Think again. Your job is to help *all* the students in your course meet the intended outcomes. So plan how you're going to do this for your limited English speakers. Begin by assessing early on the language abilities of your students. Try these measures:

1. One method is a "one-minute preview." Tear some sheets of paper into four parts and give each student a piece. Ask them no more than two questions and give them one minute (okay, two) to write their answer. The question *could* be about their language skills, but it might be better to ask them something else. That way you get a short writing sample plus information about something else, such as why they are taking the course, something they would like to learn, the types of activities they enjoy, or what they are most worried about in the course. You don't need to be an English teacher to see which students will need help. Use your common sense.

2. If your class is small, conduct a discussion early in the course. Make sure you hear each student answer a question or ask one.

3. If you are conducting a pretest for the course, include some questions that ask students if they need to improve their English or their writing skills.

4. Tell students to e-mail you if they think they will need language help or extra exam time for reading assignments or tests.

In addition to the suggestions above, consider whether or not you need to prepare a list of terms for each session or unit that might be troublemakers for English language learners. Do you need to have students arrange for tutors to assist with completing the unguided assessments? Do you need to dedicate a session or part of one to instruction on how to prepare the work you expect?

To assist English language learners learn computer concept terminology, the Marquee Series Internet Resource Center at www.emcp.net/Marquee10 includes a link to the *Computers: Understanding Technology, Fourth Edition* glossary (www.emcp.net/cut4e). This resource provides computer concepts terms and definitions in both English and Spanish.

Instructor Resources

Along with the *Instructor's Guide*, instructional materials available with *Marquee Series Microsoft Office 2010* include:

- Instructor Resources disc with electronic files for all resources included in this *Instructor's Guide*. The disc also offers the section activities model answers in live program format, and model answers for end-of-section exercises in both live program format and PDF format. Printouts of all of the end-of section PDF model answers are provided in the Assessment section of this *Instructor's Guide*.

---

[1] Excerpted from *Exceptional Teaching: Ideas in Action,* published by EMC Corporation.

- PowerPoint presentations for every section. These files are available on the Instructor Resources disc and on the student and instructor Internet Resource Centers at www.emcp.net/Marquee10.
- ExamView computerized test generator with over 600 multiple choice items to create customized Web-based or print tests.

Instructor's Resource Center at www.emcp.net/Marquee10 includes all of the materials on the Instructor Resources disc and in the *Instructor's Guide.*

Information about Microsoft Office 2010

Microsoft Office 2010 operates on and the new Windows 7 operating system, as well as on Vista and Windows XP. Because Microsoft Office 2010 represents a significant change from previous versions of Office, particularly regarding the user interface, the following information and resources will be helpful.

e-Training on the Changes in Office 2010
At its Web site (www.microsoft.com), Microsoft offers online training in the new interface at this address: http://office.microsoft.com/en-us/support/getting-started-with-office-2010-FX101822272.aspx?CTT=97

Video on the What's New in Office 2010
Microsoft Corporation offers its own downloadable video presentation on the new features in Office 2010 at this address: http://office.microsoft.com/en-us/products/cool-things-you-can-do-with-office-2010-VA101842280.aspx

Command Reference Guides
Microsoft also provides interactive guides to show you where your favorite menu and toolbar commands are located in Office 2010 at the following address: http://office.microsoft.com/en-us/outlook-help/learn-where-menu-and-toolbar-commands-are-in-office-2010-HA101794130.aspx

Additional Helpful Microsoft Web Pages
Users familiar with earlier versions of Office may find the following links helpful:
- Office 2010 frequently asked questions: http://office.microsoft.com/enus/products/office-2010-frequently-asked-questions-HA101674631.aspx
- Office 2010 menu to ribbon reference workbooks: http://office.microsoft.com/enus/templates/CL101817133.aspx?CTT=5&origin=HA101794130
- Which file format should I use in the 2010 version of Access? http://office.microsoft.com/en-us/access-help/make-the-switch-to-access-2010-RZ101791922.aspx
- Features that change in PowerPoint 2010 presentations from earlier versions: http://office.microsoft.com/en-us/powerpoint-help/make-the-switch-to-powerpoint-2010-RZ101791923.aspx
- Use Excel 2010 with earlier versions: http://office.microsoft.com/enus/excel-help/make-the-switch-to-excel-2010-RZ101809963.aspx
- Use Word 2010 to open files created in previous versions of Word: http://office.microsoft.com/en-us/word-help/make-the-switch-to-word-2010-RZ101816356.aspx

Microsoft Office 2010 Product Editions

Microsoft Office 2010 is available in the following editions:

- Microsoft Office Starter
- Office Home and Student
- Office Home and Business
- Office Professional
- Microsoft Office Professional Plus
- Microsoft Office Standard
- Microsoft Office Professional Academic

Microsoft identifies the programs included in each edition at http://office.microsoft.com/en-us/products/FX101635841033.aspx.

Microsoft Office 2010 System Requirements

This interactive text is designed for the student to complete section work on a computer running a standard installation of Microsoft Office 2010, Office Professional edition, and the Microsoft Windows 7 operating system. To effectively run this suite and operating system, your computer should be outfitted with the following:

- 1 gigahertz (GHz) processor or higher; 1 gigabyte (GB) of RAM
- DVD drive
- 15 GB of available hard-disk space
- Computer mouse or compatible pointing device

Office 2010 will also operate on computers running the Windows XP Service Pack 3 or the Windows Vista operating system.

Screen captures in this book were created using a screen resolution display setting of 1280 × 800. Refer to Windows 7, Section 2, page 38, for instructions on changing the resolution for your monitor. Windows 7, Section 2, page 40, illustrates the Microsoft Office Word ribbon at three resolutions for comparison purposes. Choose the resolution that best matches your computer; however, be aware that using a resolution other than 1280 × 800 means that your screens may not match the illustrations in this book.

Developing an Assessment Strategy

The final major phase of planning a course is to develop an assessment strategy based on the purpose of evaluation and on your philosophy of what constitutes high-quality assessments. The obvious purpose of assessing students' learning is to determine whether or not students have achieved the goals of the course and, if they have, to what degree, resulting in a grade for credits earned. Other functions of evaluation include motivating students, determining the overall effectiveness of your teaching, and meeting accreditation requirements.

What is your philosophy of assessment? In shaping one, consider these suggestions from Paradigm Publishing's *Exceptional Teaching*:

1. Assessment should contribute to students' learning by asking them to apply their skills in out-of-school or workplace situations.
2. Timing, content, and form of assessments should be planned as an integral part of the course design.
3. The purpose of every assessment should be clear.
4. The type of assessment—its content and format—should be appropriate for the purpose.

5. Assessments should be scored as consistently and objectively as possible.
6. Assessments should provide students with feedback on their learning.
7. Assessments should emphasize intellectual traits of value: analytical reading, thinking, decision making, and research skills along with individual creativity and individual intelligence.
8. Assessments should be conducted at specific, planned checkpoints.
9. Assessments should be conducted in a positive learning environment, with every effort made to lower students' test anxieties.
10. Assessments should allow students to demonstrate their accomplishment of outcomes in various ways, including ways that fit their individual learning styles.

Determining the Number, Level, and Type of Assessments

Using your philosophy of assessment as a guide, begin to formulate your evaluation and grading strategy by answering these course-level questions, as presented in *Exceptional Teaching*:

- Do I want a course pre-assessment?
- Do I want a course comprehensive assessment—one that will determine students' mastery of the major intended outcomes for the entire course?
- Do I want pre-assessments for each section or program?
- Do I want comprehensive assessments for each section or program—ones that assess students' mastery of the major intended outcomes for that program?
- Do I want interim or checkpoint assessments that assess students' mastery of intended outcomes of learning chunks within units? How many? How often?
- Once my system is in place, will my students know that I value *how* and *how well* they think?

The questions above will help you establish approximately how many assessments you wish to include and their place in the course. The next decisions concern which types of assessment to use: traditional cognitive (objective) tests and/or performance-based assessments. Each of these two major categories of tests has its best uses. Traditional cognitive tests such as multiple-choice exams usually work best for testing information recall, comprehension, and analysis. They also are reliable and efficient, and relatively easy to score. On the down side, objective-type tests are criticized for not representing how students will use their new skills in an unfamiliar setting or in the real world of work. Here's where performance-based testing rises to the fore. Requiring students to demonstrate what they have learned and to apply it in a realistic context that closely approximates an on-the-job situation measures how well students can do what the course intended to teach them. As emphasized in *Exceptional Teaching*, "Authentic, performance-based assessments ask students to integrate what they have learned and apply it to resolve an issue, solve a problem, create something new, work collaboratively, or use their written and oral communication skills. Authentic assessments stress the process of learning as well as the outcomes of learning."

Typically, instructors develop an assessment strategy that uses the strengths of both major types of assessments. The Assessment section of this *Instructor's Guide* lists the objective and performance-based testing tools available with this text and also provides a grading sheet that can be customized for your assessment plan.

Creating a Grading Plan

By choosing the types of assessments that will measure students' achievement of course and program outcomes, you will already have established a schema of the major grading components. The next step is to weight the scores as preparation for entering them into a grade calculation system, for example, an Excel spreadsheet.

Will you include nonachievement factors such as effort and attendance, in students' grades? If so, consider how to measure those elements. While it is simple to track attendance, it is not so easy to objectively evaluate effort and attitude. Some experts recommend that teachers provide regular verbal and written feedback on nonachievement factors, but confine grades to academic achievement.

The following grading plan offers a starting point as you develop your comprehensive grading strategy for a course using any one of the texts in the Marquee Series:

Average of all Knowledge Check assignments	5%
Average of all Skills Review assignments	15%
Average of all Skills Assessment assignments	20%
Average of all Marquee Challenge assignments	20%
Average of all Integrating Skills Review assignments	10%
Average of all supplemental activities and/or tests	30%

The Grading Sheet on page 41 can be used as a resource to create your own grading plan. See also the Overview of Assessment Venues available for assessing student achievement in your course on page 39.

For More Information

Much of the content of this "Planning the Course" article is based on information found in *Exceptional Teaching: Ideas in Action*. To order a copy of this resource, please visit www.emcp.com or call or email Customer Care at 800-535-6865, educate@emcp.com.

Section Overviews

The following overviews outline the learning objectives, activities, and end-of-section exercises in each section of *Marquee Office 2010*. Detailed Lesson Plan Blueprints that correspond to a traditional 16-week semester course are located on the Instructor Resource disc and the Internet Resource Center.

WINDOWS 7
Windows Section 1: Exploring Windows 7

Learning Objectives
- Navigate the Windows 7 desktop
- Perform the following actions using the mouse: point, click, double-click, and drag
- Start and close a program
- Open and close a window
- Shut down Windows 7
- Move a window
- Minimize, maximize, and restore a window
- Stack and cascade windows
- Use the snap feature to position windows on the desktop
- Change the date and time
- Use components of a dialog box
- Adjust the volume using the Speaker's slider bar
- Customize the Taskbar
- Add a gadget to the desktop
- Use the Help and Support feature
- Turn on the display of file extensions

Activities
1.1 Exploring the Windows 7 Desktop
1.2 Opening and Manipulating Windows
1.3 Exploring the Taskbar, Gadgets, and Dialog Box Components
1.4 Getting Help in Windows; Displaying File Extensions

End-of-Section Exercises
Features Summary
Knowledge Check
Skills Review
Review 1 Opening and Manipulating Windows
Review 2 Exploring the Taskbar and Gadgets
Skills Assessment
Assessment 1 Manipulating Windows
Assessment 2 Customizing the Taskbar and Adding a Gadget
Assessment 3 Restoring the Taskbar and Removing a Gadget

Windows Section 2: Maintaining Files and Customizing Windows

Learning Objectives
- Browse the contents of storage devices
- Change folder and view options
- Create a folder
- Rename a folder or file
- Select, move, copy, and paste folders or files
- Delete files/folders to and restore files/folders from the Recycle Bin
- Explore the Control Panel
- Use Search tools to find programs, folders, and/or files
- Customize the desktop
- Change screen resolution

Activities
2.1 Browsing Storage Devices and Files in a Computer Window
2.2 Changing Folder and View Options
2.3 Creating a Folder; Renaming a Folder or File
2.4 Selecting and Copying Folders and Files
2.5 Moving Folders and Files

INTERNET EXPLORER 8.0
Section 1: Browsing the Internet Using Internet Explorer 8.0

Learning Objectives
- Visit sites by typing a web address
- Use hyperlinks to navigate to web pages
- Search for information using search tools
- Narrow a search using advanced search
  options
- Download content from a web page
- Evaluate content found on a web page

Activities
1.1 Navigating the Internet Using Web
    Addresses
1.2 Finding Information Using Search
    Tools
1.3 Refining Your Search Using Advanced
    Search Tools
1.4 Downloading Content from a Web Page
1.5 Evaluating Content on the Web

End-of-Section Exercises
Features Summary
Knowledge Check
Skills Review
Review 1 Browsing the Internet and
    Navigating with Hyperlinks
Review 2 Searching for Specific Sites
Review 3 Downloading Content from a
    Web Page
Skills Assessment
Assessment 1 Visiting Web Pages for
    Current News Articles
Assessment 2 Navigating Websites for
    Theatre Programs
Assessment 3 Downloading Content on
    Ski Resorts
Assessment 4 Deleting Downloaded
    Content on the Desktop

WORD 2010

Word Section 1: Creating and Editing a Document

Learning Objectives

- Complete the word processing cycle
- Move the insertion point
- Insert, replace, and delete text
- Scroll and navigate in a document
- Select and delete text
- Use Undo and Redo
- Check spelling and grammar in a document
- Use the AutoCorrect feature
- Use the Thesaurus feature
- Change document views
- Find specific text
- Find and replace text
- Use the Help feature
- Print a document
- Close a document
- Create a document using a template
- Create and rename a folder
- Save a document in a different format

Activities

1.1 Completing the Word Processing Cycle
1.2 Moving the Insertion Point; Inserting and Deleting Text
1.3 Scrolling and Navigating in a Document
1.4 Selecting and Deleting Text; Using Undo and Redo
1.5 Checking the Spelling and Grammar in a Document

1.6 Using AutoCorrect and Thesaurus
1.7 Changing Document Views
1.8 Finding and Replacing Text
1.9 Using the Help Feature; Printing a Document
1.10 Creating a Document Using a Template
1.11 Creating and Renaming Folders; Saving a Document in a Different Format

End-of-Section Exercises

Features Summary
Knowledge Check
Skills Review
Review 1 Editing a Hawaiian Specials Document
Review 2 Editing an Agreement
Review 3 Preparing a Fax Sheet
Skills Assessment
Assessment 1 Editing a Letter
Assessment 2 Writing a Letter
Assessment 3 Preparing a Fax
Assessment 4 Finding Information on Changing Grammar Checking Options
Assessment 5 Individual Challenge: Creating a Certificate
Marquee Challenge
Challenge 1 Preparing a Business Letter
Challenge 2 Editing and Formatting a Travel Document

Word Section 2: Formatting Characters and Paragraphs

Learning Objectives

- Apply fonts and font effects
- Use Format Painter
- Repeat a command
- Align text in paragraphs
- Indent text
- Change line and paragraph spacing
- Reveal Formatting
- Find and replace formatting
- Insert bullets and numbering
- Insert symbols and special characters

- Set tabs and tabs with leaders
- Add borders and shading to text
- Insert a page border
- Apply styles
- Change the document default formatting
- Insert symbols and special characters
- Set tabs and tabs with leaders
- Add borders and shading to text
- Insert a page border
- Apply styles
- Change the document default formatting

Activities

2.1 Applying Formatting with the Font Group and the Mini Toolbar

2.2 Using the Font Dialog Box and Format Painter; Repeating a Command

2.3 Aligning and Indenting Text

2.4 Changing Line and Paragraph Spacing

2.5 Revealing Formatting; Finding and Replacing Formatting

2.6 Inserting Bullets and Numbering

2.7 Inserting Symbols and Special Characters

2.8 Setting Tabs

2.9 Setting Tabs with Leaders

2.10 Adding Borders and Shading

2.11 Applying Styles

2.12 Changing Default Document Formatting

End-of-Section Exercises

Features Summary

Knowledge Check

Skills Review

Review 1 Formatting a Petersburg, Alaska, Document

Review 2 Formatting a Vacation Package Document

Skills Assessment

Assessment 1 Formatting a Cross Country Skiing Document

Assessment 2 Preparing and Formatting a Letter

Assessment 3 Setting Leader Tabs

Assessment 4 Finding Information on Controlling Page Breaks

Assessment 5 Individual Challenge: Creating a Document with Tabbed Text

Marquee Challenge

Challenge 1 Editing and Formatting a Document on Juneau, Alaska

Challenge 2 Creating and Formatting a Flyer about a Skiing Vacation Package

Word Section 3: Formatting and Enhancing a Document

Learning Objectives

- Cut, copy, and paste text
- Use the Clipboard task pane to copy and paste items
- Change page margins, orientation, and size
- Apply a theme
- Insert a watermark, page color, and page border
- Insert page numbering
- Insert a header and footer
- Format a document in MLA Style
- Insert citations
- Create a works cited page
- Edit a source
- Use the Click and Type feature
- Vertically align text
- Insert, size, and move images
- Prepare an envelope
- Prepare labels

Activities

3.1 Cutting, Copying, and Pasting Text; Using Paste Special

3.2 Using the Clipboard Task Pane

3.3 Customizing the Page Setup; Applying a Theme

3.4 Customizing the Page and Page Background

3.5 Inserting Page Numbering, Headers, and Footers

3.6 Formatting a Document in MLA Style; Inserting Citations

3.7 Creating a Works Cited Page; Editing Sources

3.8 Using Click and Type; Vertically Aligning Text; Inserting, Sizing, and Moving an Image

3.9 Preparing an Envelope

3.10 Preparing Mailing Labels

End-of-Section Exercises
Features Summary
Knowledge Check
Skills Review
Review 1 Formatting a Fact Sheet on Juneau, Alaska
Review 2 Formatting a Document in MLA Style
Review 3 Preparing and Formatting an Announcement
Review 4 Preparing an Envelope
Review 5 Preparing Mailing Labels

Skills Assessment
Assessment 1 Formatting a Costume Rental Agreement
Assessment 2 Creating an Announcement
Assessment 3 Preparing Mailing Labels
Assessment 4 Finding Information on Creating a Picture Watermark
Assessment 5 Individual Challenge: Creating a Personal Letterhead
Marquee Challenge
Challenge 1 Formatting a Costume Document
Challenge 2 Preparing an Announcement

Word Section 4: Formatting with Special Features

Learning Objectives
- Create and modify WordArt text
- Create a drop cap
- Insert a text box and draw a text box
- Insert and modify shapes
- Use SmartArt to create organizational charts and graphics
- Create and modify tables
- Insert one file into another
- Insert a continuous section break
- Create and modify columns
- Save a document as a single file Web page
- Insert a hyperlink
- Merge letters and envelopes

Activities
4.1 Creating and Modifying WordArt Text
4.2 Creating Drop Caps and Text Boxes; Drawing Shapes
4.3 Creating SmartArt Graphics
4.4 Creating and Modifying a Table
4.5 Changing the Table Layout
4.6 Changing the Table Design
4.7 Inserting a File and Section Break; Creating and Modifying Newspaper Columns
4.8 Saving a Document as a Web Page; Creating a Hyperlink
4.9 Merging Documents and Envelopes

End-of-Section Exercises
Features Summary
Knowledge Check
Skills Review
Review 1 Formatting a First Choice Travel Document
Review 2 Preparing and Formatting an Organizational Chart
Review 3 Preparing, Modifying, and Formatting a Table
Review 4 Saving a Document as a Web Page; Inserting a Hyperlink
Review 5 Merging Letters and Envelopes
Skills Assessment
Assessment 1 Formatting a Theatre Arts Division Newsletter
Assessment 2 Creating an Organization Chart
Assessment 3 Creating a Table for the Waterfront Bistro
Assessment 4 Finding Information on Flipping and Copying Objects
Assessment 5 Individual Challenge: Locating Information and Creating a Table
Marquee Challenge
Challenge 1 Formatting a Document on Orcas Island
Challenge 2 Preparing a Flier for The Waterfront Bistro

EXCEL 2010
Excel Section 1: Analyzing Data Using Excel

Learning Objectives
- Start Excel and identify features in the Excel window
- Enter labels and values
- Use the fill handle to enter a series
- Enter formulas
- Create a formula using SUM
- Copy a formula
- Test a worksheet for accuracy
- Apply the Accounting Number format to values
- Right-align labels
- Sort a selection
- Use the Help feature
- Center a label across multiple columns
- Change the page orientation to landscape
- Preview and print a worksheet
- Display cell formulas n a worksheet
- Navigate a large worksheet using the mouse and the keyboard
- Jump to a specific cell using Go To

Activities
1.1 Completing the Excel Worksheet Cycle
1.2 Entering Labels and Values; Using Fill Options
1.3 Performing Calculations Using Formulas
1.4 Using the SUM Function

1.5 Copying Formulas
1.6 Testing the Worksheet; Improving the Worksheet Appearance; Sorting
1.7 Using Help
1.8 Previewing; Changing Page Orientation; Printing a Worksheet
1.9 Displaying Formulas; Navigating a Worksheet

End-of-Section Exercises
Features Summary
Knowledge Check
Skills Review
Review 1 Creating Labels, Values, and Formulas
Review 2 Improving the Appearance of the Worksheet; Previewing and Printing
Skills Assessment
Assessment 1 Adding Values and Formulas to a Worksheet
Assessment 2 Creating a New Workbook
Assessment 3 Creating a New Workbook
Assessment 4 Finding Information on Sorting
Assessment 5 Individual Challenge: Creating a School Budget
Marquee Challenge
Challenge1 Preparing an International Student Registration Report
Challenge 2 Preparing a Theatre Arts Target Enrollment Report

Excel Section 2: Editing and Formatting Worksheets

Learning Objectives
- Edit the contents of a cell
- Clear cells and cell formats
- Use proofing tools
- Insert and delete columns and rows
- Move and copy cells
- Use Paste Options to link cells
- Adjust column width and row height

- Change the font, size, style, and color of cells
- Apply numeric formats and adjust the number of decimal places
- Use Undo, Redo, and Repeat
- Change cell alignment and indentation
- Add borders and shading
- Copy formats using Format Painter

- Apply cell styles
- Apply a theme
- Find and replace cell entries and formats
- Freeze and unfreeze panes
- Change the zoom percentage
- Insert, move, and resize pictures and clip art

Activities

2.1 Editing and Clearing Cells; Using Proofing Tools

2.2 Inserting and Deleting Columns and Rows

2.3 Moving and Copying Cells

2.4 Adjusting Column Width and Row Height; Using AutoFit

2.5 Changing the Font, Size, Style, and Color of Cells

2.6 Formatting Numeric Cells; Adjusting Decimal Places; Using Undo and Redo

2.7 Changing the Alignment and Indentation of Cells; Using Repeat

2.8 Adding Borders and Shading; Copying Formats with Format Painter

2.9 Using Cell Styles and Themes

2.10 Using Find and Replace

2.11 Freezing Panes; Changing the Zoom

2.12 Inserting, Moving, and Resizing Pictures and Clip Art

End-of-Section Exercises

Features Summary

Knowledge Check

Skills Review

Review 1 Editing, Moving, Copying, and Clearing Cells; Performing a Spell Check; Inserting and Deleting Rows

Review 2 Adjusting Column Widths; Replacing Data; Moving Cells; Applying Formatting Features; Inserting a Picture

Skills Assessment

Assessment 1 Editing Cells; Inserting Columns; Copying Formulas; Inserting Pictures; Applying Formatting Features

Assessment 2 Completing a Formatting Worksheet

Assessment 3 Performing a Spelling Check; Adjusting Column Width; Using Find and Replace; Inserting Clip Art; Applying Formatting Features

Assessment 4 Finding the Select All Button

Assessment 5 Individual Challenge: Locating Information on Theatre Arts Programs

Marquee Challenge

Challenge 1 Creating a Direct Wages Budget Report for a Film Shoot

Challenge 2 Creating a Room Timetable

Excel Section 3: Using Functions, Setting Print Options, and Adding Visual Elements

Learning Objectives

- Create formulas with absolute addresses
- Create AVERAGE, MAX, and MIN formulas to perform statistical analysis
- Create TODAY, NOW, and DATE formulas
- Create PMT formulas to calculate loan payments
- Create and use range names
- Create an IF formula to return a result based on a logical test
- Create, edit, and format a column, pie, and line chart
- Draw shapes and text boxes
- Center a worksheet horizontally and vertically
- Modify and format charts
- Change page layout options for printing such as margins, horizontal and vertical centering, and scaling
- Manipulate a worksheet in Page Layout view
- Insert headers and footers

Activities

3.1 Creating Formulas with Absolute Addressing

3.2 Using Statistical Functions AVERAGE, COUNT, MAX, and MIN

3.3 Using Date Functions TODAY, NOW, and DATE

3.4 Using the Financial Function PMT

3.5 Creating and Using Range Names

3.6 Using the Logical IF Function

3.7 Creating a Column Chart

3.8 Creating a Pie Chart

3.9 Creating a Line Chart; Drawing Shapes

3.10 Modifying and Formatting Charts

3.11 Changing Page Layout Options

3.12 Using Page Layout View; Inserting Headers and Footers

End-of-Section Exercises

Features Summary

Knowledge Check

Skills Review

Review 1 Creating Range Names; Inserting Statistical, Date, and IF Functions; Changing Page Layout Options

Review 2 Creating Charts; Drawing Shapes

Skills Assessment

Assessment 1 Creating Statistical and IF Functions; Using Absolute References

Assessment 2 Applying the PTM Function

Assessment 3 Creating Charts; Drawing Shapes

Assessment 4 Creating Charts; Changing Page Layout; Inserting a Footer

Assessment 5 Finding Information on Chart Axis Options

Assessment 6 Individual Challenge: Social Networking Survey

Marquee Challenge

Challenge1 Creating Charts on Movie Attendance Statistics

Challenge 2 Preparing an International Student Report

Excel Section 4: Working with Multiple Worksheets, Tables, and Other File Formats

Learning Objectives

- Insert, delete, and rename a worksheet
- Format sheet tabs
- Move and copy a worksheet
- Group and ungroup worksheets
- Create 3-D references in formulas
- Link cells between worksheets
- Print multiple worksheets
- Use Page Break Preview to manipulate page breaks
- Format data as a table
- Apply table design options
- Insert rows and columns into a table
- Add a total row to a table
- Sort and filter a table by single and multiple criteria
- Insert, edit, delete, and print comments
- Create a new workbook using a template
- Open and save a workbook in a different file format
- Create a PDF/XPS copy of a worksheet

Activities

4.1 Inserting, Deleting, and Renaming a Worksheet; Formatting Sheet Tabs

4.2 Moving and Copying Worksheets; Grouping and Ungrouping Worksheets

4.3 Using 3-D References

4.4 Linking Cells; Printing Multiple Worksheets

4.5 Using Page Break Preview

4.6 Formatting Data as a Table; Applying Table Design Options

4.7 Sorting a Table by Single and Multiple Criteria

4.8 Filtering a Table

4.9 Inserting, Editing, Deleting, and Printing Comments

4.10 Creating a Workbook from a Template

4.11 Opening and Saving a Workbook in a Different File Format

4.12 Creating a PDF/XPS Copy of a Worksheet

End-of-Section Exercises

Features Summary

Knowledge Check

Skills Review

Review 1 Managing and Formatting Worksheets; Using 3-D References; Printing Multiple Worksheets

Review 2 Formatting a Table; Sorting; Filtering; and Inserting and Printing Comments

Review 3 Creating a Workbook Using a Template

Skills Assessment

Assessment 1 Inserting, Deleting, and Renaming Worksheets; Linking Worksheets

Assessment 2 Formatting a Table; Filtering; Sorting

Assessment 3 Inserting and Printing Comments

Assessment 4 Formatting Columns and Formatting a Table; Opening an Excel 2003 Workbook and Saving as an Excel 2010 Workbook

Assessment 5 Finding Information on File Formats Not Supported by Excel 2010

Assessment 6 Individual Challenge: Smartphone Shopping

Marquee Challenge

Challenge 1 Creating a Sales Invoice by Downloading a Template

Challenge 2 Importing, Formatting and Sorting a Distributor List

Integrating Programs: Word and Excel

Learning Objectives

- Copy and paste Word data into an Excel worksheet
- Link an Excel worksheet with a Word document
- Update linked data
- View linked data as an icon
- Link an Excel chart with a Word document
- Embed an Excel worksheet into a Word document
- Edit an embedded worksheet

Activities

1.1 Copying and Pasting Word Data into an Excel Worksheet

1.2 Linking an Excel Worksheet with a Word Document

1.3 Updating Linked Data; Viewing a Link

1.4 Linking an Excel Chart with a Word Document

1.5 Embedding an Excel Worksheet into a Word Document

End-of-Section Exercises

Skills Review

Review 1 Copying and Pasting Data

Review 2 Linking an Object and Editing a Linked Object

Review 3 Embedding an Object

ACCESS 2010

Access Section 1: Maintaining Data in Access Tables

Learning Objectives
- Describe how data is organized in a database
- Define field, record, table, datasheet, and database
- Start Access
- Identify features in the Access window
- Open, navigate, and close a database, table and form
- Adjust column widths
- Find and edit records
- Add and delete records
- Sort and filter records
- Move columns in a datasheet
- Preview and print a table
- Change margins
- Change the page orientation
- Use the Help feature
- Change the font size for selected records
- Hide columns in a datasheet

Activities
1.1 Understanding Database Concepts and Terminology
1.2 Exploring Access Objects and the User Interface
1.3 Adjusting Column Width; Navigating in Datasheet View
1.4 Finding and Editing Records
1.5 Adding Records to a Datasheet
1.6 Adding Records Using a Form
1.7 Deleting Records in a Datasheet and Form
1.8 Sorting Records; Moving Columns
1.9 Applying and Removing Filters
1.10 Previewing and Printing; Changing Margins and Page Orientation
1.11 Using Help; Hiding Columns in a Datasheet

End-of-Section Exercises
Features Summary
Knowledge Check
Skills Review
Review 1 Adjusting Column Widths; Finding and Editing Records; Adding and Deleting Records
Review 2 Sorting; Previewing; Changing Page Orientation; Filtering; Hiding Columns; Printing
Skills Assessment
Assessment 1 Adjusting Column Width; Finding and Editing Records; Previewing and Printing
Assessment 2 Finding, Adding, and Deleting Records; Formatting Datasheet
Assessment 3 Finding, Sorting, Filtering, and Deleting Records
Assessment 4 Finding Information on Designing a Database
Assessment 5 Individual Challenge: Creating a Job Search Company Database
Marquee Challenge
Challenge1 Updating and Printing a Catering Event Database
Challenge 2 Determining Fields and Table Names for a New Database

Access Section 2: Creating Tables and Relationships

Learning Objectives
- List guidelines for field names
- Choose an appropriate data type for a field
- Define primary key field
- Create a new database
- Create a table using a blank datasheet
- Create and modify a table in Design view
- Set the primary key for a table
- Limit the number of characters allowed in a field
- Display a descriptive title for fields by using a caption
- Display a default value in a field

- Verify data entry using a validation rule
- Restrict data entered into a filed using an input mask
- Create a Lookup list in a field
- Insert, move and delete fields
- Add a total row to a datasheet
- Describe why tables are joined in a relationship
- Create and edit a one-to-many relationship
- Define foreign key field
- Create and edit a one-to-one relationship
- Print a relationship report
- Delete a relationship

Activities

2.1 Understanding Table Design Principles and Primary Keys
2.2 Creating a New Database; Creating a Table
2.3 Creating a Table in Design View; Setting the Primary Key
2.4 Modifying Field Size, Caption, and Default Value Properties
2.5 Validating Field Entries
2.6 Creating Input Masks; Formatting a Field
2.7 Creating a Lookup List
2.8 Inserting, Moving, and Deleting Fields; Inserting a Total
2.9 Understanding Relationships; Using the Relationships Window

2.10 Creating and Editing a One-to-Many Relationship
2.11 Creating and Editing a One-to-One Relationship
2.12 Printing a Relationships Report; Deleting a Relationship

End-of-Section Exercises
Features Summary
Knowledge Check
Skills Review
Review 1 Creating and Modifying a Table in Design View
Review 2 Modifying, Moving, and Deleting Fields;
Skills Assessment
Assessment 1 Creating a Table in Design View; Creating a Lookup Field
Assessment 2 Changing Field Size; Validating Entries; Creating an Input Mask; Formatting Dates; Formatting a Datasheet
Assessment 3 Creating a New Database
Assessment 4 Finding Information on Table Templates
Assessment 5 Individual Challenge: Investigating Social Media Websites
Marquee Challenge
Challenge1 Refining Tables in a Database; Creating Relationships
Challenge 2 Creating a New Database

Access Section 3: Creating Queries, Forms, and Reports

Learning Objectives

- Create a select query using the Simple Query Wizard
- Create a select query in Design view
- Add multiple tables to a query
- Add criteria statements to a query
- Prevent columns in the query design grid from displaying in the query results datasheet
- Select records using And statement
- Select records using OR statements

- Sort the query results
- Perform calculations in a query
- Create and edit a form using the Form tool
- Add a field to a form
- Add a logo image to a form
- Resize and format an object on a form
- Create, edit, and print a report using the Report tool
- Move and resize columns in a report

Activities

3.1 Creating a Query Using the Simple Query Wizard

3.2 Creating a Query in Design View Using a Single Table

3.3 Creating a Query in Design View Using Multiple Tables

3.4 Extracting Records Using Criteria Statements; Hiding Columns

3.5 Extracting Records Using AND Criteria; Sorting Query Results

3.6 Extracting Records Using OR Criteria

3.7 Performing Calculations in a Query

3.8 Creating and Editing Forms Using Form Tools

3.9 Adding Fields to a Form from Another Table

3.10 Adding a Logo; Resizing and Editing Objects

3.11 Creating and Editing a Report

3.12 Resizing and Moving Columns in a Report

End-of-Section Exercises

Features Summary

Knowledge Check

Skills Review

Review 1 Creating a Query Using the Simple Query Wizard; Sorting a Query; Creating a Calculated Field; Extracting Records

Review 2 Creating and Modifying a Form

Review 3 Creating and Modifying a Report

Skills Assessment

Assessment 1 Creating a Query In Design View; Sorting a Query; Extracting Records Using Multiple Criteria

Assessment 2 Creating a Query and Report; Modifying a Report

Assessment 3 Creating and Modifying a Form

Assessment 4 Finding Information on Creating a Form with a Subform

Assessment 5 Individual Challenge: Researching Movies on the Internet for a New Blog

Marquee Challenge

Challenge1 Creating Queries and a Report for a Catering Events Database

Challenge 2 Creating Forms and a Report for a Custom Costume Database

Access Section 4: Summarizing Data and Calculating in Forms and Reports

Learning Objectives

- Use functions in a query to calculate statistics
- Summarize data in a crosstab query
- Create a find duplicates query
- Create a find unmatched query
- Add control objects to a form and report in Layout view
- Add a calculation to a form and report
- Move and resize control objects in a report
- Sort in a form or report

- Add grouping, subtotals, and totals in a report
- Conditionally format in a report
- Create mailing labels
- Compact and repair a database
- Back up a database

Activities

4.1 Calculating Statistics Using Functions

4.2 Summarizing Data Using a Crosstab Query

4.3 Using a Query to Find Duplicate Records

4.4 Using a Query to Find Unmatched Records
4.5 Adding Control Objects to a Form Using Layout View; Sorting in a Form
4.6 Add a Calculation to a Form
4.7 Modifying a Report in Layout View
4.8 Grouping, Sorting, and Adding Totals to a Report
4.9 Applying Conditional Formatting in a Report
4.10 Creating Mailing Labels
4.11 Compacting and Repairing a Database; Backing Up a Database

End-of-Section Exercises
Features Summary
Knowledge Check
Skills Review
Review 1 Creating a Crosstab; Find Unmatched, and Find Duplicates Query
Review 2 Adding Control Objects to a Form; Sorting a Form
Review 3 Creating and Modifying a Report; Creating a Calculated Control
Skills Assessment
Assessment 1 Adding a Calculated Control to a Form
Assessment 2 Creating and Modifying a Report; Sorting a Report
Assessment 3 Creating Mailing Labels
Assessment 4 Calculated Statistics; Creating a Crosstab Query
Assessment 5 Finding Information on Creating a Query That Asks for Input
Assessment 6 Individual Challenge: Researching Salary Statistics on the Internet and Creating a Blog Entry
Marquee Challenge
Challenge1 Summarizing Catering Event Information
Challenge 2 Summarizing Costume Rental Revenue with Conditioning Formatting

Integrating Programs: Word, Excel, and Access

Learning Objectives
- Export Access data in a table to Excel
- Export Access data in a table to Word
- Export Access data in a report to Word
- Import Excel data to a new Access table
- Link data between an Excel worksheet and an Access table
- Edit linked data

Activities
2.1 Exporting Access Data to Excel
2.2 Exporting an Access Table to Word
2.3 Exporting an Access Report to Word
2.4 Importing Data to a New Table
2.5 Linking Data to a New Table

End-of-Section Exercises
Skills Review
Review 1 Exporting Access Data to Excel
Review 2 Exporting Access Data to Word
Review 3 Exporting an Access Report to Word
Review 4 Importing Data to a New Table
Review 5 Linking Data to a New Table and Editing Linked Data

POWERPOINT 2010
PowerPoint Section 1: Preparing a Presentation

Learning Objectives
- Complete the presentation cycle
- Choose a design theme
- Add a new slide to a presentation
- Navigate in a presentation
- Insert a slide in a presentation
- Change the presentation view
- Change the slide layout
- Rearrange, delete, and hide slides
- Use the Help feature
- Check spelling in a presentation
- Use Thesaurus to display synonyms for words
- Run a presentation and use the pen during a presentation
- Add transition and sound to a presentation
- Print and preview a presentation

Activities
1.1 Completing the Presentation Cycle
1.2 Choosing a Design Theme; Creating Slides; Closing a Presentation
1.3 Opening, Navigating, and Inserting Slides in a Presentation
1.4 Changing Views; Choosing a Slide Layout
1.5 Changing the Slide Layout; Selecting and Moving a Placeholder
1.6 Rearranging, Deleting, and Hiding Slides
1.7 Using Help; Checking Spelling; Using Thesaurus
1.8 Running a Presentation; Using the Pen During a Presentation
1.9 Adding Transition and Sound
1.10 Printing and Previewing a Presentation

End-of-Section Exercises
Features Summary
Knowledge Check
Skills Review
Review 1 Creating a Presentation for Marquee Productions
Skills Assessment
Assessment 1 Preparing a Presentation for Worldwide Enterprises
Assessment 2 Preparing a Presentation for the Waterfront Bistro
Assessment 3 Finding Information on Setting Slide Show Timings
Assessment 4 Individual Challenge: Preparing a Presentation on Cancun, Mexico
Marquee Challenge
Challenge1 Preparing a Presentation on Toronto, Ontario, Canada
Challenge 2 Preparing a Presentation for Performance Threads

PowerPoint Section 2: Editing and Enhancing Slides

Learning Objectives
- Open a presentation and save it with a new name
- Increase and decrease the indent of text
- Select, cut, copy, and paste text
- Apply font and font effects
- Find and replace fonts
- Apply formatting with Format Painter
- Change alignment and line and paragraph spacing
- Change the design theme, theme color, and theme font
- Insert, size, and move images
- Insert and format clip art images
- Insert and format a SmartArt organizational chart
- Insert and format a SmartArt graphic
- Apply animation to an object in a slide

Activities
2.1 Increasing and Decreasing Indent; Cutting, Copying, and Pasting Text
2.2 Applying Fonts and Font Effects
2.3 Changing the Font at the Font Dialog Box; Replacing Fonts
2.4 Formatting with Format Painter

2.5 Changing Alignment and Line and Paragraph Spacing

2.6 Changing the Design Theme, Theme Color, and Theme Font

2.7 Inserting, Sizing, and Moving an Image

2.8 Inserting and Formatting Clip Art Images

2.9 Inserting and Formatting a SmartArt Organizational Chart

2.10 Inserting and Formatting a SmartArt Graphic

2.11 Applying Animation to Objects and Text

End-of-Section Exercises
Features Summary
Knowledge Check
Skills Review
Review 1 Editing and Formatting a Presentation for Marquee Productions

Review 2 Formatting a Presentation for Performance Threads

Skills Assessment
Assessment 1 Formatting a Presentation for Niagara Peninsula College, Theatre Arts Division

Assessment 2 Formatting a Presentation for First Choice Travel

Assessment 3 Finding Information on Converting Text to a SmartArt Graphic

Assessment 4 Individual Challenge: Locating Information and Preparing a Presentation

Marquee Challenge
Challenge1 Preparing a Presentation for Worldwide Enterprises

Challenge 2 Preparing a Presentation for The Waterfront Bistro

PowerPoint Section 3: Customizing a Presentation

Learning Objectives
- Copy and paste items using the Clipboard task pane
- Find and replace text
- Insert and format WordArt
- Draw and customize objects
- Display gridlines
- Insert text in a box
- Copy and rotate shapes
- Create and format a table
- Insert action buttons
- Insert a hyperlink
- Format with a Slide Master
- Insert headers and footers
- Add audio and video
- Set and rehearse timings for a presentation

Activities
3.1 Using the Clipboard Task Pane
3.2 Finding and Replacing Text
3.3 Inserting and Formatting WordArt
3.4 Drawing and Customizing Shapes
3.5 Displaying Gridlines; Inserting a Text Box; Copying and Rotating Shapes
3.6 Creating a Table in a Slide
3.7 Inserting Action Buttons and Hyperlinks
3.8 Formatting with a Slide Master
3.9 Inserting Headers and Footers

3.10 Adding Audio and Video
3.11 Setting and Rehearsing Timings for a Presentation

End-of-Section Exercises
Features Summary
Knowledge Check
Skills Review
Review 1 Formatting and Customizing a Biography Project Presentation

Review 2 Formatting with Slide Masters

Review 3 Formatting a Vacation Cruise Presentation to Run Automatically

Skills Assessment
Assessment 1 Formatting a Presentation for Performance Threads

Assessment 2 Formatting a Presentation for First Choice Travel

Assessment 3 Learning about Custom Shows

Assessment 4 Individual Challenge: Locating Information and Preparing a Presentation on Social Networking Sites

Marquee Challenge
Challenge1 Preparing a Project Schedule Presentation for Marquee Productions

Challenge 2 Preparing a Moroccan Tour Presentation for First Choice Travel

Integrating Programs: Word, Excel, and PowerPoint

Learning Objectives
- Export a PowerPoint presentation to a Word document
- Export a Word outline document to a PowerPoint presentation
- Link an Excel chart with a Word document and a PowerPoint presentation
- Edit a linked object
- Embed a Word table in a PowerPoint presentation
- Edit an embedded object

Activities
3.1 Exporting a PowerPoint Presentation to Word

3.2 Exporting a Word Outline to a PowerPoint Presentation

3.3 Linking an Excel Chart with a Word Document and a PowerPoint Presentation

3.4 Editing a Linked Object

3.5 Embedding and Editing a Word Table in a PowerPoint Presentation

End-of-Section Exercises
Skills Review
Review 1 Exporting a PowerPoint Presentation to Word

Review 2 Linking and Editing an Excel Chart in a PowerPoint Slide

Review 3 Embedding and Editing a Word Table in a PowerPoint Slide

Integrating Programs: Word, Excel, Access, and PowerPoint
Marquee Series Microsoft Office 2010 Brief Edition

Learning Objectives
- Export Access data to Excel and Word
- Import Excel data to a new table in Access
- Export a PowerPoint presentation to Word
- Export a Word outline to a PowerPoint presentation
- Link an Excel chart with a Word document and PowerPoint presentation
- Edit a linked Object
- Embed and edit a Word table in a PowerPoint slide
- Link data to a new Access table and edit linked data
- Embed an Excel worksheet in a Word document

Activities
Exporting Access Data to Excel

Exporting an Access Table to Word

Importing Data to a New Table

Exporting a PowerPoint Presentation to Word

Exporting a Word Outline to a PowerPoint Presentation

Linking an Excel Chart with a Word Document and a PowerPoint Presentation

Editing a Linked Object

Embedding and Editing a Word Table in a PowerPoint Slide

Linking Data to a New Table

Embedding an Excel Worksheet into a Word Document

Editing an Embedded Worksheet

End-of-Section Exercises
Skills Review
Review 1 Exporting Access Data to Excel

Review 2 Exporting an Access Report to Word

Review 3 Importing Data to a New Table

Review 4 Exporting a PowerPoint Presentation to Word

Review 5 Linking and Editing an Excel Chart with a PowerPoint Slide

Review 6 Embedding and Editing a Word Table in a PowerPoint Slide

Review 7 Linking Data to a New Table and Editing Linked Data

Review 8 Embedding an Object

Overview of Assessment Venues

The grading sheet on the following page can be used as a resource to create your grading plan. An electronic copy of this table is provided on the Instructor Resources CD, and you can alter this file to meet your specific course needs. Several venues of different types are available for assessing student achievement in your course.

Comprehension Assessments

- Knowledge Check questions appear at the end of each section. Answer keys for these items are included in this section of the *Instructor's Guide* and on the Instructor Resources CD.
- ExamView test generating software and test bank includes multiple choice items for each section of the text. Use ExamView to create web-based or print tests.
- SNAP web-based assessments include multiple choice items for each section of the text (prepared from the ExamView test bank).

Performance-Based Assessments

- Skills Review—Exercises provide additional hands-on computer exercises to reinforce learning. These exercises include some guidance, but less than the section activities. PDFs are included in this section and on the Instructor Resources CD. Live files are also available to instructors on the Instructor Resources CD.
- Skills Assessment—Framed in a workplace project perspective, these less-guided assessments evaluate students' abilities to apply section skills and concepts in solving realistic problems. They require demonstrating program skills as well as decision-making skills and include Help and Internet-based activities. PDFs are included in this section and on the Instructor Resources CD. Live files are also available on the Instructor Resources CD.
- Marquee Challenge—Culminating assessments test students' mastery of program features and their problem-solving abilities. PDFs are included in this section and on the Instructor Resources CD. Live files are also available on the Instructor Resources CD.
- Two supplemental Skills Assessment exercises are provided for Word, Excel, Access, and PowerPoint. Printouts of these assessments are provided in this section and corresponding files are available on the Instructor Resources CD.
- One supplemental Marquee Challenge is provided for each section of the text. Printouts of these assessments are provided in this section and corresponding files are available on the Instructor Resources CD.
- SNAP Skills Assessments are available to evaluate students' mastery of programs in the Microsoft Office 2010 suite.

Grading Sheet
Marquee Series Microsoft Office 2010

Program/Section	Assignment	File Name	Date Due	Grade
Information Technology Essentials	Knowledge Check			
Windows 7, Section 1: Exploring Windows 7	Activity 1.1–1.4			NA
	Knowledge Check			
	Review 1			
	Review 2			
	Assessment 1			
	Assessment 2			
	Assessment 3			
	SNAP Tutorial 1.1			
	SNAP Tutorial 1.2			
	SNAP Tutorial 1.3			
	SNAP Tutorial 1.4			
Windows 7, Section 2: Maintaining Files and Customizing Windows	Activity 2.1–2.10			NA
	Knowledge Check			
	Review 1			
	Review 2			
	Review 3			
	Review 4			
	Review 5			
	Assessment 1			
	Assessment 2			
	Assessment 3			
	Assessment 4			
	Assessment 5			
	Assessment 6			
	Assessment 7			
	SNAP Tutorial 2.1			
	SNAP Tutorial 2.2			
	SNAP Tutorial 2.3			
	SNAP Tutorial 2.4			
	SNAP Tutorial 2.5			
	SNAP Tutorial 2.6			
	SNAP Tutorial 2.7			

Program/Section	Assignment	File Name	Date Due	Grade
Internet Explorer 8.0, Section 1: Browsing the Internet Using Internet Explorer 8.0	Activity 1.1–1.5			NA
	Knowledge Check			
	Review 1			
	Review 2			
	Review 3			
	Assessment 1			
	Assessment 2			
	Assessment 3			
	Assessment 4			
	SNAP Tutorial 1.1			
	SNAP Tutorial 1.2			
	SNAP Tutorial 1.3			
	SNAP Tutorial 1.4			
Word, Section 1: Creating and Editing a Document	Activity 1.1–1.11			NA
	Knowledge Check			
	Review 1	WS1-R1-FCTHawaiianSpecials.docx		
	Review 2	WS1-R2-WEIncentiveAgt.docx		
	Review 3	WS1-R3-WEAgtFax.docx		
	Assessment 1	WS1-A1-PTMarqueeLtr.docx		
	Assessment 2	WS1-A2-WBCateringLtr.docx		
	Assessment 3	WS1-A3-WBFax.docx		
	Assessment 4	WS1-A4-FCTNorwayTour.docx		
	Assessment 5	WS1-A5-IC-Membership.docx		
	Challenge 1	WS1-C1-MPLtrtoTWB.docx		
	Challenge 2	WS1-C2-FCTRenoTahoeVac.docx		
	Supplemental Marquee Challenge	Features-WordS1SMC.docx		
	SNAP Tutorial 1.1			
	SNAP Tutorial 1.2			
	SNAP Tutorial 1.3			
	SNAP Tutorial 1.4			
	SNAP Tutorial 1.5			
	SNAP Tutorial 1.6			
	SNAP Tutorial 1.7			
	SNAP Tutorial 1.8			
	SNAP Tutorial 1.9			
	SNAP Tutorial 1.10			

Program/Section	Assignment	File Name	Date Due	Grade
	SNAP Tutorial 1.11			
	SNAP Tutorial 1.12			
Word, Section 2: Formatting Characters and Paragraphs	Activity 2.1-2.12			NA
	Knowledge Check			
	Review 1	WS2-R1-FCTPetersburg.docx		
	Review 2	WS2-R2-FCTVacPackages.docx		
	Assessment 1	WS2-A1-FCTLakeTahoeSkiing.docx		
	Assessment 2	WS2-A2-MPLtrtoNPC.docx		
	Assessment 3	WS2-A3-WEDistSch.docx		
	Assessment 4	WS2-A4-FCTVacSpecials.docx WS2-A4-PageBreaks.docx		
	Assessment 5	WS2-A5-IC-Airfare.docx		
	Challenge 1	WS2-C1-FCT-Juneau.docx		
	Challenge 2	WS2-C2-FCTSkiTahoe.docx		
	Supplemental Marquee Challenge	Program-WordS2SMC.docx		
	SNAP Tutorial 2.1			
	SNAP Tutorial 2.2			
	SNAP Tutorial 2.3			
	SNAP Tutorial 2.4			
	SNAP Tutorial 2.5			
	SNAP Tutorial 2.6			
	SNAP Tutorial 2.7			
	SNAP Tutorial 2.8			
	SNAP Tutorial 2.9			
	SNAP Tutorial 2.10			
	SNAP Tutorial 2.11			
	SNAP Tutorial 2.12			
	SNAP Tutorial 2.13			
	SNAP Tutorial 2.14			
	SNAP Tutorial 2.15			
Word, Section 3: Formatting and Enhancing a Document	Activity 3.1-3.10			NA
	Knowledge Check			
	Review 1	WS3-R1-FCTJuneau.docx		
	Review 2	WS3-R2-PTRenaissanceRpt.docx		
	Review 3	WS3-R3-MPEmpOpps01.docx WS3-R3-MPEmpOpps02.docx		
	Review 4	WS3-R4-FCTEnv.docx		

Program/Section	Assignment	File Name	Date Due	Grade
	Review 5	WS3-R5-WELabels.docx		
	Assessment 1	WS3-A1-PTAgreement.docx		
	Assessment 2	WS3-A2-NPCInternship.docx		
	Assessment 3	WS3-A3-NPCLabels.docx		
	Assessment 4	WS3-A4-MPEmpOpps-Wtrmark.docx		
	Assessment 5	WS3-A5-IC-Ltrhead.docx		
	Challenge 1	WS3-C1-PTCostumes.docx		
	Challenge 2	WS3-C2WENotice.docx		
	Supplemental Assessment 1	xxSaddleClubFlyer-WordSA1.docx		
	Supplemental Marquee Challenge	GolfReport-WordS3SMC.docx		
	SNAP Tutorial 3.1			
	SNAP Tutorial 3.2			
	SNAP Tutorial 3.3			
	SNAP Tutorial 3.4			
	SNAP Tutorial 3.5			
	SNAP Tutorial 3.6			
	SNAP Tutorial 3.7			
	SNAP Tutorial 3.8			
	SNAP Tutorial 3.9			
	SNAP Tutorial 3.10			
	SNAP Tutorial 3.11			
	SNAP Tutorial 3.12			
	SNAP Tutorial 3.13			
	SNAP Tutorial 3.14			
	SNAP Tutorial 3.15			
Word, Section 4: Formatting with Special Features	Activity 4.1-4.9			NA
	Knowledge Check			
	Review 1	WS4-R1-FCTZenithAdv.docx		
	Review 2	WS4-R2-MPProdDept.docx		
	Review 3	WS4-R3-NPCFallSch.docx		
	Review 4	WS4-R4-FCTOslo.docx WS4-R4-FCTOlso.mht		
	Review 5	WS4-R5-PTFabricLtrMD.docx WS4-R5-PTMergedEnvs.docx WS4-R5-PTMergedFabricLtrs.docx		
	Assessment 1	WS4-A1-NPCTheatreNewsltr.docx		
	Assessment 2	WS4-A2-PTDesignDept.docx		
	Assessment 3	WS4-A3-WBLunchOptions.docx		
	Assessment 4	WS4-A4-WEStockholderMtg.docx		

Program/Section	Assignment	File Name	Date Due	Grade
	Assessment 5	WS4-A5-IC-CarRentalInfo.docx		
	Challenge 1	WS4-C1-FCTOrcasIsland.docx		
	Challenge 2	WS4-C2-WBFlier.docx		
	Supplemental Assessment 2	xxEventsNewsletter-WordSA2.docx		
	Supplemental Marquee Challenge	Minerals-WordS4SMC.docx		
	SNAP Tutorial 4.1			
	SNAP Tutorial 4.2			
	SNAP Tutorial 4.3			
	SNAP Tutorial 4.4			
	SNAP Tutorial 4.5			
	SNAP Tutorial 4.6			
	SNAP Tutorial 4.7			
	SNAP Tutorial 4.8			
	SNAP Tutorial 4.9			
	SNAP Tutorial 4.10			
	SNAP Tutorial 4.11			
Excel, Section 1: Analyzing Data Using Excel	Activity 1.1-1.9			NA
	Knowledge Check			
	Review 1	ES1-R1-WBQtrlyIncome.xlsx		
	Review 2	ES1-R1-WBQtrlyIncome.xlsx		
	Assessment 1	ES1-A1-MPTravelCosts.xlsx		
	Assessment 2	ES1-A2-PTCostumeCont.xlsx		
	Assessment 3	ES1-A3-WEGGProjRev.xlsx		
	Assessment 4	ES1-A4-WBInventory.xlsx		
	Assessment 5	ES1-A5-SchoolBudget.xlsx		
	Challenge 1	ES1-C1-NPCIntlRegRpt.xlsx		
	Challenge 2	ES1-C2-NPCTargetEnrolRpt.xlsx		
	Supplemental Marquee Challenge	TopsandBottoms-ExcelS1SMC.xlsx		
	SNAP Tutorial 1.1			
	SNAP Tutorial 1.2			
	SNAP Tutorial 1.3			
	SNAP Tutorial 1.4			
	SNAP Tutorial 1.5 SNAP Tutorial 1.6			
Excel, Section 2: Editing and Formatting Worksheets	Activity 2.1-2.12			NA

Program/Section	Assignment	File Name	Date Due	Grade
	Knowledge Check			
	Review 1	ES2-R1-WBInvToNPC.xlsx		
	Review 2	ES2-R1-WBInvToNPC.xlsx		
	Assessment 1	ES2-A1-PTMarqCost.xlsx		
	Assessment 2	ES2-A2-PTMarqCostInv.xlsx		
	Assessment 3	ES2-A3-WEMBRev.xlsx		
	Assessment 4	ES2-A4-WBInventory.xlsx		
	Assessment 5	ES2-A5-TheatreArts.xlsx		
	Challenge 1	ES2-C1-MPLocBudg.xlsx		
	Challenge 2	ES2-C2-NPCRoomSch.xlsx		
	Supplemental Marquee Challenge	EmployeeWages-ExcelS2SMC.xlsx		
	SNAP Tutorial 2.1			
	SNAP Tutorial 2.2			
	SNAP Tutorial 2.3			
	SNAP Tutorial 2.4			
	SNAP Tutorial 2.5			
	SNAP Tutorial 2.6			
	SNAP Tutorial 2.7			
	SNAP Tutorial 2.8			
	SNAP Tutorial 2.9			
Excel, Section 3: Using Functions, Setting Print Options, and Adding Visual Elements	Activity 3.1-3.12			NA
	Knowledge Check			
	Review 1	ES3-R1-WBQtrRev.xlsx		
	Review 2	ES3-R1-WBQtrRev.xlsx		
	Assessment 1	ES3-A1-FCTSalesComm.xlsx		
	Assessment 2	ES3-A2-WELoan.xlsx		
	Assessment 3	ES3-A3-NPCGrades.xlsx		
	Assessment 4	ES3-A4-FCTEurope.xlsx		
	Assessment 5	ES3-A5-FCTEurope.xlsx		
	Assessment 6	ES3-A6-SocialNetSurvey.xlsx		
	Challenge 1	ES3-C1-MPMovieStats.xlsx		
	Challenge 2	ES3-C2-NPCTop10.xlsx		
	Supplemental Marquee Challenge	LendingHands-ExcelS3SMC.xlsx		
	Supplemental Assessment 1	xxInsuranceReport-ExcelSA1.xlsx		
	SNAP Tutorial 3.1			
	SNAP Tutorial 3.2			

Program/Section	Assignment	File Name	Date Due	Grade
	SNAP Tutorial 3.3			
	SNAP Tutorial 3.4			
	SNAP Tutorial 3.5			
	SNAP Tutorial 3.6			
	SNAP Tutorial 3.7			
	SNAP Tutorial 3.8			
	SNAP Tutorial 3.9			
Excel, Section 4: Working with Multiple Worksheets, Formatting Sheet Tabs	Activity 4.1-4.12			NA
	Knowledge Check			
	Review 1	ES4-R1-WBPayroll.xlsx		
	Review 2	ES4-R2-WBInventory.xlsx		
	Review 3	ES4-R3-PTStmntNov30.xlsx		
	Assessment 1	ES4-A1-NPCInternGrades.xlsx		
	Assessment 2	ES4-A2-PTMarqueeSch.xlsx		
	Assessment 3	ES4-A3-PTMarqueeSch.xlsx		
	Assessment 4	ES4-A4-PTRentalCost.xlsx		
	Assessment 5	ES4-A5-FileFormats.xlsx		
	Assessment 6	ES4-A6-Smartphones.xlsx		
	Challenge 1	ES4-C1-WBInvFCT.xlsx		
	Challenge 2	ES4-C2-WEDistributors.xlsx		
	Supplemental Assessment 2	xxStock-ExcelSA2.xlsx		
	Supplemental Marquee Challenge	ScoopItUp-ExcelS4SMC.xlsx		
	SNAP Tutorial 4.1			
	SNAP Tutorial 4.2			
	SNAP Tutorial 4.3			
	SNAP Tutorial 4.4			
	SNAP Tutorial 4.5			
	SNAP Tutorial 4.6			
	SNAP Tutorial 4.7			
	SNAP Tutorial 4.8			
	SNAP Tutorial 4.9			
	SNAP Tutorial 4.10			
	SNAP Tutorial 4.11			
	SNAP Tutorial 4.12			
Integrating Programs: Word and Excel	Activity 1.1-1.5			NA
	Review 1	Int1-R1-NPCExcelScores.xlsx		

Program/Section	Assignment	File Name	Date Due	Grade
	Review 2	Int1-R2-NPCExcelChart.xlsx Int1-R2-NPCWordEnroll.docx		
	Review 3	Int1-R3-WERevMemo.docx		
Access, Section 1: Maintaining Data in Access Tables	Activity 1.1-1.11			NA
	Knowledge Check			
	Review 1	WEEmployees1.accdb		
	Review 2	WEEmployees1.accdb		
	Assessment 1	NPCGrades1.accdb		
	Assessment 2	WBInventory1.accdb		
	Assessment 3	PTCostumeInv1.accdb		
	Assessment 4	AS1-A4-TableMemo.docx		
	Assessment 5	JobSearchInfo1.accdb		
	Challenge 1	WBSpecialEvents1.accdb		
	Challenge 2	AS1-C2-PTCostumes.docx		
	Supplemental Marquee Challenge	JustShoes-AccessS1SMC.accdb		
	SNAP Tutorial 1.1			
	SNAP Tutorial 1.2			
	SNAP Tutorial 1.3			
	SNAP Tutorial 1.4			
	SNAP Tutorial 1.5			
	SNAP Tutorial 1.6			
	SNAP Tutorial 1.7			
	SNAP Tutorial 1.8			
Access, Section 2: Creating Tables and Relationships	Activity 2.1-2.12			NA
	Knowledge Check			
	Review 1	WEEmployees2.accdb		
	Review 2	WEEmployees2.accdb		
	Assessment 1	NPCGrades2.accdb		
	Assessment 2	PTCostumeInv2.accdb		
	Assessment 3	FCTExpenses.accdb		
	Assessment 4	WBEvents2.accdb		
	Assessment 5	NewWeb20_2.accdb		
	Challenge 1	WEPurchases2.accdb AS2-C1-Memo.docx		
	Challenge 2	AS2-C2-PTCostumes.docx AS2-C2-PTCostumes.accdb		
	Supplemental Marquee Challenge	Tri-StateDentalGroup-AccessS2SMC.accdb		
	SNAP Tutorial 2.1			

Program/Section	Assignment	File Name	Date Due	Grade
	SNAP Tutorial 2.2			
	SNAP Tutorial 2.3			
	SNAP Tutorial 2.4			
	SNAP Tutorial 2.5			
	SNAP Tutorial 2.6			
	SNAP Tutorial 2.7			
Access, Section 3: Creating Queries, Forms, and Reports	Activity 3.1-3.9			NA
	Knowledge Check			
	Review 1	WEEmployees3.accdb		
	Review 2	WEEmployees3.accdb		
	Review 3	WEEmployees3.accdb		
	Assessment 1	NPCGrades3.accdb		
	Assessment 2	PTCostumeInv3.accdb		
	Assessment 3	PTCostumeInv3.accdb		
	Assessment 4	WEVendors3.accdb		
	Assessment 5	AS3-Movies.accdb		
	Challenge 1	WBSpecialEvents3.accdb		
	Challenge 2	AS3-C2-PTCostumes.accdb		
	Supplemental Assessment 1	InventoryForm-AccessSA1.accdb InventoryforSale-AccessSA1.accdb FordInventory-AccessSA1.accdb		
	Supplemental Marquee Challenge	Tri-StateDentalGroup-AccessS3SMC .accdb		
	SNAP Tutorial 3.1			
	SNAP Tutorial 3.2			
	SNAP Tutorial 3.3			
	SNAP Tutorial 3.4			
	SNAP Tutorial 3.5			
	SNAP Tutorial 3.6			
	SNAP Tutorial 3.7			
	SNAP Tutorial 3.8			
	SNAP Tutorial 3.9			
	SNAP Tutorial 3.10			
Access, Section 4: Summarizing Data and Calculating in Forms and Reports	Activity 4.1-4.11			NA
	Knowledge Check			
	Review 1	WEEmployees4.accdb		
	Review 2	WEEmployees4.accdb		
	Review 3	WEEmployees4.accdb		

Program/Section	Assignment	File Name	Date Due	Grade
	Assessment 1	PTCostumeInv4.accdb		
	Assessment 2	WEDistributors4.accdb		
	Assessment 3	WEDistributors4.accdb		
	Assessment 4	WBInventory4.accdb		
	Assessment 5	WEEmployees4.accdb		
	Assessment 6	AS4-SalaryStats.accdb		
	Challenge 1	WBSpecialEvents4.accdb		
	Challenge 2	PTCostumeInv4.accdb		
	Supplemental Assessment 2	WEEmployees4-AssessSA2.accdb		
	Supplemental Marquee Challenge	FitnessNFun-AccessS4AMC.accdb		
	SNAP Tutorial 4.1			
	SNAP Tutorial 4.2			
	SNAP Tutorial 4.3			
	SNAP Tutorial 4.4			
	SNAP Tutorial 4.5			
	SNAP Tutorial 4.6			
Integrating Programs: Word, Excel, and Access	Activity 2.1-2.5			NA
	Review 1	Int2-R1-CostumeInventory.xlsx		
	Review 2	Int2-R2-InventoryList.rtf		
	Review 3	Int2-R3-CostumeInventory.xlsx		
	Review 4	Int2-PTCostumes.accdb		
	Review 5	Int2-FCTCommissions.accdb		
PowerPoint, Section 1: Preparing a Presentation	Activity 1.1-1.10			NA
	Knowledge Check			
	Review 1	PS1-R1-MPTeamMtg.pptx		
	Assessment 1	PS1-A1-WEExecMtg.pptx		
	Assessment 2	PS1-A2-TWBServices.pptx		
	Assessment 3	PS1-A3-MPProj.pptx		
	Assessment 4	PS1-A4-IC-Cancun.pptx		
	Challenge 1	PS1-C1-FCTToronto.pptx		
	Challenge 2	PS1-C2-PTCostumeMtg.pptx		
	Supplemental Marquee Challenge	Accounting-PPS1SMC.pptx		
	SNAP Tutorial 1.1			
	SNAP Tutorial 1.2			
	SNAP Tutorial 1.3			
	SNAP Tutorial 1.4			

Program/Section	Assignment	File Name	Date Due	Grade
	SNAP Tutorial 1.5			
	SNAP Tutorial 1.6			
	SNAP Tutorial 1.7			
	SNAP Tutorial 1.8			
	SNAP Tutorial 1.9			
	SNAP Tutorial 1.10			
PowerPoint, Section 2: Editing and Enhancing Slides	Activity 2.1-2.11			NA
	Knowledge Check			
	Review 1	PS2-R1-MPAnnualMtg.pptx		
	Review 2	PS2-R2-PTPres.pptx		
	Assessment 1	PS2-A1-NPCTheatreArts.pptx		
	Assessment 2	PS2-A2-FCTVacations.pptx		
	Assessment 3	PS2-A3-FCTVacations.pptx		
	Assessment 4	PS2-A4.pptx		
	Challenge 1	PS2-C1-WEDist.pptx		
	Challenge 2	PS2-C2-TWBInfo.pptx		
	Supplemental Assessment 1	xxFundRaiser-PPSA1.pptx		
	Supplemental Marquee Challenge	FitnessNFun-PPS2SMC.pptx		
	SNAP Tutorial 2.1			
	SNAP Tutorial 2.2			
	SNAP Tutorial 2.3			
	SNAP Tutorial 2.4			
	SNAP Tutorial 2.5			
	SNAP Tutorial 2.6			
	SNAP Tutorial 2.7			
PowerPoint, Section 3: Customizing a Presentation	Activity 3.1-3.11			NA
	Knowledge Check			
	Review 1	PS3-R1-MPBiography.pptx		
	Review 2	PS3-R2-MPAnnualMtg.pptx		
	Review 3	PS3-R3-FCTCruise.pptx		
	Assessment 1	PS3-A1-PTCostumes.pptx		
	Assessment 2	PS3-A2-FCTSouthernTours.pptx		
	Assessment 3	PS3-A3-FCTSouthernTours.pptx		
	Assessment 4	PS3-A4-IC-SocialNetwork.pptx		
	Challenge 1	PS3-C1-MPProdSch.pptx		
	Challenge 2	PS3-C2-FCTMorocco.pptx		

Program/Section	Assignment	File Name	Date Due	Grade
	Supplemental Assessment 2	xxClubMeeting-PPSA2.pptx		
	Supplemental Marquee Challenge	CafeShopandMore-PPS3SMC.pptx		
	SNAP Tutorial 3.1			
	SNAP Tutorial 3.2			
	SNAP Tutorial 3.3			
	SNAP Tutorial 3.4			
	SNAP Tutorial 3.5			
	SNAP Tutorial 3.6			
	SNAP Tutorial 3.7			
	SNAP Tutorial 3.8			
	SNAP Tutorial 3.9			
	SNAP Tutorial 3.10			
Integrating Programs: Word, Excel, and PowerPoint	Activity 3.1-3.5			NA
	Review 1	Int3-R1-FCTVacations.pptx		
	Review 2	Int3-R2-NPCEnroll.pptx Int3-R2-NPCEnrollChart.xlsx		
	Review 3	Int3-R3-NPCEnroll.pdf		

Marquee Series Microsoft Office 2010 Brief Edition

Program/Section	Assignment	File Name	Date Due	Grade
Integrating Programs: Word, Excel, Access, and PowerPoint	Activity 1.1-1.11			NA
	Review 1	Int-R1-CostumeInventory.xlsx		
	Review 2	Int-R2-CostumeInventory.rtf		
	Review 3	Int.PTCostumes.accdb		
	Review 4	Int-R4-FCTVacSpecials.pptx		
	Review 5	Int-R5-NPCEnroll.pptx Int-R5-NPCEnrollChart.xlsx		
	Review 6	Int-R6-NPCEnroll.pptx		
	Review 7	Int-R7-FCTBookings.xlsx		
	Review 8	Int-R8-WERevMemo.docx		

Information Technology Essentials

Knowledge Check Answer Key

1.	What are the four segments of the information processing cycle?	input, processing, output, storage	page 1
2.	Besides the keyboard, mouse, and storage devices, list five devices that can be used to enter information into a computer.	touchpad, touchscreen, scanner, tablet, joystick, digital camera, microphone, bar code reader	pages 2-4
3.	What part of the computer handles the tasks of calculating formulas and editing documents?	central processing unit (CPU)	page 4
4.	What advantage do dual-core and quad-core processors have over single-core processors?	They process instructions simultaneously	page 4
5.	What is the technical name for the volatile computer workspace that is erased whenever the power is turned off?	random access memory (RAM)	page 4
6.	Which storage device has no motor or other moving parts?	flash drive or solid-state hard drive	page 6
7.	What type of port allows up to 127 hardware devices to be connected to the computer host at 480 Mbps?	USB 2.0 port (Universal Serial Bus)	page 6
8.	What type of software can be copied freely and has no license agreement?	open-source	page 13
9.	What is the basic purpose for a computer network?	sharing information	page 14
10.	What two terms describe the "data requester" and "data provider" in a LAN?	client and server	pages 14-15
11.	What is the name of the connector used on a network cable?	RJ-45	page 18
12.	What is the basic protocol that allows all computers on the Internet to interact?	TCP/IP	page 17
13.	What protocol and application can you use if you need to transfer a file that is too large to email?	File Transfer Protocol (FTP)	page 20
14.	List at least three types of malware.	virus, worm, Trojan, spyware	pages 21-22
15.	What term describes the act of illegally sharing a software application with someone else?	software piracy	page 26

Windows 7 Section 1

Knowledge Check Answer Key

1.	This mouse term refers to tapping the left mouse button twice in quick succession.	double-click	page 3
2.	Click this button on a window Title bar to reduce the window to a task button on the Taskbar.	Minimize	page 6
3.	Click this button on a window Title bar to expand the window so it fills the entire screen.	Maximize	page 6
4.	Click the time located at the right side of the Taskbar and then click this option to open the Date and Time dialog box.	Change date and time settings	page 8
5.	This is the name of a mini program that you can display on the desktop for information at a glance, such as a calendar.	gadget	page 8
6.	Windows Help and Support is accessed from this button on the Taskbar.	Start	page 12

Windows 7 Section 2

Knowledge Check Answer Key

1.	Navigate to any other device or folder from the current device and folder using the Navigation pane or this bar in the Computer window.	Address	page 20
2.	Specify the option to open each folder in its own window at this dialog box.	Folder Options	page 22
3.	Click this button on the toolbar to create a new folder in the Computer window.	New folder	page 24
4.	Change the display of files and folders in the Computer window to List or Details using this button on the toolbar.	Views	page 26
5.	To select adjacent files, click the first file, hold down this key, and then click the last file.	Shift	page 26
6.	To select nonadjacent files, click the first file, hold down this key, and then click any other desired files.	Ctrl	page 26
7.	Click this button to display in the Content pane the files in the previous folder viewed.	Back	page 27
8.	Click this option at the Organize button drop-down list to move the selected files.	Cut	page 28
9.	Files deleted from the hard drive are sent here.	Recycle Bin	page 30
10.	Open this window to display a list of categories or icons in which you can customize the appearance and functionality of your computer.	Control Panel	page 34
11.	Type a search criterion in this text box at the Start menu to locate a program.	Search	page 36
12.	Customize the desktop such as by changing the background, screen saver, and color option at this window.	Personalization	page 38

Internet Explorer 8.0 Section 1

Knowledge Check Answer Key

1.	Type a URL in this bar at the Internet Explorer window.	Address	page 2
2.	The letters *URL* stand for this.	Uniform Resource Locator	page 2
3.	Click this button on the Internet Explorer toolbar to display the previous web page.	Back	page 3
4.	Click in this box located at the right end of the Internet Explorer Navigation bar to locate web pages using a keyword or phrase.	Instant Search	page 4
5.	Reduce the number of search results by looking for these options at the search engine's website.	Advanced Search	page 6
6.	Download an image from a website to a file on your computer by right-clicking the image and selecting this option at the shortcut menu.	Save Picture As	page 8

Word Section 1

Knowledge Check Answer Key

1.	This area on the screen contains tabs and commands divided into groups.	ribbon	page 7
2.	Click this tab to display the Backstage view.	File tab	page 7
3.	Use this keyboard command to move the insertion point to the beginning of the document.	Ctrl + Home	page 11
4.	To select a sentence, hold down this key and then click anywhere in the sentence.	Ctrl key	page 14
5.	This toolbar contains the Undo and Redo buttons.	Quick Access toolbar	page 15
6.	To begin checking the spelling and grammar in a document, click this tab and then click the Spelling & Grammar button in the Proofing group.	Review tab	page 16
7.	This feature automatically detects and corrects some typographical errors.	AutoCorrect	page 18
8.	Use this feature to find synonyms for a word.	Thesaurus	page 18
9.	Display a document in this view for easy viewing and reading.	Full Screen Reading	page 20
10.	The *Navigation Pane* check box is located in this group in the View tab.	Show group	page 21
11.	Click this button at the Find and Replace dialog box to replace all occurrences of text.	Replace All	page 22
12.	Click this option at the New tab Backstage view to display available templates.	Sample templates	page 26
13.	Click this button on the Open dialog box toolbar to create a new folder.	New folder	page 28
14.	Select nonadjacent documents at the Open dialog box by holding down this key while clicking each document name.	Ctrl key	page 28

Word Section 2

Knowledge Check Answer Key

1.	The Bold button is located in this group in the Home tab.	Font	page 42
2.	Click this button in the Font group and then click the *UPPERCASE* option to change selected text to uppercase letters.	Change Case	page 42
3.	Press these keys on the keyboard to italicize selected text.	Ctrl + I	page 45
4.	The *Small caps* option is located in this section of the Font dialog box.	Effects	page 45
5.	Click this button in the Paragraph group in the Home tab to align text at the right margin.	Align Text Right	page 46
6.	Indent text from the left margin by dragging the Left Indent marker on this.	Ruler	page 46
7.	The Line and Paragraph Spacing button displays in this group in the Home tab.	Paragraph	page 48
8.	This is the keyboard shortcut to display the Reveal Formatting task pane.	Shift + F1	page 50
9.	Click this button at the Find and Replace dialog box to display additional options.	More	page 50
10.	Click this button in the Paragraph group in the Home tab to number selected paragraphs.	Numbering	page 52
11.	Create multiple-level bulleted or numbered paragraphs with options from this button.	Multilevel List	page 53
12.	Display the Symbol palette by clicking this tab and then clicking the Symbol button in the Symbols group.	Insert	page 54
13.	This is the name of the button that displays at the left side of the Ruler.	Alignment	page 56
14.	Set tabs at the Tabs dialog box or using this.	Ruler	page 56
15.	Click this button in the Font group in the Home tab to remove paragraph formatting from selected text.	Clear Formatting	page 57
16.	These can be added to a tab to help guide the reader's eyes across the page.	leaders	page 58
17.	Insert a page border with options at this dialog box with the Page Border tab selected.	Borders and Shading	page 60
18.	A document contains a number of predesigned formats grouped into sets called this.	Quick Styles	page 62
19.	To change the Quick Styles set, click this button in the Styles group in the Home tab, point to *Style Set*, and then click the desired Quick Styles at the side menu.	Changes Styles	page 62
20.	At a new document, this is the default line spacing.	1.15	page 64

Word Section 3

Knowledge Check Answer Key

1.	The Cut button is located in this group in the Home tab.	Clipboard	page 86
2.	Click this button to insert copied text in the document.	Paste	page 86
3.	Click this to display the Clipboard task pane.	Clipboard dialog box launcher	page 88
4.	Click this tab to display the Margins button.	Page Layout	page 90
5.	This is the default measurement for the top, bottom, left, and right margins.	1 inch	page 90
6.	This is the default page orientation.	portrait	page 90
7.	This is the default page size.	8.5" x 11"	page 90
8.	A document theme is a set of formatting choices that includes a font theme, an effects theme, and this.	color theme	page 90
9.	This term refers to lightened text or image that displays behind text.	watermark	page 92
10.	The Cover Page button is located in the Pages group in this tab.	Insert	page 92
11.	Insert a page break by clicking the Page Break button in the Pages group in the Insert tab or with this keyboard shortcut.	Ctrl + Enter	page 93
12.	Insert a footer by clicking the Footer button in this group in the Insert tab.	Header & Footer	page 94
13.	The initials MLA refer to this type of report style generally used in the humanities and English.	Modern Language Association	page 96
14.	General MLA style guidelines recommend this measurement for the top, bottom, left, and right margins.	1 inch	page 96
15.	General MLA style guidelines recommend this line spacing.	2	page 96
16.	The Insert Citation button is located in this tab.	References	page 97
17.	In an MLA report, this page is an alphabetic list of the books, journal articles, web pages, or other sources referenced in the document.	Works Cited page	page 100
18.	Use this feature to position the mouse pointer at the left margin, center of the page, or right margin.	Click and Type	page 102
19.	This is the default page alignment.	Top of page	page 102
20.	Change page alignment with the *Vertical alignment* option at this dialog box.	Page Setup	page 102
21.	The Clip Art button displays in this group in the Insert tab.	Illustrations	page 103
22.	Click this button in the Picture Tools Format tab to choose a wrapping style.	Position	page 104
23.	When changing the size of an image, maintain the image proportions by holding down this key while dragging a corner sizing handle.	Shift	page 105
24.	To display the Envelopes and Labels dialog box, click this tab and then click the Envelopes button or the Labels button.	Envelopes	page 106

Word Section 4

Knowledge Check Answer Key

1.	Use this feature to distort or modify text to conform to a variety of shapes.	WordArt	page 130
2.	This is the first letter of the first word of a paragraph that is set into a paragraph.	drop cap	page 132
3.	When you draw a shape in a document, this tab becomes active.	Drawing Tools Format	page 130
4.	Insert a text box by clicking the Text Box button in this group in the Insert tab.	Text	page 132
5.	To display a menu of SmartArt choices, click the Insert tab and then click the SmartArt button in this group.	Illustrations	page 136
6.	In a SmartArt graphic, click this button in the Create Graphic group to close the *Type your text here* window.	Text Pane	page 136
7.	You can create a table using the Table button in the Insert tab or with options at this dialog box.	Insert Table	page 140
8.	Press this key to move the insertion point to the next cell in a table.	Tab	page 140
9.	Press these keys to move the insertion point to the previous cell in a table.	Shift + Tab	page 140
10.	To insert a row in a table above the current row, click this button in the Rows & Columns group in the Table Tools Layout tab.	Insert Above	page 141
11.	Merge selected cells in a table by clicking the Merge Cells button in this group.	Merge	page 141
12.	Rotate text in a cell by clicking this button in the Alignment group in the Table Tools Layout tab.	Text Directions	page 142
13.	Use this button in the Text group in the Insert tab to insert one file into another.	Object	page 146
14.	Insert a section break in a document with options at this button drop-down list.	Breaks	page 146
15.	To display the Columns dialog box, click the Page Layout tab, click the Columns button, and then click this option at the drop-down list.	More columns	page 147
16.	If you want to save a Word document as a single file web page, choose this option at the *Save as type* option box drop-down list at the Save As dialog box.	Single File Web (*.mht; *.mhtml)	page 148
17.	To navigate to a hyperlinked document or website, hold down this key while clicking the hyperlink.	Ctrl	page 149
18.	A merge generally takes two documents—the main document and this.	data source	page 150
19.	Use buttons in this tab to merge documents.	Mailings	page 150

Excel Section 1

Knowledge Check Answer Key

1.	This area contains commands and features for performing actions divided into tabs and groups.	ribbon	page 5
2.	This area displays the formula stored within the cell (not the result).	Formula bar	page 5
3.	The cell pointer changes to this when pointing at the small black square at the bottom right corner of the active cell.	thin black cross	page 9
4.	This is the term for the method used to create a formula by typing the equals sign and operator symbols while clicking reference cells between the typed symbols.	pointing method	page 12
5.	This would be the formula entry to divide the contents of cell C6 by the contents in cell C12.	C6/C12	page 13
6.	This term is used to refer to the values identified within parentheses in the SUM function.	argument	page 14
7.	The SUM function button is located in this group in the Home tab.	Editing	page 14
8.	Do this action if Excel suggests the wrong range after clicking the Sum button.	Drag to select the correct range	page 14
9.	This button appears after copied cells are pasted into the destination range.	Paste Options (Ctrl)	page 16
10.	This is the term for the formulas entered beside or below a worksheet that are designed to verify the worksheet's accuracy.	proof formula	page 18
11.	This format adds a dollar sign, a comma in the thousands place, and two decimal places to each value in the selected range.	Accounting Number Format button	page 20
12.	Click the Sort & Filter button in the Editing group in the Home tab and then click this option at the drop-down list to display the Sort dialog box.	Custom Sort	page 20
13.	This keyboard shortcut will open the Excel Help window when pointing to a button.	F1	page 22
14.	Display this tab in Backstage view to change the page orientation.	Print	page 24
15.	Open this dialog box to type a cell reference to which you want to move the active cell.	Go to	page 28

Excel Section 2

Knowledge Check Answer Key

1.	Use this feature to remove everything from a cell including text and formats.	Clear All	page 40
2.	Make a cell active anywhere in this row to insert a new row between 11 and 12.	12	page 42
3.	Make a cell active anywhere in this column to insert a new column between E and F.	F	page 42
4.	This is the term for adjusting a column width to the length of the longest entry.	AutoFit Column Width	page 46
5.	This term refers to the feature where Excel shows the results of a format option while pointing to the option in a drop-down list or gallery.	Live Preview	page 48
6.	By default, cells are initially set to this numeric style format.	General	page 50
7.	Click this button in the Alignment group of the Home tab to center cells vertically between the top and bottom cell boundaries.	Middle Align	page 53
8.	Click this button in the Clipboard group of the Home tab to copy the formats of the active cell.	Format Painter	page 55
9.	This feature stores predefined format options.	Cell Styles	page 56
10.	This feature stores a set of colors, fonts, and effects that can be applied to the entire worksheet.	themes	page 56
11.	Make this cell active to freeze rows 1 through 5.	A6	page 62
12.	List two methods for changing the zoom magnification to view more cells in the current window.	Drag Zoom slider bar Drag Zoom In OR Drag Zoom Out	page 63
13.	Click this tab and button to search for art on Office Online.	Insert tab/Clip Art button	page 64
14.	Click this button in the Illustrations group to insert an image stored in a file.	Picture	page 65

Excel Section 3

Knowledge Check Answer Key

1.	This symbol next to a column or row number means the reference is absolute.	$	page 80
2.	AVERAGE and COUNT are two of the functions grouped in this function category.	Statistical	page 82
3.	This Date and Time function inserts the current date (without the time) in the active cell.	TODAY	page 84
4.	This financial function returns the payment for a loan based on a constant interest rate and period of time for repayment.	PMT	page 86
5.	A range name is typed in this box at the left end of the Formula bar.	Name box	page 88
6.	The IF function is found in this category of functions in the Function Library.	Logical button	page 90
7.	This type of chart is used to illustrate each data point as a proportion of the total.	Pie chart	page 94
8.	When a chart is selected, these three contextual Chart Tools tabs appear.	Design, Layout, Format	pages 92-95
9.	This button in the Illustrations group is used when you want to draw a star.	Shapes	page 96
10.	Page Setup options such as custom margins can be changed using the Page Layout tab or while viewing a preview of how the worksheet will print in this view.	Print tab, Backstage view	page 100
11.	You can type header or footer text directly in the worksheet while viewing the worksheet in this view.	Page Layout	page 102
12.	This code is inserted in the header or footer when you click the File Name button in the Header & Footer Elements group.	&[File]	page 103

Excel Section 4

Knowledge Check Answer Key

1.	A new workbook initially contains this many sheets.	3	page 122
2.	Perform this action with the mouse while pointing at a sheet tab to change the worksheet name.	right-click the sheet tab, click Rename, or double-click sheet tab	page 122
3.	Perform this action with multiple sheets to apply the same formatting options to all of them in one operation.	Group worksheets	page 124
4.	Hold down this key while dragging a sheet tab to copy the sheet.	Ctrl	page 124
5.	The formula =SUM('Jan:Jun'!G4) includes this type of reference.	3-D	page 126
6.	A link to a cell in another worksheet can be created by typing this kind of entry into the destination cell.	=	page 128
7.	Page breaks are displayed as broken or solid blue lines in this view.	Page Break Preview	page 132
8.	Click this button in the Styles group in the Home tab to define an area of a worksheet as an independent range that can be formatted and managed separately from the rest of the worksheet.	Format as Table	page 134
9.	Select this option from the Sort & Filter list to open a dialog box in which to define more than one sort column.	Custom Sort	page 136
10.	This term refers to temporarily hiding rows that do not meet a specified criterion.	filter	page 138
11.	Use this feature to type additional information about a cell that appears in a pop-up box when the cell pointer is positioned over the cell.	comment	page 140
12.	Predesigned formatted worksheets that have labels and formulas created for specific uses can be accessed at this tab in Backstage view.	New tab	page 142
13.	This is the default file format for Excel workbooks.	XML	page 144
14.	Opening a workbook created in an earlier version of Excel causes Excel to switch to this mode.	Compatibility	page 144
15.	This type of file requires the Adobe Reader program to view.	PDF	page 148

Access Section 1

Knowledge Check Answer Key

1.	Access opens with this view displayed.	New tab in Backstage view	page 4
2.	This term describes a single unit of information about a person place, item, or event.	record	page 4
3.	This term describes all of the data about one subject in a table.	field	page 4
4.	This object is created first before any other objects in a database.	table	page 4
5.	This database object is used to display or print data from one or more tables in a specific layout or format.	report	page 9
6.	Click this button at the Column Width dialog box to set the column width to the length of the longest entry in the column.	Best Fit	page 12
7.	Press this key to turn on Edit mode in a datasheet.	F2	page 14
8.	This object provides a user-friendly interface with which you can edit, view, or print data by working with only one record at a time.	forms	page 18
9.	Access displays a message box requesting confirmation when a record is about to be deleted because this feature is not available for a Delete operation.	undo	page 20
10.	When more than one column is selected for a sort operation, Access sorts first by this column.	leftmost column	page 22
11.	This feature temporarily hides records in the datasheet that do not meet the specified criteria.	filter	page 24
12.	This page layout orientation rotates the printout to print wider than it is tall.	landscape	page 27
13.	Display this dialog box to set your own custom margins.	Page Setup	page 27
14.	These are the steps to hide a column in a datasheet.	right-click field name in header row, then click *Hide Fields*	page 28
15.	This keyboard command selects all records in the datasheet.	Ctrl + A or Ctrl + Shift + spacebar	page 29

Access Section 2

Knowledge Check Answer Key

1.	A field name can contain this number of characters.	64	page 43
2.	Assign a field this data type if the field will contain dollar values that you do not want rounded off in calculations.	Currency	page 43
3.	This is the term for the field in a table that must contain unique information for each record.	Primary key	page 48
4.	Enter a value in this field property if you want the value to appear automatically in the field whenever a new record is created.	Default Value	page 50
5.	Enter a statement in this field property to prevent data that does not meet the range or other criteria from being entered into the field.	Validation rule	page 52
6.	This is the field property that controls data as it is being entered by ensuring data typed in the field conforms to the code entered in the property box.	input mask	page 54
7.	This field property controls how data is displayed after it has been accepted for entry in the field.	Format	page 54
8.	This is the name of the wizard used to create a drop-down list in a field.	Input Mask wizard	page 54
9.	This button can be used to add a SUM function to the bottom of a numeric field in the datasheet.	Totals	page 59
10.	One table in a relationship is referred to as the primary table. The other table is referred to as this.	related table	page 62
11.	In this type of relationship one table can have only one record with a matching field value in the common field while the other table can have several records with a matching field value.	one-to-many	page 62
12.	This is the term for the black line that displays between the common field name in the two field list boxes after a relationship has been created.	join line	pages 64-65
13.	This type of relationship is created when the field used to join the two tables is the primary key in both tables.	one-to-one	page 64
14.	Turn this relationship option on to make sure new records are added first to the primary table before a record with a matching value in the common field can be added to the related table.	Referential Integrity	pages 64-65
15.	Click this button in the Relationships window to print a hard copy of the relationships.	Relationship Report	page 66

Access Section 3

Knowledge Check Answer Key

1.	This is the name of the wizard used to facilitate creating a query to select records from a table.	Simple Query Wizard	page 84
2.	Click this button to show the query results datasheet after creating a query using Design view.	Run	page 86
3.	Type this entry in the *AnnualSalary* criteria row in the query design grid to extract records of employees who earn more than $40,000.	>40000	page 91
4.	Click the check box in this row in the query design grid to prevent a column from being displayed in the query results datasheet.	Show	page 91
5.	Multiple criteria typed in the same *Criteria* row in the query design grid become this type of statement.	AND	page 92
6.	Multiple criteria typed in different *Criteria* rows in the query design grid become this type of statement.	OR	page 94
7.	This entry in a blank field text box in the query design grid would add the values in a field named *RegHours* to the values in a field named *OTHours* and title the column in the query results datasheet *TotalHours*.	TotalHours: [RegHours]+ [OTHours]	page 96
8.	Click this button in the Query Tools Design tab to change a field's format to display in Currency.	Property Sheet	page 97
9.	These three tabs become active when the form is displayed in Layout view.	Form Layout Tools	page 98
10.	Create a form using this method if you want the ability to specify the form's layout before the form is generated.	Form Wizard	page 99
11.	A form or report is comprised of a series of objects referred to by this term.	Controls	page 99
12.	This button opens the Field List pane to add fields from another table to the form.	Add Existing Fields	page 100
13.	A form created using the Form button adds this object next to the title so you can easily add an image such as a company logo.	logo container control	page 102
14.	List two items that are added to the top of a report automatically when the report is generated using the Report tool.	title, current day, date, time	page 104
15.	A report's page orientation can be changed from portrait to landscape at this Report Layout Tools tab.	Report Layout Tools Page Setup	page 105

Access Section 4

Knowledge Check Answer Key

1.	Click this button in the Query Tools Design tab to add a row to the design grid from which you can choose an aggregate function such as Sum.	Totals	page 132
2.	This query wizard can be used to sum data that is grouped by two fields.	Crosstab Query Wizard	page 134
3.	This query wizard could be created to produce a list of customers who have placed more than one order.	Find Duplicates Query Wizard	page 135
4.	Use this query wizard to produce a list of employees who have no absences reported in an Absences table.	Find Unmatched Query Wizard	page 136
5.	Click this button in the Controls group to add a picture to a form that you have saved in a file with a *.jpg* file extension.	Image	page 140
6.	Descriptive text can be added to a form or report using this control.	label control object	page 140
7.	Use this button in the Controls group to add a calculation to a form.	Text Box	page 142
8.	A formula for a calculated control is entered in this property box.	Control Source	page 142
9.	To format a calculated control object to display the values in Currency, open this task pane.	Property Sheet	page 143
10.	To sort records in a form display the form in this view.	Layout	page 146
11.	Click this Report Layout Tools tab to change a report to landscape.	Setup	page 146
12.	Click this button to open a pane at the bottom of the work area in which you can specify a field by which to group records.	Group & Sort	page 146
13.	Click this button in the Group, Sort, and Total pane to add subtotals to a group.	More Options	page 148
14.	This button is used to format values in a report based on whether the values meet a specified criterion.	Conditional Formatting	page 150
15.	Start this wizard to assist with generating names and addresses for a mailing.	Label Wizard	page 153
16.	Open this dialog box to turn on the *Compact on Close* option for a database.	Current Database	page 155

PowerPoint Section 1

Knowledge Check Answer Key

1.	To run a presentation beginning with Slide 1, click the Slide Show tab and then click this button.	From Beginning	page 6
2.	The Save button is located on this toolbar.	Quick Access	page 6
3.	The Normal view contains the Slides/Outline pane, the Slide pane, and this pane.	Notes	page 8
4.	The New Slide button is located in this tab.	Home	page 9
5.	The Zoom slider bar is located at the right side of this bar.	Status	page 14
6.	Click the Microsoft PowerPoint Help button and this displays.	PowerPoint Help window	page 21
7.	Use this feature to find synonyms, antonyms, and related words for a particular word.	Thesaurus	page 22
8.	The Spelling button is located in the Proofing group in this tab.	Review	page 21
9.	Move the mouse while running a presentation and this toolbar displays.	Slide Show	page 24
10.	Press this key on the keyboard to change to a black screen while running a presentation.	B	page 25
11.	Press this key on the keyboard to end a presentation without running all of the slides.	Esc	page 27
12.	Add transitions and sounds to a presentation with options in this tab.	Transitions	page 28
13.	Specify the length of a transition using the *Duration* option located in this group in the Transitions tab.	Timing	page 29
14.	You can print up to this number of slides on a single piece of paper.	9	page 30

PowerPoint Section 2

Knowledge Check Answer Key

1.	Save an existing presentation with a new name at this dialog box.	Save As	page 46
2.	Increase the text level indent by clicking the Increase List Level button or by pressing this key on the keyboard.	Tab	page 46
3.	Decrease the text level indent by clicking the Decrease List Level button or by pressing these keys on the keyboard.	Shift + Tab	page 46
4.	The Cut button is located in this group in the Home tab.	Clipboard	page 47
5.	This is the keyboard shortcut to copy selected text.	Ctrl + C	page 47
6.	Press these keys on the keyboard to select all text in a placeholder.	Ctrl + A	page 47
7.	Use this feature to apply the same formatting in more than one location in a slide or slides.	Format Painter	page 52
8.	Click this button in the Paragraph group in the Home tab to change the text alignment to right.	Align Text Right	page 54
9.	Change the vertical alignment of text in a placeholder with options from this button drop-down list.	Align Text	page 54
10.	This dialog box contains options for changing line spacing and text alignment, indentation, and spacing.	Paragraph	page 54
11.	Click this tab to display the Themes group.	Design	page 56
12.	Use buttons in this tab to change the color of the selected picture, apply a picture style, arrange the picture, and size the picture.	Picture Tools Format	page 58
13.	Display the Clip Art task pane by clicking the Insert tab and then clicking the Clip Art Pane button in this group.	Images	page 62
14.	Use this feature to create an organizational chart or a variety of graphic diagrams.	SmartArt	page 64
15.	The Effect Options button is located in this tab.	Animations	page 68

PowerPoint Section 3

Knowledge Check Answer Key

1.	Display this task pane to collect and paste multiple items.	Clipboard	page 84
2.	The Replace button is located in this group in the Home tab.	Editing	page 86
3.	Use this feature to distort or modify text and to conform text to a variety of shapes.	WordArt	page 88
4.	When you insert a shape in a slide, this tab is available for formatting the shape.	Drawing Tools Format tab	page 90
5.	These are horizontal and vertical dashed lines that you can display on a slide.	gridlines	page 92
6.	To copy a shape, hold down this key while dragging the shape.	Ctrl	page 93
7.	Use this feature for displaying columns and rows of data.	Table	page 94
8.	These are drawn objects that have a routine attached to them.	Action buttons	page 96
9.	Create a hyperlink by clicking the Hyperlink button in this group in the Insert tab.	Links group	page 97
10.	When you click the Hyperlink button in the Insert tab, this dialog box displays.	Insert Hyperlink	page 97
11.	Create footer text that displays at the bottom of all slides with options at this dialog box.	Header and Footer	page 100
12.	Click this button in the Insert tab to insert a video clip.	Insert Video	page 102
13.	The Audio button is located in this group in the Insert tab.	Media	page 103
14.	When the desired time displays on the Recording toolbar, click this button on the Recording toolbar to display the next slide.	Next	page 104
15.	Click this button on the Recording toolbar to reset the clock back to zero for the current slide.	Repeat	page 104

HAWAIIAN SPECIALS

White Sands Charters

Sail on the spectacular Pacific Pride and visit out-of-the-way bays populated by some of Hawaii's most colorful residents. Naturalist guides help you spot humpback whales during the winter and spring seasons. Guides will also introduce you to the delightful denizens of Molokini Crater or other premier snorkeling spots. The Pacific Pride departs at 7:00 a.m. and returns at 1:00 p.m. Voyages to Molokini depart at 8:00 a.m. and return at 12:00 noon.

Air Adventures

Experience beautiful coastlines and magnificent waterfalls, and fly inside an active volcano. For an adventure that will last a lifetime, fly in Hawaii's newest and most modern jet helicopter. Each air adventure includes:

- An expert pilot
- An air-conditioned cabin
- Exclusive remote landing sites
- Video with CD sound that puts you in the picture

Air Adventures puts you in a luxurious helicopter designed specifically for touring, with all seating facing forward offering 180-degree visibility.

Deep Sea Submarines

Journey through Hawaii's natural undersea world in a high-tech submarine to discover the island's unique marine species and explore the mysteries of the sea. Choose from the following exciting adventures:

Island Expedition: An introduction to submarine travel and Hawaii's natural marine world

Island Discovery: An early morning or late afternoon dive, with special savings

Ultimate Adventure: Deep Sea Submarines' most celebrated dive, featuring a skilled team of scuba divers

All Deep Sea Submarines boats are environmentally friendly, air-conditioned vessels, with state-of-the-art equipment on board.

Snorkeling Fantasies

Don't settle for an ordinary snorkeling trip—experience a Snorkeling Fantasies adventure instead!

- Fun and fascinating! Discover sea turtles, amazing fish, and beautiful coral with a knowledgeable marine researcher as your guide.

WS1-R1-FCTHawaiianSpecials(Review1).docx (1 of 2)

- An adventure that suits your style. Snorkel in beautiful, out-of-the-way bays while on a sunset sail.
- Great value. Just bring your towel and sunscreen—we supply everything from snorkeling gear to drinks and lunch.

Bicycle Safari

Travel 38 miles downhill from the summit to the sea. View the volcano and coast through lava fields and emerald green fields. Your downhill experience includes:

- Custom-built bicycle
- Free hotel pickup
- Two volcano guides
- Vista dining
- Tour of the Orchid Flower Farm

The bicycle tour begins at the top of the volcano, where you watch the sun rise over the majestic mountain. The downhill trip requires only 400 yards of pedaling, allowing you to relax and enjoy the beautiful scenery.

Luau Legends

Enjoy a spectacular Hawaiian dinner show featuring sumptuous prime rib and authentic Hawaiian buffet. This uniquely Hawaiian experience includes a traditional lei greeting, extraordinary food and beverages, magic music of the islands, and Hawaii's finest performers. Join us each evening beginning at 7:30 p.m. for an evening of delicious Hawaiian food and spectacular performances.

WS1-R1-FCTHawaiianSpecials(Review1).docx (2 of 2)

FAX

To:		From:	Student Name
	Scott Drysdale		
Fax:	(213) 555-3349	Pages:	3
Phone:	(213) 555-3400	Date:	(current date)
Re:	Incentive Agreement	CC:	

[ ] Urgent   [ ] For Review   [ ] Please Comment   [X] Please Reply   [ ] Please Recycle

Comments:

Please review the Incentive Agreement and then call me so we can schedule an appointment.

(current date)

WS1-R3-WEAgtFax(Review3).docx

RETENTION INCENTIVE AGREEMENT

This agreement is made and entered into on this _____ day of _____, 2012, between Carol Shepard and Worldwide Enterprises. Carol Shepard and Worldwide Enterprises agree to the following:

- Carol Shepard was hired by Worldwide Enterprises on the _____ day of _____ 2012.
- Carol Shepard was hired in the position of _____.
- Worldwide Enterprises desires to retain the services of Carol Shepard and Carol Shepard desires to continue providing services to Worldwide Enterprises for a minimum of three (3) years.

Upon signing this Agreement, Worldwide Enterprises agrees to provide Carol Shepard with a Retention Incentive if any of the two following conditions occur:

- Worldwide Enterprises terminates the services of Carol Shepard for any reason except for criminal misconduct committed by Carol Shepard against Worldwide Enterprises or abandonment by Carol Shepard of the responsibilities of the job within three (3) years of signing this Agreement.
- Carol Shepard provides services to Worldwide Enterprises for a period of three (3) years from the signing of this Agreement.

Upon completion of three (3) years of employment, Carol Shepard shall receive Retention Incentive from Worldwide Enterprises in one (1) payment within five (5) business days of the occurrence of any of the two conditions stated above.

_____
Carol Shepard

_____
Worldwide Enterprises Representative

WS1-R2-WEIncentiveAgt(Review2).docx

The Waterfront Bistro
3104 Rivermist Drive
Buffalo, NY 14280

(current date)

Marquee Productions
Mr. Josh Hart, Locations Director
955 South Alameda Street
Los Angeles, CA 90037

Mr. Hart:

The Waterfront Bistro is a full-service catering company with a number of menus for breakfast, lunch, and dinner as well as morning and afternoon snacks. The price ranges are as follows: breakfast ($3 – 10), lunch ($5 – 15), dinner ($8 – 20), snacks ($3 – 7).We will offer a discount of 5% on all meals if you cater for the duration of the filming. For your information, I would like to fax you a variety of menu options. I am very interested in meeting your catering needs, and we pride ourselves on accommodating our customer's needs.

Sincerely,

Dana Hirsch

WS1-A2-WBCateringLtr(Assessment2).docx

Performance Threads

*Proudly serving the entertainment
industry for over 20 years!*

(Current date)

Camille Matsui
Production Assistant
Marquee Productions
955 South Alameda Street
Los Angeles, CA 90037

Dear Ms. Matsui:

We received your letter concerning the period movie your company will begin filming this summer. Performance Threads can costume all the actors for this movie. We have an extensive staff of histor cal researchers, designers, and seamstresses. We pride ourselves on the authenticity of our costumes.

The costume research will take approximately two to three weeks. If appropriate costumes cannot be found, costumes will be sewn. Please anticipate five working days to sew a costume. We will need you to include the number of costumes and approximate sizes. A price estimate will be provided before the costumes are purchased or sewn.

Sincerely,

Bobbie Sinclair
Business Manager

4011 Bridgewater Street ✂ Niagara Falls, ON L2E 2T6 ✂ (905) 555-2971

WS1-A1-PTMarqueeLtr(Assessment1).docx

FAX

To: Josh Hart

Fax: (612) 555-2009

Phone: (612) 555-2005

Re: Catering

From: Dana Hirsch

Pages: 11

Date: (current date)

CC:

☐ Urgent ☒ Please Comment ☐ For Review ☐ Please Reply ☐ Please Recycle

Comments:

[Type comments]

(current date)

Norway in a Nutshell Tour

When touring Norway, you must include these fabulous day-excursion through some of the most magnificent scenery in Norway. On the Norway in a Nutshell tour, you leave Bergen in the morning by train and travel to Voss. From there the train climbs to the great mountain plateau, which separates the western fjords from East Norway. In Myrdal you change trains and then travel down the many sharp curves on the famous Flam Railway, know as one of the most spectacular train rides in the world. You will pass lofty, snow-capped mountains, thundering waterfalls, and peaceful green meadows in the valley below. After a stay in Flam, you continue the trip on a ship in some of the most beautiful fjords in Norway. After cruising along the fjords, you take a bus back to Voss, where a train is ready to take you back to Bergen.

Marquee PRODUCTIONS

V: 612 555 2005
F: 612 555 2009
info@emcp.net
www.emcp.net/marquee

(Current date) *(press Enter three times)*

Ms. Dana Hirsch *(press Shift + Enter)*
The Waterfront Bistro *(press Shift + Enter)*
3104 Rivermist Drive *(press Shift + Enter)*
Buffalo, NY 14280 *(press Enter)*

Dear Ms. Hirsch: *(press Enter)*

We will be filming a movie in and around Toronto and Buffalo from July 7 to August 30, 2012. During that time, we will require catering services for cast and crew members. The services we request include breakfast, mid-morning snack, lunch, and afternoon snack for each day of filming, including weekends. *(press Enter)*

Please send information on your breakfast and lunch catering menus and snack choices. We are interested in pricing for meals and snacks for approximately 45 people for the duration of the filming. If you have any questions about our catering needs, please contact me by telephone at (612) 555-2005 or e-mail at JoshH@emcp.net. *(press Enter)*

Sincerely, *(press Enter twice)*

Josh Hart *(press Shift + Enter)*
Locations Director *(press Enter)*

SN

955 South Alameda Street ▪ Los Angeles, CA 90037

WS1-C1-MPLtrtoTWB(Challenge1).docx

VACATIONING IN RENO AND LAKE TAHOE

Reno and Lake Tahoe are home to more snow, more ski resorts, and more nightlife than any other ski destination in North America. Come visit our area and experience a vast diversity of ski terrain, scenic beauty, and entertainment options. Getting to Reno and Lake Tahoe is as easy as taking one of over 250 flights that arrive daily at the Reno/Tahoe International Airport. Getting to your accommodations can be as quick as a ten-minute shuttle ride to a hotel casino in Reno or less than a scenic hour through the Sierra foothills to a variety of Lake Tahoe properties. All of the ski slopes are between 45 and 90 minutes from the Reno Airport. Getting around is easy with a variety of transportation options.

Destinations

Convenience and great locations make Incline Village and Crystal Bay desirable destinations at Lake Tahoe. Situated between Squaw Valley and Heavenly ski resorts, the two villages, along with other great resorts such as Mt. Rose and Diamond Peak, are just minutes away. Just 30 miles from Reno/Tahoe International Airport, the villages are central to all of the Lake Tahoe ski resorts. Diamond Peak offers 2,000 acres of classic Nordic terrain, over 35 kilometers of groomed tracks and skating lanes with incredible views of Lake Tahoe. The resort also boasts a 6.2 million dollar complex including an eight-lane indoor swimming pool, cardiovascular and strength-training center, aerobic studio, and gym. Additional recreational offerings include sledding, sleigh rides, snowshoeing, bowling, and a movie theater.

North Lake Tahoe is a favored destination for discriminating vacationers. Visit this beautiful area for the epic powder, seven resorts, downhill and cross-country skiing, and unlimited dining choices—all for affordable prices. Consider trying ice skating at the world's highest ice rink, snowmobiling and snowshoeing in the backcountry, or touring Lake Tahoe on an authentic paddle-wheeler. Visit one of 80 restaurants boasting award-winning cuisine in lakeshore and alpine settings. Visit the historic town of Truckee, an old railroad and logging community with quaint shops and sights.

Lake Tahoe South Shore is the ideal destination for variety with an amazing selection of skiing for all skill levels. Almost endless lodging possibilities await you with over 95 luxurious hotels and casinos, all-suite resorts, motels, condominiums, cabins, and homes. Tour the Sierra backcountry on a snowmobile, take a paddle-wheeler cruise to Emerald Bay, try a peaceful sleigh ride, or see the sights from a dogsled.

WS1-C2-FCTRenoTahoeVac(Challenge2).docx

PETERSBURG, ALASKA

Petersburg, Alaska, located on Mitkoff Island, is considered Alaska's Little Norway. Petersburg grew up around a salmon cannery and sawmill built by Peter Buschmann between 1897 and 1899. Petersburg is named after Peter Buschmann and part of its charm lies in its magnificent setting and the Scandinavian design of some of its buildings and houses.

Services

Downtown merchants sell a variety of products including gifts and souvenirs, hunting and fishing gear and licenses, camping supplies, groceries, hardware, marine supplies, automotive parts, and clothing. Unique and colorful gifts and clothes imported from Norway are available at some specialty shops. Artwork by local artists is sold at downtown shops and at an art gallery located near the ferry terminal.

The business district contains two banks, several restaurants, a laundry, a movie theater, and a bookstore. The U.S. Post Office and the U.S. Forest Service ranger district office are both located in the federal office building. Other merchants in Petersburg offer nearly all visitor services, including gas stations and car repair, air taxi services and charters, car rentals, RV parking, propane, and boat repairs and rentals.

Visitor Attractions

Visit the Clausen Memorial Museum at Second and Fram Streets to view exhibits that explain local fishing history and Petersburg's Norwegian heritage. The museum is open daily May through September.

The recently restored Sons of Norway Hall is one of the prominent downtown landmarks. It is a favorite location for artists and photographers. The hall is on the National Register of Historic Places and is open for visitors on special occasions.

Mitkoff Island offers a picnic area at Sandy Beach located north of Petersburg. Sandy Beach has a good view of Frederick Sound and offers covered picnic shelters. Camping is not allowed at the picnic grounds.

Walk through any of the boat harbors and you will usually find a friendly fisherman who will explain some of the fishing gear and fishing boats docked in the harbor. Freshly caught local seafood is often available at the local markets and also is served at local restaurants.

Walking Tours

Petersburg offers several attractive walks. The city's Main Street contains brass inlays of area birds and animals, and boasts recently planted trees, custom light poles and benches, and picnic tables along Harbor Way. A boardwalk connects Mountain View Manor with the local ballpark. Other walks are the Loop Walk, Hammer Slough Walk, Harbor Walk, and the Three Lakes Loop Road Walk.

Accommodations

Accommodations in and around Petersburg include three hotels, several bed and breakfast establishments, a Forest Service campground, and several remote Forest Service cabins. Tent City, a municipal campground near the airport, is used primarily by the many transient cannery workers who flock to Petersburg during the summer and is not recommended for tourists.

Drivers can generally park recreational vehicles anywhere within the National Forest boundary, provided they do not interfere with logging operations. Camping or recreational vehicle parking in the city limits is discouraged. If you are planning to stay in a hotel, U.S. Forest Service cabin, or on the Alaska marine highway, you will need to make a reservation.

Transportation

Daily jet service is available from Seattle, Ketchikan, and Juneau to Petersburg. Commuter airline flights are also available from Ketchikan, Wrangell, or Juneau. The airport and seaplane base are close to town and can accommodate private aircraft. A helicopter charter service also operates at the airport.

The Alaska marine highway offers another option for traveling to Petersburg. Petersburg is one of the main stops and service is frequent during the summer. The ferry terminal is a short walk from downtown, and taxi service is available.

IF YOU WOULD LIKE MORE INFORMATION ON TRAVELING IN ALASKA, CHECK WITH A FIRST CHOICE TRAVEL REPRESENTATIVE.

Student Name
7/21/20102
3:14 PM

SOUTH LAKE TAHOE—CROSS COUNTRY SKI AREAS

Camp Richardson Resort Cross Country Ski Center

The center offers over 50 km of groomed trails with skating lanes. Ski the shoreline of Lake Tahoe or enjoy a sleigh ride or the snow play area. Rentals and lessons are available.

Lake Tahoe Winter Sports Center

Beginner and intermediate skiers will find groomed trails that wander around the golf course, ideal for that first time.

South Lake Tahoe Parks & Recreation

The South Lake Parks and Recreation Department maintains 10 km of groomed trails for practicing your striding or skating skills. A minimal fee makes this an excellent choice for a few hours of skiing.

Kirkwood Cross Country

Kirkwood Cross Country has 80 km of trails on 4,200 acres in three trail networks. Interpretive nature signs explain the variety of wildlife, winter vegetation, and surrounding vistas. A special children's area is located near the Cross Country Day Lodge.

OREGON

For a relaxing, comfortable, and affordable vacation, consider renting a condominium, house, cabin, or chalet. All vacation properties are near skiing and gaming excitement and provide the comfort and privacy of home in Oregon's beautiful mountain setting. All properties come fully equipped with kitchens, fireplaces, televisions, and decks or patios.

FAST FACTS

- Type of property: mountain recreational resort
- Telephone: (503) 555-3985
- Fax: (503) 555-2301
- Property locations: Parkdale, Rhododendron, Sandy

RATES AND PACKAGES

Accommodations	No. Persons	Daily Price
Studio/one bedroom	2 to 4	$75 to $125
Two bedrooms	4 to 6	$95 to $225
Three bedrooms	6 to 8	$135 to $300
Four bedrooms	8 to 12	$160 to $400
Five/six bedrooms	10 to 16	$250 to $500

NEVADA

Poised in the heart of the High Sierra ski bowl, the legendary Mountain Chateau Resort is a wonderful mixture of rustic mountain elegance with refined comfort. Every guest room has a spectacular view of Lake Tahoe. Dine in the Lake Side Dining Room.

FAST FACTS

- Type of property: lakefront resort hotel
- Telephone: (775) 555-7990
- Fax: (775) 555-7121
- Number of rooms: 150 lake-view rooms

RATES AND PACKAGES

Package	Length	Price
Tuck 'n' Roll	3 days/2 nights	$269
Ski Sneak	4 days/3 nights	$409
Take a Break	6 days/5 nights	$649
Ultimate	8 days/7 nights	$1,009

Additional accommodations are available at the Ste. Thérèse Chateau and Silver Creek Resort. For information, please contact Carlos Nuñez.

WORLDWIDE ENTERPRISES
Distribution Schedule
Two by Two

United States ....May 10
Canada ....June 7
Japan..July 26
Australia/New Zealand ....August 2
Mexico..September 20

WS2-A3-WEDistSch(Assessment3).docx

Marquee
PRODUCTIONS

V: 612 555 2005
F: 612 555 2009
info@emcp.net
www.emcp.net/marquee

April 16, 2012

Cal Rubine
Chair, Theatre Arts Division
Niagara Peninsula College
2199 Victoria Street
Niagara-on-the-Lake, ON L0S 1J0

Dear Mr. Rubine:

Marquee Productions will be filming in and around the city of Toronto during the summer of 2010. We would like to use approximately 20 theatre interns to assist in the shoot. The interns will perform a variety of tasks including acting as extras, assisting the camera crew, working with set designers on set construction, and providing support to the production team. Interns can work approximately 15 to 30 hours per week and will be compensated at minimum wage. I would ask that you screen interested students and then send approximately 20 names to me. If you have any questions, you may contact me at (612) 555-2005 or you can send the names by e-mail to me at NevaSW@emcp.net.

Sincerely,

Neva Smith-Wilder
Educational Liaison

955 South Alameda Street ▪ Los Angeles, CA 90037

WS2-A2-MPLtrtoNPC(Assessment2).docx

VACATION SPECIALS

Ocean Vista Cruise Lines

Sign up today for an eight-day, seven-night cruise of the Alaska Inside Passage on the beautiful new Pacific Sky cruise ship. This inaugural trip begins May 5 in Seattle, Washington, and ends back in Seattle on May 12.

The Pacific Sky cruises through Glacier Bay and the Inside Passage and pays visits to the Alaskan Ports of Skagway, Haines, and Juneau. The Pacific Sky also stops in the beautiful port city of Vancouver, British Columbia.

On this exciting cruise, you will

- Behold some of the world's most majestic scenery
- Visit colorful Gold Rush towns
- Observe fascinating wildlife
- Be subjected to a dazzling display by the Northern Lights
- Listen to the "singing of the ice"
- Walk on a glacier
- Hike through a forest of hemlocks
- Helicopter or seaplane down "rivers of ice"
- Canoe through a wildlife preserve while eagles soar overhead

Space is limited on this inaugural voyage of the Pacific Sky so make your reservations today! You can make reservations through April 15, 2012, and secure the reservation with a deposit of $250 per person. Deposits are refundable until the final payment date of May 1, 2012. Cruise rates including port charges and government fees begin as low as $950 per person based on a double-occupancy cabin. Choose the Category below that best fits your cruising style:

Category H $975 USD
Inside stateroom
Two lower beds

Category D $1,275 USD
Deluxe ocean view stateroom
Spacious outside stateroom with window
Sitting area and two lower beds

Category B $1,315 USD
Superior deluxe ocean view stateroom
Spacious outside stateroom with window
Sitting area and two lower beds

Category S $1,510 USD
Superior deluxe suite
Large ocean view suite with private balcony
Sitting area and two lower beds

Category P $2,750 USD
Three-room Presidential suite
Large ocean view with two private balconies
Sitting area and two bedrooms

Getaway Weekends

You could spend the weekend grocery shopping or cleaning closets or you could take off on a romantic three-day adventure—without breaking the bank! On a moment's notice you can be taking in the sights and sounds of London or skiing down the slopes of a ski resort in beautiful Utah.

From February through April, we are offering a three-night vacation package to London beginning as low as $449 per person. This fantastic price includes airfare from New York to London and hotel lodging for three nights. For a small fee, you can rent a car and spend time visiting sights in and around London.

Scenic Park City Mountain Resort, host to many of the 2002 Winter Olympic games, is a mere half-hour drive from Utah's Salt Lake City International Airport. First Choice Travel is offering a three day ski vacation package for prices beginning as low as $327. The three-day vacation package includes airfare, lodging, transfer, and a two-day ski lift pass.

First Choice Planner

First Choice Travel presents the 2012 First Choice Planner—your personal guide to over 50 special offers from our First Choice partners. Hang on to your copy and use it whenever you travel this summer and fall. You can save money and multiply the First Choice points you earn. The more you travel this year, the faster you can accumulate First Choice points and enjoy extra travel benefits throughout the year.

Specials offered by First Choice Travel include all reference codes you need when you make your arrangements with a First Choice Travel representative. First Choice partners include airlines, car rental companies, hotels, and cruise lines.

As you think about your travel needs for this year, consider the following specials:
- Earn 1,000 First Choice points for each round-trip airfare you book with First Choice Travel.
- Earn 500 First Choice points when you rent a car for two or more consecutive days through First Choice Travel.

Preventing Page Breaks and Widows/Orphans

In order to prevent page breaks between paragraphs, you first select the paragraphs that you want to keep together on a single page. Navigate to the Page Layout tab, click the Paragraph dialog box launcher, and then click the Line and Page Breaks tab. Click the Keep with next check box.

A professional-looking document never ends a page with just one line of a new paragraph or begins a page with only the last line of a paragraph from the previous page. The last line of a paragraph by itself at the top of a page is known as an orphan. The first line of a paragraph by itself at the bottom of a page is known as a widow. Select the paragraphs in which you want to prevent widows and orphans. Navigate to the Page Layout tab, click the Paragraph dialog box launcher, and then click the Line and Page Breaks tab. Click the Widow/Orphan control check box.

WS2-A4-PageBreaks(Assessment4).docx

- Earn 5,000 First Choice points when you book a cruise through First Choice Travel.
- Earn 100 First Choice points for each day you stay in a First Choice Travel partner hotel.
- Earn 50 First Choice points for each sightseeing excursion you book with First Choice Travel.

Let First Choice Travel take care of all your travel needs.

WS2-A4-FCTVacSpecials(Assessment4).docx (3 of 3)

Transportation

City buses transport visitors in and around Juneau as well as to and from the airport. Visitors can also choose to take a taxi or airport shuttle. In the summertime, a shuttle service is available between Juneau and the Alaska Marine Highway system ferry terminal at Auke Bay.

Museums

Juneau is the proud home to the Alaska State Museum, featuring permanent displays of Eskimo and Southeast Indian artifacts. The museum also offers changing displays of Alaska's political and natural history.

Visit the Juneau Douglas City Museum and learn about Juneau's history. Exhibits include features on gold mining and Juneau's historic past. A small admission fee is charged to adults. Children under the age of 18 are admitted free of charge.

The Alaska Maritime Heritage Foundation, a nonprofit group, is planning to build a tall ship for Alaska. It will be used to train sailors and people with disabilities in seamanship, environmental studies, goodwill trips, and charter work.

Visitor Attractions

Walking, hiking, and biking trails abound in and around Juneau. Scenic flights take visitors over the spectacular ice fields and the Glacier Bay National Monument. Take an exciting boat ride along Juneau's wilderness waterways.

Tour buses take visitors to Mendenhall Glacier where they can climb moraines left by receding glaciers, hike nearby trails, and visit the U.S. Forest Service observatory where guides and exhibits explain glacier features. Visitors can also reach the glacier by driving or taking a charter flight.

Reminders of Juneau's past abound in the city. The Davis Log Cabin, built in 1881, was the community's first church and is now the visitor information center. Consider a visit to the St. Nicholas Russian Orthodox Church, which was built in 1894 and is considered the oldest original Orthodox Church in Southeast Alaska. Other city attractions include the Juneau Douglas City Museum, the pioneer cemetery, and the Wickersham House.

Student Name

WS3-R1-FCTJuneau(Review1).docx (2 of 3)

JUNEAU, ALASKA

Juneau, Alaska's capital since 1900, sits at the base of Mt. Juneau. This capital blends its history as a mining town with old storefronts and saloons with the modern architecture of government and Native corporations.

History

In the late 1800s, gold became the foundation of Juneau. The town contained a variety of gold mines with the Alaska-Juneau, or A-J, mine the most successful. The A-J mine buildings are still visible above town. Other gold mines include the Treadwell Mine complex at Douglas and the Alaska-Gastineau mine south of town. A massive cave-in occurred at Treadwell in 1917 and the mine closed. When gold content dropped below profitable margins in 1921, the Alaska-Gastineau mine closed. The A-J mine continued operations until World War II, when labor shortages and high costs forced its closure.

Visitor Centers

Located in downtown Juneau, the Davis Log Cabin Information Center is operated by the Juneau Convention and Visitors Bureau. A free brochure is available at the center that includes a walking tour map and information about other Alaska communities. The Davis Cabin is open every day in the summer.

The USFS Information Center is located at the corner of Eagan Drive and Willoughby Avenue. Visitors can view films and videos on Glacier Bay National Park, bald eagles, humpback whales, the Tongass National Forest, mountain goats, Admiralty Island, Dall sheep, and life in logging camps.

The Mendenhall Glacier Visitor Center is located at the base of the glacier and is open every day in the summer from 9 a.m. to 6 p.m. Visitors can take a guided tour and learn about moraine ecology. Films and videos are available that provide information on the glacier and mountain goats.

Student Name

WS3-R1-FCTJuneau(Review1).docx (1 of 3)

Student Name
Instructor Name
Course Title
(current date)

Renaissance Costumes

The Renaissance period was a series of cultural and literary movements that took place in the fourteenth, fifteenth, and sixteenth centuries in Europe. The word *renaissance* means "rebirth" and originated with the belief that Europeans had rediscovered the intellectual and cultural superiority of the Greek and Roman cultures. The Renaissance period was preceded by the Middle Ages, also known as the "Dark Ages," which began with the collapse of the Roman Empire in the fifth century (Gerard).

Renaissance education was designed to produce a person well-versed in humanities, mathematics, science, sports, and art. The Renaissance person had extensive knowledge in many fields, explored beyond the boundaries of learning and geographical knowledge, and embraced free thought and skepticism. Artists, writers, explorers, architects, and scientists were motivated by a revival in classical Greek and Roman culture and a return to classical values. During the Middle Ages, interest in culture and learning was primarily confined to theologians, philosophers, and writers. During the Renaissance period, however, people from all social, political, and economic classes involved themselves in the study of classical literature and art.

Renaissance costume developed in Italy and was introduced to Western Europe following the invasion of Italy by Charles VIII of France in 1494 (Brooke). Due to the warmer climate in Italy, simpler styles evolved independently from those of the rest of

WS3-R2-PTRenaissanceRpt(Review2).docx (1 of 3)

3

The Mendenhall Valley, located outside Juneau and below the Mendenhall Glacier, contains a residential area, a commercial business complex, and the Juneau Airport. Across Gastineau Channel from downtown Juneau is Douglas, a community that served the Treadwell Mine, but is now a part of incorporated Juneau.

Visitor Services

Juneau offers a variety of comforts and services to visitors. Two major commercial areas offer several hotels and stores. One area, located downtown, caters to tourists' tastes for mementos, from souvenirs to Native arts, crafts, and contemporary art. The other area, located near the airport, offers lodging, camping, and picnicking facilities.

Accommodations in and around Juneau include hostels, bed and breakfast facilities, budget motels, and luxurious hotels. Restaurants offer food to satisfy a variety of palates, and eateries range from fast food to steak and seafood houses.

Points of Interest

Alaska State Museum .... Downtown
Davis Log Cabin Visitor Center ....Downtown
Mendenhall Glacier.............. 14 miles from Juneau
St. Nicholas Russian Orthodox Church........ Downtown
U.S. Forest Service Infomation Center Centennial Building
Gastineau Salmon Hatchery..............3 miles from Juneau

Student Name

WS3-R1-FCTJuneau(Review1).docx (3 of 3)

Works Cited

Brooke, Iris. A History of Renaissance Costumes. New York: Hudson River Publishing
House, 2009.

Gerard, Marcus. "History of the Renaissance Period." European History: Western European
Civilization (2012): 13-17.

Europe. Men's clothing consisted of low-necked tunics and chemises and women's clothing consisted of simple and low-necked gowns called "Juliet" gowns. During the middle of the fifteenth century, clothing assumed a more natural appearance. Women wore dresses with attached bodices and skirts. Men's doublets became shorter and hosiery became more prominent. Interest by women in gothic headdresses declined and instead they trimmed their hair with veils, ribbons, and jewels. Lace and perfume became more prevalent during the Renaissance period.

Early in the Renaissance period, women's dress included a long, rigid, cone-shaped corset reaching below the waist to a "V" in the front. Women's gowns expanded below the waistline and by the middle sixteenth century were supported by hoops made of wire that were held together with ribbons. This hoop skirt, called a *farthingale*, reached its maximum width around the early seventeenth century and then changed to a cartwheel or drum shape. Ballooned sleeves and circular lace collars also typified the early seventeenth century costume. Men's clothing had a similar look with puffed-out hose, balloon sleeves, padded doublets, and large ruff collars.

EMPLOYMENT OPPORTUNITIES

Working in the Movie Industry

Wednesday, March 14, 2012

7:00 to 8:30 p.m.

Sponsored by

Marquee
PRODUCTIONS

WS3-R3-MPEmpOpps02(Review3).docx

EMPLOYMENT OPPORTUNITIES

Working in the Movie Industry

Wednesday, March 14, 2012

7:00 to 8:30 p.m.

Sponsored by
Marquee Productions

WS3-R3-MPEmpOpps01(Review3).docx

Worldwide Enterprises
(Student Name)
1112-1583 Broadway
New York, NY 10110

Worldwide Enterprises
(Student Name)
1112-1583 Broadway
New York, NY 10110

Worldwide Enterprises
(Student Name)
1112-1583 Broadway
New York, NY 10110

Worldwide Enterprises
(Student Name)
1112-1583 Broadway
New York, NY 10110

Worldwide Enterprises
(Student Name)
1112-1583 Broadway
New York, NY 10110

Worldwide Enterprises
(Student Name)
1112-1583 Broadway
New York, NY 10110

Worldwide Enterprises
(Student Name)
1112-1583 Broadway
New York, NY 10110

Worldwide Enterprises
(Student Name)
1112-1583 Broadway
New York, NY 10110

Worldwide Enterprises
(Student Name)
1112-1583 Broadway
New York, NY 10110

Worldwide Enterprises
(Student Name)
1112-1583 Broadway
New York, NY 10110

Worldwide Enterprises
(Student Name)
1112-1583 Broadway
New York, NY 10110

Worldwide Enterprises
(Student Name)
1112-1583 Broadway
New York, NY 10110

Worldwide Enterprises
(Student Name)
1112-1583 Broadway
New York, NY 10110

Worldwide Enterprises
(Student Name)
1112-1583 Broadway
New York, NY 10110

Worldwide Enterprises
(Student Name)
1112-1583 Broadway
New York, NY 10110

Worldwide Enterprises
(Student Name)
1112-1583 Broadway
New York, NY 10110

Worldwide Enterprises
(Student Name)
1112-1583 Broadway
New York, NY 10110

Worldwide Enterprises
(Student Name)
1112-1583 Broadway
New York, NY 10110

Worldwide Enterprises
(Student Name)
1112-1583 Broadway
New York, NY 10110

Worldwide Enterprises
(Student Name)
1112-1583 Broadway
New York, NY 10110

Worldwide Enterprises
(Student Name)
1112-1583 Broadway
New York, NY 10110

Worldwide Enterprises
(Student Name)
1112-1583 Broadway
New York, NY 10110

Worldwide Enterprises
(Student Name)
1112-1583 Broadway
New York, NY 10110

Worldwide Enterprises
(Student Name)
1112-1583 Broadway
New York, NY 10110

Worldwide Enterprises
(Student Name)
1112-1583 Broadway
New York, NY 10110

Worldwide Enterprises
(Student Name)
1112-1583 Broadway
New York, NY 10110

Worldwide Enterprises
(Student Name)
1112-1583 Broadway
New York, NY 10110

Worldwide Enterprises
(Student Name)
1112-1583 Broadway
New York, NY 10110

Worldwide Enterprises
(Student Name)
1112-1583 Broadway
New York, NY 10110

Worldwide Enterprises
(Student Name)
1112-1583 Broadway
New York, NY 10110

First Choice Travel
(Student Name)
3588 Ventura Boulevard
Los Angeles, CA 90102

Chris Greenbaum
Marquee Productions
955 South Alameda Street
Los Angeles, CA 90037

COSTUME RENTAL AGREEMENT

Marquee Productions agrees this ___ day of _____, 20__, to rent from Performance Threads those costumes numbered _____, beginning the ___ day of _____, 20__, and ending the ___ day of _____, 20__, upon the following terms and conditions:

1. **Rent:** Marquee Productions agrees to pay rent in the amount of $_____ per day for the above listed costumes.

2. **Inspection of Costume:** Marquee Productions agrees that an inspection of the above listed costumes was performed and accepts the condition of each one in its present state.

3. **Alterations:** Marquee Productions agrees not to make alterations or do or cause to be done any alterations without prior written consent.

4. **Marquee Productions Agrees:**

   a. To keep said costumes in clean and sanitary condition.

   b. To not intentionally or negligently destroy, deface, or damage any part of said costumes.

   c. To return said costumes in reasonable and wearable condition.

5. **Security Deposit:** Marquee Productions has deposited the sum of _____ dollars, receipt of which is hereby acknowledged, which sum shall be refunded to Marquee Productions upon return of costumes in the manner earlier described.

WS3-A1-PTAgreement(Assessment1).docx (1 of 2)

---

6. **Obligations:** Marquee Productions shall fully perform obligations hereunder:

   a. Marquee Productions shall rent costumes for _____ weeks or longer from date hereof.

   b. Marquee Productions shall clean and restore said costumes and return the same to Performance Threads in their initial condition except for reasonable wear and tear.

   c. Marquee Productions shall have remedied or repaired any damage to said costumes.

IN WITNESS WHEREOF, the Marquee Productions has hereunto set his/her hand and seal the day and year first above written.

_____
Performance Threads Representative

_____
Marquee Productions Representative

WS3-A1-PTAgreement(Assessment1).docx (1 of 2)

NIAGARA PENINSULA COLLEGE

Internship Opportunities

June 18 through August 30, 2012

Marquee Productions, Toronto Office

Contact Cal Rubine, Theatre Arts Division

WS3-A2-NPCInternship(Assessment2).docx

Niagara Peninsula College (Student Name) 2199 Victoria Street Niagara-on-the-Lake, ON L0S 1J0	Niagara Peninsula College (Student Name) 2199 Victoria Street Niagara-on-the-Lake, ON L0S 1J0	Niagara Peninsula College (Student Name) 2199 Victoria Street Niagara-on-the-Lake, ON L0S 1J0
Niagara Peninsula College (Student Name) 2199 Victoria Street Niagara-on-the-Lake, ON L0S 1J0	Niagara Peninsula College (Student Name) 2199 Victoria Street Niagara-on-the-Lake, ON L0S 1J0	Niagara Peninsula College (Student Name) 2199 Victoria Street Niagara-on-the-Lake, ON L0S 1J0
Niagara Peninsula College (Student Name) 2199 Victoria Street Niagara-on-the-Lake, ON L0S 1J0	Niagara Peninsula College (Student Name) 2199 Victoria Street Niagara-on-the-Lake, ON L0S 1J0	Niagara Peninsula College (Student Name) 2199 Victoria Street Niagara-on-the-Lake, ON L0S 1J0
Niagara Peninsula College (Student Name) 2199 Victoria Street Niagara-on-the-Lake, ON L0S 1J0	Niagara Peninsula College (Student Name) 2199 Victoria Street Niagara-on-the-Lake, ON L0S 1J0	Niagara Peninsula College (Student Name) 2199 Victoria Street Niagara-on-the-Lake, ON L0S 1J0
Niagara Peninsula College (Student Name) 2199 Victoria Street Niagara-on-the-Lake, ON L0S 1J0	Niagara Peninsula College (Student Name) 2199 Victoria Street Niagara-on-the-Lake, ON L0S 1J0	Niagara Peninsula College (Student Name) 2199 Victoria Street Niagara-on-the-Lake, ON L0S 1J0
Niagara Peninsula College (Student Name) 2199 Victoria Street Niagara-on-the-Lake, ON L0S 1J0	Niagara Peninsula College (Student Name) 2199 Victoria Street Niagara-on-the-Lake, ON L0S 1J0	Niagara Peninsula College (Student Name) 2199 Victoria Street Niagara-on-the-Lake, ON L0S 1J0
Niagara Peninsula College (Student Name) 2199 Victoria Street Niagara-on-the-Lake, ON L0S 1J0	Niagara Peninsula College (Student Name) 2199 Victoria Street Niagara-on-the-Lake, ON L0S 1J0	Niagara Peninsula College (Student Name) 2199 Victoria Street Niagara-on-the-Lake, ON L0S 1J0
Niagara Peninsula College (Student Name) 2199 Victoria Street Niagara-on-the-Lake, ON L0S 1J0	Niagara Peninsula College (Student Name) 2199 Victoria Street Niagara-on-the-Lake, ON L0S 1J0	Niagara Peninsula College (Student Name) 2199 Victoria Street Niagara-on-the-Lake, ON L0S 1J0
Niagara Peninsula College (Student Name) 2199 Victoria Street Niagara-on-the-Lake, ON L0S 1J0	Niagara Peninsula College (Student Name) 2199 Victoria Street Niagara-on-the-Lake, ON L0S 1J0	Niagara Peninsula College (Student Name) 2199 Victoria Street Niagara-on-the-Lake, ON L0S 1J0
Niagara Peninsula College (Student Name) 2199 Victoria Street Niagara-on-the-Lake, ON L0S 1J0	Niagara Peninsula College (Student Name) 2199 Victoria Street Niagara-on-the-Lake, ON L0S 1J0	Niagara Peninsula College (Student Name) 2199 Victoria Street Niagara-on-the-Lake, ON L0S 1J0

WS3-A3-NPCLabels(Assessment3).docx

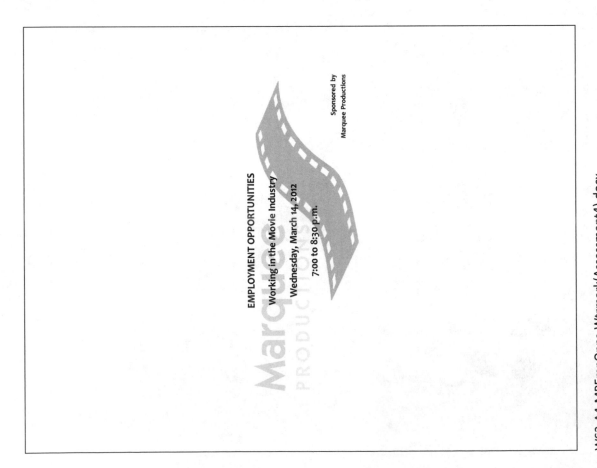

Zenith Adventures

We are excited to announce that First Choice Travel has teamed with Zenith Adventures to provide our clients with thrilling, adrenaline-producing, extreme outdoor adventures. You can choose from a variety of exciting adventures, including Antarctic expedition cruises, tall-ship sailing, and bicycling tours. Many of our trips are appropriate for beginners, so get out and enjoy an amazing outdoor adventure with family and friends!

Zenith Adventures	Length	Price
Antarctic Exploration	7 days	$4,399
Weddell Sea Adventure	10 days	$6,899
Falkland Islands Journey	14 days	$7,699
Sailing Spectacular	14 days	$8,999

ANTARCTIC ZENITH ADVENTURES

Travel with our Antarctic experts, cruise on our state-of-the-art ships, and experience Antarctica in all of its grandeur. We use ice-rated expedition ships custom-designed for your comfort and safety. Each ship can carry up to 100 passengers and provides excellent viewing for watching whales, seabirds, and icebergs as well as facilities for educational presentations by our Antarctic experts. For our more adventurous clients, we offer additional activities such as snowshoeing, sea-kayaking, and camping on the Antarctic ice. Plan on a shore excursion where you can view penguin rookeries, seal colonies, and places of historical and scientific interest. To carry you to the Antarctic shore, we use inflatable boats that can carry 12 to 15 people. After a thrilling day on shore, we will take you back to the ship where you can enjoy a delicious meal prepared by our gourmet chefs. Our Antarctic travel experts are naturalists, historians, and adventurers committed to providing you with a fabulous Antarctic adventure.

First Choice Travel is teaming with Zenith Adventures to provide our clients with thrilling and extreme outdoor adventures.

TALL-SHIP ADVENTURES

Visit exotic and spectacular locations in the South Pacific aboard the *Laura Devon*, a luxurious tall ship. On your tall-ship adventure, seek out the hidden Pacific by sailing the trade winds to discover the undisturbed cultures and beauty of remote islands and communities. Our tall-ship sailing adventure combines exotic exploration and timeless romance. You can sign on for the challenge of an ocean voyage with blue water sailing or a more leisurely island voyage sailing through tropical paradises. For many, tall-ship sailing is the ultimate in escapist adventuring. Sailing on the magnificent *Laura Devon*, combined with the sparkling beauty of the South Pacific, makes for the adventure of a lifetime.

Zenith Adventures	Length	Price
Vanuatu Exploration	10 days	$1,599
Tahiti to Cook Islands	14 days	$2,899
Fiji to Vanuatu	14 days	$2,299
Tonga to Fiji	16 days	$3,999

BICYCLING ADVENTURES

A bicycle is the perfect form of transportation for a travel adventure. Sign up for one of our bicycle tours and travel at your own pace, interact with village residents, stay healthy and fit, and know

that your adventure has a minimal effect on the environment. We offer bicycle tours ranging from a leisurely trip through the Loire Valley of France to a mountain-bike expedition in the Atlas Mountains in Morocco. Our Zenith Adventures bicycle guides provide you with historical and educational information about the region in which you are traveling. They also take care of luggage and transportation needs and maintain your bicycle. We are confident that we can provide the bicycle adventure of a lifetime!

Zenith Adventures	Length	Price
Loire Valley Tour	7 days	$1,999
Tuscan Village Tour	8 days	$2,499
Atlas Trek Extreme	9 days	$2,899
Great Wall of China	14 days	$3,299

Adventure with us!

UPCOMING ADVENTURES

Beginning next year, Zenith Adventures, together with First Choice Travel, will offer volunteer vacation opportunities. Tentative volunteer adventures include building village and mountain paths, building homes, and helping the families of trail porters improve village facilities. Our volunteer adventures will provide you with an exciting vacation and a rewarding volunteer experience. The group size will be limited to a maximum of 15 and participants will be required to raise a minimum amount of money to contribute to the program and local charities. All charities have been carefully screened to ensure that funds are well managed and distributed fairly. Look for more information in our next newsletter and consider a rewarding volunteer adventure.

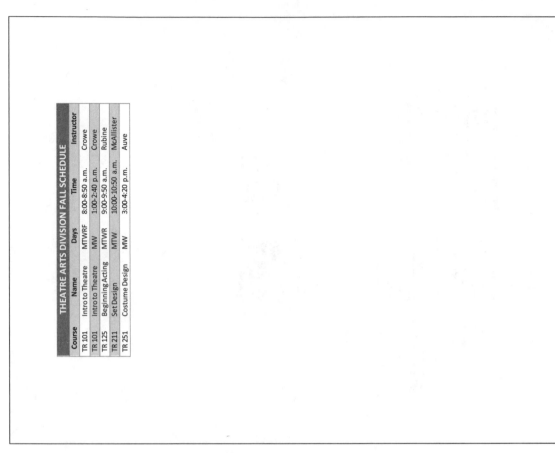

THEATRE ARTS DIVISION FALL SCHEDULE

Course	Name	Days	Time	Instructor
TR 101	Intro to Theatre	MTWRF	8:00-8:50 a.m.	Crowe
TR 101	Intro to Theatre	MW	1:00-2:40 p.m.	Crowe
TR 125	Beginning Acting	MTWR	9:00-9:50 a.m.	Rubine
TR 211	Set Design	MTW	10:00-10:50 a.m.	McAllister
TR 251	Costume Design	MW	3:00-4:20 p.m.	Auve

WS4-R3-NPCFallSch(Review3).docx

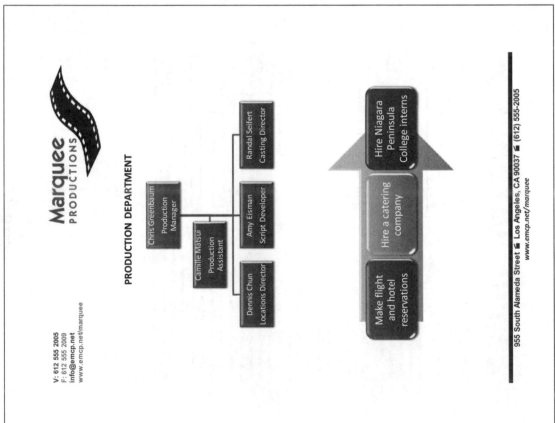

WS4-R2-MPProdDept(Review2).docx

Oslo, Norway

History

The founding of Oslo took place in the turbulent period between the Viking Age and Norway's Catholic Middle Ages. Many remnants and ruins from ancient Oslo can be found in Memorial Park. The city has a fascinating, interesting, and dramatic history.

Oslo's population was substantially reduced during the time of the Black Death in 1348, which claimed over fifty percent of the inhabitants. This epidemic also had political consequences for Norway, which was reduced to a province of Denmark. During this period, Copenhagen was the actual capital of Norway. Oslo was also greatly affected by the Lutheran Protestant Reformation of 1537, with religious conflicts, political separation from the Catholic Church, and the foundation of a Protestant National Church. Many ruins of churches and monasteries bear witness to this process.

Oslo was completely destroyed by fire in 1624. Following intense renewal and advanced city planning in the spirit of the Renaissance, a new city was created and named Christiania. In 1814 Norway was united with Sweden, and Christiania experienced strong economic and political growth. In 1905 the union with Sweden was dissolved and Norway gained its independence. The original name of Oslo was reinstated in 1924.

Population

Oslo is the capital of Norway and has more than 500,000 inhabitants. Approximately 900,000 people live in the Greater Oslo area, representing twenty percent of the total population of Norway.

Commerce and Industry

The working population of Oslo distributed according to occupation includes: industry, 16%; building and construction, 6%; transport, 9%; trade, services, and tourism, 69%.

Climate

Oslo's climate is temperate in the autumn and warm in spring and summer. Snow falls for three to five months in the winter. Skiing conditions are good in the hills around Oslo between December and April. From May to July, the weather can be quite warm with long periods of sunshine. Drought can also occur from time to time. Statistically speaking, Oslo is Scandinavia's sunniest capital.

Holiday, Sport, and Leisure

Oslo is surrounded by forest and fjord. Preserving the fjord and the area surrounding the city for leisure and outdoor pursuits is an important part of Oslo's political tradition. Some of the major sports events in Oslo include the Grete Waitz Race, Holmenkollen Relay, Oslo Marathon, and the Holmenkollen Ski Festival. Oslo includes over 2,000 kilometers of prepared ski trails for cross-country skiing and a number of ski lifts for alpine skiing.

Sightseeing Tours

You can choose from a variety of sightseeing tours in and around the Oslo area. Take a two-hour cruise that leaves from Pier 3 in front of the Oslo City Hall and then enjoy a dinner at the Restaurant Lanternen. Sign up for a three-hour bus tour of Vigeland Sculpture Park, the Holmenkollen Ski Jump, the Viking ships, and the Kon-Tiki Raft.

Additional Information on Norway

WS4-R4-FCTOslo(Review4).pdf

Oslo, Norway

History

The founding of Oslo took place in the turbulent period between the Viking Age and Norway's Catholic Middle Ages. Many remnants and ruins from ancient Oslo can be found in Memorial Park. The city has a fascinating, interesting, and dramatic history.

Oslo's population was substantially reduced during the time of the Black Death in 1348, which claimed over fifty percent of the inhabitants. This epidemic also had political consequences for Norway, which was reduced to a province of Denmark. During this period, Copenhagen was the actual capital of Norway. Oslo was also greatly affected by the Lutheran Protestant Reformation of 1537, with religious conflicts, political separation from the Catholic Church, and the foundation of a Protestant National Church. Many ruins of churches and monasteries bear witness to this process.

Oslo was completely destroyed by fire in 1624. Following intense renewal and advanced city planning in the spirit of the Renaissance, a new city was created and named Christiania. In 1814 Norway was united with Sweden, and Christiania experienced strong economic and political growth. In 1905 the union with Sweden was dissolved and Norway gained its independence. The original name of Oslo was reinstated in 1924.

Population

Oslo is the capital of Norway and has more than 500,000 inhabitants. Approximately 900,000 people live in the Greater Oslo area, representing twenty percent of the total population of Norway.

Commerce and Industry

The working population of Oslo distributed according to occupation includes: industry, 16%; building and construction, 6%; transport, 9%; trade, services, and tourism, 69%.

Climate

Oslo's climate is temperate in the autumn and warm in spring and summer. Snow falls for three to five months in the winter. Skiing conditions are good in the hills around Oslo between December and April. From May to July, the weather can be quite warm with long periods of sunshine. Drought can also occur from time to time. Statistically speaking, Oslo is Scandinavia's sunniest capital.

Holiday, Sport, and Leisure

Oslo is surrounded by forest and fjord. Preserving the fjord and the area surrounding the city for leisure and outdoor pursuits is an important part of Oslo's political tradition. Some of the major sports events in Oslo include the Grete Waitz Race, Holmenkollen Relay, Oslo Marathon, and the Holmenkollen Ski Festival. Oslo includes over 2,000 kilometers of prepared ski trails for cross-country skiing and a number of ski lifts for alpine skiing.

Sightseeing Tours

You can choose from a variety of sightseeing tours in and around the Oslo area. Take a two-hour cruise that leaves from Pier 3 in front of the Oslo City Hall and then enjoy a dinner at the Restaurant Lanternen. Sign up for a three-hour bus tour of Vigeland Sculpture Park, the Viking ships, the Holmenkollen Ski Jump, and the Kon-Tiki Raft.

WS4-R4-FCTOslo(Review4,Step6).docx

Mr. Frank Tolentino
Royal Fabrics and Supplies
3220 Wilson Avenue
Toronto, ON M4C 3S3

Performance Threads

Proudly serving the entertainment industry for over 20 years!

January 9, 2012

«AddressBlock»

«GreetingLine»

We have a contract to design and sew approximately 50 costumes for a movie production company. Most of the costumes will require wool fabric in brown and gray. We need to purchase approximately 200 yards of brown worsted wool fabric and 75 yards of gray worsted wool fabric. In addition to the wool fabric, we also need to purchase 300 yards of linen material in beige that is 55% linen and 45% nylon.

Please send us a fax with a list of prices for the wool and linen fabrics. Along with the prices, we also need to know the availability of the fabrics and the earliest shipping dates. To have time to complete all of the costumes, we need the fabric in our office no later than the end of next month.

Send the pricing and availability information to our fax number (905) 555-2998. If you have any questions or need to talk to a designer, please call our office at (905) 555-2971. We value our relationship with your company, «Title» «Last_Name», and look forward to receiving your fax.

Sincerely,

Camilla Yong
Design Manager

4011 Bridgewater Street ✂ Niagara Falls, ON L2E 2T6 ✂ (905) 555-2971

Mrs. Anna Strassburg
Millwood Fabrics
550 Jane Street
Toronto, ON M4B 2C7

Mrs. Andrea Jones-Leigh
JL Fabrics and Crafts
1230 Sheppard Avenue
Toronto, ON M6H 4J2

Performance Threads

Proudly serving the entertainment industry for over 20 years!

January 9, 2012

Mr. Frank Tolentino
Royal Fabrics and Supplies
3220 Wilson Avenue
Toronto, ON M4C 3S3

Dear Mr. Tolentino:

We have a contract to design and sew approximately 50 costumes for a movie production company. Most of the costumes will require wool fabric in brown and gray. We need to purchase approximately 200 yards of brown worsted wool fabric and 75 yards of gray worsted wool fabric. In addition to the wool fabric, we also need to purchase 300 yards of linen material in beige that is 55% linen and 45% nylon.

Please send us a fax with a list of prices for the wool and linen fabrics. Along with the prices, we also need to know the availability of the fabrics and the earliest shipping dates. To have time to complete all of the costumes, we need the fabric in our office no later than the end of next month.

Send the pricing and availability information to our fax number (905) 555-2998. If you have any questions or need to talk to a designer, please call our office at (905) 555-2971. We value our relationship with your company, Mr. Tolentino, and look forward to receiving your fax.

Sincerely,

Camilla Yong
Design Manager

4011 Bridgewater Street ✂ Niagara Falls, ON L2E 2T6 ✂ (905) 555-2971

WS4-R5-PTMergedFabricLtrs(Review5).docx (1 of 4)

Mr. Donald Enslow
Premiere Fabrics and Design
8744 Huron Street
London, ON N5V 2K8

WS4-R5-PTMergedEnvs(Review5).docx (4 of 4)

Performance Threads

Proudly serving the entertainment industry for over 20 years!

January 9, 2012

Mrs. Andrea Jones-Leigh
JL Fabrics and Crafts
1230 Sheppard Avenue
Toronto, ON M6H 4J2

Dear Mrs. Jones-Leigh:

We have a contract to design and sew approximately 50 costumes for a movie production company. Most of the costumes will require wool fabric in brown and gray. We need to purchase approximately 200 yards of brown worsted wool fabric and 75 yards of gray worsted wool fabric. In addition to the wool fabric, we also need to purchase 300 yards of linen material in beige that is 55% linen and 45% nylon.

Please send us a fax with a list of prices for the wool and linen fabrics. Along with the prices, we also need to know the availability of the fabrics and the earliest shipping dates. To have time to complete all of the costumes, we need the fabric in our office no later than the end of next month.

Send the pricing and availability information to our fax number (905) 555-2998. If you have any questions or need to talk to a designer, please call our office at (905) 555-2971. We value our relationship with your company, Mrs. Jones-Leigh, and look forward to receiving your fax.

Sincerely,

Camilla Yong
Design Manager

4011 Bridgewater Street ✂ Niagara Falls, ON L2E 2T6 ✂ (905) 555-2971

WS4-R5-PTMergedFabricLtrs(Review5).docx (2 of 4)

Performance Threads

Proudly serving the entertainment industry for over 20 years!

January 9, 2012

Mrs. Anna Strassburg
Millwood Fabrics
550 Jane Street
Toronto, ON M4B 2C7

Dear Mrs. Strassburg:

We have a contract to design and sew approximately 50 costumes for a movie production company. Most of the costumes will require wool fabric in brown and gray. We need to purchase approximately 200 yards of brown worsted wool fabric and 75 yards of gray worsted wool fabric. In addition to the wool fabric, we also need to purchase 300 yards of linen material in beige that is 55% linen and 45% nylon.

Please send us a fax with a list of prices for the wool and linen fabrics. Along with the prices, we also need to know the availability of the fabrics and the earliest shipping dates. To have time to complete all of the costumes, we need the fabric in our office no later than the end of next month.

Send the pricing and availability information to our fax number (905) 555-2998. If you have any questions or need to talk to a designer, please call our office at (905) 555-2971. We value our relationship with your company, Mrs. Strassburg, and look forward to receiving your fax.

Sincerely,

Camilla Yong
Design Manager

4011 Bridgewater Street ✂ Niagara Falls, ON L2E 2T6 ✂ (905) 555-2971

WS4-R5-PTMergedFabricLtrs(Review5).docx (3 of 4)

Theatre Arts Division

Division Description

Niagara Peninsula College's award-winning Theatre Arts Division offers a curriculum designed to provide students with a thorough exposure to all aspects of the theatre arts. Each student is assigned to a faculty advisor and works with that advisor to plan coursework that will transfer to a four-year college. Students enroll in coursework across a variety of topics, including acting, history of theatre, scenery design, composition, and communication. Transfer students from the theatre program usually do well in a university setting because of the general education they receive at Niagara Peninsula College. The philosophy of the Theatre Arts Division is to offer a sequential program where students can emphasize "backstage" as well as "onstage" courses. Students need to earn at least 65 semester credits to complete both the acting sequence and the technical theatre sequence.

Theatre graduates make valuable employees in any field. Meeting deadlines, working closely with associates, developing and implementing projects, performing under pressure, and developing creative problem-solving strategies are work skills theatre students use daily. The Niagara Peninsula College theatre experience can be the

> The Niagara Peninsula College theatre experience can be the beginning of a lifelong interest in the art of theatre.

beginning of a lifelong interest in the art of theatre.

Division Faculty

Three full-time instructors teach in the Theatre Arts Division along with a number of part-time instructors. The three full-time instructors are:

Cal Rubine, Chair: Mr. Rubine has been involved in over 150 shows as a director, scene designer, actor, and/or producer. His most recent acting included roles in *To Kill a Mockingbird* and *Rent*. As the artistic director of the Niagara Repertory Theatre, he has taken five productions overseas on tours to Brazil, Panama, and Argentina. He has served on international educational theatre committees and presented papers at several national and international regional conferences. He has received numerous awards for acting, directing, and designing.

Gina Simmons: A member of the Theatre Arts Division at Niagara Peninsula College for over 20 years, Ms. Simmons has served as the vice-chair of programs for the Northeast Institute for Theatre Arts and has written and directed numerous musicals. She has directed over 15 regional theatre productions and designed scenery for several national plays. Ms. Simmons has also designed shows for Niagara Peninsula College and directed

---

Performance Threads

Proudly serving the entertainment industry for over 20 years!

January 9, 2012

Mr. Donald Enslow
Premiere Fabrics and Design
8744 Huron Street
London, ON N5V 2K8

Dear Mr. Enslow:

We have a contract to design and sew approximately 50 costumes for a movie production company. Most of the costumes will require wool fabric in brown and gray. We need to purchase approximately 200 yards of brown worsted wool fabric and 75 yards of gray worsted wool fabric. In addition to the wool fabric, we also need to purchase 300 yards of linen material in beige that is 55% linen and 45% nylon.

Please send us a fax with a list of prices for the wool and linen fabrics. Along with the prices, we also need to know the availability of the fabrics and the earliest shipping dates. To have time to complete all of the costumes, we need the fabric in our office no later than the end of next month.

Send the pricing and availability information to our fax number (905) 555-2998. If you have any questions or need to talk to a designer, please call our office at (905) 555-2971. We value our relationship with your company, Mr. Enslow, and look forward to receiving your fax.

Sincerely,

Camilla Yong
Design Manager

4011 Bridgewater Street ✂ Niagara Falls, ON L2E 2T6 ✂ (905) 555-2971

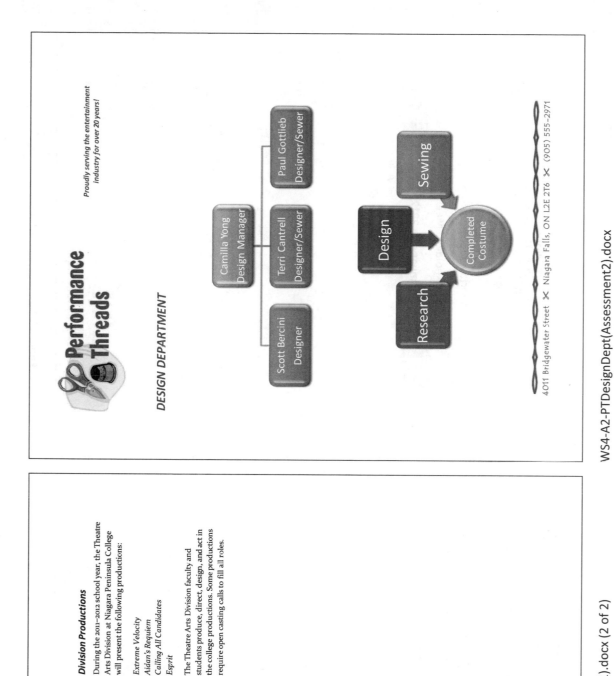

Performance Threads

Proudly serving the entertainment industry for over 20 years!

DESIGN DEPARTMENT

Camilla Yong
Design Manager

Scott Bercini
Designer

Terri Cantrell
Designer/Sewer

Paul Gottlieb
Designer/Sewer

Research — Design — Sewing — Completed Costume

4011 Bridgewater Street ✂ Niagara Falls, ON L2E 2T6 ✂ (905) 555-2971

WS4-A2-PTDesignDept(Assessment2).docx

---

the original historical pageant for Niagara-on-the-Lake.

Joseph Pivens: Mr. Pivens has had a long career in theatre in Ontario, New York, and Europe. He has acted in a variety of local and regional productions, including *Our Town*, *Who's Afraid of Virginia Woolf*, and *Death of a Salesman*. He received the Distinguished Acting award from the Northeast Theatre Group. Mr. Pivens joined the faculty at Niagara Peninsula College in 1990.

Division Productions

During the 2011–2012 school year, the Theatre Arts Division at Niagara Peninsula College will present the following productions:

Extreme Velocity
Aidan's Requiem
Calling All Candidates
Esprit

The Theatre Arts Division faculty and students produce, direct, design, and act in the college productions. Some productions require open casting calls to fill all roles.

WS4-A1-NPCTheatreNewsltr(Assessment1).docx (2 of 2)

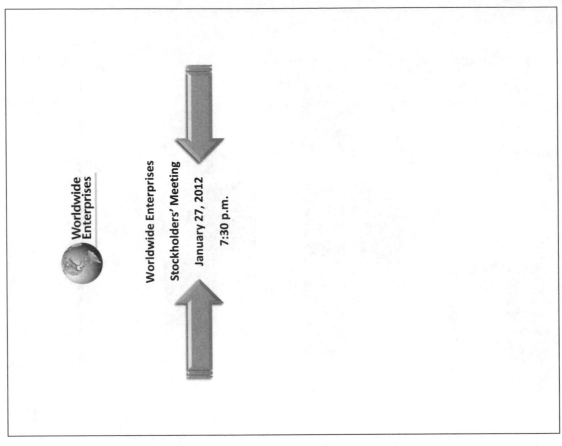

CATERED LUNCH OPTIONS			
Option	Contents	Cost Per Person	Discount Price
Option A: Hot	Vegetarian quiche, Caesar salad, vegetables, dressing, dessert, and beverages	$11.75	$10.95
Option B: Deli	Turkey or ham sandwiches, chips, vegetables, dressing, brownies, and beverages	$9.75	$9.30
Option C: Continental	Bagels, rolls, cream cheese, vegetables, dressing, cookies, and beverages	$8.95	$8.50

Worldwide Enterprises

Worldwide Enterprises

Stockholders' Meeting

January 27, 2012

7:30 p.m.

WS4-A4-WEStockholderMtg(Assessment4).docx

WS4-A3-WBLunchOptions(Assessment3).docx

The Waterfront Bistro
Condensed Quarterly Statement of Income
For the Quarter Ended September 30, 2011
In Thousands

	Jul	Aug	Sep	Total
Sales	$ 51.20	$ 53.70	$ 55.60	$ 160.50
Cost of Goods Sold	$ 35.20	$ 44.80	$ 45.70	$ 125.70
Gross Margin	$ 16.00	$ 8.90	$ 9.90	$ 34.80
Advertising Expense	$ 2.10	$ 2.10	$ 2.10	$ 6.30
Wages and Benefits Expense	$ 10.20	$ 9.40	$ 10.60	$ 30.20
Miscellaneous and Overhead Expense	$ 1.30	$ 1.30	$ 1.30	$ 3.90
Total Expenses	$ 13.60	$ 12.80	$ 14.00	$ 40.40
Net Income Before Taxes	$ 2.40	$ (3.90)	$ (4.10)	$ (5.60)
Taxes	$ 0.53	$ (0.86)	$ (0.90)	$ (1.23)
Net Income After Taxes	$ 1.87	$ (3.04)	$ (3.20)	$ (4.37)

ES1-R1-WBQtrlyIncome(Review1).xlsx

The Waterfront Bistro
Condensed Quarterly Statement of Income
For the Quarter Ended September 30, 2011
In Thousands

	Jul	Aug	Sep	Total
Sales	$ 51.2	$ 53.7	$ 55.6	$ 160.5
Cost of Goods Sold	$ 35.2	$ 44.8	$ 45.7	$ 125.7
Gross Margin	$ 16.0	$ 8.9	$ 9.9	$ 34.8
Advertising Expense	$ 2.1	$ 2.1	$ 2.1	$ 6.3
Wages and Benefits Expense	$ 10.2	$ 9.4	$ 10.6	$ 30.2
Miscellaneous and Overhead Expense	$ 1.3	$ 1.3	$ 1.3	$ 3.9
Total Expenses	$ 13.6	$ 12.8	$ 14.0	$ 40.4
Net Income Before Taxes	$ 2.4	$ (3.9)	$ (4.1)	$ (5.6)
Taxes	$ 0.5	$ (0.9)	$ (0.9)	$ (1.2)
Net Income After Taxes	$ 1.9	$ (3.0)	$ (3.2)	$ (4.4)

ES1-R1-WBQtrlyIncome(Review2).xlsx

Performance Threads
Contract Quotation
Costume Rental and Alteration Fees
For Marquee Productions Location Film Shoot
July 11 to August 31, 2011

Item	Quantity	Unit Cost	Number of Days	Extended Cost
Renaissance period costume rentals	17	$ 88.50	50	$ 75,225.00
On-site alteration fees	17	$ 110.00	N/A	$ 1,870.00
TOTAL CONTRACT QUOTATION:				$ 77,095.00

ES1-A2-PTCostumeCont(Assessment2).xlsx

Marquee Productions
Remote Location Travel Costs
July 11 to August 31, 2011

Item Description	Quantity	Unit Cost	Number of Days	Extended Cost
Return Airfare to/from LAX	48	$ 588.15	N/A	$ 28,231.20
Hotel	24	$ 76.20	52	$ 95,097.60
Daily Expense Allowance	48	$ 27.00	52	$ 67,392.00
TOTAL				$ 190,720.80

ES1-A1-MPTravelCosts(Assessment1).xlsx

North American Distribution for Worldwide Enterprises
Projected Distribution Revenue Schedule
Going Global, Release Date of September 2, 2011

	Preview Cities		
City	Projected Sales in Thousands	Rate	Estimated Revenue
Atlanta	33.1	15%	$ 4,965
Denver	19.6	15%	$ 2,940
Los Angeles	47.1	15%	$ 7,065
Montreal	17.3	15%	$ 2,595
New York	41.9	15%	$ 6,285
Toronto	29.2	15%	$ 4,380
Wichita	11.2	15%	$ 1,680
Total Revenue for Preview Cities:			$ 29,910

	General Release Cities		
City	Projected Sales in Thousands	Rate	Estimated Revenue
Boston	26.9	10%	$ 2,690
Calgary	15.8	10%	$ 1,580
Dallas	18.7	10%	$ 1,870
Des Moines	10.4	10%	$ 1,040
Milwaukee	12.6	10%	$ 1,260
Orlando	29.6	10%	$ 2,960
Philadelphia	21.4	10%	$ 2,140
Tuscon	15.3	10%	$ 1,530
Vancouver	31.7	10%	$ 3,170
Total Revenue for General Release Cities:			$ 18,240

Total Revenue for Film:			$ 48,150

ES1-A3-WEGGProjRev(Assessment3).xlsx

The Waterfront Bistro
Standard Stock Items

Item	Unit	Supplier Name	Rep
Allspice	case	Chapman Wholesale Foods	Kelsey
Baking Powder	case	Chapman Wholesale Foods	Kelsey
Baking Soda	case	Chapman Wholesale Foods	Kelsey
Bananas	case	Tropic Fruits Ltd.	Jay
Beef	side	KLM Meats	Sven
Broccoli	case	Wholesale Produce Inc.	Jamie
Brussel Sprouts	flat	Wholesale Produce Inc.	Jamie
Butternut Squash	case	JL Enterprises	Leigh
Cantaloupe	case	Tropic Fruits Ltd.	Jay
Carrots	25 lb bag	JL Enterprises	Leigh
Cauliflower	case	Wholesale Produce Inc.	Jamie
Celery	case	Wholesale Produce Inc.	Jamie
Chicken	case	KLM Meats	Sven
Cinnamon	case	Chapman Wholesale Foods	Kelsey
Cloves	case	Chapman Wholesale Foods	Kelsey
English Muffins	flat	Paul's Bakery Foods Inc.	Maria
Garlic	10 lb bag	JL Enterprises	Leigh
Green Beans	case	Wholesale Produce Inc.	Jamie
Green Peppers	case	Wholesale Produce Inc.	Jamie
Iceburg Lettuce	case	Wholesale Produce Inc.	Jamie
Kaiser Rolls	flat	Paul's Bakery Foods Inc.	Maria
Lake Erie Perch	flat	Lakeshore Fishery	Claude
Nutmeg	25 lb bag	Chapman Wholesale Foods	Kelsey
Onions	case	JL Enterprises	Leigh
Oranges	case	Tropic Fruits Ltd.	Jay
Pineapple	case	Tropic Fruits Ltd.	Jay
Pita Wraps	flat	Paul's Bakery Foods Inc.	Maria
Pork	side	KLM Meats	Sven
Potatoes	50 lb bag	JL Enterprises	Leigh
Radishes	case	Wholesale Produce Inc.	Jamie
Red Peppers	case	Wholesale Produce Inc.	Jamie
Romaine Lettuce	case	Wholesale Produce Inc.	Jamie
Swordfish	case	Lakeshore Fishery	Claude
Tomatoes	case	Wholesale Produce Inc.	Jamie
Tortilla Wraps	flat	Paul's Bakery Foods Inc.	Maria
White Bread	flat	Paul's Bakery Foods Inc.	Maria
White Flour	25 lb bag	Chapman Wholesale Foods	Kelsey
White Sugar	25 lb bag	Chapman Wholesale Foods	Kelsey
Whole Wheat Bread	flat	Paul's Bakery Foods Inc.	Maria
Whole Wheat Flour	25 lb bag	Chapman Wholesale Foods	Kelsey
Yellow Peppers	case	Wholesale Produce Inc.	Jamie

ES1-A4-WBInventory(Assessment4,Step4).xlsx

Niagara Peninsula College
International Student Registrations
for the 2011/2012 Academic Year
Report Date: (Current Date)

ID #	Last Name	First Name	Home Country	Program	Semester	Credit Hours	Fee per Hour	Tuition Fee
241588	Cano	Sergio	Spain	BIS11	1	45	432	$ 19,440.00
241578	Flannigan	Maren	Ireland	BIS11	1	60	432	$ 25,920.00
241856	Chou	Terry	China	BMK12	1	45	432	$ 19,440.00
286953	Zhang	Joseph	China	BIN32	2	45	432	$ 19,440.00
274586	Alivero	Maria	Mexico	CMP12	2	45	432	$ 19,440.00
268451	Torres	Phillip	Ecuador	CTN14	2	60	432	$ 25,920.00
234851	Davis	Caitlyn	Australia	OAM24	3	60	432	$ 25,920.00
299635	Muir	Christa	Australia	GRD13	4	30	432	$ 12,960.00
247523	North	Marlo	Bahamas	HTC24	2	30	432	$ 12,960.00
277458	Cervinka	Mary	Croatia	TTM14	4	30	432	$ 12,960.00

TOTAL INTERNATIONAL STUDENT FEES: $ 194,400.00

Prepared by: (Student Name)

ES1-C1-NPCIntlRegRpt(Challenge1).xlsx

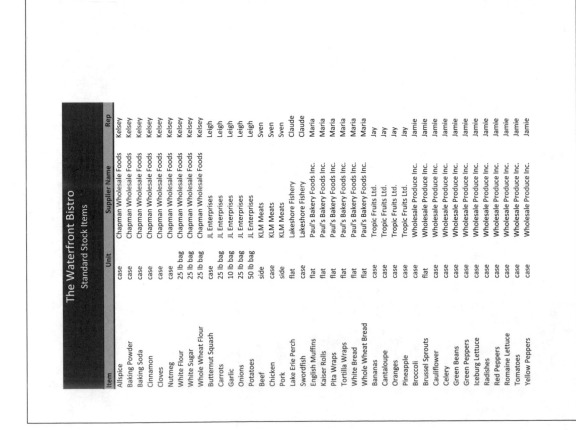

The Waterfront Bistro
Standard Stock Items

Item	Unit	Supplier Name	Rep
Allspice	case	Chapman Wholesale Foods	Kelsey
Baking Powder	case	Chapman Wholesale Foods	Kelsey
Baking Soda	case	Chapman Wholesale Foods	Kelsey
Cinnamon	case	Chapman Wholesale Foods	Kelsey
Cloves	case	Chapman Wholesale Foods	Kelsey
Nutmeg	case	Chapman Wholesale Foods	Kelsey
White Flour	25 lb bag	Chapman Wholesale Foods	Kelsey
White Sugar	25 lb bag	Chapman Wholesale Foods	Kelsey
Whole Wheat Flour	25 lb bag	Chapman Wholesale Foods	Kelsey
Butternut Squash	case	JL Enterprises	Leigh
Carrots	25 lb bag	JL Enterprises	Leigh
Garlic	10 lb bag	JL Enterprises	Leigh
Onions	25 lb bag	JL Enterprises	Leigh
Potatoes	50 lb bag	JL Enterprises	Leigh
Beef	side	KLM Meats	Sven
Chicken	case	KLM Meats	Sven
Pork	side	KLM Meats	Sven
Lake Erie Perch	flat	Lakeshore Fishery	Claude
Swordfish	case	Lakeshore Fishery	Claude
English Muffins	flat	Paul's Bakery Foods Inc.	Maria
Kaiser Rolls	flat	Paul's Bakery Foods Inc.	Maria
Pita Wraps	flat	Paul's Bakery Foods Inc.	Maria
Tortilla Wraps	flat	Paul's Bakery Foods Inc.	Maria
White Bread	flat	Paul's Bakery Foods Inc.	Maria
Whole Wheat Bread	flat	Paul's Bakery Foods Inc.	Maria
Bananas	case	Tropic Fruits Ltd.	Jay
Cantaloupe	case	Tropic Fruits Ltd.	Jay
Oranges	case	Tropic Fruits Ltd.	Jay
Pineapple	case	Tropic Fruits Ltd.	Jay
Broccoli	case	Wholesale Produce Inc.	Jamie
Brussel Sprouts	flat	Wholesale Produce Inc.	Jamie
Cauliflower	case	Wholesale Produce Inc.	Jamie
Celery	case	Wholesale Produce Inc.	Jamie
Green Beans	case	Wholesale Produce Inc.	Jamie
Green Peppers	case	Wholesale Produce Inc.	Jamie
Iceburg Lettuce	case	Wholesale Produce Inc.	Jamie
Radishes	case	Wholesale Produce Inc.	Jamie
Red Peppers	case	Wholesale Produce Inc.	Jamie
Romaine Lettuce	case	Wholesale Produce Inc.	Jamie
Tomatoes	case	Wholesale Produce Inc.	Jamie
Yellow Peppers	case	Wholesale Produce Inc.	Jamie

ES1-A4-WBInventory(Assessment4,Step6).xlsx

Niagara Peninsula College
Target Student Enrollments
For the 2012/2013 Academic Year
Theatre Arts Division

Academic chair: Cal Rubine

Report date: (current date)
Prepared by: (student name)

Program Name	Program Code	Semester Offering	Actual Enrollment 2010/2011	Target
Theatre Arts: Acting	TAA12	1 2 3 4	210	200
Theatre Arts: Stage Management	TAM23	1 2	55	58
Theatre Arts: Lighting & Effects	TAL42	1 2	67	75
Theatre Arts: Production	TAP32	1 2 3 4	221	188
Theatre Arts: Sound	TAS14	1 2	38	39
Theatre Arts: Business Management	TAB25	1 2 3 4	64	48

ESTIMATED ENROLLMENTS FOR 2012/2013: 608

Invoice (Review2)

The Waterfront B·I·S·T·R·O

3104 Rivermist Drive
Buffalo, NY 14280
716 555 3166

Invoice

To: Niagara Peninsula College
2199 Victoria Street
Niagara-on-the-Lake, ON L0S 1J0

Date: 18-Dec-09
PO No. TA-11-643

Attention: Cal Rubine

Re: Theatre Arts Christmas Party
Friday, December 16, 2011

Item	No. of Persons	Price per Person	Total
Buffet Lunch	36	15.23	$ 548.28
French Onion Soup			
Rolls and Butter			
Tossed Salad			
Prime Rib			
Seafood Pasta			
Mixed Vegetables			
Dessert			
Coffee and Tea			
Assorted Juice			
Mineral Water			
Sweet Tray	36	4.89	176.04
Cookies and Squares			
Coffee and Tea			
Delivery and Setup			65.00
Total			$ 789.32

Note: All prices include tax.
Terms: Due upon receipt of invoice payable in U.S. funds.

ES2-R1-WBInvToNPC(Review2).xlsx

Invoice (Review1)

3104 Rivermist Drive
Buffalo, NY 14280
716 555 3166

Invoice

To: Niagara Peninsula College
2199 Victoria Street
Niagara-on-the-Lake, ON L0S 1J0

Date: 18-Dec-09
PO No. TA-11-643

Attention: Cal Rubine

Re: Theatre Arts Christmas Party
Friday, December 16, 2011

Item	No. of Pers	Price per Person	Total
Buffet Lunch	32	15.23	487.36
French Onion Soup			
Rolls and Butter			
Tossed Salad			
Prime Rib			
Mixed Vegetables			
Dessert			
Coffee and Tea			
Milk			
Assorted Juice			
Mineral Water			
Sweet Tray	32	4.89	156.48
Cookies and Squares			
Coffee			
Donuts			
Delivery and Setup			65
Total			

Note: All prices include tax.
Terms: Due upon receipt of invoice payable in U.S. funds.

ES2-R1-WBInvToNPC(Review1).xlsx

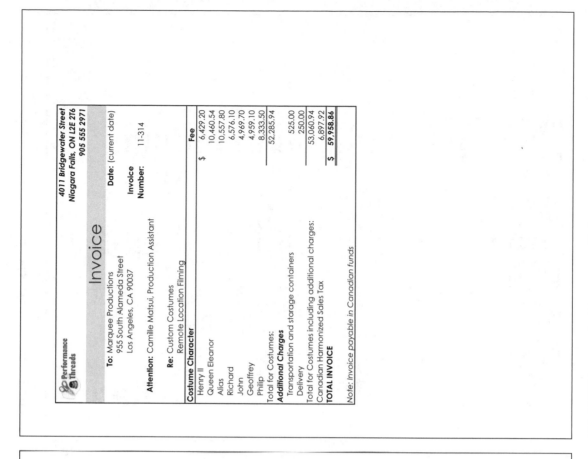

Performance Threads

4011 Bridgewater Street
Niagara Falls, ON L2E 2T6
905 555 2971

Invoice

Date: (current date)

Invoice Number: 11-314

To: Marquee Productions
955 South Alameda Street
Los Angeles, CA 90037

Attention: Camille Matsui, Production Assistant

Re: Custom Costumes
Remote Location Filming

Costume Character	Fee
Henry II	$ 6,429.20
Queen Eleanor	10,460.54
Alias	10,557.80
Richard	6,576.10
John	4,969.70
Geoffrey	4,959.10
Philip	8,333.50
Total for Costumes:	52,285.94
Additional Charges	
Transportation and storage containers	525.00
Delivery	250.00
Total for Costumes including additional charges:	53,060.94
Canadian Harmonized Sales Tax	6,897.92
TOTAL INVOICE	$ 59,958.86

Note: Invoice payable in Canadian funds

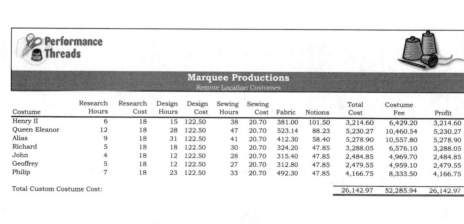

Performance Threads

Marquee Productions
Remote Location Costumes

Costume	Research Hours	Research Cost	Design Hours	Design Cost	Sewing Hours	Sewing Cost	Fabric	Notions	Total Cost	Costume Fee	Profit
Henry II	6	18	15	122.50	38	20.70	381.00	101.50	3,214.60	6,429.20	3,214.60
Queen Eleanor	12	18	28	122.50	47	20.70	523.14	88.23	5,230.27	10,460.54	5,230.27
Alias	9	18	31	122.50	41	20.70	412.30	58.40	5,278.90	10,557.80	5,278.90
Richard	5	18	18	122.50	30	20.70	324.20	47.85	3,288.05	6,576.10	3,288.05
John	4	18	12	122.50	28	20.70	315.40	47.85	2,484.85	4,969.70	2,484.85
Geoffrey	5	18	12	122.50	27	20.70	312.80	47.85	2,479.55	4,959.10	2,479.55
Philip	7	18	23	122.50	33	20.70	492.30	47.85	4,166.75	8,333.50	4,166.75
Total Custom Costume Cost:									26,142.97	52,285.94	26,142.97

Worldwide Enterprises
Revenue Schedule

Date:	(current date)				
Film:	The Endangered Monarch Butterfly				
Production Company:	Marquee Productions				

Venue	Location	Release Category	Box Office Sales	Worldwide Percentage	Gross Revenue
Cinema Plus	Boston	General	$ 23,198,000	10.00%	$ 2,319,800
Movie Mania	Des Moines	General	13,125,000	10.00%	1,312,500
Picture House	Tucson	General	21,245,000	10.00%	2,124,500
Cinema Plus	Orlando	General	27,422,000	10.00%	2,742,200
Reels 'R Us	Milwaukee	General	17,810,000	10.00%	1,781,000
Cinema Plus	Philadelphia	General	23,400,000	10.00%	2,340,000
Reels 'R Us	Dallas	General	15,975,000	10.00%	1,597,500
Cinema Magic	Vancouver	General	13,125,000	10.00%	1,312,500
Cinema Magic	Calgary	General	12,225,000	10.00%	1,222,500
Picture House	Denver	Preview	21,200,000	15.00%	3,180,000
Cinema Plus	Los Angeles	Preview	36,675,000	15.00%	5,501,250
Cinema Magic	Montreal	Preview	20,650,000	15.00%	3,097,500
Cinema Plus	New York	Preview	23,645,000	15.00%	3,546,750
Cinema Magic	Toronto	Preview	19,650,000	15.00%	2,947,500
Movie Mania	Wichita	Preview	12,450,000	15.00%	1,867,500
Cinema Plus	Atlanta	Preview	32,475,000	15.00%	4,871,250
Total:			**$ 334,270,000**		**$ 41,764,250**

ES2-A3-WEMBRev(Assessment3).xlsx

The Waterfront Bistro
Standard Stock Items

Item	Unit	Supplier Name	Rep
Butternut Squash	case	JL Enterprises	Leigh
Potatoes	50 lb bag	JL Enterprises	Leigh
Carrots	25 lb bag	JL Enterprises	Leigh
Onions	25 lb bag	JL Enterprises	Leigh
Garlic	10 lb bag	JL Enterprises	Leigh
Green Peppers	case	Wholesale Produce Inc.	Jamie
Red Peppers	case	Wholesale Produce Inc.	Jamie
Yellow Peppers	case	Wholesale Produce Inc.	Jamie
Radishes	case	Wholesale Produce Inc.	Jamie
Celery	case	Wholesale Produce Inc.	Jamie
Broccoli	case	Wholesale Produce Inc.	Jamie
Cauliflower	case	Wholesale Produce Inc.	Jamie
Tomatoes	case	Wholesale Produce Inc.	Jamie
Green Beans	case	Wholesale Produce Inc.	Jamie
Brussel Sprouts	flat	Wholesale Produce Inc.	Jamie
Iceburg Lettuce	case	Wholesale Produce Inc.	Jamie
Romaine Lettuce	case	Wholesale Produce Inc.	Jamie
Bananas	case	Tropic Fruits Ltd.	Jay
Pineapple	case	Tropic Fruits Ltd.	Jay
Oranges	case	Tropic Fruits Ltd.	Jay
Cantaloupe	case	Paul's Bakery Foods Inc.	Maria
White Bread	flat	Paul's Bakery Foods Inc.	Maria
Whole Wheat Bread	flat	Paul's Bakery Foods Inc.	Maria
Kaiser Rolls	flat	Paul's Bakery Foods Inc.	Maria
English Muffins	flat	Paul's Bakery Foods Inc.	Maria
Pita Wraps	flat	Paul's Bakery Foods Inc.	Maria
Tortilla Wraps	flat	Paul's Bakery Foods Inc.	Maria
Beef	side	KLM Meats	Sven
Pork	side	KLM Meats	Sven
Chicken	case	KLM Meats	Sven
Swordfish	case	Lakeshore Fishery	Claude
Lake Erie Perch	flat	Lakeshore Fishery	Claude
White Flour	25 lb bag	Chapman Wholesale Foods	Kelsey
Whole Wheat Flour	25 lb bag	Chapman Wholesale Foods	Kelsey
White Sugar	25 lb bag	Chapman Wholesale Foods	Kelsey
Baking Powder	case	Chapman Wholesale Foods	Kelsey
Baking Soda	case	Chapman Wholesale Foods	Kelsey
Cinnamon	case	Chapman Wholesale Foods	Kelsey
Nutmeg	case	Chapman Wholesale Foods	Kelsey
Cloves	case	Chapman Wholesale Foods	Kelsey
Allspice	case	Chapman Wholesale Foods	Kelsey

ES2-A4-WBInventory(Assessment4).xlsx

Marquee Excel 2010 Section 2 Model Answers

Niagara Peninsula College

Room: T1101

Period Covered: January 1 to April 30

Time	Monday	Tuesday	Wednesday	Thursday	Friday
8:00 AM	SM100-01 Prasad	AC215-03 McLean (lab)		MG210-01 Spelberger	SM240-03 Prasad
9:00 AM			LE100-03 Das		
10:00 AM	LE253-03 Das			SM355-02 Prasad	SD350-04 Attea
11:00 AM					
12:00 PM	SD451-01 Attea	PD250-02 Kemper	**Common Period**	PD320-03 Kemper	
1:00 PM					LE310-02 Das
2:00 PM	PD340-02 Kemper	MG410-03 Spelberger	AC478-01 Simmons	AC480-01 Simmons (lab)	
3:00 PM			AC140-01 Chou		
4:00 PM	MG150-02 Spelberger	SM165-01 Prasad			MG210-01 Spelberger
5:00 PM					

Use of this facility is restricted to staff and registered students only of Niagara Peninsula College. Failure to abide by this policy is considered a serious violation of the college's code of conduct.

Note 1:	Monday through Thursday evenings, room is booked for Continuing Education department.
Note 2:	Room is booked 8:00 AM to 5:00 PM the second Saturday of each month for the local community theatre group.

ES2-C2-NPCRoomSch(Challenge2).xlsx

Marquee PRODUCTIONS

Remote Location Film Shoot
July 11 to August 31, 2011

Personnel	Site Prep Days	Shoot Days	Cleanup Days	Daily Rate	Extended Cost
		Direct Wages Budget			
Crew	9	32	2	1,275	$ 54,825
Cast	0	32	0	13,775	$ 440,800
Actor Assistants	0	32	0	3,250	$ 104,000
Extras	0	19	0	2,800	$ 53,200
Cleaners	9	32	5	875	$ 40,250
Security	7	32	5	3,750	$ 165,000
Administration	9	32	5	1,275	$ 58,650
			Total Direct Wages Budget		$ 916,725

Estimated Daily Rates	
Subject to Change	
Crew	1,275
Cast	13,775
Actor Assistants	3,250
Extras	2,800
Cleaners	875
Security	3,750
Administration	1,275

ES2-C1-MPLocBudg(Challenge1).xlsx

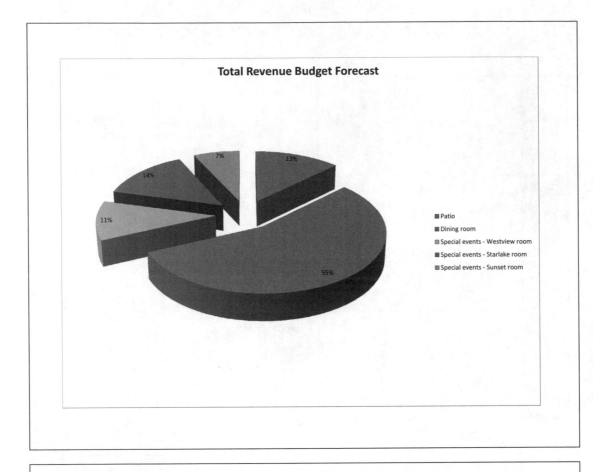

Total Revenue Budget Forecast

- Patio
- Dining room
- Special events - Westview room
- Special events - Starlake room
- Special events - Sunset room

ES3-R1-WBQtrRev(Review2,Step2).xlsx

The Waterfront Bistro
Quarterly Revenue Budget Forecast

Room	Qtr1	Qtr2	Qtr3	Qtr4	Total
Patio	28,135	22,100	73,455	65,412	189,102
Dining room	192,540	204,510	198,475	224,755	820,280
Special events - Westview room	36,750	27,450	42,785	51,875	158,860
Special events - Starlake room	55,475	37,850	48,750	62,175	204,250
Special events - Sunset room	28,450	19,875	22,550	31,850	102,725
TOTAL	341,350	311,785	386,015	436,067	1,475,217
Proof Total	1,475,217				
Average revenue	68,270	62,357	77,203	87,213	295,043
Maximum revenue	192,540	204,510	198,475	224,755	820,280
Minimum revenue	28,135	19,875	22,550	31,850	102,725
Date created	10-Nov-2011				
Next revision date	25-Oct-2012				
Quarterly minimum target	350,000				
Revenue target not met by	-8650	-38215	0	0	

ES3-R1WBQtrRev(Reveiw1)

ES3-R1-WBQtrRev(Review1).xlsx

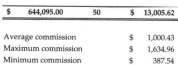

First Choice Travel
Sales Agent Commission Report

Sales agent	Total value of travel bookings	Number of cruises booked	Commission
Lopez, D.	$ 72,185.00	1	$ 1,263.24
El-Kerdi, S.	$ 61,475.00	5	$ 1,383.19
Fournier, W.	$ 31,485.00	0	$ 550.99
Bhayana, M.	$ 52,684.00	3	$ 921.97
Mennill, S.	$ 23,685.00	1	$ 414.49
Doxtator, V.	$ 34,875.00	7	$ 784.69
Redick, L.	$ 22,145.00	0	$ 387.54
Ashby, W.	$ 63,895.00	5	$ 1,437.64
De Papp, Q.	$ 57,642.00	3	$ 1,008.74
O'Donovan, R.	$ 37,478.00	2	$ 655.87
Karamek, F.	$ 61,485.00	8	$ 1,383.41
Postovic, W.	$ 72,665.00	10	$ 1,634.96
Bistany, W.	$ 52,396.00	5	$ 1,178.91
Total	$ 644,095.00	50	$ 13,005.62

Average commission	$	1,000.43
Maximum commission	$	1,634.96
Minimum commission	$	387.54

Commission Parameters

Number of cruises booked	Commission
0 to 4	1.75%
5 and over	2.25%

Note: Agent commission is paid as a percentage of the total value of travel bookings. The percent paid is based on the number of cruises booked. For example, an agent with 7 cruise bookings receives 2.25% commission on travel bookings whereas an agent with only 2 cruise bookings receives 1.75%.

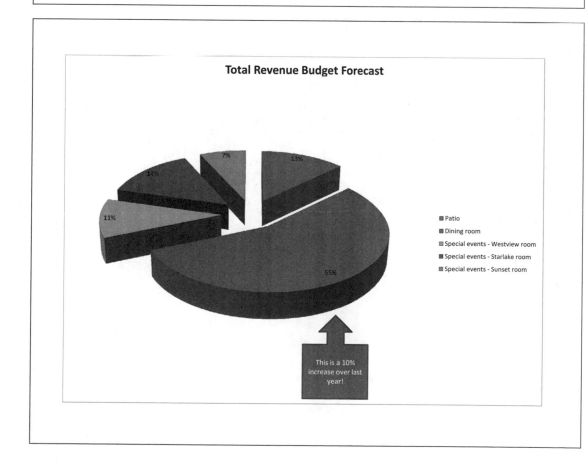

Niagara Peninsula College
Grades Analysis
Theatre Arts Division

Course	A+	A	B	C	D	F	Total Students
AC140-01	6	8	16	14	7	5	56
AC215-03	5	13	20	17	8	10	73
AC330-02	4	11	15	16	8	8	62
AC478-01	2	8	11	16	3	2	42
AC480-01	1	4	9	13	6	2	35
Totals:	18	44	71	76	32	27	268

Theatre Arts Grades Analysis
All Courses

A+ 7%
A 16%
B 27%
C 28%
D 12%
F 10%

Lowest failure rate since 2008!

Worldwide Enterprises

	Guaranty Funds Group	Kilkarney Finance Co.
Interest Rate (per annum)	7.75%	9.25%
Amortization (years)	18	15
Principal Amount Borrowed	$1,050,000	$1,050,000
Monthly Payment	($9,028.99)	($10,806.52)
(includes interest and principal)		
Total Payments on Loan	$ (1,950,262.25)	$ (1,945,173.43)

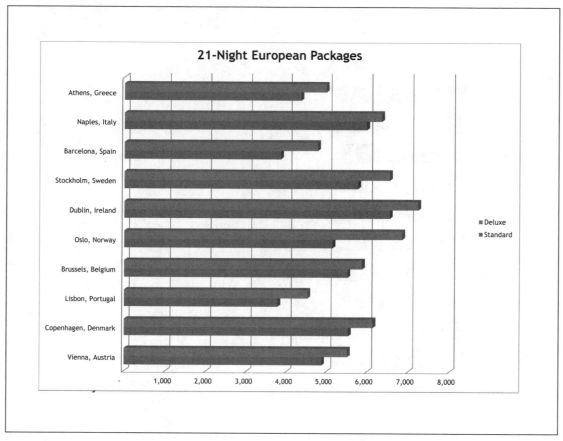

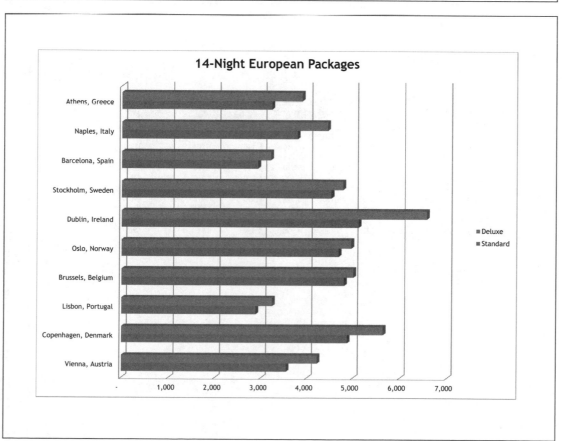

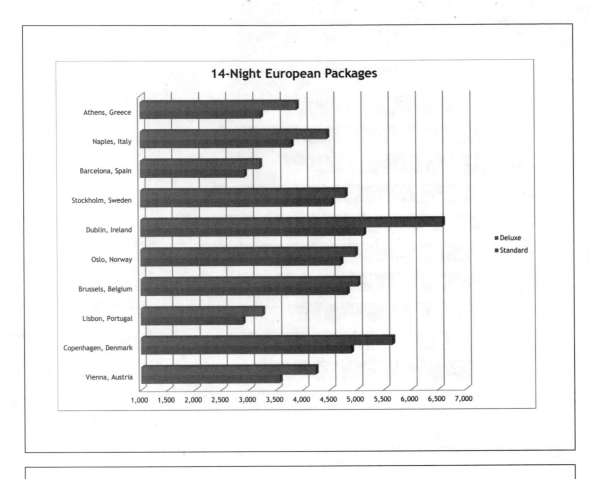

14-Night European Packages

European Packages

European Destinations	14 nights		21 nights		Air Fare Only	Single Surcharge
	Standard	Deluxe	Standard	Deluxe		
Vienna, Austria	3,550	4,220	4,880	5,520	978	450
Copenhagen, Denmark	4,880	5,640	5,540	6,140	1,104	510
Lisbon, Portugal	2,880	3,240	3,775	4,520	855	460
Brussels, Belgium	4,811	5,010	5,520	5,875	965	495
Oslo, Norway	4,694	4,965	5,150	6,850	856	495
Dublin, Ireland	5,120	6,570	6,550	7,240	978	495
Stockholm, Sweden	4,533	4,785	5,775	6,550	978	495
Barcelona, Spain	2,920	3,200	3,850	4,775	688	510
Naples, Italy	3,785	4,450	5,985	6,350	845	450
Athens, Greece	3,222	3,885	4,350	4,990	963	450

Student Name

ES3-A4FCTEurope(Assessment4,Step13)

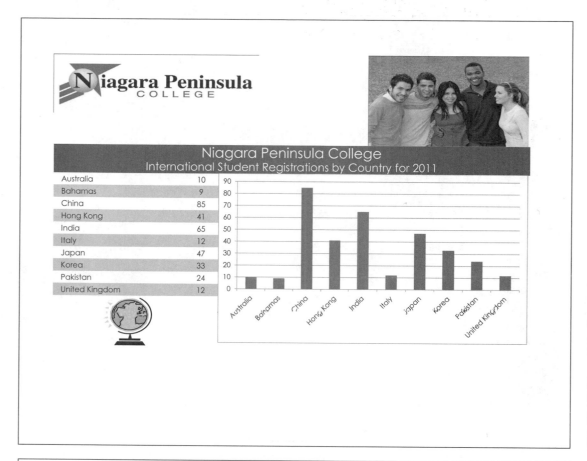

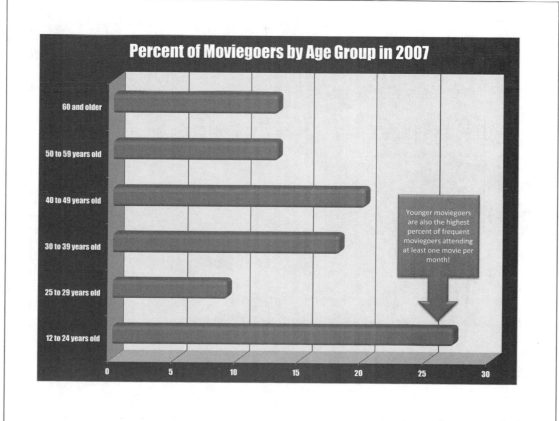

The Waterfront Bistro
Standard Stock Items

Item	Unit	Supplier Name	Rep
Brussel Sprouts	flat	Wholesale Produce Inc.	Jamie
White Bread	flat	Paul's Bakery Foods Inc.	Maria
Whole Wheat Bread	flat	Paul's Bakery Foods Inc.	Maria
Kaiser Rolls	flat	Paul's Bakery Foods Inc.	Maria
English Muffins	flat	Paul's Bakery Foods Inc.	Maria
Pita Wraps	flat	Paul's Bakery Foods Inc.	Maria
Tortilla Wraps	flat	Paul's Bakery Foods Inc.	Maria
Lake Erie Perch	flat	Lakeshore Fishery	Claude

ES4-R2-WBInventory(Review2,Step4).xlsx

The Waterfront Bistro
Payroll Summary

Employee		Total Hours	Overtime Hours	Gross Pay
Lou	Cortez	174	16	$ 1,501.50
Jasmine	Hill	162	3	$ 1,348.88
Heather	Kiley	160	0	$ 1,320.00
Dayna	McGuire	167	7	$ 1,406.63
Carla	Modano	152	0	$ 1,254.00
Tyler	Santini	161	2	$ 1,336.50
Pat	Soulliere	154	0	$ 1,270.50
Moira	Su-Lin	152	0	$ 1,254.00
Toni	Williams	151	0	$ 1,245.75
Total		1433	28	$ 11,937.75

ES4-R1-WBPayroll(Review1).xlsx

Marquee Excel 2010 Section 4 Model Answers

The Waterfront Bistro
Standard Stock Items

Item	Unit	Supplier Name	Rep
Allspice	case	Chapman Wholesale Foods	Kelsey
Baking Powder	case	Chapman Wholesale Foods	Kelsey
Baking Soda	case	Chapman Wholesale Foods	Kelsey
Cinnamon	case	Chapman Wholesale Foods	Kelsey
Cloves	case	Chapman Wholesale Foods	Kelsey
Nutmeg	case	Chapman Wholesale Foods	Kelsey
White Flour	25 lb bag	Chapman Wholesale Foods	Kelsey
White Sugar	25 lb bag	Chapman Wholesale Foods	Kelsey
Whole Wheat Flour	25 lb bag	Chapman Wholesale Foods	Kelsey
Butternut Squash	case	JL Enterprises	Leigh
Carrots	25 lb bag	JL Enterprises	Leigh
Garlic	10 lb bag	JL Enterprises	Leigh
Onions	25 lb bag	JL Enterprises	Leigh
Potatoes	50 lb bag	JL Enterprises	Leigh
Beef	side		Sven
Chicken	case		Sven
Pork	side		Sven
Lake Erie Perch			Claude
Swordfish	ca	...s Inc.	Claude
English Muffins	fl	...ods Inc.	Maria
Kaiser Rolls	fl	...ods Inc.	Maria
Pita Wraps	flat	Paul's Bakery Foods Inc.	Maria
Tortilla Wraps	flat	Paul's Bakery Foods Inc.	Maria
White Bread	flat	Paul's Bakery Foods Inc.	Maria
Whole Wheat Bread	flat	Paul's Bakery Foods Inc.	Maria
Bananas	case	Tropic Fruits Ltd.	Jay
Cantaloupe	case	Tropic Fruits Ltd.	Jay
Oranges	case	Tropic Fruits Ltd.	Jay
Pineapple	case	Tropic Fruits Ltd.	Jay
Broccoli	case	Wholesale Produce Inc.	Jamie
Brussel Sprouts	flat	Wholesale Produce Inc.	Jamie
Cauliflower	case	Wholesale Produce Inc.	Jamie
Celery	case	Wholesale Produce Inc.	Jamie
Green Beans	case	Wholesale Produce Inc.	Jamie
Green Peppers	case	Wholesale Produce Inc.	Jamie
Iceburg Lettuce	case	Wholesale Produce Inc.	Jamie
Radishes	case	Wholesale Produce Inc.	Jamie
Red Peppers	case	Wholesale Produce Inc.	Jamie
Romaine Lettuce	case	Wholesale Produce Inc.	Jamie
Tomatoes	case	Wholesale Produce Inc.	Jamie
Yellow Peppers	case	Wholesale Produce Inc.	Jamie

Student Name:
This item is difficult to source. Dana, should we consider an alternative product?

Student Name:
Dana, is this the right unit for this item?

ES4-R2-WBInventory(Review2,Step10).xlsx

The Waterfront Bistro

3104 Rivermist Drive
Buffalo, NY 14280

Phone: (716) 555-3166
Fax: (716) 555-3190
E-mail: accounts@wfbistro.emcp.net

Statement

Statement #: 101
Date: November 30, 2012
Customer ID: PT-Sinclair

Bill To: Bobbie Sinclair

Performance Threads
4011 Bridgewater Street
NIAGARA FALLS, ON L2E 2T6

Date	Type	Invoice #	Description	Amount	Payment	Balance
11/10/2012	Dir Mtg	2462	Catering Services	$ 726.60		$ 726.60
			Total			$ 726.60

Reminder: Please include the statement number on your check.
Terms: Balance due in 30 days.

REMITTANCE

Customer Name: Performance Threads
Customer ID: PT-Sinclair
Statement #: 101
Date: November 30, 2012
Amount Due: $726.50
Amount Enclosed:

Page 1

ES4-R3-PTStmntNov30(Review3).xlsx

Performance
Threads

Costume Production Schedule						
Marquee Productions						
	Research		Design		Production		Final Delivery
Costume	Start Date	End Date	Start Date2	End Date3	Start Date4	End Date5	Date
Geoffrey	15-May	17-May	12-Jun	16-Jun	25-Jun	30-Jun	9-Jul
Henry II	20-May	21-May	10-Jun	13-Jun	24-Jun	28-Jun	9-Jul
John	30-May	31-May	10-Jun	13-Jun	24-Jun	28-Jun	9-Jul
Philip	19-May	22-May	12-Jun	16-Jun	27-Jun	30-Jun	9-Jul

ES4-A2-PTMarqueeSch(Assessment2,Step5).xlsx

| Niagara Peninsula Community College ||||
| Theatre Arts Co-op Internships ||||
Student Name	Student Number	Co-op Grade P (Pass)/F (Fail)	Date Co-op Grade Entered
Yiu, Terry	138-456-749	P	2/24/2011
Bastow, Maren	111-785-156	P	2/24/2011
Gagne, Martine	378-159-746	P	2/25/2011
Ennis, Amado	348-876-486	P	2/25/2011
Lirette, Marek	498-657-134	P	2/27/2011
Westine, Jesse	348-674-881	F	2/27/2011
Rees, Karen	489-746-315	P	3/2/2011
Vanbeek, Chris	349-587-659	P	3/2/2011
MacKay, Sue	498-315-678	P	3/2/2011

ES4-A1-NPCInternGrades(Assessment1).xlsx

Costume Production Schedule
Marquee Productions

Costume	Research		Design		Production		Final Delivery
	Start Date	End Date	Start Date			End Date	Date
Henry II	20-May	21-May	10-Jun			28-Jun	9-Jul
Queen Eleanor	6-May	10-May	3-Jun			21-Jun	7-Jul
Alias	13-May	15-May	5-Jun			13-Jun	5-Jul
Richard	27-May	29-May	5-Jun			13-Jun	5-Jul
John	30-May	31-May	10-Jun			28-Jun	9-Jul
Geoffrey	15-May	17-May	12-Jun			30-Jun	9-Jul
Philip	19-May	22-May	12-Jun			30-Jun	9-Jul

Student Name: Sue is not yet done with the research. Design may not be able to start June 10.

Student Name: These dates may need adjustment due to overlapping projects.

ES4-A3-PTMarqueeSch(Assessment3).xlsx

Costume Production Schedule
Marquee Productions

Costume	Research		Design		Production		Final Delivery
	Start Date	End Date	Start Date2	End Date3	Start Date4	End Date5	Date
Alias	13-May	15-May	5-Jun	7-Jun	10-Jun	13-Jun	5-Jul
Richard	27-May	29-May	5-Jun	7-Jun	10-Jun	13-Jun	5-Jul
Queen Eleanor	6-May	10-May	3-Jun	7-Jun	17-Jun	21-Jun	7-Jul
Geoffrey	15-May	17-May	12-Jun	16-Jun	25-Jun	30-Jun	9-Jul
Henry II	20-May	21-May	10-Jun	13-Jun	24-Jun	28-Jun	9-Jul
John	30-May	31-May	10-Jun	13-Jun	24-Jun	28-Jun	9-Jul
Philip	19-May	22-May	12-Jun	16-Jun	27-Jun	30-Jun	9-Jul

ES4-A2-PTMarqueeSch(Assessment2,Step8).xlsx

INVOICE

The Waterfront Bistro

3104 Rivermist Drive
Buffalo, NY 14280
P: 716.555.3166 F: 716.555.3190
www.emcp.net/wfbistro

INVOICE NO.	2463
DATE	(current date)
CUSTOMER ID	FCT-Torres

TO
Alex Torres
First Choice Travel
4277 Yonge Street
Toronto, ON M4P 2E6
416.555.9834

SHIP TO
2100 Victoria Street
Niagara-on-the-Lake, ON L0S 1J0
FCT-Torres

QTY	ITEM #	DESCRIPTION	UNIT PRICE	DISCOUNT	LINE TOTAL
16		Lunches	$ 18.23		$ 291.68
16		Desserts	5.31		84.96
16		Beverages	1.87		29.92
1		Delivery and setup	65.00		65.00
				SUBTOTAL	$ 471.56
				SALES TAX	6%
				TOTAL	$ 499.85

ES4-C1-WBInvFCT(Challenge1).xlsx

Performance Threads

Costume Rentals

CostumeID	Description	DailyRentalFee	DateOut	DateIn	DaysRented	TotalDue
A-101	Val Wingfield	$112.75	7/7/2011	7/31/2011	24	$ 2,706.00
A-102	Eunice Billings	$112.75	7/7/2011	7/15/2011	8	$ 902.00
A-110	Tony Salvatore	$112.75	7/15/2011	8/12/2011	28	$ 3,157.00
A-122	Celia Gopf	$112.75	8/1/2011	8/30/2011	29	$ 3,269.75
A-130	Jade Norwich	$112.75	8/12/2011	8/31/2011	19	$ 2,142.25
A-144	Kelly Williams	$102.50	5/2/2011	6/11/2011	40	$ 4,100.00
A-152	Hannah Sorenti	$115.50	6/1/2011	7/12/2011	41	$ 4,735.50
A-160	William Mercer	$122.00	7/7/2011	7/10/2011	3	$ 366.00
A-162	Jorge Nevada	$131.50	8/1/2011	8/30/2011	29	$ 3,813.50
A-166	Catherine Bellfield	$141.00	8/1/2011	8/30/2011	29	$ 4,089.00
A-170	Vincent Dudikoff	$112.75	8/12/2011	8/22/2011	10	$ 1,127.50
A-176	Pietro Gorski	$115.50	5/2/2011	6/10/2011	39	$ 4,504.50
A-180	Robert Foullette	$102.50	7/15/2011	7/31/2011	16	$ 1,640.00
A-188	Jade Sorbet	$115.50	8/1/2011	8/22/2011	21	$ 2,425.50
A-190	Xavier Vanderkof	$141.00	8/12/2011	8/31/2011	19	$ 2,679.00
A-198	Nanci Lasertol	$122.00	7/22/2011	8/15/2011	24	$ 2,928.00
D-101	Simba	$255.00	7/1/2011	7/31/2011	30	$ 7,650.00
D-102	Timon	$166.00	7/1/2011	7/31/2011	30	$ 4,980.00
D-103	Poombah	$128.00	7/1/2011	7/31/2011	30	$ 3,840.00
D-104	Rafiki	$138.00	7/1/2011	7/31/2011	30	$ 4,140.00
D-105	Nala	$144.00	7/1/2011	7/31/2011	30	$ 4,320.00
D-106	Zazu	$155.00	7/1/2011	7/31/2011	30	$ 4,650.00
D-107	Scar	$144.00	7/1/2011	7/31/2011	30	$ 4,320.00
D-108	Mufasa	$224.00	7/1/2011	7/31/2011	30	$ 6,720.00
D-201	Belle	$175.00	10/1/2011	11/15/2011	45	$ 7,875.00
D-202	Beast	$237.00	10/1/2011	11/15/2011	45	$ 10,665.00
D-203	Gaston	$190.00	10/1/2011	11/15/2011	45	$ 8,550.00
D-204	Maurice	$155.00	10/1/2011	11/15/2011	45	$ 6,975.00
D-205	Lumiere	$188.00	10/1/2011	11/15/2011	45	$ 8,460.00
D-206	Cogsworth	$192.00	10/1/2011	11/15/2011	45	$ 8,640.00
D-207	Mrs. Potts	$210.00	10/1/2011	11/15/2011	45	$ 9,450.00
D-208	Chip	$189.00	10/1/2011	11/15/2011	45	$ 8,505.00
S-101	Macbeth	$175.50	5/12/2011	6/30/2011	49	$ 8,599.50
S-102	Lady Macbeth	$195.00	5/12/2011	6/30/2011	49	$ 9,555.00
S-106	Hamlet	$125.00	7/1/2011	7/31/2011	30	$ 3,750.00
S-110	Othello	$125.00	7/22/2011	8/31/2011	40	$ 5,000.00
S-118	King Lear	$145.50	8/1/2011	9/10/2011	40	$ 5,820.00
S-122	Richard III	$135.00	8/1/2011	9/10/2011	40	$ 5,400.00
S-130	Romeo	$140.00	9/1/2011	10/15/2011	44	$ 6,160.00
S-131	Juliet	$140.00	9/1/2011	10/15/2011	44	$ 6,160.00
Total						**$ 204,770.00**

ES4-A4-PTRentalCost(Assessment4).xlsx

	Worldwide Enterprises		North American Distributor List				
Name	**Mailing Address**	**City**	**State**	**ZIP code**	**Telephone**	**Fax**	
Olypmic Cinemas	P. O. Box 1439	Calgary	AB	T2C 3P7	403-651-4587	403-651-4589	
LaVista Cinemas	111 Vista Road	Phoenix	AZ	86355-6014	602-555-6231	602-555-6233	
West Coast Movies	P. O. Box 298	Vancouver	BC	V6Y 1N9	604-555-3548	604-555-3549	
Marquee Movies	1011 South Alameda Street	Los Angeles	CA	90045	612-555-2398	612-555-2377	
Sunfest Cinemas		Tampa	FL	33562	813-555-3185	813-555-3177	
Liberty Cinemas	P. O. Box 998	Atlanta	GA	73125	404-555-8113	404-555-2349	
O'Shea Movies	59 Erie	Oak Park	IL	60302	312-555-7719	312-555-7381	
Midtown Moviehouse	1033 Commercial Street	Emporia	KS	66801	316-555-7013	316-555-7022	
All Nite Cinemas	2188 3rd Street	Louisville	KY	40201	502-555-4238	502-555-4240	
Eastown Movie House	P. O. Box 722	Cambridge	MA	2142	413-555-0981	413-555-0226	
Riverview Cinemas	1011-848 Sheppard Street	Winnipeg	MB	R2P 0N6	204-555-6538	204-555-6533	
New Age Movies	73 Killarney Road	Moncton	NB	E1B 2Z9	506-555-8376	506-555-8377	
EastCoast Cinemas	62 Mountbatten Drive	St.John's	NF	A1A 3X9	709-555-8349	709-555-8366	
Hillman Cinemas	55 Kemble Avenue	Baking Ridge	NJ	7920	201-555-1147	201-555-1143	
Seaboard Movie House Inc.	P. O. Box 1005	Dartmouth	NS	B2V 1Y8	902-555-3948	902-555-3950	
Northern Reach Movies	P. O. Box 34	Yellowknife	NW	X1A 2N9	867-555-6314	867-555-6316	
Mainstream Movies	P. O. Box 33	Buffalo	NY	14601	212-555-3269	212-555-3270	
Victory Cinemas	12119 South 23rd	Buffalo	NY	14288	212-555-8746	212-555-8748	
Waterfront Cinemas	P. O. Box 3255	New York	NY	14288	212-555-3845	212-555-3947	
Westview Movies	1112 Broadway	New York	NY	10119	212-555-4875	212-555-4877	
Mooretown Movies	P. O. Box 11	Dublin	OH	43107	614-555-8134	614-555-8339	
Millennium Movies	4126 Yonge Street	Toronto	ON	M2P 2B8	416-555-9335	416-555-9338	
Redwood Cinemas	P. O. Box 112F	Portland	OR	97466-3359	503-555-8641	503-555-8633	
Wellington 10	1203 Tenth Southwest	Philadelphia	PA	19178	215-555-9045	215-555-9048	
Waterdown Cinemas	575 Notre Dame Street	Summerside	PE	C1N 1T8	902-555-8374	902-555-8376	
MountainView Movies	5417 RoyalMount Avenue	Montreal	PQ	H4P 1H8	514-555-3584	514-555-3585	
Danforth Cinemas	P. O. Box 22	Columbia	SC	29201	803-555-3487	803-555-3421	
Plains Cinema House	P. O. Box 209	Regina	SK	S4S 5Y9	306-555-1247	305-555-1248	
Century Cinemas	3687 Avenue K	Arlington	TX	76013	817-555-2116	817-555-2119	
Countryside Cinemas	22 Hillside Street	Bennington	VT	5201	802-555-1469	802-555-1470	
Northern Stars Movies	811 Cook Street	Whitehorse	YK	Y1A 2S4	867-555-6598	867-555-6599	

ES4-C2-WEDistributors(Challenge2).xlsx

Theatre Arts Division Student Enrollment

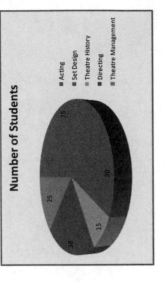

Number of Students

Legend: Acting, Set Design, Theatre History, Directing, Theatre Management

75, 30, 15, 25, 38

2199 Victoria Street ◊ *Niagara-on-the-Lake* ◊ *ON L0S 1J0* ◊ *(905) 555-2183*
www.emcp.net/npcollege.ca

Int1-R2-NPCWordEnroll(Review2,Step7).docx

Beginning Theatre
Fall Term
Acting Scores

Student	Scene 1	Scene 2	Scene 3	Average
Bastow, Maren	3.50	2.75	3.25	3.2
Bodine, Rod	2.00	2.00	2.50	2.2
Colbert, Sherrie	4.00	3.00	3.25	3.4
Ennis, Amado	4.00	3.50	3.75	3.8
Gagne, Martine	2.50	2.75	3.00	2.8
Remy, David	2.50	1.75	2.00	2.1
Snowden, Lee	3.50	2.00	2.50	2.7
Yiu, Terry	3.50	3.00	3.50	3.3

Int1-R1-NPCExcelScores(Review1).xlsx

Spring Term

Area of Emphasis	# of Students
Acting	98
Set Design	25
Theatre History	23
Directing	52
Theatre Management	10

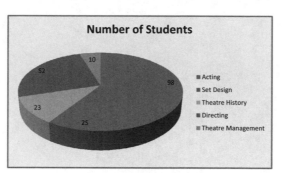

Fall Term

Area of Emphasis	# of Students
Acting	75
Set Design	30
Theatre History	15
Directing	38
Theatre Management	25

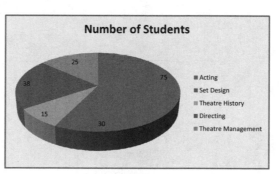

Worldwide Enterprises

Date: August 13, 2012

To: Sam Vestering, Manager

From: Heidi Pasqual, Financial Officer

Subject: July Revenues

The table below shows the box office sales, percentages, and revenue for the previous month. The box office sales are lower than anticipated for the summer season.

July Revenues			
Theatre Company	Box Office Sales	Percentage	Revenue
Cinema House	$1,356,000	5.0%	$67,800
Cinema Plus	$2,450,000	5.0%	$122,500
Movie Mania	$1,635,000	7.5%	$122,625
Picture House	$950,000	5.0%	$47,500
Reels 'R Us	$1,050,000	5.0%	$52,500

Int1-R3-WERevMemo(Review3,Step5).docx

Niagara Peninsula COLLEGE

Theatre Arts Division Student Enrollment

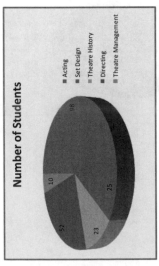

Number of Students

- ■ Acting
- ■ Set Design
- ■ Theatre History
- ■ Directing
- ■ Theatre Management

98
10
52
23
25

2199 Victoria Street ✧ Niagara-on-the-Lake ✧ ON L0S 1J0 ✧ (905) 555-2183
www.emcp.net/npcollege.ca

Int1-R2-NPCWordEnroll(Review2,Step15).docx

Worldwide Enterprises

Date: September 3, 2012

To: Sam Vestering, Manager

From: Heidi Pasqual, Financial Officer

Subject: August Revenues

The table below shows the box office sales, percentages, and revenue for the previous month. The box office sales are lower than anticipated for the summer season.

Theatre Company	August Revenues		
	Box Office Sales	Percentage	Revenue
Cinema House	$1,575,000	5.0%	$78,750
Cinema Plus	$2,375,000	5.0%	$118,750
Movie Mania	$1,750,000	7.5%	$131,250
Picture House	$1,100,000	5.0%	$55,000
Reels 'R Us	$1,255,000	5.0%	$62,750

Int1-R3-WERevMemo(Review3,Step10).docx

Employees

EmployeeID	LastName	FirstName	MiddleInitial	BirthDate	HireDate
1000	Vestering	Sam	L	2/18/1957	7/22/2002
1005	Deptulski	Roman	W	3/12/1948	8/15/2002
1010	Postma	Hanh	A	12/10/1952	1/30/2002
1015	Besterd	Lyle	C	10/15/1959	5/17/2003
1020	Doxtator	Angela	B	5/22/1963	8/3/2003
1025	Biliski	Jorge	N	6/18/1970	12/1/2003
1030	Hicks	Thom	P	7/27/1977	1/22/2004
1040	Lafreniere	Guy	F	9/14/1972	3/10/2005
1045	Yiu	Terry	M	6/18/1961	1/31/2006
1050	Zakowski	Carl	W	12/22/1987	2/9/2006
1060	McKnight	Donald	Z	1/6/1964	6/22/2007
1065	Liszniewski	Norm	M	11/16/1970	2/6/2008
1070	Jhawar	Balfor	R	9/3/1973	11/22/2009
1075	Fitchett	Mike	L	4/18/1966	1/19/2010
1080	Couture	Leo	S	1/8/1978	1/27/2010
1085	Armine	Yousef	J	11/19/1990	3/14/2010
1090	Quinte	Maria	D	4/16/1991	11/29/2010
1095	Kllarney	Patrick	J	2/27/1985	12/12/2010

WEEmployees1(Review1).accdb (1 of 2)

Employees

Department	AnnualSalary
North American Distribution	$69,725.00
Overseas Distribution	$72,750.00
European Distribution	$69,725.00
North American Distribution	$45,651.00
North American Distribution	$45,558.00
North American Distribution	$44,892.00
Overseas Distribution	$42,824.00
Overseas Distribution	$45,395.00
European Distribution	$42,238.00
European Distribution	$44,387.00
European Distribution	$42,126.00
North American Distribution	$43,695.00
Overseas Distribution	$44,771.00
Overseas Distribution	$42,857.00
European Distribution	$43,659.00
European Distribution	$42,177.00
Overseas Distribution	$42,177.00
North American Distribution	$42,177.00

WEEmployees1(Review1).accdb (2 of 2)

SM100-01Grades

StudentNo	LastName	FirstName	Grade
111-785-156	Bestow	Maren	C
118-487-578	Ardre	Ian	D
137-845-746	Krowlton	Sherri	C
138-456-749	Yiu	Terry	A+
146-984-137	Rhodes	Tari	A+
157-457-856	Dwyer	Barbara	B
184-457-156	Van Este	Doranda	C
197-486-745	Koning	Jeffrey	F
198-744-149	Lysenko	Earl	C
211-745-856	Ut-rig	Andrew	D
217-458-687	HLsson	Ahmad	A+
221-689-478	Bhullar	Ash	A
229-658-412	Mrsior	Melanie	B
255-158-498	Gibson	Kevin	C
274-658-986	Weollatt	Bentley	B
314-745-856	Morgan	Bruce	B
321-487-659	Loewen	Richard	F
325-841-469	Clements	Russell	A
326-945-745	Hodgson	Catherine	B
328-746-985	Po teous	Louis	D
329-685-457	Turpela	Murray	C
344-745-812	Isowski	Alija	A
348-876-486	Ennis	Armado	D
349-856-745	Buziak	Claudette	B
349-874-658	Relieffe	Susan	C
359-845-475	Collyer	Sandra	D
378-159-746	Gagne	Martine	B

Page 1

Employees   7/11/2012

Department	LastName	FirstName	MiddleInitial	BirthDate	HireDate	AnnualSalary
European Distribution	Armine	Yousef	J	11/19/1990	3/14/2010	$42,177.00
European Distribution	Couture	Leo	S	1/8/1978	1/27/2010	$43,659.00
European Distribution	McKnight	Donald	Z	1/6/1964	6/22/2007	$42,126.00
European Distribution	Postma	Hanh	A	12/10/1952	1/30/2002	$69,725.00
European Distribution	Yiu	Terry	M	6/18/1961	1/31/2006	$42,238.00
European Distribution	Zakowski	Carl	W	12/22/1987	2/9/2006	$44,387.00
North American Distribution	Besterd	Lyle	C	10/15/1959	5/17/2003	$45,651.00
North American Distribution	Biliski	Jorge	N	6/18/1970	12/1/2003	$44,892.00
North American Distribution	Doxtator	Angela	B	5/22/1963	8/3/2003	$45,558.00
North American Distribution	Kilarney	Patrick	J	2/27/1985	12/12/2010	$42,177.00
North American Distribution	Liszniewski	Norm	M	11/16/1970	2/6/2008	$43,695.00
North American Distribution	Vestering	Sam	L	2/18/1957	7/22/2002	$69,725.00
Overseas Distribution	Deptulski	Roman	W	3/12/1948	8/15/2002	$72,750.00
Overseas Distribution	Fitchett	Mike	L	4/18/1966	1/19/2010	$42,857.00
Overseas Distribution	Hicks	Thom	P	7/27/1977	1/22/2004	$42,824.00
Overseas Distribution	Jhawar	Balfor	R	9/3/1973	11/22/2009	$44,771.00
Overseas Distribution	Lafreniere	Guy	F	9/14/1972	3/10/2005	$45,395.00
Overseas Distribution	Quinte	Maria	D	4/16/1991	11/29/2010	$42,177.00

Page 1

InventoryList 7/22/2012

ItemNo	ItemDescription	Unit	SupplierCode
001	Butternut Squash	case	4
002	Potatoes	50 lb bag	4
003	Carrots	25 lb bag	4
004	Onions	25 lb bag	4
005	Garlic	10 lb bag	3
006	Green Peppers	case	3
007	Red Peppers	case	3
008	Yellow Peppers	case	4
009	Radishes	case	4
010	Celery	case	3
011	Broccoli	case	3
012	Cauliflower	case	4
013	Tomatoes	case	4
014	Green Beans	case	3
015	Brussel Sprouts	flat	4
016	Iceburg Lettuce	case	3
017	Romaine Lettuce	case	3
018	Bananas	case	2
019	Pineapple	case	2
020	Oranges	case	2
021	Cantaloupe	case	2
022	White Bread	flat	1
023	Whole Wheat Bread	flat	1
024	Kaiser Rolls	flat	1
025	English Muffins	flat	1
027	Tortilla Wraps	flat	1
028	Beef	side	7
029	Pork	side	7
030	Chicken	case	6
032	Swordfish	case	8
034	Ketchup	gallon	10
035	Mustard	gallon	10
036	Mayonnaise	gallon	10
037	Green Relish	gallon	10
038	Barbecue Sauce	case	15
039	White Flour	25 lb bag	11
040	Whole Wheat Flour	25 lb bag	11
041	White Sugar	25 lb bag	11
042	Baking Powder	case	12
043	Baking Soda	case	12
044	Cinnamon	case	12
045	Nutmeg	case	12
046	Cloves	case	12
047	Allspice	case	12
048	Seasoned Salt	case	12

Page 1

WBInventory1(Assessment2).accdb (1 of 2)

InventoryList 7/22/2012

ItemNo	ItemDescription	Unit	SupplierCode
049	Salt	case	12
050	Pepper	case	12
051	Atlantic Scallops	case	9
052	Lake Trout	case	9
053	Panini Rolls	flat	1

Page 2

WBInventory1(Assessment2).accdb (2 of 2)

CostumeNo	DateOut	DateIn	CostumeTitle	DailyRentalFee
G-105			Bartender	$89.00
G-103			Cowboy (blue)	$112.00
G-104			Cowboy (green)	$112.00
G-110			Doctor	$85.00
G-108			Fireman	$180.00
G-109			Paramedic	$155.00
G-106			Policeman	$120.00
G-107			RCMP Officer	$215.00
G-102			Sheriff (black)	$120.00
G-101			Sheriff (gray)	$120.00
A-176	5/2/2011	6/10/2011	Pietro Gorski	$115.50
A-144	5/2/2011	6/11/2011	Kelly Williams	$99.50
A-152	6/1/2011	7/12/2011	Hannah Sorenti	$115.50
D-108	7/1/2011	7/31/2011	Mufasa	$215.50
D-105	7/1/2011	7/31/2011	Nala	$188.75
D-103	7/1/2011	7/31/2011	Pumbaa	$112.75
D-104	7/1/2011	7/31/2011	Rafiki	$144.50
D-107	7/1/2011	7/31/2011	Scar	$198.75
D-101	7/1/2011	7/31/2011	Simba	$224.75
D-102	7/1/2011	7/31/2011	Timon	$85.50
D-106	7/1/2011	7/31/2011	Zazu	$85.50
A-160	7/7/2011	7/10/2011	William Mercer	$122.00
A-102	7/7/2011	7/15/2011	Eunice Billings	$124.50
A-101	7/7/2011	7/31/2011	Val Wingfield	$124.50
A-180	7/15/2011	7/31/2011	Robert Foullette	$102.50
A-110	7/15/2011	8/12/2011	Tony Salvatore	$124.50
A-198	7/22/2011	8/15/2011	Nanci Lasertol	$122.00
A-188	8/1/2011	8/22/2011	Jade Sorbet	$115.50
A-166	8/1/2011	8/30/2011	Catherine Bellfield	$141.00
A-122	8/1/2011	8/30/2011	Celia Gopf	$124.50
A-162	8/1/2011	8/30/2011	Jorge Nevada	$131.50
A-170	8/12/2011	8/22/2011	Vincent Dudkoff	$124.50
A-130	8/12/2011	8/31/2011	Jade Norwich	$124.50
A-190	8/12/2011	8/31/2011	Xavier Vanderkof	$141.00
S-131	9/1/2011	10/15/2011	Juliet	$140.00
S-130	9/1/2011	10/15/2011	Romeo	$140.00
D-202	10/1/2011	11/15/2011	Beast	$237.00
D-201	10/1/2011	11/15/2011	Belle	$175.00
D-208	10/1/2011	11/15/2011	Chip	$189.00
D-206	10/1/2011	11/15/2011	Cogsworth	$192.00
D-203	10/1/2011	11/15/2011	Gaston	$190.00
D-205	10/1/2011	11/15/2011	Lumiere	$188.00
D-204	10/1/2011	11/15/2011	Maurice	$155.00

PTCostumeInv1(Assessment3).accdb (1 of 2)

CostumeNo	DateOut	DateIn	CostumeTitle	DailyRentalFee
D-207	10/1/2011	11/15/2011	Mrs. Potts	$210.00

PTCostumeInv1(Assessment3).accdb (2 of 2)

Marquee Access 2010 Section 1 Model Answers

WBSpecialEvents1(Challenge1).accdb (1 of 2)

CateringContracts   7/22/2012

RoomBooked	LastName	FirstName	ContactPhone	Event	DateOfEvent
Starlake	Hillmore	Cecily	716 555 6598	Business Meetin	1/15/2011
Westview	Fontaine	Mario	716 555 1886	Engagement Part	1/20/2011
Westview	Corriveau	Frances	716 555 3256	Birthday Party	1/23/2011
Sunset	Kressman	Weston	716 555 4219	Wedding	2/28/2011
Westview	Fagan	Orlando	716 555 3694	25th Wedding A	3/10/2011
Westview	Pockovic	Kim	905 555 3698	Birthday Party	3/18/2011
Starlake	Gill	Lane	416 555 3264	Business Meetin	3/29/2011
Westview	Bresque	Percy	716 555 1248	50th Wedding A	4/12/2011
Sunset	Santore	Max	905 555 3264	Wedding	4/28/2011
Sunset	Hamid	Omar	716 555 8796	Engagement Part	5/8/2011
Starlake	Russell	Dana	716 555 4965	Birthday Party	5/30/2011
Starlake	Szucs	Walter	905 555 6998	Birthday Party	6/10/2011
Starlake	Griffin	Nicole	905 555 4166	25th Wedding A	6/17/2011
Sunset	Doucet	Zack	716 555 3488	Wedding	6/20/2011
Westview	Golinsky	Jesse	716 555 4218	Business Meetin	6/26/2011
Sunset	Jin Ping	Cora	716 555 7774	Baby Shower	7/10/2011
Sunset	McMaster	Elizabeth	716 555 9442	Engagement Part	7/11/2011
Starlake	Pavelich	Reed	716 555 2286	Wedding	7/25/2011
Westview	Juanitez	Alfredo	716 555 4668	Business Meetin	7/31/2011
Westview	Spriet	Cora	905 555 1623	Wedding	8/8/2011
Starlake	Vezina	Sean	716 555 3846	Business Meetin	8/12/2011
Sunset	Graham	William	716 555 8694	25th Wedding A	8/15/2011
Sunset	Kosjovic	Helena	716 555 3441	Engagement Bru	8/16/2011
Starlake	Borman	Pieter	716 555 6994	Business Meetin	8/22/2011

Page 1

WBSpecialEvents1(Challenge1).accdb (2 of 2)

CateringContracts   7/22/2012

Guests	PerPersonCharge	SpecialMenu	DepositReceived
35	$21.95	☐	☐
177	$28.95	☑	☑
85	$25.95	☑	☑
266	$28.95	☑	☑
88	$28.95	☑	☐
62	$35.95	☐	☑
71	$21.95	☑	☑
62	$32.95	☐	☑
157	$25.95	☑	☑
85	$28.95	☐	☐
36	$26.95	☑	☐
42	$28.95	☐	☐
54	$31.95	☑	☑
168	$28.95	☑	☑
57	$24.95	☑	☑
62	$21.95	☑	☑
75	$27.95	☑	☐
110	$33.50	☑	☑
49	$23.95	☐	☑
150	$26.95	☐	☑
24	$23.75	☐	☑
80	$24.95	☐	☑
56	$22.95	☐	☑
41	$24.95	☑	☑

Page 2

Performance Threads Custom Costume Database
Table and Field Name Structure

This Challenge assessment would be well suited to a paired or team activity.
You may want to instruct students to create this document in the same format as the database diagram
shown in Figure 1.3.

NOTES to Instructors: Answers will vary. Key concepts to watch for:
  ✓ Tables are provided a logical name (no spaces)
  ✓ Fields are broken down into the smallest units of information (no spaces in names)
  ✓ Each table contains a unique field suitable for a primary key
  ✓ Information from the additional notes is added
  ✓ Students might choose to create an additional table for the hours. Encourage various answers
     and discussion in class and emphasize there is no one right answer.
  ✓ At this stage, students are not expected to know how to join tables in relationships; therefore, if
     the student duplicates customer or seamstress names in tables consider this acceptable. This
     project will be worked on again in the next section at which time these will be corrected.

Some of the field names below are long—at this stage look to see that the student is describing the field
appropriately. Shortening the names will be discussed in section 2.

Table 1 – Customers
CustomerID
FirstName
LastName
StreetAddress
City
StateOrProvince
ZIPorPostalCode
HomePhone
BusinessPhone
CellPhone

Table 2 – Costume_Orders
CostumeID
Description
CustomerID
ContractPrice
SignedContract
DepositAmount
SeamstressID
EstimatedHrs_Research
EstimatedHrs_Design
EstimatedHrs_Production
ActualHrs_Research
ActualHrs_Design
ActualHrs_Production

Table 3 – Contract_Seamstresses
SeamstressID
FirstName
LastName
StreetAddress
City
StateOrProvince
ZIPorPostalCode
HomePhone
BusinessPhone
CellPhone

Table 4 – Ship_To
CustomerID
CostumeID
ShipStreetAddress
ShipCity
ShipStateorProvince
ShipZIPorPostalCode
ShipTelephone
*ShipCarrier
ShippingCharge

*Students may recognize that good database
design would have a separate table to store the
carrier names and may include a ShipCarrierID
here instead.*

AS1-C2-PTCostumes(Challenge2).docx

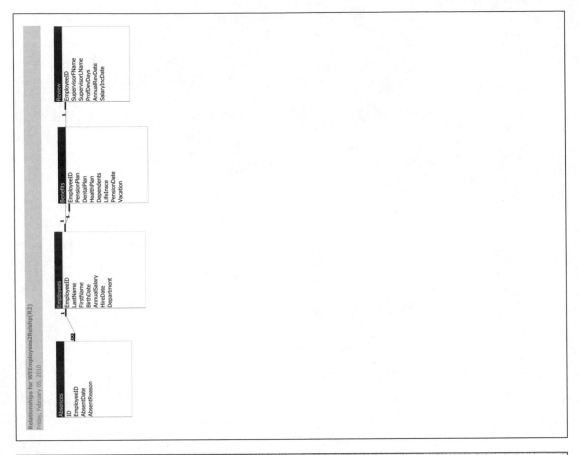

Relationships for WEEmployees2Relshp(R.2)
Friday, February 05, 2010

Review
EmployeeID
SupervisorFName
SupervisorLName
ProfDevDays
AnnualRevDate
SalaryIncDate

Benefits
EmployeeID
PensionPlan
DentalPlan
HealthPlan
Dependents
LifeInsce
PensionDate
Vacation

Employees
EmployeeID
LastName
FirstName
BirthDate
AnnualSalary
HireDate
Department

Absences
ID
EmployeeID
AbsentDate
AbsentReason

WEEmployees2Relshp(Review2).accdb

	Review				7/12/2012

EmployeeID	Supervisor First Name	Supervisor Last Name	Professional Development Days	Annual Review Date	Salary Increase Date
1013	Sam	Vestering	5	10-Feb-11	01-Sep-11
1030	Roman	Deptulski	10	22-Jan-12	22-Jul-12
1040	Celesta	Ruiz	8	10-Mar-12	01-Sep-12
1043	Roman	Deptulski	6	15-Aug-11	01-Feb-12

Page 1

WEEmployees2Relshp(Review1).accdb

Marquee Access 2010 Section 2 Model Answers

CostumeNo	CostumeTitle	DailyRentalFee	DateOut	DateIn
A-101	Val Wingfield	$124.50	Thursday, July 07, 2011	Sunday, July 31, 2011
A-102	Eunice Billings	$124.50	Thursday, July 07, 2011	Friday, July 15, 2011
A-110	Tony Salvatore	$124.50	Friday, July 15, 2011	Friday, August 12, 2011
A-122	Celia Gopf	$124.50	Monday, August 01, 2011	Tuesday, August 30, 2011
A-130	Jade Norwich	$124.50	Friday, August 12, 2011	Wednesday, August 31, 2011
A-144	Kelly Williams	$99.50	Monday, May 02, 2011	Saturday, June 11, 2011
A-152	Hannah Sorenti	$115.50	Wednesday, June 01, 2011	Tuesday, July 12, 2011
A-160	William Mercer	$122.00	Thursday, July 07, 2011	Sunday, July 10, 2011
A-162	Jorge Nevada	$131.50	Monday, August 01, 2011	Tuesday, August 30, 2011
A-166	Catherine Bellfield	$141.00	Monday, August 01, 2011	Tuesday, August 30, 2011
A-170	Vincent Dudkoff	$124.50	Friday, August 12, 2011	Monday, August 22, 2011
A-176	Pietro Gorski	$115.50	Monday, May 02, 2011	Friday, June 10, 2011
A-180	Robert Foullette	$102.50	Friday, July 15, 2011	Sunday, July 31, 2011
A-188	Jade Sorbet	$115.50	Monday, August 01, 2011	Monday, August 22, 2011
A-190	Xavier Vanderkof	$141.00	Friday, August 12, 2011	Wednesday, August 31, 2011
A-198	Nanci Lasertol	$122.00	Friday, July 22, 2011	Monday, August 15, 2011
D-101	Simba	$224.75	Friday, July 01, 2011	Sunday, July 31, 2011
D-102	Timon	$85.50	Friday, July 01, 2011	Sunday, July 31, 2011
D-103	Pumbaa	$112.75	Friday, July 01, 2011	Sunday, July 31, 2011
D-104	Rafiki	$144.50	Friday, July 01, 2011	Sunday, July 31, 2011
D-105	Nala	$188.75	Friday, July 01, 2011	Sunday, July 31, 2011
D-106	Zazu	$85.50	Friday, July 01, 2011	Sunday, July 31, 2011
D-107	Scar	$198.75	Friday, July 01, 2011	Sunday, July 31, 2011
D-108	Mufasa	$215.50	Friday, July 01, 2011	Sunday, July 31, 2011
D-201	Belle	$175.00	Saturday, October 01, 2011	Tuesday, November 15, 2011
D-202	Beast	$237.00	Saturday, October 01, 2011	Tuesday, November 15, 2011
D-203	Gaston	$190.00	Saturday, October 01, 2011	Tuesday, November 15, 2011
D-204	Maurice	$155.00	Saturday, October 01, 2011	Tuesday, November 15, 2011
D-205	Lumiere	$188.00	Saturday, October 01, 2011	Tuesday, November 15, 2011
D-206	Cogsworth	$192.00	Saturday, October 01, 2011	Tuesday, November 15, 2011
D-207	Mrs. Potts	$210.00	Saturday, October 01, 2011	Tuesday, November 15, 2011
D-208	Chip	$189.00	Saturday, October 01, 2011	Tuesday, November 15, 2011

PTCostumeInv2(Assessment2).accdb (1 of 2)

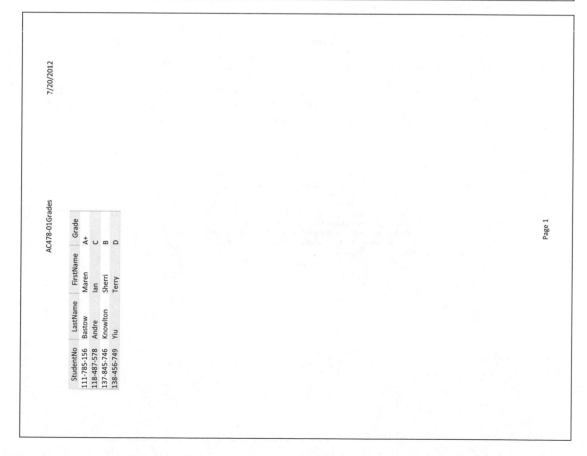

StudentNo	LastName	FirstName	Grade
111-785-156	Bastow	Maren	A+
118-487-578	Andre	Ian	C
137-845-746	Knowlton	Sherri	B
138-456-749	Yiu	Terry	D

NPCGrades2(Assessment1).accdb

EventID	Title	Start Time	End Time	Location	Description
1	Sailing Regatta	6/10/2011	6/12/2011	Buffalo Yacht Club	Daily races at yacht club
2	Sunfest Festival	7/29/2011	7/31/2011	Broderick Park	Celebration of world cultures with music, crafts, and cuisine

WBEvents2(Assessment3).accdb

CostumeNo	CostumeTitle	DailyRentalFee	DateOut	DateIn
G-101	Sheriff (gray)	$120.00		
G-102	Sheriff (black)	$120.00		
G-103	Cowboy (blue)	$112.00		
G-104	Cowboy (green)	$112.00		
G-105	Bartender	$89.00		
G-106	Policeman	$120.00		
G-107	RCMP Officer	$215.00		
G-108	Fireman	$180.00		
G-109	Paramedic	$155.00		
G-110	Doctor	$85.00		
S-101	Macbeth	$175.50	Thursday, May 12, 2011	Thursday, June 30, 2011
S-102	Lady Macbeth	$195.00	Thursday, May 12, 2011	Thursday, June 30, 2011
S-106	Hamlet	$125.00	Friday, July 01, 2011	Sunday, July 31, 2011
S-110	Othello	$125.00	Friday, July 22, 2011	Wednesday, August 31, 2011
S-118	King Lear	$145.50	Monday, August 01, 2011	Saturday, September 10, 2011
S-122	Richard III	$135.00	Monday, August 01, 2011	Saturday, September 10, 2011
S-130	Romeo	$140.00	#########################	Saturday, October 15, 2011
S-131	Juliet	$140.00	#########################	Saturday, October 15, 2011

PTCostumeInv2(Assessment2).accdb (2 of 2)

Purchases

7/20/2012

PurchaseOrderNo	VendorNo	PurchaseDate	Amount	ShipMethod
6540	115	19-Feb-11	$556.88	Fedex
6541	125	10-Mar-11	$556.99	UPS
6542	100	28-Feb-11	$1,255.87	Fedex
6543	100	13-Mar-11	$965.33	Express Freight
6544	120	25-Mar-11	$1,000.15	Global Transport
6545	130	28-Mar-11	$865.24	Fedex
6546	110	31-Mar-11	$554.78	Express Freight
6547	115	09-Apr-11	$869.42	Global Transport
6548	110	22-Apr-11	$10,265.88	Fedex
6549	115	31-May-11	$2,354.55	UPS
6550	100	10-Jun-11	$349.78	Fedex
6551	125	15-Jun-11	$367.42	Express Freight

Page 1

WEPurchases2(Challenge1).accdb

Expenses

7/12/2012

ID	Emp ID	First Name	Last Name	Position	Manager	Expense Date	Description	Total Claimed
1	LA-104	Terry	Blessing	President	Not required	26-May-11	Travel expenses to Toronto office for meeting	$2,344.10

Page 1

FCTExpenses2(Assessment3).accdb

Performance Threads Custom Costume Database
Table and Field Properties Structure

NOTES to Instructors: Answers will vary. Key concepts to watch for:

- Look for appropriate data types
- Students should employ as many of the properties learned in section 2 as possible in reasonable assumptions.
- Look for:
  - o Field sizes used to limit entries on fields such as IDs or State/Province
  - o Input masks on date, telephone, and postal code fields
  - o Validation rules that match assumptions
  - o Captions to label the fields more descriptively or insert spaces between words in the datasheet
- Assumptions should be documented and clearly state a business rule.
  - o Examples: Minimum contract for a custom costume is $500
  - Minimum hours for research is 3 hours
- Lookup lists to lookup data in another table was not taught in this section; however, students may have prior knowledge or find information in Help. Appropriate places for a lookup to another table is the CustomerID in the Costume_Orders and Ship_To tables and the SeamtressID in the Costume_Orders table.

**Note: Caption property entries not included in model answer below. Results by student will vary depending on field name abbreviations adopted by the student.

**NOTE: Field names in the tables below are longer in some cases since abbreviations by individuals will vary. Watch that students use abbreviations that are generally understood and that he/she included captions for the datasheet view and documented captions below.

Table 1 – Customers

CustID	Text	Field size = 3	Primary key field
FirstName	Text	Field size = 20	
LastName	Text	Field size = 30	
Street	Text	Field size = 50	
City	Text	Field size = 30	
StateOrProv	Text	Field size = 2	
ZIPCode	Text	Field size = 10; Input mask	
HPhone	Text	Field size = 14; Input mask	
BusPhone	Text	Field size = 14; Input mask	
Cell	Text	Field size = 14; Input mask	

Table 2 – Costume_Orders

CostumeID	Text	Text – field size = 3	Primary key field
Description	Memo		
CustID	Text	Field size = 3 (NOTE: This should be the same as the Customers table)	
ContPrice	Currency	Validation Rule >=500	
		Validation Text "Enter a value greater than or equal to $500.00"	
		Assumption: minimum contract price is	

AS2-C2PTCostumes(C2).docx   Page 1 of 4

AS2-C2-PTCostumes(Challenge2).docx (1 of 4)

Worldwide Enterprises
WEPurchases2.accdb Database

NOTES to Instructors: Answers will vary in memo. Key concepts to watch for:

Purchases table:

- *PurchaseOrderNo* - data type changed to Text; Field size changed to 4
- *VendorNo* - field size changed to 3
- *PurchaseDate* - format and input mask changed to Medium Date
- *Amount* – validation rule >=300.00; validation text has an appropriate message
- *ShipMethod* – lookup list containing the values: UPS, Fedex, Express Freight, Global Transport; lookup properties – limit to list set to Yes; allow value list edits = No

Vendors table:

- *VendorNo* – field size changed to 3
- *StateOrProv* – field size changed to 2
- *Telephone* – field size changed to 14; input mask for telephone with area code
- *Fax* – field size changed to 14; input mask for telephone with area code

Relationship created is a one-to-many relationship with Vendors as the primary table and Purchases as the related table. Referential integrity should be turned on.

Memo(Challenge1).docx

	Validation Text "Enter a value greater than or equal to $25.00"
	Assumption: A minimum shipping charge of $25 applies to all orders

AS2-C2-PTCostumes(Challenge2).docx (3 of 4)

DueDate	Date/Time	$500.00 for custom costume
		Format = Medium Date
		Input Mask = Medium Date
SignedContract	Yes/No	Default Value = Yes
Deposit	Currency	Validation Rule >=100
		Validation Text "Enter a value greater than or equal to $100.00"
		Assumption: Customers must pay a minimum deposit of $100.00 before work on costume is started
SeamstressID	Text	Field size = 3 (NOTE: This should be the same as the Contract_Seamstresses table)
EstHrs_Research	Number	
EstHrs_Design	Number	
EstHrs_Prod	Number	
ActualHrs_Research	Number	
ActualHrs_Design	Number	
ActualHrs_Prod	Number	

Table 3 – Contract_Seamstresses

SeamstressID	Text	Field size = 3 Primary key field
FirstName	Text	Field size = 20
LastName	Text	Field size = 30
Street	Text	Field size = 50
City	Text	Field size = 30
StateOrProv	Text	Field size = 2
ZIPCode	Text	Field size = 10; Input mask
HPhone	Text	Field size = 14; Input mask
BusPhone	Text	Field size = 14; Input mask
Cell	Text	Field size = 14; Input mask

Table 4 – Ship_To

CustID	Text	Field size = 3 NOTE: This should be the same as Customers table
CostumeID	Text	Text – field size = 3 Primary key field NOTE: This should be the same as the Costume_Orders table
Description	Memo	
ShipStreet	Text	Field size = 50
ShipCity	Text	Field size = 30
ShipStateorProv	Text	Field size = 2
ShipZIPCode	Text	Field size = 10; Input mask
ShipPhone	Text	Field size = 14; Input mask
ShipCarrier	Lookup wizard	Lookup list created with names of carriers; Limited List: No edits allowed Assumption: Company only ships using Express Freight, Purolator Courier, and USPS
ShipCharge	Currency	Validation Rule >=25

AS2-C2-PTCostumes(Challenge2).docx (2 of 4)

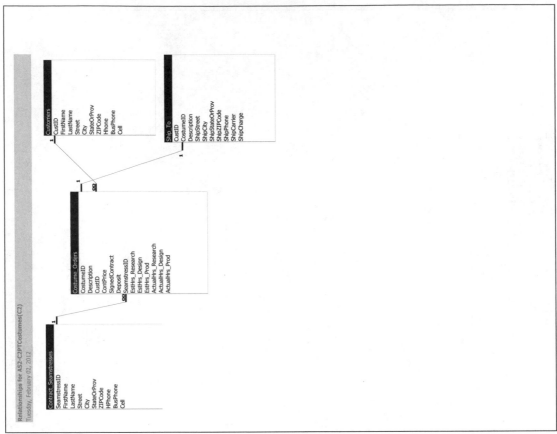

AS2-C2-PTCostumes(Challenge2,Step9).accdb

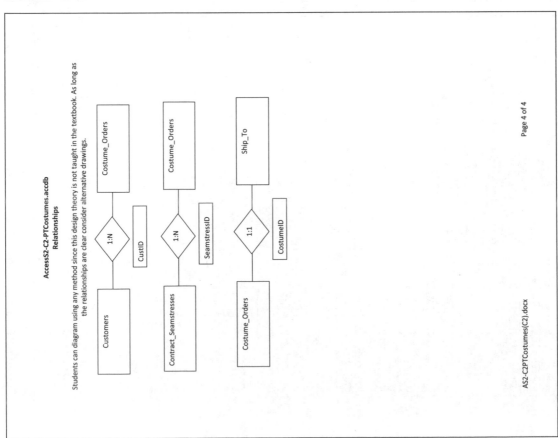

AS2-C2-PTCostumes(Challenge2).docx (4 of 4)

EmployeeID	FirstName	LastName	HireDate	AnnualSalary	Life Insurance	MonthlySalary
1085	Yousef	Armine	3/14/2010	$42,177.00	$125,000.00	$3,514.75
1083	Drew	Arnold	6/22/2010	$43,659.00	$75,000.00	$3,638.25
1080	Leo	Couture	1/27/2010	$43,659.00	$150,000.00	$3,638.25
1073	Marsha	Judd	11/30/2009	$44,771.00	$200,000.00	$3,730.92
1095	Patrick	Kilarney	12/12/2010	$42,177.00	$200,000.00	$3,514.75
1040	Guy	Lafreniere	3/10/2005	$45,395.00	$200,000.00	$3,782.92
1065	Norm	Liszniewski	2/6/2008	$43,695.00	$150,000.00	$3,641.25
1060	Donald	McKnight	6/22/2007	$42,126.00	$175,000.00	$3,510.50
1063	Charlotte	McPhee	2/6/2008	$43,695.00	$100,000.00	$3,641.25
1043	Enzo	Morano	8/15/2005	$48,750.00	$200,000.00	$4,062.50
1053	Shauna	O'Connor	4/15/2007	$43,695.00	$85,000.00	$3,641.25
1090	Maria	Quinte	11/29/2010	$42,177.00	$150,000.00	$3,514.75
1093	Luis	Vaquez	12/5/2010	$42,177.00	$185,000.00	$3,514.75
1045	Terry	Yiu	1/31/2006	$42,238.00	$50,000.00	$3,519.83
1050	Carl	Zakowski	2/9/2006	$44,387.00	$125,000.00	$3,698.92

EmployeeID	FirstName	LastName	HireDate	AnnualSalary	Life Insurance	MonthlySalary
1085	Yousef	Armine	3/14/2010	$42,177.00	$125,000.00	$3,514.75
1083	Drew	Arnold	6/22/2010	$43,659.00	$75,000.00	$3,638.25
1015	Lyle	Besterd	5/17/2003	$45,651.00	$185,000.00	$3,804.25
1025	Jorge	Biliski	12/1/2003	$44,892.00	$200,000.00	$3,741.00
1023	Aleksy	Bulinkski	10/10/2003	$51,450.00	$100,000.00	$4,287.50
1013	Gregg	Chippewa	2/10/2003	$48,650.00	$200,000.00	$4,054.17
1080	Leo	Couture	1/27/2010	$43,659.00	$150,000.00	$3,638.25
1005	Roman	Deptulski	8/15/2002	$72,750.00	$150,000.00	$6,062.50
1020	Angela	Doxtator	8/3/2003	$45,558.00	$200,000.00	$3,796.50
1030	Thom	Hicks	1/22/2004	$42,824.00	$75,000.00	$3,568.67
1073	Marsha	Judd	11/30/2009	$44,771.00	$200,000.00	$3,730.92
1095	Patrick	Kilarney	12/12/2010	$42,177.00	$200,000.00	$3,514.75
1040	Guy	Lafreniere	3/10/2005	$45,395.00	$200,000.00	$3,782.92
1065	Norm	Liszniewski	2/6/2008	$43,695.00	$150,000.00	$3,641.25
1060	Donald	McKnight	6/22/2007	$42,126.00	$175,000.00	$3,510.50
1063	Charlotte	McPhee	2/6/2008	$43,695.00	$100,000.00	$3,641.25
1043	Enzo	Morano	8/15/2005	$48,750.00	$200,000.00	$4,062.50
1053	Shauna	O'Connor	4/15/2007	$43,695.00	$85,000.00	$3,641.25
1090	Maria	Quinte	11/29/2010	$42,177.00	$150,000.00	$3,514.75
1003	Celesta	Ruiz	8/5/2002	$41,875.00	$200,000.00	$3,489.58
1033	Dina	Titov	1/10/2004	$45,655.00	$125,000.00	$3,804.58
1093	Luis	Vaquez	12/5/2010	$42,177.00	$185,000.00	$3,514.75
1000	Sam	Vestering	7/22/2002	$69,725.00	$100,000.00	$5,810.42
1045	Terry	Yiu	1/31/2006	$42,238.00	$50,000.00	$3,519.83
1050	Carl	Zakowski	2/9/2006	$44,387.00	$125,000.00	$3,698.92

Annual Review and Salary Increase Dates

Worldwide Enterprises

EmployeeID	1013
Supervisor First Name	Sam
Supervisor Last Name	Vestering
Professional Development Days	5
Annual Review Date	10-Feb-11
Salary Increase Date	01-Sep-11

EmployeeID	1015
Supervisor First Name	Sam
Supervisor Last Name	Vestering
Professional Development Days	4
Annual Review Date	17-May-11
Salary Increase Date	01-Aug-11

EmployeeID	1020
Supervisor First Name	Celesta
Supervisor Last Name	Ruiz
Professional Development Days	8
Annual Review Date	03-Aug-12
Salary Increase Date	01-Oct-12

EmployeeID	1023
Supervisor First Name	Sam

WEEmployees3(Review2).accdb (1 of 6)

Supervisor Last Name	Vestering
Professional Development Days	6
Annual Review Date	15-Oct-12
Salary Increase Date	15-Nov-12

EmployeeID	1025
Supervisor First Name	Roman
Supervisor Last Name	Deptulski
Professional Development Days	5
Annual Review Date	01-Dec-12
Salary Increase Date	01-Jan-13

EmployeeID	1030
Supervisor First Name	Roman
Supervisor Last Name	Deptulski
Professional Development Days	10
Annual Review Date	22-Jan-12
Salary Increase Date	22-Jul-12

EmployeeID	1033
Supervisor First Name	Roman
Supervisor Last Name	Deptulski
Professional Development Days	5
Annual Review Date	01-Jan-12
Salary Increase Date	05-Feb-12

EmployeeID	1040

WEEmployees3(Review2).accdb (2 of 6)

WEEmployees3(Review2).accdb (3 of 6)

Supervisor First Name	Celesta
Supervisor Last Name	Ruiz
Professional Development Days	8
Annual Review Date	10-Mar-12
Salary Increase Date	01-Sep-12

EmployeeID	1043
Supervisor First Name	Roman
Supervisor Last Name	Deptulski
Professional Development Days	6
Annual Review Date	15-Aug-11
Salary Increase Date	01-Feb-12

EmployeeID	1045
Supervisor First Name	Celesta
Supervisor Last Name	Ruiz
Professional Development Days	6
Annual Review Date	01-Jan-12
Salary Increase Date	05-Feb-12

EmployeeID	1050
Supervisor First Name	Sam
Supervisor Last Name	Vestering
Professional Development Days	5
Annual Review Date	09-Feb-11
Salary Increase Date	01-Apr-11

WEEmployees3(Review2).accdb (4 of 6)

EmployeeID	1053
Supervisor First Name	Sam
Supervisor Last Name	Vestering
Professional Development Days	8
Annual Review Date	15-Apr-11
Salary Increase Date	15-Jun-11

EmployeeID	1060
Supervisor First Name	Roman
Supervisor Last Name	Deptulski
Professional Development Days	6
Annual Review Date	25-Jun-11
Salary Increase Date	15-Aug-11

EmployeeID	1063
Supervisor First Name	Celesta
Supervisor Last Name	Ruiz
Professional Development Days	5
Annual Review Date	10-Feb-11
Salary Increase Date	10-Apr-11

EmployeeID	1065
Supervisor First Name	Sam
Supervisor Last Name	Vestering
Professional Development Days	8

Annual Review Date: 10-Feb-11
Salary Increase Date: 10-Apr-11

EmployeeID: 1073
Supervisor First Name: Roman
Supervisor Last Name: Deptulski
Professional Development Days: 5
Annual Review Date: 30-Nov-11
Salary Increase Date: 01-Jan-12

EmployeeID: 1080
Supervisor First Name: Roman
Supervisor Last Name: Deptulski
Professional Development Days: 5
Annual Review Date: 27-Jan-11
Salary Increase Date: 01-Mar-11

EmployeeID: 1083
Supervisor First Name: Celesta
Supervisor Last Name: Ruiz
Professional Development Days: 8
Annual Review Date: 22-Jun-11
Salary Increase Date: 01-Aug-11

EmployeeID: 1085
Supervisor First Name: Celesta

WEEmployees3(Review2).accdb (5 of 6)

Supervisor Last Name: Ruiz
Professional Development Days: 5
Annual Review Date: 14-Mar-11
Salary Increase Date: 01-May-11

EmployeeID: 1090
Supervisor First Name: Sam
Supervisor Last Name: Vestering
Professional Development Days: 6
Annual Review Date: 30-Nov-11
Salary Increase Date: 10-Jan-12

EmployeeID: 1093
Supervisor First Name: Sam
Supervisor Last Name: Vestering
Professional Development Days: 5
Annual Review Date: 10-Dec-11
Salary Increase Date: 01-Feb-12

EmployeeID: 1095
Supervisor First Name: Celesta
Supervisor Last Name: Ruiz
Professional Development Days: 5
Annual Review Date: 15-Dec-11
Salary Increase Date: 01-Feb-12

WEEmployees3(Review2).accdb (6 of 6)

Employee ID	First Name	Last Name	Hire Date	Life Insurance	Annual Salary	Monthly Salary
1000	Sam	Vestering	7/22/2002	$100,000.00	$69,725.00	$5,810.42
1045	Terry	Yiu	1/31/2006	$50,000.00	$42,238.00	$3,519.83
1050	Carl	Zakowski	2/9/2006	$125,000.00	$44,387.00	$3,698.92

Page 2 of 2

Worldwide Enterprises — Salary and Life Insurance Report

Friday, July 20, 2012
11:56:53 AM

Employee ID	First Name	Last Name	Hire Date	Life Insurance	Annual Salary	Monthly Salary
1085	Yousef	Armine	3/14/2010	$125,000.00	$42,177.00	$3,514.75
1083	Drew	Arnold	6/22/2010	$75,000.00	$43,659.00	$3,638.25
1015	Lyle	Besterd	5/17/2003	$185,000.00	$45,651.00	$3,804.25
1025	Jorge	Biliski	12/1/2003	$200,000.00	$44,892.00	$3,741.00
1023	Aleksy	Bulinkski	10/10/2003	$100,000.00	$51,450.00	$4,287.50
1013	Gregg	Chippewa	2/10/2003	$200,000.00	$48,650.00	$4,054.17
1080	Leo	Couture	1/27/2010	$150,000.00	$43,659.00	$3,638.25
1005	Roman	Deptulski	8/15/2002	$150,000.00	$72,750.00	$6,062.50
1020	Angela	Doxtator	8/3/2003	$200,000.00	$45,558.00	$3,796.50
1030	Thom	Hicks	1/22/2004	$75,000.00	$42,824.00	$3,568.67
1073	Marsha	Judd	11/30/2009	$200,000.00	$44,771.00	$3,730.92
1095	Patrick	Kilarney	12/12/2010	$200,000.00	$42,177.00	$3,514.75
1040	Guy	Lafreniere	3/10/2005	$200,000.00	$45,395.00	$3,782.92
1065	Norm	Liszniewski	2/6/2008	$150,000.00	$43,695.00	$3,641.25
1060	Donald	McKnight	6/22/2007	$175,000.00	$42,126.00	$3,510.50
1063	Charlotte	McPhee	2/6/2008	$100,000.00	$43,695.00	$3,641.25
1043	Enzo	Morano	8/15/2005	$200,000.00	$48,750.00	$4,062.50
1053	Shauna	O'Connor	4/15/2007	$85,000.00	$43,695.00	$3,641.25
1090	Maria	Quinte	11/29/2010	$150,000.00	$42,177.00	$3,514.75
1003	Celesta	Ruiz	8/5/2002	$200,000.00	$41,875.00	$3,489.58
1033	Dina	Titov	1/10/2004	$125,000.00	$45,655.00	$3,804.58
1093	Luis	Vaquez	12/5/2010	$185,000.00	$42,177.00	$3,514.75

Page 1 of 2

CostumeNo	CostumeTitle	DailyRentalFee	DateOut	DateIn
A-101	Val Wingfield	$124.50	7/7/2011	7/31/2011
A-102	Eunice Billings	$124.50	7/7/2011	7/15/2011
A-110	Tony Salvatore	$124.50	7/15/2011	8/12/2011
A-122	Celia Gopf	$124.50	8/1/2011	8/30/2011
A-130	Jade Norwich	$124.50	8/12/2011	8/31/2011
A-144	Kelly Williams	$99.50	5/2/2011	6/11/2011
A-152	Hannah Sorenti	$115.50	6/1/2011	7/12/2011
A-160	William Mercer	$122.00	7/7/2011	7/10/2011
A-162	Jorge Nevada	$131.50	8/1/2011	8/30/2011
A-166	Catherine Bellfield	$141.00	8/1/2011	8/30/2011
A-170	Vincent Dudkoff	$124.50	8/12/2011	8/22/2011
A-176	Pietro Gorski	$115.50	5/2/2011	6/10/2011
A-180	Robert Foullette	$102.50	7/15/2011	7/31/2011
A-188	Jade Sorbet	$115.50	8/1/2011	8/22/2011
A-190	Xavier Vanderkof	$141.00	8/12/2011	8/31/2011
A-198	Nanci Lasertol	$122.00	7/22/2011	8/15/2011
D-101	Simba	$224.75	7/1/2011	7/31/2011
D-102	Timon	$85.50	7/1/2011	7/31/2011
D-103	Pumbaa	$112.75	7/1/2011	7/31/2011
D-104	Rafiki	$144.50	7/1/2011	7/31/2011
D-105	Nala	$188.75	7/1/2011	7/31/2011
D-106	Zazu	$85.50	7/1/2011	7/31/2011
D-107	Scar	$198.75	7/1/2011	7/31/2011
D-108	Mufasa	$215.50	7/1/2011	7/31/2011
D-201	Belle	$175.00	10/1/2011	11/15/2011
D-202	Beast	$237.00	10/1/2011	11/15/2011
D-203	Gaston	$190.00	10/1/2011	11/15/2011
D-204	Maurice	$155.00	10/1/2011	11/15/2011
D-205	Lumiere	$188.00	10/1/2011	11/15/2011
D-206	Cogsworth	$192.00	10/1/2011	11/15/2011
D-207	Mrs. Potts	$210.00	10/1/2011	11/15/2011
D-208	Chip	$189.00	10/1/2011	11/15/2011
G-101	Sheriff (gray)	$120.00		
G-102	Sheriff (black)	$120.00		
G-103	Cowboy (blue)	$112.00		
G-104	Cowboy (green)	$112.00		
G-105	Bartender	$89.00		
G-106	Policeman	$120.00		
G-107	RCMP Officer	$215.00		
G-108	Fireman	$180.00		
G-109	Paramedic	$155.00		
G-110	Doctor	$85.00		
S-101	Macbeth	$175.50	5/12/2011	6/30/2011

Page 1

PTCostumeInv3(Assessment2).accdb (1 of 2)

StudentNo	FirstName	LastName	AC215-03Grades.Grade	LE253-03Grades.Grade	SM100-01Grades.Grade
217-458-687	Ahmad	Husson	A+	A+	A+

Page 1

NPCGrades3(Assessment1).accdb

Summer2011Rentals

7/20/2012

CostumeNo	DateOut	DateIn	CostumeTitle	DailyRentalFee
S-106	7/1/2011	7/31/2011	Hamlet	$125.00
D-108	7/1/2011	7/31/2011	Mufasa	$215.50
D-105	7/1/2011	7/31/2011	Nala	$188.75
D-103	7/1/2011	7/31/2011	Pumbaa	$112.75
D-104	7/1/2011	7/31/2011	Rafiki	$144.50
D-107	7/1/2011	7/31/2011	Scar	$198.75
D-101	7/1/2011	7/31/2011	Simba	$224.75
D-102	7/1/2011	7/31/2011	Timon	$85.50
D-106	7/1/2011	7/31/2011	Zazu	$85.50
A-160	7/7/2011	7/10/2011	William Mercer	$122.00
A-102	7/7/2011	7/15/2011	Eunice Billings	$124.50
A-101	7/7/2011	7/31/2011	Val Wingfield	$124.50
A-180	7/15/2011	7/31/2011	Robert Foullette	$102.50
A-110	7/15/2011	8/12/2011	Tony Salvatore	$124.50
A-198	7/22/2011	8/15/2011	Nanci Lasertol	$122.00
S-110	7/22/2011	8/31/2011	Othello	$125.00
A-188	8/1/2011	8/22/2011	Jade Sorbet	$115.50
A-166	8/1/2011	8/30/2011	Catherine Bellfield	$141.00
A-122	8/1/2011	8/30/2011	Celia Gopf	$124.50
A-162	8/1/2011	8/30/2011	Jorge Nevada	$131.50
S-118	8/1/2011	9/10/2011	King Lear	$145.50
S-122	8/1/2011	9/10/2011	Richard III	$135.00
A-170	8/12/2011	8/22/2011	Vincent Dudkoff	$124.50
A-130	8/12/2011	8/31/2011	Jade Norwich	$124.50
A-190	8/12/2011	8/31/2011	Xavier Vanderkof	$141.00

PTCostumeInv3(Assessment3).accdb

CostumeInventory

7/20/2012

CostumeNo	CostumeTitle	DailyRentalFee	DateOut	DateIn
S-102	Lady Macbeth	$195.00	5/12/2011	6/30/2011
S-106	Hamlet	$125.00	7/1/2011	7/31/2011
S-110	Othello	$125.50	7/22/2011	8/31/2011
S-118	King Lear	$145.50	8/1/2011	9/10/2011
S-122	Richard III	$135.00	8/1/2011	9/10/2011
S-130	Romeo	$140.00	9/1/2011	10/15/2011
S-131	Juliet	$140.00	9/1/2011	10/15/2011

Page 2

PTCostumeInv3(Assessment2).accdb (2 of 2)

Marquee Access 2010 Section 3 Model Answers

145

Vendors and Purchases

Worldwide Enterprises

Vendor No	100
Vendor Name	First Choice Travel (Los Angeles)
Street Address	3588 Ventura Boulevard
City	Los Angeles
State or Province	CA
ZIP or PostalCode	90102
Telephone	213-555-0962
Fax	213-555-0964
URL	www.emcp.com/fc-travel

Purchase_Order_No	Purchase_Date	Amount
6542	28-Feb-11	$1,255.87
6543	13-Mar-11	$965.33
6550	10-Jun-11	$349.78

Vendor No	110
Vendor Name	First Choice Travel (Toronto)
Street Address	4277 Yonge Street
City	Toronto
State or Province	ON
ZIP or PostalCode	M4P 2E6
Telephone	416-555-4511
Fax	416-555-4512
URL	www.emcp.com/fc-travel/toronto

WEVendors3(Assessment4).accdb (1 of 4)

Purchase_Order_No	Purchase_Date	Amount
6546	31-Mar-11	$554.78
6548	22-Apr-11	$10,265.88

Vendor No	115
Vendor Name	The Waterfront Bistro
Street Address	3104 Rivermist Drive
City	Buffalo
State or Province	NY
ZIP or PostalCode	14280
Telephone	716-555-3166
Fax	716-555-3160
URL	www.emcp.com/wfbistro

Purchase_Order_No	Purchase_Date	Amount
6540	19-Feb-11	$556.88
6547	11-Apr-11	$869.42
6549	31-May-11	$2,354.55

Vendor No	120
Vendor Name	Marquee Productions
Street Address	955 South Alameda Street
City	Los Angeles
State or Province	CA
ZIP or PostalCode	90037

WEVendors3(Assessment4).accdb (2 of 4)

City	Niagara-on-the-Lake
State or Province	ON
ZIP or PostalCode	L0S 1J0
Telephone	905-555-2183
Fax	905-555-2183
URL	www.emcp.com/npcollege

Purchase_Order_No	Purchase_Date	Amount
6545	28-Mar-11	$865.24

Telephone	612-555-2005
Fax	612-555-2009
URL	www.emcp.com/marquee

Purchase_Order_No	Purchase_Date	Amount
6544	25-Mar-11	$1,000.15

Vendor No	125
Vendor Name	Performance Threads
Street Address	4011 Bridgewater Street
City	Niagara Falls
State or Province	ON
ZIP or PostalCode	L2E 2T6
Telephone	905-555-2971
Fax	905-555-2970
URL	www.emcp.com/perthreads

Purchase_Order_No	Purchase_Date	Amount
6541	10-Mar-11	$556.99
6551	15-Jun-11	$367.42

Vendor No	130
Vendor Name	Niagara Peninsula College
Street Address	2199 Victoria Street

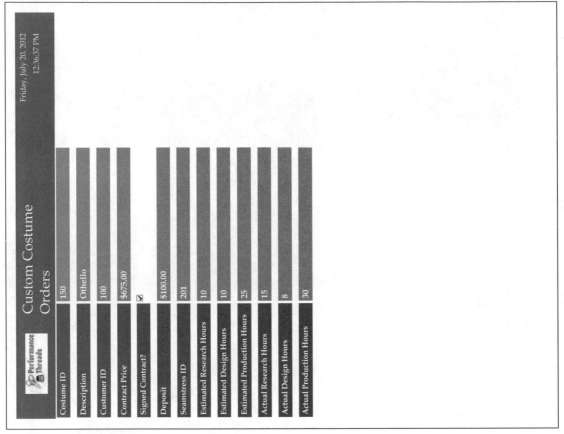

Custom Costume Orders — Performance Threads

Friday, July 20, 2012 12:36:37 PM

Costume ID	150
Description	Othello
Customer ID	100
Contract Price	$675.00
Signed Contract?	☑
Deposit	$100.00
Seamstress ID	201
Estimated Research Hours	10
Estimated Design Hours	10
Estimated Production Hours	25
Actual Research Hours	15
Actual Design Hours	8
Actual Production Hours	30

AS3-C2-PTCostumes(Challenge2).accdb (1 of 2)

Catering Event Revenue

The Waterfront B·I·S·T·R·O

Thursday, August 12, 2010
3:02:55 PM

Last Name	Event	Date of Event	Guests	Per Person Charge	Event Total
Hillmore	Business Meeting	1/15/2011	35	$21.95	$768.25
Fontaine	Engagement Party	1/20/2011	177	$28.95	$5,124.15
Corriveau	Birthday Party	1/23/2011	85	$25.95	$2,205.75
Kressman	Wedding	2/28/2011	266	$28.95	$7,700.70
Fagan	25th Wedding Anniversary	3/10/2011	88	$28.95	$2,547.60
Pockovic	Birthday Party	3/18/2011	62	$35.95	$2,228.90
Gill	Business Meeting	3/29/2011	71	$21.95	$1,558.45
Bresque	50th Wedding Anniversary	4/12/2011	62	$32.95	$2,042.90
Santore	Wedding	4/28/2011	157	$25.95	$4,074.15
Hamid	Engagement Party	5/8/2011	85	$28.95	$2,460.75
Torrance	Business Meeting	5/15/2011	26	$23.95	$622.70
Russell	Birthday Party	5/30/2011	36	$26.95	$970.20
Szucs	Birthday Party	6/10/2011	42	$28.95	$1,215.90
Griffin	25th Wedding Anniversary	6/17/2011	54	$31.95	$1,725.30
Doucet	Wedding	6/20/2011	168	$28.95	$4,863.60
Golinsky	Business Meeting	6/26/2011	57	$24.95	$1,422.15
Jin Ping	Baby Shower	7/10/2011	62	$21.95	$1,360.90
McMaster	Engagement Party	7/11/2011	75	$27.95	$2,096.25
Pavelich	Wedding	7/25/2011	110	$31.95	$3,514.50
Juanitez	Business Meeting	7/31/2011	49	$23.95	$1,173.55
				$552.00	$49,676.65

WBSpecialEvents3(Challenge1).accdb

Costume ID	155
Description	Hamlet
Customer ID	110
Contract Price	$1,100.00
Signed Contract?	☑
Deposit	$500.00
Seamstress ID	205
Estimated Research Hours	15
Estimated Design Hours	10
Estimated Production Hours	40
Actual Research Hours	12
Actual Design Hours	9
Actual Production Hours	41

AS3-C2-PTCostumes(Challenge2).accdb (2 of 2)

Marquee Access 2010 Section 3 Model Answers

NoAbsences

7/22/2010

EmployeeID	FirstName	LastName
1003	Celesta	Ruiz
1005	Roman	Deptulski
1013	Gregg	Chippewa
1015	Lyle	Besterd
1020	Angela	Doxtator
1043	Enzo	Morano
1063	Charlotte	McPhee
1080	Leo	Couture
1085	Yousef	Armine
1093	Luis	Vaquez

Page 1

WEEmployees4(Review1,Step6).accdb

DupAbsences

7/12/2012

EmployeeID	ID	Absent Date	Absent Reason
1023	24	3/18/2011	Personal leave day
1023	21	3/15/2011	Bereavement
1023	20	3/14/2011	Bereavement
1025	5	2/3/2011	Sick Day
1025	4	2/2/2011	Sick Day
1025	3	2/1/2011	Sick Day
1030	6	2/5/2011	Bereavement
1030	7	2/6/2011	Bereavement
1060	23	3/16/2011	Sick Day
1060	22	3/15/2011	Sick Day
1073	11	2/25/2011	Sick Day
1073	9	2/12/2011	Sick Day
1083	14	2/27/2011	Sick Day
1083	1	1/15/2011	Sick Day
1083	27	3/29/2011	Jury Duty
1083	26	3/28/2011	Jury Duty
1090	2	1/15/2011	Jury Duty
1090	10	2/22/2011	Sick Day
1095	18	3/11/2011	Sick Day
1095	13	2/26/2011	Sick Day

Page 1

WEEmployees4(Review1).accdb

Employee Salaries

Employee ID	First Name	Last Name	Hire Date	Department	Annual Salary	Monthly Salary
1000	Sam	Vestering	7/22/2002	North American Distribution	$69,725.00	$5,810.42
1003	Celesta	Ruiz	8/5/2002	North American Distribution	$41,875.00	$3,489.58
1005	Roman	Deptulski	8/15/2002	Overseas Distribution	$72,750.00	$6,062.50
1013	Gregg	Chippewa	2/10/2003	European Distribution	$48,650.00	$4,054.17
1015	Lyle	Besterd	5/17/2003	North American Distribution	$45,651.00	$3,804.25
1020	Angela	Doxtator	8/3/2003	North American Distribution	$45,558.00	$3,796.50
1023	Aleksy	Bulinkski	10/10/2003	European Distribution	$51,450.00	$4,287.50
1025	Jorge	Biliski	12/1/2003	North American Distribution	$44,892.00	$3,741.00
1030	Thom	Hicks	1/22/2004	Overseas Distribution	$42,824.00	$3,568.67
1033	Dina	Titov	1/10/2004	North American Distribution	$45,655.00	$3,804.58
1040	Guy	Lafreniere	3/10/2005	Overseas Distribution	$45,395.00	$3,782.92
1043	Enzo	Morano	8/15/2005	North American Distribution	$48,750.00	$4,062.50
1045	Terry	Yiu	1/31/2006	European Distribution	$42,238.00	$3,519.83
1050	Carl	Zakowski	2/9/2006	European Distribution	$44,387.00	$3,698.92
1053	Shauna	O'Connor	4/15/2007	North American Distribution	$43,695.00	$3,641.25
1060	Donald	McKnight	6/22/2007	European Distribution	$42,126.00	$3,510.50
1063	Charlotte	McPhee	2/6/2008	North American Distribution	$43,695.00	$3,641.25
1065	Norm	Liszniewski	2/6/2008	North American Distribution	$43,695.00	$3,641.25
1073	Marsha	Judd	11/30/2009	North American Distribution	$44,771.00	$3,730.92
1080	Leo	Couture	1/27/2010	European Distribution	$43,659.00	$3,638.25
1083	Drew	Arnold	6/22/2010	North American Distribution	$43,659.00	$3,638.25
1085	Yousef	Armine	3/14/2010	European Distribution	$42,177.00	$3,514.75
1090	Maria	Quinte	11/29/2010	Overseas Distribution	$42,177.00	$3,514.75

WEEmployees4(Review3).accdb (1 of 2)

Employees — Worldwide Enterprises

Employee ID	1095
Last Name	Kilarney
First Name	Patrick
Birth Date	2/27/1985
Annual Salary	$42,177.00
Vacation Pay	$1,687.08
Hire Date	12/12/2010
Department	North American Distribution

Contact the Help Desk at extension 436 if you need assistance using this form.

WEEmployees4(Review2).accdb

Costume Inventory

Costume No:	D-202
Costume Title:	Beast
Date Out:	10/1/2011
Date In:	11/15/2011
Daily Rental Fee:	$237.00
Fee with Tax:	$11.85

Costume No:	D-201
Costume Title:	Belle
Date Out:	10/1/2011
Date In:	11/15/2011
Daily Rental Fee:	$175.00
Fee with Tax:	$8.75

Costume No:	D-203
Costume Title:	Gaston
Date Out:	10/1/2011
Date In:	11/15/2011
Daily Rental Fee:	$190.00
Fee with Tax:	$9.50

Costume No:	D-204
Costume Title:	Maurice
Date Out:	10/1/2011
Date In:	11/15/2011
Daily Rental Fee:	$155.00
Fee with Tax:	$7.75

Costume No:	D-205
Costume Title:	Lumiere

PTCostumeInv4(Assessment1).accdb (1 of 11)

Employee ID	First Name	Last Name	Hire Date	Department	Annual Salary	Monthly Salary
1093	Luis	Vaquez	12/5/2010	North American Distribution	$42,177.00	$3,514.75
1095	Patrick	Kilarney	12/12/2010	North American Distribution	$42,177.00	$3,514.75

WEEmployees4(Review3).accdb (2 of 2)

Costume No:	S-131
Costume Title:	Juliet
Date Out:	9/1/2011
Date In:	10/15/2011
Daily Rental Fee:	$140.00
Fee with Tax:	$7.00

Costume No:	A-190
Costume Title:	Xavier Vanderkof
Date Out:	8/12/2011
Date In:	8/31/2011
Daily Rental Fee:	$141.00
Fee with Tax:	$7.05

Costume No:	A-130
Costume Title:	Jade Norwich
Date Out:	8/12/2011
Date In:	8/31/2011
Daily Rental Fee:	$124.50
Fee with Tax:	$6.23

Costume No:	A-170
Costume Title:	Vincent Dudkcff
Date Out:	8/12/2011
Date In:	8/22/2011
Daily Rental Fee:	$124.50
Fee with Tax:	$6.23

Costume No:	S-122
Costume Title:	Richard III
Date Out:	8/1/2011
Date In:	9/10/2011

Date Out:	10/1/2011
Date In:	11/15/2011
Daily Rental Fee:	$188.00
Fee with Tax:	$9.40

Costume No:	D-206
Costume Title:	Cogsworth
Date Out:	10/1/2011
Date In:	11/15/2011
Daily Rental Fee:	$192.00
Fee with Tax:	$9.60

Costume No:	D-207
Costume Title:	Mrs. Potts
Date Out:	10/1/2011
Date In:	11/15/2011
Daily Rental Fee:	$210.00
Fee with Tax:	$10.50

Costume No:	D-208
Costume Title:	Chip
Date Out:	10/1/2011
Date In:	11/15/2011
Daily Rental Fee:	$189.00
Fee with Tax:	$9.45

Costume No:	S-130
Costume Title:	Romeo
Date Out:	9/1/2011
Date In:	10/15/2011
Daily Rental Fee:	$140.00
Fee with Tax:	$7.00

PTCostumeInv4(Assessment1).accdb (4 of 11)

Daily Rental Fee: $135.00
Fee with Tax: $6.75

Costume No: S-118
Costume Title: King Lear
Date Out: 8/1/2011
Date In: 9/10/2011
Daily Rental Fee: $145.50
Fee with Tax: $7.28

Costume No: A-188
Costume Title: Jade Sorbet
Date Out: 8/1/2011
Date In: 8/22/2011
Daily Rental Fee: $115.50
Fee with Tax: $5.78

Costume No: A-166
Costume Title: Catherine Bellfield
Date Out: 8/1/2011
Date In: 8/30/2011
Daily Rental Fee: $141.00
Fee with Tax: $7.05

Costume No: A-162
Costume Title: Jorge Nevada
Date Out: 8/1/2011
Date In: 8/30/2011
Daily Rental Fee: $131.50
Fee with Tax: $6.58

Costume No: A-122

PTCostumeInv4(Assessment1).accdb (5 of 11)

Costume Title: Celia Gopf
Date Out: 8/1/2011
Date In: 8/30/2011
Daily Rental Fee: $124.50
Fee with Tax: $6.23

Costume No: S-110
Costume Title: Othello
Date Out: 7/22/2011
Date In: 8/31/2011
Daily Rental Fee: $125.00
Fee with Tax: $6.25

Costume No: A-198
Costume Title: Nanci Lasertol
Date Out: 7/22/2011
Date In: 8/15/2011
Daily Rental Fee: $122.00
Fee with Tax: $6.10

Costume No: A-180
Costume Title: Robert Foullette
Date Out: 7/15/2011
Date In: 7/31/2011
Daily Rental Fee: $102.50
Fee with Tax: $5.13

Costume No: A-110
Costume Title: Tony Salvatore
Date Out: 7/15/2011
Date In: 8/12/2011
Daily Rental Fee: $124.50
Fee with Tax: $6.23

PTCostumeInv4(Assessment1).accdb (6 of 11)

Costume No:	A-160
Costume Title:	William Mercer
Date Out:	7/7/2011
Date In:	7/10/2011
Daily Rental Fee:	$122.00
Fee with Tax:	$6.10

Costume No:	A-102
Costume Title:	Eunice Billings
Date Out:	7/7/2011
Date In:	7/15/2011
Daily Rental Fee:	$124.50
Fee with Tax:	$6.23

Costume No:	A-101
Costume Title:	Val Wingfield
Date Out:	7/7/2011
Date In:	7/31/2011
Daily Rental Fee:	$124.50
Fee with Tax:	$6.23

Costume No:	D-106
Costume Title:	Zazu
Date Out:	7/1/2011
Date In:	7/31/2011
Daily Rental Fee:	$85.50
Fee with Tax:	$4.28

Costume No:	D-103
Costume Title:	Pumbaa
Date Out:	7/1/2011

PTCostumeInv4(Assessment1).accdb (7 of 11)

Date In:	7/31/2011
Daily Rental Fee:	$112.75
Fee with Tax:	$5.64

Costume No:	D-101
Costume Title:	Simba
Date Out:	7/1/2011
Date In:	7/31/2011
Daily Rental Fee:	$224.75
Fee with Tax:	$11.24

Costume No:	D-102
Costume Title:	Timon
Date Out:	7/1/2011
Date In:	7/31/2011
Daily Rental Fee:	$85.50
Fee with Tax:	$4.28

Costume No:	D-105
Costume Title:	Nala
Date Out:	7/1/2011
Date In:	7/31/2011
Daily Rental Fee:	$188.75
Fee with Tax:	$9.44

Costume No:	D-107
Costume Title:	Scar
Date Out:	7/1/2011
Date In:	7/31/2011
Daily Rental Fee:	$198.75
Fee with Tax:	$9.94

Form 1 (8 of 11)

Costume No:	S-106
Costume Title:	Hamlet
Date Out:	7/1/2011
Date In:	7/31/2011
Daily Rental Fee:	$125.00
Fee with Tax:	$6.25

Costume No:	D-108
Costume Title:	Mufasa
Date Out:	7/1/2011
Date In:	7/31/2011
Daily Rental Fee:	$215.50
Fee with Tax:	$10.78

Costume No:	D-104
Costume Title:	Rafiki
Date Out:	7/1/2011
Date In:	7/31/2011
Daily Rental Fee:	$144.50
Fee with Tax:	$7.23

Costume No:	A-152
Costume Title:	Hannah Sorenti
Date Out:	6/1/2011
Date In:	7/12/2011
Daily Rental Fee:	$115.50
Fee with Tax:	$5.78

Costume No:	S-102
Costume Title:	Lady Macbeth
Date Out:	5/12/2011
Date In:	6/30/2011
Daily Rental Fee:	$195.00

Form 2 (9 of 11)

| Fee with Tax: | $9.75 |

Costume No:	S-101
Costume Title:	Macbeth
Date Out:	5/12/2011
Date In:	6/30/2011
Daily Rental Fee:	$175.50
Fee with Tax:	$8.78

Costume No:	A-176
Costume Title:	Pietro Gorski
Date Out:	5/2/2011
Date In:	6/10/2011
Daily Rental Fee:	$115.50
Fee with Tax:	$5.78

Costume No:	A-144
Costume Title:	Kelly Williams
Date Out:	5/2/2011
Date In:	6/11/2011
Daily Rental Fee:	$99.50
Fee with Tax:	$4.98

Costume No:	G-102
Costume Title:	Sheriff (black)
Date Out:	
Date In:	
Daily Rental Fee:	$120.00
Fee with Tax:	$6.00

| Costume No: | G-109 |
| Costume Title: | Paramedic |

Costume No: G-103
Costume Title: Cowboy (blue)
Date Out:
Date In:
Daily Rental Fee: $112.00
Fee with Tax: $5.60

Costume No: G-101
Costume Title: Sheriff (gray)
Date Out:
Date In:
Daily Rental Fee: $120.00
Fee with Tax: $6.00

Costume No: G-110
Costume Title: Doctor
Date Out:
Date In:
Daily Rental Fee: $85.00
Fee with Tax: $4.25

Costume No: G-104
Costume Title: Cowboy (green)
Date Out:
Date In:
Daily Rental Fee: $112.00
Fee with Tax: $5.60

Check for damage/repairs upon return

PTCostumeInv4(Assessment1).accdb (11 of 11)

Date Out:
Date In:
Daily Rental Fee: $155.00
Fee with Tax: $7.75

Costume No: G-108
Costume Title: Fireman
Date Out:
Date In:
Daily Rental Fee: $180.00
Fee with Tax: $9.00

Costume No: G-107
Costume Title: RCMP Officer
Date Out:
Date In:
Daily Rental Fee: $215.00
Fee with Tax: $10.75

Costume No: G-106
Costume Title: Policeman
Date Out:
Date In:
Daily Rental Fee: $120.00
Fee with Tax: $6.00

Costume No: G-105
Costume Title: Bartender
Date Out:
Date In:
Daily Rental Fee: $89.00
Fee with Tax: $4.45

PTCostumeInv4(Assessment1).accdb (10 of 11)

Waterdown Cinemas
575 Notre Dame Street
Summerside, PE C1N 1T8

Millennium Movies
4126 Yonge Street
Suite 302
Toronto, ON M2P 2B8

Olympic Cinemas
P. O. Box 1439
188 Riverbrook Road SE
Calgary, AB T2C 3P7

Northern Stars Movies
811 Cook Street
Whitehorse, YK Y1A 2S4

Seaboard Movie House Inc.
P. O. Box 1005
696 Colby Drive
Dartmouth, NS B2V 1Y8

Mountain View Movies
5417 Royalmount Avenue
Montreal, PQ H4P 1H8

Plains Cinema House
P. O. Box 209
46 Prospect Place
Regina, SK S4S 5Y9

Northern Reach Movies
P. O. Box 34
Yellowknife, NW X1A 2N9

East Coast Cinemas
62 Mountbatten Drive
St. John's, NF A1A 3X9

New Age Movies
73 Killarney Road
Moncton, NB E1B 2Z9

Riverview Cinemas
1011-848 Sheppard Street
Winnipeg, MB R2P 0N6

West Coast Movies
P. O. Box 298
7348 Granville Drive
Vancouver, BC V6Y 1N9

Canadian Distributors by Province

Thursday, July 22, 2010
2:27:34 PM

ID	Company Name	Street Address	City	Province	PostalCode	Telephone	Fax
7	Olympic Cinemas	P. O. Box 1439	Calgary	AB	T2C 3P7	403-555-4587	403-555-4589
12	West Coast Movies	P. O. Box 298	Vancouver	BC	V6Y 1N9	604-555-3548	604-555-3549
9	Riverview Cinemas	1011-848 Sheppard Street	Winnipeg	MB	R2P 0N6	204-555-6538	204-555-6533
4	New Age Movies	73 Killarney Road	Moncton	NB	E1B 2Z9	506-555-8376	506-555-8377
1	East Coast Cinemas	62 Mountbatten Drive	St. John's	NF	A1A 3X9	709-555-8349	709-555-8366
10	Seaboard Movie House Inc.	P. O. Box 1005	Dartmouth	NS	B2V 1Y8	902-555-3948	902-555-3950
5	Northern Reach Movies	P. O. Box 34	Yellowknife	NW	X1A 2N9	867-555-6314	867-555-6316
2	Millennium Movies	4126 Yonge Street	Toronto	ON	M2P 2B8	416-555-9335	416-555-9338
11	Waterdown Cinemas	575 Notre Dame Street	Summerside	PE	C1N 1T8	902-555-8374	902-555-8376
3	Mountain View Movies	5417 Royalmount Avenue	Montreal	PQ	H4P 1H8	514-555-3584	514-555-3585
8	Plains Cinema House	P. O. Box 209	Regina	SK	S4S 5Y9	306-555-1247	305-555-1248
6	Northern Stars Movies	811 Cook Street	Whitehorse	YK	Y1A 2S4	867-555-6598	867-555-6599

PromptedDept   7/12/2012

EmployeeID	FirstName	LastName	HireDate	Department
1005	Roman	Deptulski	8/15/2002	Overseas Distribution
1030	Thom	Hicks	1/22/2004	Overseas Distribution
1040	Guy	Laffreniere	3/10/2005	Overseas Distribution
1090	Maria	Quinte	11/29/2010	Overseas Distribution

Page 1

WEEmployees4(Assessment5).accdb

PurchaseItems_Crosstab   7/12/2012

ItemDescription	Total Of Amount	Qtr 1	Qtr 2
Butternut Squash	$197.78	$65.14	$132.64
Cantaloupe	$48.75	$48.75	
Carrots	$119.14	$47.69	$71.45
English Muffins	$22.47		$22.47
Green Peppers	$103.23	$55.12	$48.11
Kaiser Rolls	$35.12		$35.12
Lake Erie Perch	$178.94	$178.94	
Pita Wraps	$33.85		$33.85
Potatoes	$252.29	$68.91	$183.38
Swordfish	$419.24	$229.57	$189.67
White Bread	$88.14		$88.14
Whole Wheat Bread	$145.94		$145.94

Page 1

WBInventory4(Assessment4).accdb

Costume Rental Revenue by Month

Date Out by Month	Costume No	Costume Title	Date In	Days Rented	Rental Fee
May 2011					
5/12/2011	S-101	Macbeth	6/30/2011	49	$9,115.47
5/2/2011	A-176	Pietro Gorski	6/10/2011	39	$4,774.77
5/12/2011	S-102	Lady Macbeth	6/30/2011	49	$10,128.30
5/2/2011	A-144	Kelly Williams	6/11/2011	40	$4,218.80
					$28,237.34
June 2011					
6/1/2011	A-152	Hannah Sorenti	7/12/2011	41	$5,019.63
					$5,019.63
July 2011					
7/7/2011	A-160	William Mercer	7/10/2011	3	$387.96
7/15/2011	A-110	Tony Salvatore	8/12/2011	28	$3,695.16
7/1/2011	D-105	Nala	7/31/2011	30	$6,002.25
7/7/2011	A-102	Eunice Billings	7/15/2011	8	$1,055.76
7/1/2011	D-107	Scar	7/31/2011	30	$6,320.25
7/22/2011	A-198	Nanci Laserrol	8/15/2011	24	$3,103.68
7/1/2011	D-101	Simba	7/31/2011	30	$7,147.05
7/1/2011	D-102	Timon	7/31/2011	30	$2,718.90
7/7/2011	A-101	Val Wingfield	7/31/2011	24	$3,167.28
7/1/2011	D-104	Rafiki	7/31/2011	30	$4,595.10
7/1/2011	D-106	Zazu	7/31/2011	30	$2,718.90
7/15/2011	A-180	Robert Foullette	7/31/2011	16	$1,738.40
7/22/2011	S-110	Othello	8/31/2011	40	$5,300.00
7/1/2011	D-108	Mufasa	7/31/2011	30	$6,852.90
7/1/2011	S-106	Hamlet	7/31/2011	30	$3,975.00
7/1/2011	D-103	Pumbaa	7/31/2011	30	$3,585.45
					$62,364.04
August 2011					
8/12/2011	A-170	Vincent Dudkoff	8/22/2011	10	$1,319.70

Page

PTCostumeInv4(Challenge2).accdb (1 of 2)

Revenue by Type of Event by Quarter

Event	Quarter 1	Quarter 2	Quarter 3	Total Revenue
Wedding	$7,700.70	$8,937.75	$3,514.50	$20,152.95
Engagement Party	$5,124.15	$2,460.75	$2,096.25	$9,681.15
Birthday Party	$4,434.65	$2,186.10		$6,620.75
Business Meeting	$2,326.70	$2,044.85	$1,173.55	$5,545.10
25th Wedding Anniversary	$2,547.60	$1,725.30		$4,272.90
50th Wedding Anniversary		$2,042.90		$2,042.90
Baby Shower			$1,360.90	$1,360.90
	$22,133.80	**$19,397.65**	**$8,145.20**	**$49,676.65**

WBSpecialEvents4(Challenge1).accdb

Date Out by Month	Costume No	Costume Title	Date In	Days Rented	Rental Fee
8/1/2011	S-122	Richard III	9/10/2011	40	$5,724.00
8/1/2011	A-122	Celia Gopf	8/30/2011	29	$3,827.33
8/12/2011	A-130	Jade Norwich	8/31/2011	19	$2,507.63
8/1/2011	S-118	King Lear	9/10/2011	40	$6,169.20
8/12/2011	A-190	Xavier Vanderkof	8/31/2011	19	$2,839.74
8/1/2011	A-188	Jade Sorbet	8/22/2011	21	$2,571.03
8/1/2011	A-166	Catherine Bellfield	8/30/2011	29	$4,334.34
8/1/2011	A-162	Jorge Nevada	8/30/2011	29	$4,042.31
					$33,334.58

September 2011					
9/1/2011	S-130	Romeo	10/15/2011	44	$6,529.62
9/1/2011	S-131	Juliet	10/15/2011	44	$6,529.60
					$13,059.22

October 2011					
10/1/2011	D-207	Mrs. Potts	11/15/2011	45	$10,017.00
10/1/2011	D-206	Cogsworth	11/15/2011	45	$9,158.40
10/1/2011	D-205	Lumiere	11/15/2011	45	$8,967.60
10/1/2011	D-204	Maurice	11/15/2011	45	$7,393.50
10/1/2011	D-203	Gaston	11/15/2011	45	$9,063.00
10/1/2011	D-202	Beast	11/15/2011	45	$11,304.90
10/1/2011	D-201	Belle	11/15/2011	45	$8,347.50
10/1/2011	D-208	Chip	11/15/2011	45	$9,015.30
					$73,267.20
					$215,282.28

40

PTCostumeInv4(Challenge2).accdb (2 of 2)

The Waterfront Bistro Inventory List

Item_No	Item	Unit	Supplier Code
1	Butternut Squash	case	4
2	Potatoes	50 lb bag	4
3	Carrots	25 lb bag	4
4	Onions	25 lb bag	4
5	Garlic	10 lb bag	3
6	Green Peppers	case	3
7	Red Peppers	case	3
8	Yellow Peppers	case	3
9	Radishes	case	4
10	Celery	case	3
11	Broccoli	case	3
12	Cauliflower	case	4
13	Tomatoes	case	4
14	Green Beans	case	3
15	Brussel Sprouts	flat	4
16	Iceberg Lettuce	case	3
17	Romaine Lettuce	case	3
18	Bananas	case	2
19	Pineapple	case	2
20	Oranges	case	2
21	Cantaloupe	case	2
22	White Bread	flat	1
23	Whole Wheat Bread	flat	1
24	Kaiser Rolls	flat	1
25	English Muffins	flat	1
26	Pita Wraps	flat	1
27	Tortilla Wraps	flat	1
28	Beef	side	7
29	Pork	side	7
30	Chicken	case	6
31	Tuna	case	8
32	Swordfish	case	8
33	Lake Erie Perch	flat	8
34	Ketchup	gallon	10
35	Mustard	gallon	10

Int2-R2-InventoryList(Review2).rtf

Costume_No	Character	Daily_Rental_Fee	Date_Out	Date_In
A-101	Val Wingfield	$110.00	07-Jul-10	31-Jul-10
A-102	Eunice Billings	$110.00	07-Jul-10	15-Jul-10
A-110	Tony Salvatore	$120.00	15-Jul-10	12-Aug-10
A-122	Celia Gopf	$125.00	01-Aug-10	30-Aug-10
A-130	Jade Norwich	$110.00	12-Aug-10	31-Aug-10
A-144	Kelly Williams	$105.00	02-May-10	11-Jun-10
A-152	Hannah Sorenti	$115.50	01-Jun-10	12-Jul-10
A-160	William Mercer	$122.50	07-Jul-10	10-Jul-10
A-162	Jorge Nevada	$131.50	01-Aug-10	30-Aug-10
A-166	Catherine Bellfield	$141.50	01-Aug-10	30-Aug-10
A-170	Vincent Dudkoff	$110.00	12-Aug-10	22-Aug-10
A-176	Pietro Gorski	$115.50	02-May-10	10-Jun-10
A-180	Robert Foullette	$99.50	15-Jul-10	31-Jul-10
A-188	Jade Sorbet	$115.50	01-Aug-10	22-Aug-10
A-190	Xavier Vanderkof	$141.00	12-Aug-10	31-Aug-10
A-198	Nanci Lasertol	$122.00	22-Jul-10	15-Aug-10

Int2-R1-CostumeInventory(Review1).xlsx

DesignHours

Costume	Research	Design	Sewing
Val Wingfield	6	15	38
Eunice Billings	12	28	47
Tony Salvatore	9	31	41
Celia Gopf	5	18	30
Jade Norwich	7	23	33

Page 1

Int2-PTCostumes(Review4).accdb

Costume Inventory

Thursday, February 04, 2010 11:02:18 PM

Costume_No	Character	Daily_Rental_Fee	Date_Out	Date_In
A-101	Val Wingfield	$110.00	7/7/2010	7/31/2010
A-102	Eunice Billings	$110.00	7/7/2010	7/15/2010
A-110	Tony Salvatore	$110.00	7/15/2010	8/12/2010
A-122	Celia Gopf	$110.00	8/1/2010	8/30/2010
A-130	Jade Norwich	$110.00	8/12/2010	8/31/2010
A-144	Kelly Williams	$99.50	5/2/2010	6/11/2010
A-152	Hannah Sorenti	$115.50	6/1/2010	7/12/2010
A-160	William Mercer	$122.50	7/7/2010	7/10/2010
A-162	Jorge Nevada	$131.50	8/1/2010	8/30/2010
A-166	Catherine Bellfield	$141.50	8/1/2010	8/30/2010
A-170	Vincent Dudkoff	$110.00	8/12/2010	8/22/2010
A-176	Pietro Gorski	$115.50	5/2/2010	6/10/2010
A-180	Robert Foullette	$99.50	7/15/2010	7/31/2010
A-188	Jade Sorbet	$115.50	8/1/2010	8/22/2010
A-190	Xavier Vanderkof	$141.00	8/12/2010	8/31/2010
A-198	Nanci Lasertol	$122.00	7/22/2010	8/15/2010
		$1,864.00		

Int2-R3-CostumeInventory(Review3).xlsx

LinkedCommissions

Sales Agent	Total Bookings	Commission
Sanderson, T.	$43,189	$1,296
Williamson, L.	$55,198	$1,656
Forbrege, A.	$23,459	$704
Bhayana, M.	$48,975	$1,469
Mennill, S.	$29,657	$890
Giuliani, K.	$63,198	$1,896
Redick, L.	$22,945	$688
Ashby, W.	$55,347	$1,660
De Papp, Q.	$50,981	$1,529
Lampkin, R.	$28,671	$860
Borje, J.	$65,317	$1,960
Putnam, N.	$66,198	$1,986

Page 1

Int2-FCTCommissions(Review5).accdb

Sales Agent	Total Bookings		Commission	
Sanderson, T.	$	43,189	$	1,296
Williamson, L.	$	55,198	$	1,656
Forbrege, A.	$	23,459	$	704
Bhayana, M.	$	48,975	$	1,469
Mennill, S.	$	29,657	$	890
Giuliani, K.	$	63,198	$	1,896
Redick, L.	$	22,945	$	688
Ashby, W.	$	55,347	$	1,660
De Papp, Q.	$	50,981	$	1,529
Lampkin, R.	$	28,671	$	860
Borje, J.	$	65,317	$	1,960
Putnam, N.	$	66,198	$	1,986

Int2-R5-FCTBookings(Review5).xlsx

7/12/2012

ACCOUNTING POLICIES
- Cash Equivalents
- Short-Term Investments
- Inventory Valuation
- Property and Equipment
- Foreign Currency Translation

INVENTORIES
- Products
- Raw Material
- Equipment
- Buildings

WORLDWIDE ENTERPRISES
Executive Meeting

FINANCIAL INSTRUMENTS
- Investments
- Derivative Instruments
- Credit Risks
- Fair Value of Instruments

EMPLOYEE PLANS
- Stock Options
- Bonus Plan
- Savings and Retirement Plan
- Defined Benefits Plan
- Foreign Subsidiaries

1

7/12/2012

Resources
- Location Contacts
- Movie Extras
- Catering Company
- Lodging
- Transportation Rentals

Filming Sites
- Gardiner Expressway
- Kings Mill Park
- Island Airport
- Royal Ontario Museum
- Black Creek Pioneer Village
- Additional Sites

Marquee Productions
Location Team Meeting

Current Status
- Overview of Project
- Tasks on Schedule
- Tasks behind Schedule

Key Issues
- Equipment Rental
- Budget Overruns
- Transportation Concerns
- Location Agreement

1

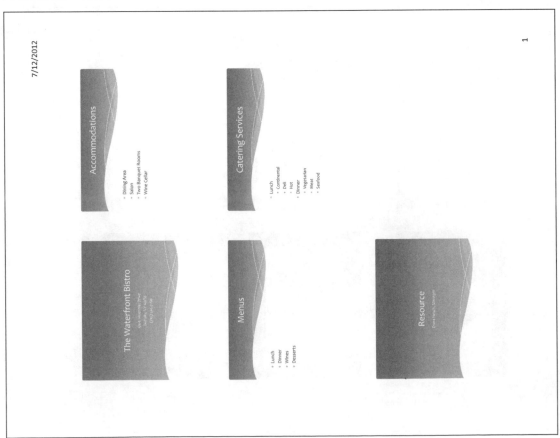

PS1-C1-FCTToronto(Challenge1).pptx

PS1-A2-TWBServices(Assessment2).pptx

Sewing Projects
- Costumes for current production at Lafferty Performing Arts Theatre
- Research for Pantages Art Group
- Medieval and Regency period costumes for Marquee Productions

Performance Threads
Costuming Meeting

Medieval Costume: Men
Cotton tunic with decorative trim in various colors on sleeves, neck, and bottom of tunic.

Medieval Costume: Women
Cotton dress with gathered neckline, wide extended sleeves, full skirt with overbodice laces, and decorative trim down the front.

Regency Costume: Men
Double-breasted waistcoat with high collar and white linen cravat with rolled hem.

Regency Costume: Women
High-waisted bodice with puff sleeves over long sleeves with ruffled cuffs, skirt with sash tie and slight train, and three bands of trim.

1

PS1-C2-PTCostumeMtg(Challenge2).pptx

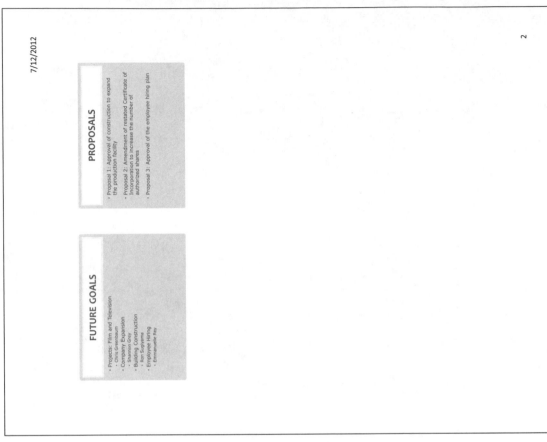

7/12/2012

PS2-R1-MPAnnualMtg(Review1).pptx (2 of 2)

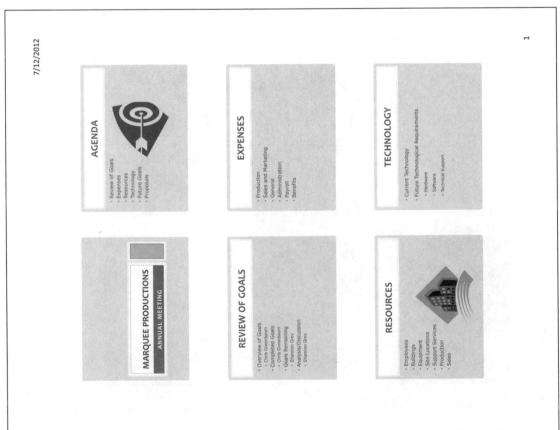

7/12/2012

PS2-R1-MPAnnualMtg(Review1).pptx (1 of 2)

Marquee PowerPoint 2010 Section 2 Model Answers

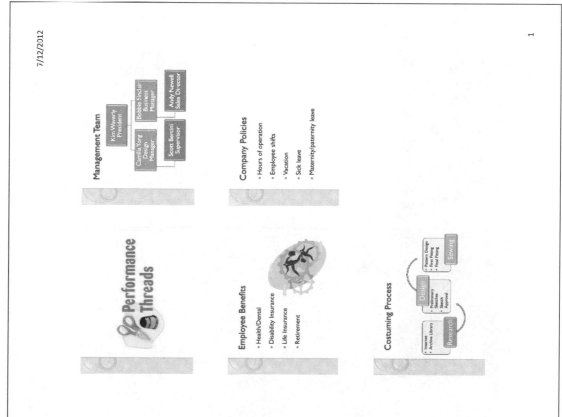

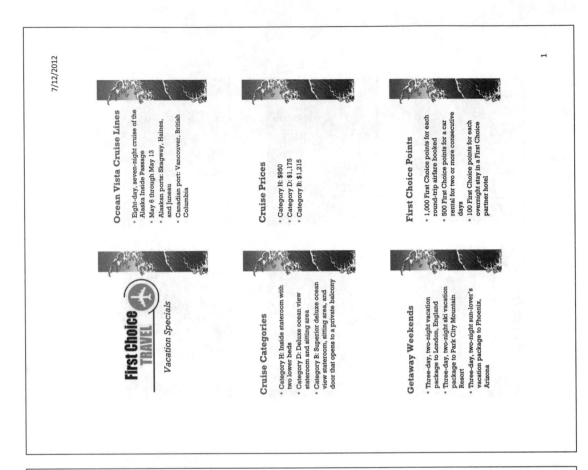

PS2-A2-FCTVacations(Assessment2).pptx

PS2-A1-NPCTheatreArts(Assessment1).pptx (2 of 2)

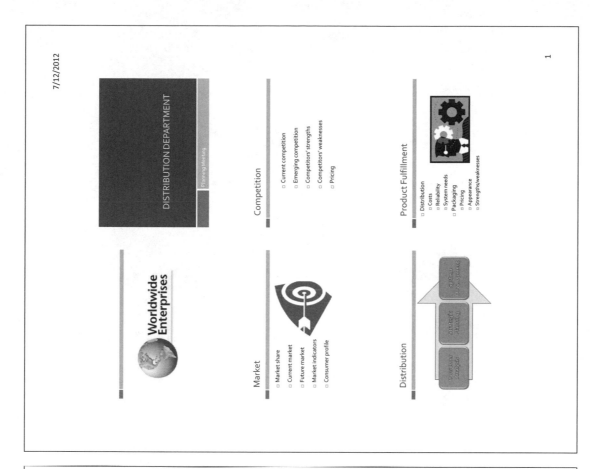

PS2-C1-WEDist(Challenge1).pptx

PS2-A3-FCTVacations(Assessment3).pptx

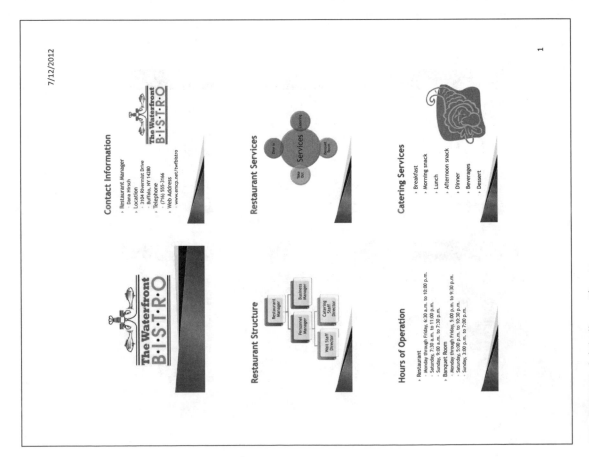

PS2-C2-TWBInfo(Challenge2).pptx

Marquee PowerPoint 2010 Section 2 Model Answers

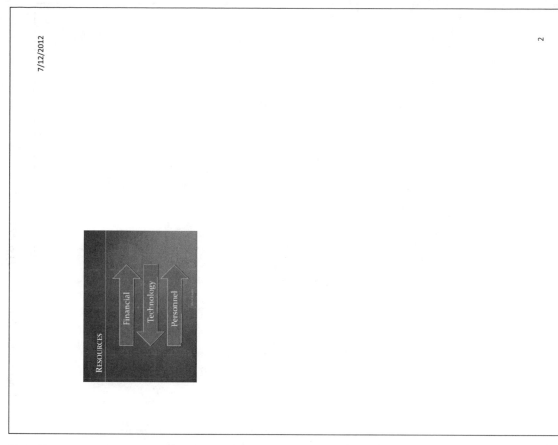

MARQUEE PRODUCTIONS
Annual Meeting

AGENDA
- Review of Goals
- Resources
- Financial
- Future Goals
- Technology
- Proposals

REVIEW OF GOALS
- Overview of Goals
- Completed Goals
- Goals Remaining
- Analysis/Discussion

RESOURCES
- Employees
- Buildings
- Equipment
- Site Locations
- Support Services
- Production
- Sales

FINANCIAL
- Real Estate Taxes
- Management Fees
- Revenue
  - Forecast/Actual
  - Gross Margin
- Profit
- Expenses

FUTURE GOALS
- Projects: Film and Television
  - Chris Greenbaum
- Company Expansion
  - Shannon Grey
- Building Construction
  - Ron Sugiyama
- Employee Hiring
  - Emmanuelle Rey

PS3-R2-MPAnnualMtg(Review2).pptx (1 of 2)

TECHNOLOGY
- Current Technology
- Future Technological Requirements
- Hardware
- Software
- Technical Support

PROPOSALS
- Proposal 1: Approval of construction to expand the production facility
- Proposal 2: Amendment of restated Certificate of Incorporation to increase the number of authorized shares
- Proposal 3: Approval of the employee hiring plan

EXPENSES
- Production
- Sales and Marketing
- General
- Administration
  - Payroll
  - Benefits

PS3-R2-MPAnnualMtg(Review2).pptx (2 of 2)

First Choice TRAVEL

Vacation Cruise

Ocean Vista Cruise Lines

- Eight-day, seven-night cruise of the Alaska Inside Passage
- May 6 through May 13
- Alaskan ports: Skagway, Haines, and Juneau
- Canadian port: Vancouver, British Columbia

Cruise Categories

- Category H: Inside stateroom with two lower beds
- Category D: Deluxe ocean view stateroom with stateroom and sitting area
- Category B: Superior deluxe ocean view stateroom, sitting area, and door that opens to a private balcony

Cruise Prices

- Category H: $950
- Category D: $1,175
- Category B: $1,215

First Choice Points

- 1,000 First Choice points for each round-trip airfare booked
- 500 First Choice points for a car rental for two or more consecutive days
- 100 First Choice points for each overnight stay in a First Choice partner hotel

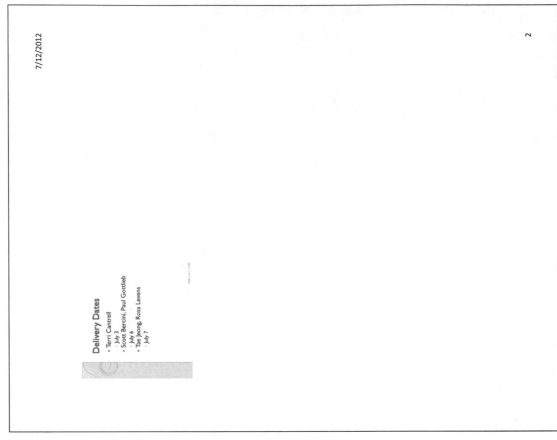

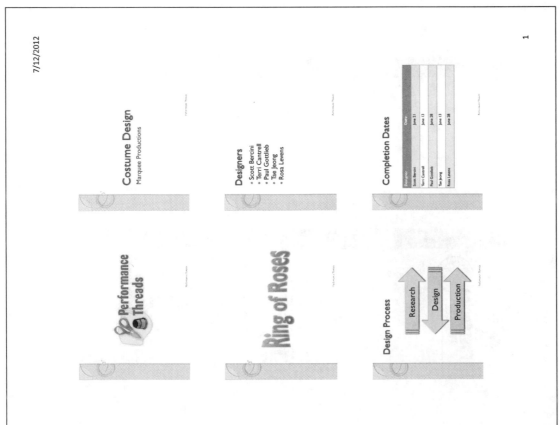

New Zealand Tour
- Round-trip airfare from Los Angeles to Auckland, New Zealand
- 14 days and 13 nights in New Zealand
- Summer and winter tours
- Prices from $2399 to $3199

Accommodations
- Auckland—Moreland Hotel
- Queenstown—Regency Hotel
- Christchurch—Cornwall Plaza

Highlights
- Auckland Harbour Yacht Cruise
- Coromandel Peninsula Excursion
- Christchurch Historical Tour
- Maori Celebration Dinner

2

PS3-A2-FCTSouthernTours(Assessment2).pptx (2 of 2)

Australia

First Choice Travel
Southern Tours

Accommodations
- Sydney—Royal Arms Resort
- Melbourne—Queens Plaza
- Cairns—Lofton Regency Hotel

Australia Tour
- Round-trip airfare from Los Angeles to Sydney, Australia
- 14 days and 13 nights in Australia
- Summer and winter tours
- Prices from $2599 to $3599

New Zealand

Highlights
- Melbourne City Tour
- Great Barrier Reef Cruise
- Sydney Comprehensive Tour
- Sydney Harbour Cruise

1

PS3-A2-FCTSouthernTours(Assessment2).pptx (1 of 2)

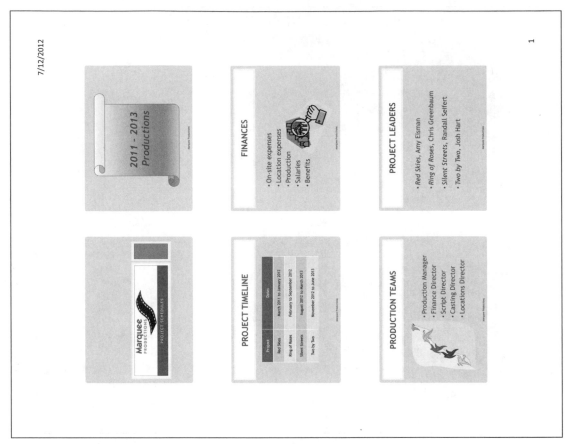

PS3-C1-MPProdSch(Challenge1).pptx

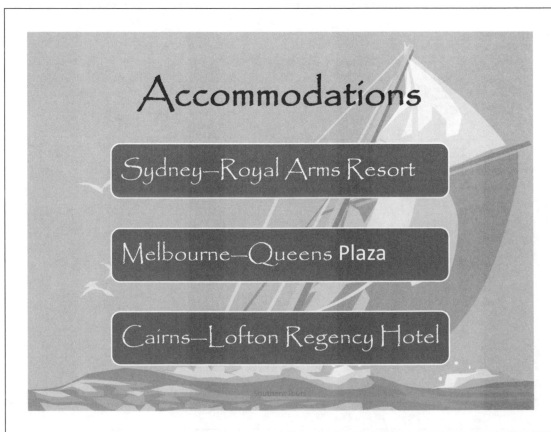

PS3-A3-FCTSouthernTours(Assessment3).pptx

MOROCCO FACTS

Location: Northern Africa
Government: Constitutional monarchy
Population: Approximately 35 million
Official language: Arabic
Capital: Rabat

Morocco Tour

ACCOMMODATIONS

× Casablanca: Royal Meridien
× Fez: Zalagh Plaza
× Erfoud: Le Berbere Resort
× Ouarzazate: Belere Palace
× Marrakesh: Saadi Hotel

SCENIC HIGHLIGHTS

× Barbary Coast
× Route de Fez
× Middle Atlas Range
× High Atlas Range
× Ziz and Todra Gorges
× Dades Valley
× Tizi-n-Tichka Pass

DATES AND PRICES

Dates	Land and Air	Land Only
January 17 through 27	$2,359	$1,599
March 8 through 18	$2,359	$1,599
June 6 through 16	$2,119	$1,399
September 20 through 30	$2,119	$1,399

ITINERARY

× Casablanca: Three days, two nights
× Fez: Three days, two nights
× Erfoud: Two days, one night
× Marrakesh: Two days, one night

PS3-C2-FCTMorocco(Challenge2).pptx

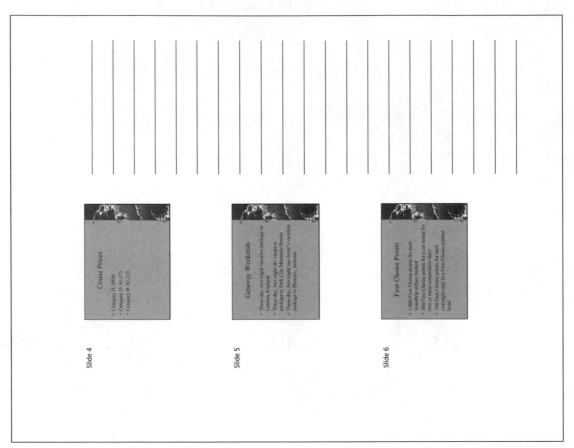

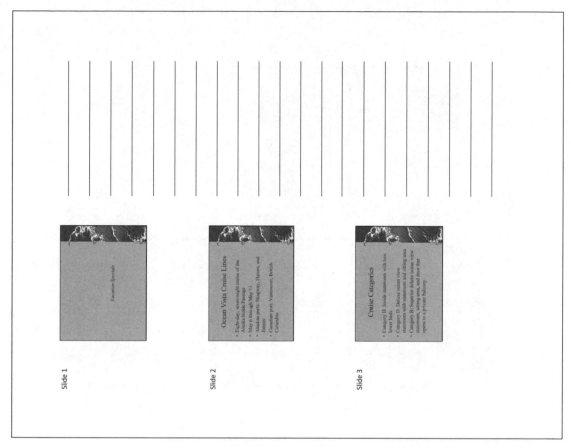

Int3-R1-FCTVacations(Review1,Step8).pptx

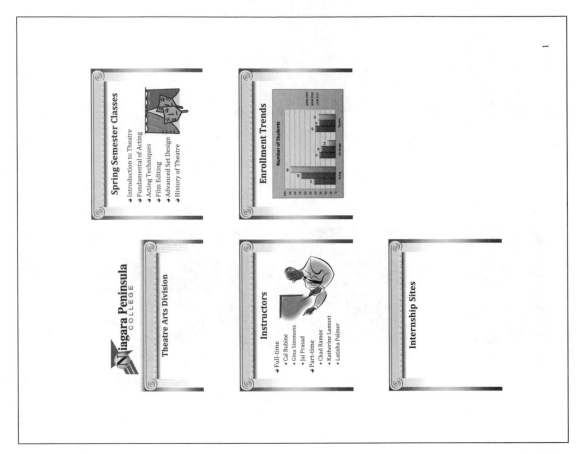

Int3-R2-NPCEnroll(Review2,Step9).pptx

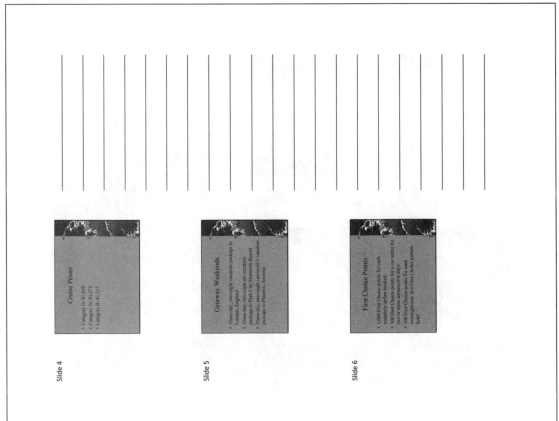

Int3-R1-FCTVacSpecials(Review1,Step10).docx (2 of 2)

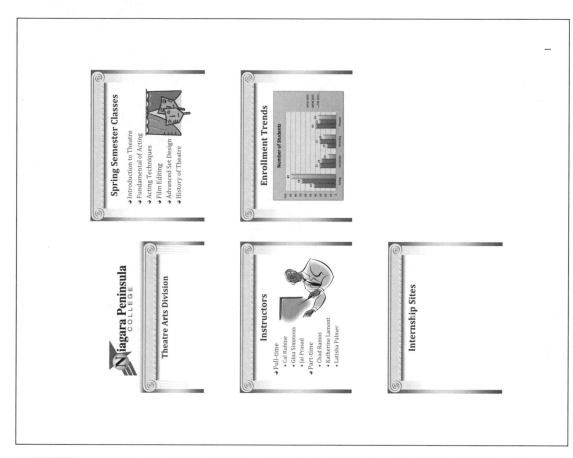

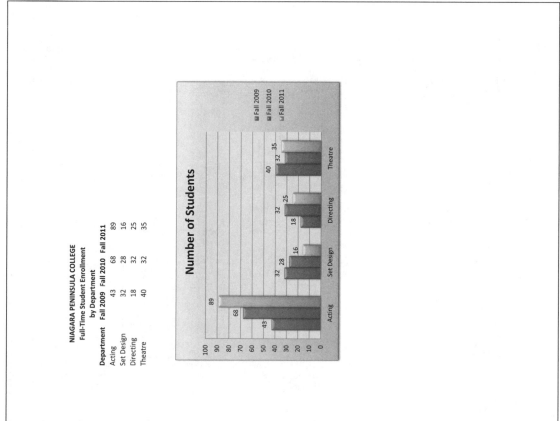

Int3-R2-NPCEnroll(Review2,Step18).pptx

Int3-R2-NPCEnrollChart(Review2,Step15).xlsx

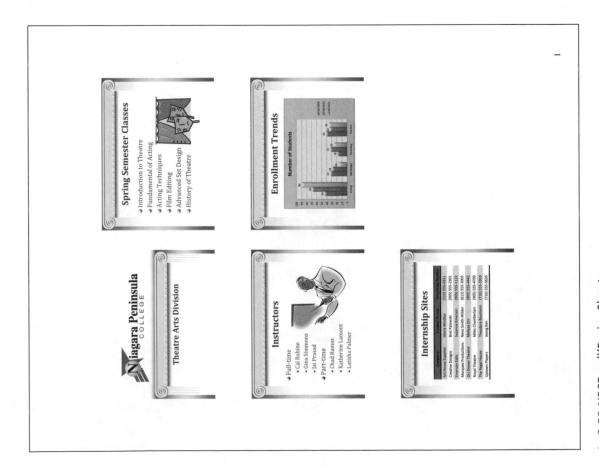

Int3-R3-NPCEnroll(Review3).pptx

Costume Inventory

Thursday, February 18, 20108:57

Costume_No	Character	Daily_Rental_Fee	Date_Out	Date_In
A-101	Val Wingfield	$110.00	7/7/2010	7/31/2010
A-102	Eunice Billings	$110.00	7/7/2010	7/15/2010
A-110	Tony Salvatore	$110.00	7/15/2010	8/12/2010
A-122	Celia Gopf	$110.00	8/1/2010	8/30/2010
A-130	Jade Norwich	$110.00	8/12/2010	8/31/2010
A-144	Kelly Williams	$99.50	5/2/2010	6/11/2010
A-152	Hannah Sorenti	$115.50	6/1/2010	7/12/2010
A-160	William Mercer	$122.50	7/7/2010	7/10/2010
A-162	Jorge Nevada	$131.50	8/1/2010	8/30/2010
A-166	Catherine Bellfield	$141.50	8/1/2010	8/30/2010
A-170	Vincent Dudkoff	$110.00	8/12/2010	8/22/2010
A-176	Pietro Gorski	$115.50	5/2/2010	6/10/2010
A-180	Robert Foullette	$99.50	7/15/2010	7/31/2010
A-188	Jade Sorbet	$115.50	8/1/2010	8/22/2010
A-190	Xavier Vanderkof	$141.00	8/12/2010	8/31/2010
A-198	Nanci Lasertol	$122.00	7/22/2010	8/15/2010
		$1,864.00		

Int-R2-CostumeInventory(Review2).rtf

Costume_No	Character	Daily_Rental_Fee	Date_Out	Date_In
A-101	Val Wingfield	$110.00	07-Jul-10	31-Jul-10
A-102	Eunice Billings	$110.00	07-Jul-10	15-Jul-10
A-110	Tony Salvatore	$120.00	15-Jul-10	12-Aug-10
A-122	Celia Gopf	$125.00	01-Aug-10	30-Aug-10
A-130	Jade Norwich	$110.00	12-Aug-10	31-Aug-10
A-144	Kelly Williams	$105.00	02-May-10	11-Jun-10
A-152	Hannah Sorenti	$115.50	01-Jun-10	12-Jul-10
A-160	William Mercer	$122.50	07-Jul-10	10-Jul-10
A-162	Jorge Nevada	$131.50	01-Aug-10	30-Aug-10
A-166	Catherine Bellfield	$141.50	01-Aug-10	30-Aug-10
A-170	Vincent Dudkoff	$110.00	12-Aug-10	22-Aug-10
A-176	Pietro Gorski	$115.50	02-May-10	10-Jun-10
A-180	Robert Foullette	$99.50	15-Jul-10	31-Jul-10
A-188	Jade Sorbet	$115.50	01-Aug-10	22-Aug-10
A-190	Xavier Vanderkof	$141.00	12-Aug-10	31-Aug-10
A-198	Nanci Lasertol	$122.00	22-Jul-10	15-Aug-10

Int-R1-CostumeInventory(Review1).xlsx

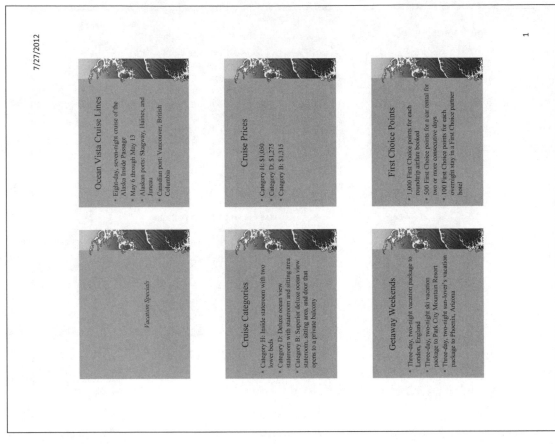

Vacation Specials

Ocean Vista Cruise Lines
- Eight-day, seven-night cruise of the Alaska Inside Passage
- May 6 through May 13
- Alaskan ports: Skagway, Haines, and Juneau
- Canadian port: Vancouver, British Columbia

Cruise Categories
- Category H: Inside stateroom with two lower beds
- Category D: Deluxe ocean view stateroom with stateroom and sitting area
- Category B: Superior deluxe ocean view stateroom, sitting area, and door that opens to a private balcony

Cruise Prices
- Category H: $1,050
- Category D: $1,275
- Category B: $1,315

Getaway Weekends
- Three-day, two-night vacation package to London, England
- Three-day, two-night ski vacation package to Park City Mountain Resort
- Three-day, two-night sun-lover's vacation package to Phoenix, Arizona

First Choice Points
- 1,000 First Choice points for each roundtrip airfare booked
- 500 First Choice points for a car rental for two or more consecutive days
- 100 First Choice points for each overnight stay in a First Choice partner hotel

Int-R4-FCTVacations(Review3).pptx

DesignHours

Costume	Research	Design	Sewing
Val Wingfield	6	15	38
Eunice Billings	12	28	47
Tony Salvatore	9	31	41
Celia Gopf	5	18	30
Jade Norwich	7	23	33

Page 1

DesignHours(Review3).accdb

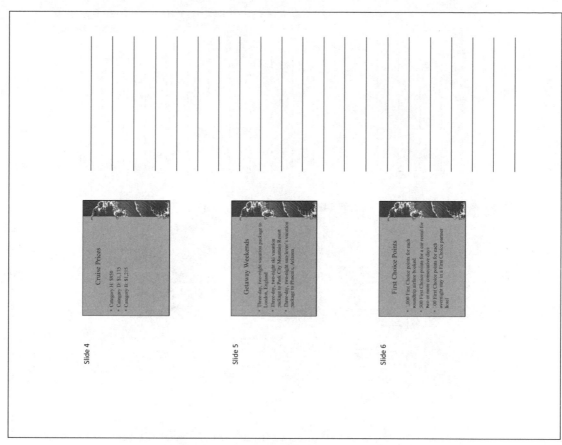

Slide 4

Cruise Prices
* Category H: $950
* Category D: $1,175
* Category B: $1,215

Slide 5

Getaway Weekends
* Three-day, two-night vacation package to London, England
* Three-day, two-night ski vacation package to Park City Mountain Resort
* Three-day, two-night sun-lover's vacation package to Phoenix, Arizona

Slide 6

First Choice Points
* 1,000 First Choice points for each roundtrip airfare booked
* 500 First Choice points for a car rental for two or more consecutive days
* 100 First Choice points for each overnight stay at a First Choice partner hotel

Slide 1

Vacation Specials

Slide 2

Ocean Vista Cruise Lines
* Eight-day, seven-night cruise of the Alaska Inside Passage
* May 6 through May 13
* Alaskan ports: Skagway, Haines, and Juneau
* Canadian port: Vancouver, British Columbia

Slide 3

Cruise Categories
* Category H: Inside stateroom with two lower beds
* Category D: Deluxe ocean view stateroom with stateroom and sitting area
* Category B: Superior deluxe ocean view stateroom, sitting area, and door that opens to a private balcony

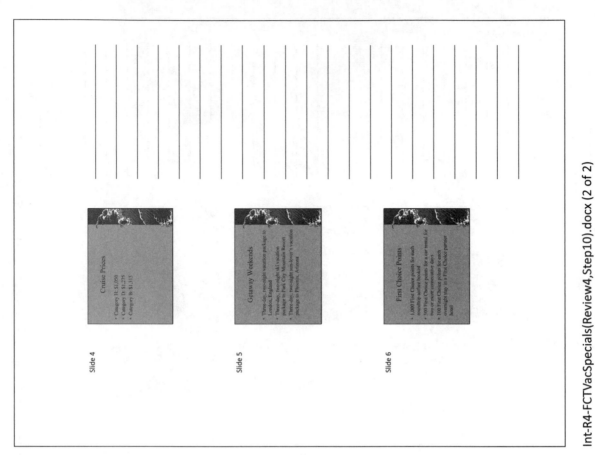

Slide 1

Slide 2

Slide 3

Slide 4

Slide 5

Slide 6

Niagara Peninsula College
COLLEGE

Theatre Arts Division

Instructors
→ Full-time
  • Cal Rubine
  • Gina Simmons
  • Jai Prasad
→ Part-time
  • Chad Ramos
  • Katherine Lamont
  • Latisha Palmer

Internship Sites

Spring Semester Classes
→ Introduction to Theater
→ Fundamental of Acting
→ Acting Techniques
→ Film Editing
→ Advanced Set Design
→ History of Theater

Enrollment Trends
Number of Students

NIAGARA PENINSULA COLLEGE
Full-Time Student Enrollment
by Department

Department	Fall 2009	Fall 2010	Fall 2011
Acting	43	68	89
Set Design	32	28	16
Directing	18	32	25
Theatre	40	32	35

Number of Students

Fall 2009
Fall 2010
Fall 2011

Sales Agent	Total Bookings	Commission
Sanderson, T.	$43,189.00	
Williamson, L.	$55,198.00	
Forbrege, A.	$23,459.00	
Bhayana, M.	$48,975.00	
Mennill, S.	$29,657.00	
Giuliani, K.	$63,198.00	
Redick, L.	$22,945.00	
Ashby, W.	$55,347.00	
De Papp, Q.	$50,981.00	
Lampkin, R.	$28,671.00	
Borje, J.	$65,317.00	
Putnam, N.	$66,198.00	

Page 1

Int-R7-FCTBookings(Review7).xlsx

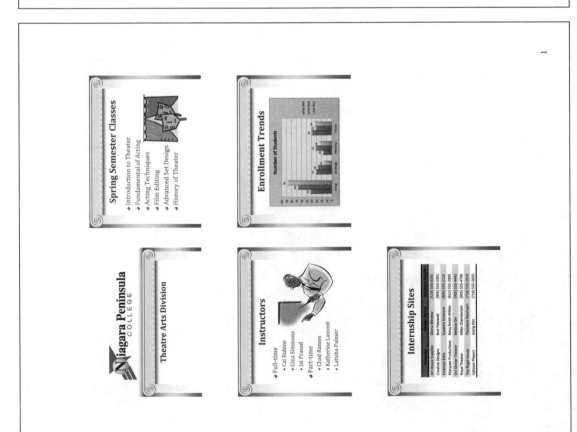

Int-R6-NPCEnroll(Review6).pptx

LinkedCommissions

2/18/2012

Sales Agent	Total Bookings	Commission
Sanderson, T.	$43,189	$1,296
Williamson, L.	$55,198	$1,656
Forbrege, A.	$23,459	$704
Bhayana, M.	$48,975	$1,469
Mennill, S.	$29,657	$890
Giuliani, K.	$63,198	$1,896
Redick, L.	$22,945	$688
Ashby, W.	$55,347	$1,660
De Papp, Q.	$50,981	$1,529
Lampkin, R.	$28,671	$860
Borje, J.	$65,317	$1,960
Putnam, N.	$66,198	$1,986

LinkedCommissions(Review7,Step6)

Sales Agent	Total Bookings	Commission
Sanderson, T.	$ 43,189	$ 1,296
Williamson, L.	$ 55,198	$ 1,656
Forbrege, A.	$ 23,459	$ 704
Bhayana, M.	$ 48,975	$ 1,469
Mennill, S.	$ 29,557	$ 890
Giuliani, K.	$ 63,198	$ 1,896
Redick, L.	$ 22,345	$ 688
Ashby, W.	$ 55,347	$ 1,660
De Papp, Q.	$ 50,381	$ 1,529
Lampkin, R.	$ 28,571	$ 860
Borje, J.	$ 65,317	$ 1,960
Putnam, N.	$ 66,198	$ 1,986

LinkedCommissions(Review7,Step13)

**Worldwide
Enterprises**

Date: September 2, 2012

To: Sam Vestering, Manager

From: Heidi Pasqual, Financial Officer

Subject: August Revenues

The table below shows the box office sales, percentages, and revenue for the previous month. The box office sales are lower than anticipated for the summer season.

Theatre Company	August Revenues		
	Box Office Sales	Percentage	Revenue
Cinema House	$1,575,000	5.0%	$78,750
Cinema Plus	$2,375,000	5.0%	$118,750
Movie Mania	$1,750,000	7.5%	$131,250
Picture House	$1,100,000	5.0%	$55,000
Reels 'R Us	$1,255,000	5.0%	$62,750

Int-R8-WERevMemo(Review8).docx

Grading Rubrics

Windows 7 Section 1 Skills Reviews Grading Rubrics

Review 1: Opening and Manipulating Windows
(No file involved)

Steps	Tasks	Criterion/Criteria	Value	Score
1-4	**Accuracy/ Familiarization**	Click Start, click Documents, click Start & click Computer (restore each window if necessary), drag Computer window by Title bar to make active, click Documents title bar to make active	4	
5-9	**Accuracy/ Familiarization**	Right-click blank are on Taskbar & choose Cascade, click minimize button on Documents Title bar & then on Computer Title bar to minimize them, click on Thumbnails for Computer & Documents window, in turn, to restore them	5	
10-13	**Accuracy/ Familiarization**	Drag Documents window to top of screen to maximize & then drag down to restore, drag Documents window off right edge of screen to snap it & Computer window off left edge of screen to snap it	3	
14-15	**Accuracy**	Close Documents & Computer windows	13	
		TOTAL POINTS: 25		

Review 2: Exploring the Taskbar and Gadgets
(No file involved)

Steps	Tasks	Criterion/Criteria	Value	Score
1-3	**Options/ Accuracy**	Click time display in notification area, click Change date and time settings, advance calendar one month, click OK twice	3	
4-5	**Command/ Accuracy**	Click Start, follow path to open Notepad, close Notepad	4	
6	**Command/ Customization**	Right-click blank area of desktop, click Gadgets, double-click clock gadget if available	3	
		TOTAL POINTS: 10		

Windows 7 Section 1 Skills Assessments Grading Rubric

Assessment 1: Manipulating Windows
(No file involved)

Steps	Tasks	Criterion/Criteria	Value	Score
1-7	**Command, Accuracy & Familiarization**	Click Start & click Pictures, click Start & click Music, stack windows, make Pictures active & minimize it, minimize Music window, restore Pictures & Music	7	
8-9	**Accuracy/ Familiarization**	Arrange windows side-by-side using Snap, close Music & Pictures windows	3	
		TOTAL POINTS: 10		

Assessment 2: Customizing the Taskbar and Adding a Gadget
(No file involved)

Steps	Tasks	Criterion/Criteria	Value	Score
1-2	**Options/ Accuracy**	Display Date and Time dialog, move time one hour ahead, close dialog	2	
3	**Command**	Increase volume by dragging Speaker slider bar	2	
4	**Command, Options & Customization**	Display Taskbar and Start Menu Properties dialog, change Taskbar location, close dialog	2	
5-6	**Command/ Customization**	Open Gadgets window & add gadget (user-selected), re-position, change options (user-selected)	4	
		TOTAL POINTS: 10		

Assessment 3: Restoring the Taskbar and Removing a Gadget
(No file involved)

Steps	Tasks	Criterion/Criteria	Value	Score
1	**Options/ Accuracy**	Display Date and Time dialog, change settings back to current date and time	3	
2-3	**Command**	Display Speakers slide bar and drag slider bar back to original position	2	
4	**Command/ Customization**	Remove gadgets added to the desktop	5	
		TOTAL POINTS: 10		

Windows 7 Section 2 Skills Reviews Grading Rubrics

Review 1: Browsing Devices and Changing the View
(No file involved)

Steps	Tasks	Criterion/Criteria	Value	Score
1-10	**Command, Accuracy & Options**	Open Computer window, change view to Large Icons, change folder option (open each folder in own window), display storage medium (user-selected), display WindowsS2 folder, change view to Details, close Windows S2 & storage medium windows, change folder option (open in same window), change view to Tiles, close Computer window	10	
		TOTAL POINTS: 10		

Review 2: Creating a Folder
(No file involved)

Steps	Tasks	Criterion/Criteria	Value	Score
1-5	**Command, Accuracy & Folder/File Management**	Open Computer window, display storage medium (user-selected), right-click in Content pane & use New to create folder, name folder, close window	5	
		TOTAL POINTS: 5		

Review 3: Selecting, Copying, Moving, and Deleting Files
FCTBookings.xlsx, FCTPackages.docx, WEExcelRevenues.xlsx, WERevChart.xlsx, FCTCCSkiing.docx, FCTNorwayTour.docx

Steps	Tasks	Criterion/Criteria	Value	Score
1-4	**Command, Accuracy & Options**	Open Computer window, display storage medium (user-selected), display WindowsS2 folder, change view to List	4	
5-14	**File/Folder Management, Accuracy, Command & Editing**	Click an Excel file, hold Shift & click a Word document, right-click group & Copy, click Back, open Worksheets folder by double-clicking, right-click & Paste, click Back, click an Excel file, hold Ctrl & click another Excel file, click Organize & click cut, click Back, open Worksheets folder by double-clicking, click Organize & click Paste	12	
15-18	**Accuracy, File/Folder Management & Editing**	Use right-down pointing arrow in Address bar to go to WindowsS2 folder, click Word document, hold Ctrl & click another Word document, press Delete & click Yes, close Computer window	4	
		TOTAL POINTS: 20		

Review 4: Renaming a File
WETable01.docx, WEPreviewDistribution.docx, WETable02.docx, WEGeneralDistribution.docx

Steps	Tasks	Criterion/Criteria	Value	Score
1-3	**Command/ Accuracy**	Open Computer window, display storage medium (user-selected), display WindowsS2 folder	3	
4-6	**File/Folder Management, Accuracy & Command**	Right-click Word document & rename, right-click another Word document & rename, close window	7	
		TOTAL POINTS: 10		

Review 5: Searching for Files
(No single specific file involved)

Steps	Tasks	Criterion/Criteria	Value	Score
1-2	**Command/ Accuracy**	Open Computer window, display storage medium (user-selected), display WindowsS2 folder	3	
3-6	**Command, Editing & Accuracy**	In Search text box use wildcard search (*rev*), press Esc to clear search, use wildcard search (*excel*), close Computer window	4	
7-9	**Command, Editing & Accuracy**	Click Start, use wildcard search (*word*), observe results, click desktop to close Start menu	3	
		TOTAL POINTS: 10		

Windows 7 Section 2 Skills Assessments Grading Rubrics

Assessment 1: Managing Folders and Files
PTExcelOctPayroll.xlsx, PTWordOctPayroll.docx, PTMarqueeLetter.docx, PTAGreement.docx, CostumeAgreement.docx

Steps	Tasks	Criterion/Criteria	Value	Score
1-9	**Folder/File Management, Options & Accuracy**	On storage medium (user-selected) create new folder, display WindowsS2 folder & change view to List (if necessary), copy all files beginning with "PT" to new folder & view new folder, create subfolder, move two files (Excel, Word) into new subfolder, delete file from first new folder, rename two files (Word) in first new folder	10	
		TOTAL POINTS: 10		

Assessment 2: Managing Folders and Files

FCTBookings.xlsx, FCTSalesCommissions.xlsx, FCTIslandFlights.docx, FCTPackages.docx

Steps	Tasks	Criterion/Criteria	Value	Score
1-11	**Folder/File Management, Options & Accuracy**	On storage medium (user-selected) create new folder, display WindowsS2 folder, copy all files beginning with "FCT" to FirstChoiceTravel folder, display that folder & change view to List, create two new subfolders, from FirstChoiceTravel folder move two Excel files to two different subfolders, move Back, delete a file, rename a file	15	
		TOTAL POINTS: 15		

Assessment 3: Managing Folders and Files

WEOutline.docx

Steps	Tasks	Criterion/Criteria	Value	Score
1-7	**Folder/File Management, Options & Accuracy**	On storage medium (user-selected) create new folder, display WindowsS2 folder, copy all files beginning with "WE" to new folder, display new folder & change view to List, delete a file, go Back, rename folder	10	
		TOTAL POINTS: 10		

Assessment 4: Deleting Folders and Files

(No file involved)

Steps	Tasks	Criterion/Criteria	Value	Score
1-4	**Folder/File Management & Accuracy**	On storage medium (user-selected) delete 3 folders	5	
		TOTAL POINTS: 5		

Assessment 5: Copying Folders from the Student CD to Your Device

(No specific file involved)

Steps	Tasks	Criterion/Criteria	Value	Score
1-8	**Folder/File Management & Accuracy**	Display contents of Marquee student CD & contents of Word folder in Content pane, select all subfolders & copy to storage medium (user-selected), display contents of Excel folder & copy subfolders to Excel folder on storage medium, go through same process for Access & PowerPoint folders, copy AudioandVideo folder to storage medium, display & copy all subfolders of Integrating to storage medium	15	
		TOTAL POINTS: 15		

Assessment 6: Searching for Information on User Accounts
WS2-UserAccounts.docx

Steps	Tasks	Criterion/Criteria	Value	Score
1-3	**Research & Folder/File Management**	Use Help and Support to learn about user accounts, create new folder on storage medium	3	
4-6	**Writing, Editing, Organization & Finishing**	Create memo on research describing different user accounts & making recommendation, save & print	7	
		TOTAL POINTS: 10		

Assessment 7: Searching for Information on Windows Libraries
WS2Libraries.docx

Steps	Tasks	Criterion/Criteria	Value	Score
1-3	**Research, Writing & Editing**	After using Help and Support to learn about Windows libraries create memo that addresses Step 3a-3d	7	
4-5	**Organization/ Finishing**	Save & print memo	3	
		TOTAL POINTS: 10		

Internet Explorer 8 Skills Reviews Grading Rubrics

Review 1: Browsing the Internet and Navigating with Hyperlinks
(No file involved)

Steps	Tasks	Criterion/Criteria	Value	Score
1-2	**Command/ Accuracy**	Open Internet Explorer, navigate to Smithsonian	2	
3-5	**Accuracy/ Navigation**	Click two separate links to read topics (user-selected), click Back button to Smithsonian home page	3	
		TOTAL POINTS: 5		

Review 2: Searching for Specific Sites
(No file involved)

Steps	Tasks	Criterion/Criteria	Value	Score
1-2	**Research / Searching**	In IE, use Instant Search to look for mountain climbing websites, click link from results (user-selected)	3	
3-4	**Navigation, Searching & Accuracy**	Navigate to Yahoo!, use advanced search options for .com's on mountain climbing in B.C., Canada & visit at least two sites of interest (user-selected)	7	
		TOTAL POINTS: 10		

Review 3: Downloading Content from a Web Page
ParasailImage1.gif or ParasailImage1.jpg, HawaiiMap1.gif or HawaiiMap1.jpg

Steps	Tasks	Criterion/Criteria	Value	Score
1-5	**Research, Searching & Command**	Use favorite search engine to search for sites on parasailing in Hawaii to find a site that has parasailing image preferred (user-selected), download to desktop and save with specific name; search for maps of Hawaii, browse images found & download one to desktop to save with specific name, close IE	10	
		TOTAL POINTS: 10		

Internet Explorer 8 Skills Assessments Grading Rubrics

Assessment 1: Visiting Web Pages for Current News Articles
(No file involved)

Steps	Tasks	Criterion/Criteria	Value	Score
1-5	**Research/ Navigation**	Go to N Y Times website, scan headlines for today's publication, click link to interesting article (user-selected) & read; go to USA Today site, click link to interesting article (user-selected) & read	5	
		TOTAL POINTS: 5		

Assessment 2: Navigating Websites for Theatre Programs
(No file involved)

Steps	Tasks	Criterion/Criteria	Value	Score
1-4	**Research/ Navigation**	Go to York University's website, locate page for Theatre Department & read about the program; go to New York University's site, use NYU A-Z search in About section, locate page for Department of Drama & read about program, click links to detail pages	**10**	
		TOTAL POINTS: 10		

Assessment 3: Downloading Content on Ski Resorts
UtahResortImage1.gif or UtahResortImage1.jpg

Steps	Tasks	Criterion/Criteria	Value	Score
1-2	**Research / Searching**	Visit website of interest that contains image of resort or mountains (user-selected)	**2**	
3-4	**Command**	Download image to desktop & save with specific name, close IE	**3**	
		TOTAL POINTS: 5		

Assessment 4: Deleting Downloaded Content on the Desktop
(UtahResortImage1.gif or UtahResortImage1.jpg)

Steps	Tasks	Criterion/Criteria	Maximum Value	Score*
1-2	**Folder/File Management & Accuracy**	At Windows 7 desktop, right-click image saved, show shortcut menu & delete (answer Yes to dialog), delete all other downloaded files saved to desktop	**5**	
		TOTAL POINTS: 5		

Word Section 1 Skills Reviews Grading Rubrics

Review 1: Editing a Hawaiian Specials Document
WS1-R1-FCTHawaiianSpecials.docx

Steps	Tasks	Criterion/Criteria	Value	Score
1	**Folder/File Management**	Create folder	2	
2	**Organization**	Open Document, use Save As	2	
3-4	**Typing**	Type text (word, sentence)	3	
5-10	**Editing**	Select and delete text & bullet point, use Undo	4	
11	**Accuracy**	Spelling and grammar check	2	
12-13	**Editing**	Create and use AutoCorrect entry	3	
14	**Editing/Feature**	Use Thesaurus to change two words	2	
15	**Organization**	Re-save, print, and close document	2	
		TOTAL POINTS: 20		

Review 2: Editing an Agreement
WS1-R2-WEIncentiveAgt.docx

Steps	Tasks	Criterion/Criteria	Value	Score
1	**Organization**	Open document, use Save As	2	
2	**Accuracy**	Spelling and grammar check	2	
3-4	**Editing**	Use Replace for two different words	4	
5	**Organization**	Re-save, print, and close document	2	
		TOTAL POINTS: 10		

Review 3: Preparing a Fax Sheet
WS1-R3-WEAftFax.docx

Steps	Tasks	Criterion / Criteria	Value	Score
1	**Feature**	Use specific Word template	3	
2	**Typing / Accuracy**	Type text in specific template fields, type text in placeholder	5	
3-4	**Organization**	Re-save, print, and close document	2	
		TOTAL POINTS: 10		

Word Section 1 Skills Assessments Grading Rubrics

Assessment 1: Editing a Letter
WS1-A1-PTMarqueeLtr.docx

Steps	Tasks	Criterion/Criteria	Value	Score
1	**Organization**	Open document, use Save As	2	
2	**Writing**	Write paragraph of text based on bullet points	9	
3	**Editing / Feature**	Use Thesaurus to replace a word	2	
4	**Organization**	Re-save, print, and close document	2	
		TOTAL POINTS: 15		

Assessment 2: Writing a Letter
WS1-A2-WBCatering.docx

Steps	Tasks	Criterion/Criteria	Value	Score
1	**Feature**	Use specific Word template	3	
1	**Writing**	Write a letter based on points shown in paragraph	8	
2	**Organization**	re-save, print, and close document	4	
		TOTAL POINTS: 15		

Assessment 3: Preparing a Fax
WS1-A3-WBFax.docx

Steps	Tasks	Criterion/Criteria	Value	Score
1	**Feature**	Use specific Word template	3	
1	**Typing/ Accuracy**	Type text in specific template fields, type text in placeholder	8	
2	**Organization**	Re-save, print, and close document	4	
		TOTAL POINTS: 15		

Assessment 4: Finding Information on Changing Grammar Checking Options
WS1-A4-FCTNorwayTour.docx

Steps	Tasks	Criterion/Criteria	Value	Score
1	**Organization**	Open document, use Save As	2	
2 & 4	**Feature**	Change a Word Proofing Option	4	
3	**Accuracy**	Spelling and grammar check	2	
5	**Organization**	Re-save, print, and close document	2	
		TOTAL POINTS: 10		

Assessment 5: Individual Challenge (Creating a Certificate)
WS1-A5-IC-Membership.docx

Steps	Tasks	Criterion/Criteria	Value	Score
1	**Feature**	Use specific Word template	3	
2	**Typing**	Type text in specific template fields	5	
2	**Organization**	re-save, print, and close document	2	
		TOTAL POINTS: 10		

Word Section 1 Marquee Challenges Grading Rubrics

Challenge 1: Preparing a Business Letter
WS1-C1-MPLtrtoWB.docx

Steps	Tasks	Criterion/Criteria	Value	Score
1	**Organization**	Open document, use Save As	**2**	
2	**Typing/ Accuracy**	Type/reproduce letter shown (Figure 1.6) accurately	**4**	
3	**Accuracy / Organization**	Spelling and grammar check (not a *required* step), and re-save, print, and close document	**4**	
		TOTAL POINTS: 10		

Challenge 2: Editing and Formatting a Travel Document
WS1-C2-FCTRenoTahoeVac.docx

Steps	Tasks	Criterion/Criteria	Value	Score
1	**Organization**	Open document, use Save As	**2**	
2	**Formatting**	Use Word formatting features to display document as shown in Fig. 1.7	**5**	
2	**Editing**	Use Replace for two words (incl. using More button)	**4**	
2	**Accuracy**	Spelling and grammar check	**2**	
3	**Organization**	Re-save, print, and close document	**2**	
		TOTAL POINTS: 15		

Word Section 2 Skills Reviews Grading Rubrics

Review 1: Formatting a Petersburg, Alaska, Document
WS2-R1-FCTPetersburg.docx

Steps	Tasks	Criterion/Criteria	Value	Score
1	**Organization**	Open Document, use Save As	2	
2-3	**Formatting**	Select document, change font size and color, change title to specific font	3	
4	**Formatting**	Change heading font, use Format Painter	2	
5	**Formatting**	Use Font dialog to apply effect	2	
6	**Formatting**	Apply text effect	2	
7-8	**Formatting**	Change alignment of two paragraphs	2	
9	**Formatting**	Change alignment and indent paragraph, use Format Painter on several paragraphs	3	
10	**Formatting, Typing & Command**	Use Enter key, change alignment, typing, use commands to insert date and time	5	
11-13	**Formatting & Command**	Select document, alter line spacing, alter paragraph spacing, use Repeat command	5	
14	**Formatting**	Insert page border	2	
15	**Organization**	Re-save, print, and close document	2	
		TOTAL POINTS: 30		

Review 2: Formatting a Vacation Package Document
WS2-R2-FCTVacPackages.docx

Steps	Tasks	Criterion/Criteria	Value	Score
1	**Organization**	Open Document, use Save As	2	
2	**Formatting**	Select document, change line & paragraph spacing	2	
3-4	**Formatting/ Command**	Select two different sets of paragraphs, use Indent, apply bullets	4	
5-6	**Editing**	Use Replace twice (with More) to replace fonts	3	
7	**Typing/ Command**	Type text (and insert symbols)	2	
8-9	**Formatting/ Typing**	Set tabs and type two sets of tabular data	4	
10-11	**Formatting**	Select two separate sets of tabular data and apply borders and shading	2	
12-13	**Formatting**	Apply Heading style to different text	2	
14	**Formatting**	Change Quick Style, apply paragraph spacing style	2	
15	**Organization**	Re-save, print, and close document	2	
		TOTAL POINTS: 25		

Word Section 2 Skills Assessments Grading Rubrics

Assessment 1: Formatting a Cross Country Skiing Document
WS2-A1-FCTLakeTahoeSkiing.docx

Steps	Tasks	Criterion/Criteria	Value	Score
1	**Organization**	Open Document, use Save As	2	
2a-2c	**Formatting**	Change font in three places	3	
2d-2f	**Formatting**	Change line and paragraph spacing, different places	3	
2g	**Formatting**	Indent and change alignment, several paragraphs	3	
2h	**Formatting**	Center title, apply shading	2	
2i	**Formatting**	Apply shading & insert border, several places	3	
2j	**Formatting**	Insert specific page border	2	
3	**Organization**	Re-save, print, and close document	2	
		TOTAL POINTS: 20		

Assessment 2: Preparing and Formatting a Letter
WS2-A2-MPLtrtoNPC.docx

Steps	Tasks	Criterion/Criteria	Value	Score
1	**Organization**	Open Document, use Save As	2	
2	**Writing**	Write a (properly formatted) business letter, using information provided	8	
3	**Formatting**	Change font for entire letter, justify align paragraphs	3	
4	**Organization**	Re-save, print, and close document	2	
		TOTAL POINTS: 15		

Assessment 3: Setting Leader Tabs
WS2-A3-WEDistSch.docx

Steps	Tasks	Criterion/Criteria	Value	Score
1	**Typing**	Type title text as shown	2	
1a	**Formatting**	Use center, bold, and italics	2	
1b	**Formatting/ Typing**	Set tabs, type tabbed text	6	
1c	**Formatting**	Change font, change paragraph spacing	3	
2-3	**Organization**	Save as, print, and close document	2	
		TOTAL POINTS: 15		

Assessment 4: Finding Information on Controlling Page Breaks
WS2-A4-PageBreaks.docx), WS2-A4-FCTVacSpecials.docx

Steps	Tasks	Criterion/Criteria	Value	Score
1-2	**Research/ Writing**	After using Help, create document that includes a title and three paragraphs (Steps 2b, 2c, 2d)	**5**	
3	**Formatting**	Format to enhance document appeal (user-chosen)	**4**	
4-5	**Organization**	Save as, print, and close document	**2**	
6-7	**Organization**	Open Document, use Save As	**2**	
8	**Formatting**	Select document, change font	**2**	
9-10	**Editing**	Use Replace in two separate operations	**2**	
11	**Accuracy**	Spelling and grammar check	**2**	
12	**Formatting/ Command**	Select heading & text, use widow/orphan command	**4**	
13-14	**Organization**	Save as, print specific page, close document	**2**	
		TOTAL POINTS: 25		

Assessment 5: Individual Challenge (Creating a Document with Tabbed Text)
WS2-A5-IC-Airfare.docx

Steps	Tasks	Criterion/Criteria	Value	Score
1-2	**Research, Formatting & Writing**	Use Internet to research airlines/airfare, set tabs, type data in tabular format	**8**	
3	**Writing/ Formatting**	Create heading, apply paragraph border and/or shading	**3**	
4	**Formatting**	Apply page border	**2**	
5-6	**Organization**	Save as, print, and close document	**2**	
		TOTAL POINTS: 15		

Word Section 2 Marquee Challenges Grading Rubrics

Challenge 1: Editing and Formatting a Document on Juneau, Alaska
WS2-C1-FCTJuneau.docx

Steps	Tasks	Criterion/Criteria	Value	Score
1	**Organization**	Open Document, use Save As	2	
2	**Formatting**	Apply Heading styles, change Quick Styles set, color and font	3	
3	**Formatting**	Use Word formatting commands to display document as shown in Fig. 2.10	6	
4	**Accuracy/ Organization**	Spelling and grammar check (*not required*), re-save, print, and close document	4	
		TOTAL POINTS: 15		

Challenge 1: Creating and Formatting a Flyer about a Skiing Vacation Package
WS2-C2-FCTSkiTahoe.docx

Steps	Tasks	Criterion/Criteria	Value	Score
1	**Typing/ Formatting**	Type document shown in Fig. 2.11, apply specific formatting (font, page border, paragraph spacing, and bullets)	6	
2-3	**Accuracy/ Organization**	Spelling and grammar check (*not required*), re-save, print, and close document	4	
		TOTAL POINTS: 10		

Word Section 3 Skills Reviews Grading Rubrics

Review 1: Formatting a Fact Sheet on Juneau, Alaska
WS3-R1-FCTJuneau.docx

Steps	Tasks	Criterion/Criteria	Value	Score
1	**Organization**	Open Document, use Save As	2	
2	**Formatting**	Select document, change to No Spacing style	2	
3-4	**Editing**	Use Replace twice	2	
5-6	**Editing**	Select & move two sets of paragraphs	2	
7-8	**Organization/ Editing**	Open a second document, display Clipboard task pane	2	
9-11	**Editing**	Three select & copy operations involving paragraphs, headings, and columns	4	
12-18	**Organization/ Editing**	Switch to original document, perform three distinct paste operations, clear Clipboard task pane, close second document	5	
19	**Formatting**	Change all margins	2	
20-21	**Formatting**	Apply Heading 1 Heading styles (several instances)	4	
22	**Formatting**	Change to Quick Style, apply paragraph style	2	
23	**Formatting**	Apply theme	2	
24-25	**Formatting/ Typing**	Insert page numbering style (header), and footer (and type first and last name)	3	
26	**Formatting**	Insert watermark	2	
27	**Formatting/ Command**	Select heading & text, use widow/orphan command	4	
28	**Organization**	Re-save, print, and close document	2	
		TOTAL POINTS: 40		

Review 2: Formatting a Document in MLA Style

WS3-R2-PTRenaissanceRpt.docx

Steps	Tasks	Criterion/Criteria	Value	Score
1	**Organization/ Accuracy**	Open Document & Save As, ensure MLA style selected	3	
3	**Formatting**	Select document, change font, line spacing, and paragraph spacing	3	
4	**Typing**	Type name and other text, top of document	2	
5	**Formatting**	Insert header, change font	3	
6-7	**Typing**	Type text at two specific places in document	2	
8	**Formatting/ Command**	Insert works cited page, end of document	2	
9-10	**Editing/ Command**	Change a source, update works cited page	3	
11	**Formatting**	Perform several steps (paragraph spacing, font, line spacing, centering, indenting) on works cited page	5	
12	**Organization**	Re-save, print, and close document	2	
		TOTAL POINTS: 25		

Review 3: Preparing and Formatting an Announcement

WS3-R3-MPEmpOpps01.docx, WS3-R3-MPEmpOpps02.docx

Steps	Tasks	Criterion/Criteria	Value	Score
1	**Formatting/ Typing**	In blank document, use Click and Type, type text shown (Fig. 3.5)	3	
2-3	**Formatting**	Select two different sets of text, change font	3	
4	**Formatting/ Command**	Change vertical alignment	2	
5-7	**Organization/ Finishing**	Save & print document, re-save under new name	2	
8	**Formatting/ Command**	Change vertical alignment	2	
9	**Formatting**	Insert, size & position user-chosen clip art image	3	
10	**Editing/ Formatting**	Delete text, insert and size & position specific image	3	
11	**Organization**	Re-save, print, and close document	2	
		TOTAL POINTS: 20		

Review 4: Preparing an Envelope

WS3-R4-FCTEnv.docx

Steps	Tasks	Criterion/Criteria	Value	Score
1	**Command/ Typing**	In blank document, insert envelope & type specific text	3	
2	**Organization**	Save, print, and close envelope document	2	
		TOTAL POINTS: 5		

Review 5: Preparing Mailing Labels

WS3-R5-WELabels.docx

Steps	Tasks	Criterion/Criteria	Value	Score
1	**Command/ Typing**	In blank document, insert/prepare sheet of labels using specific labels option, type text	3	
2	**Organization**	Re-save, print, and close labels document	2	
		TOTAL POINTS: 5		

Word Section 3 Skills Assessments Grading Rubrics

Assessment 1: Formatting a Costume Rental Agreement

WS3-A1-PTAgreement.docx

Steps	Tasks	Criterion/Criteria	Value	Score
1	**Organization**	Open Document, use Save As	2	
2	**Editing**	Use Replace command	2	
3	**Editing/ Formatting**	Move a section of text & renumber it	2	
4	**Formatting**	Select document, change font	2	
5	**Formatting**	Change top margin	2	
6	**Formatting/ Typing**	Insert specific footer, type first & last name	3	
7	**Organization**	Re-save, print, and close document	2	
		TOTAL POINTS: 15		

Assessment 2: Creating an Announcement

WS3-A2-NPCInternship.docx

Steps	Tasks	Criterion/Criteria	Value	Score
1	**Typing**	In blank document, type text shown in Fig. 3.6	3	
2	**Formatting**	Change font, font size, font colour (user-chosen)	4	
3	**Formatting**	Change line spacing for document	2	
4	**Formatting**	Insert, size & position user-chosen clip art image	4	
5	**Organization**	Re-save, print, and close document	2	
		TOTAL POINTS: 15		

Assessment 3: Preparing Mailing Labels

WS3-A3-NPCLabels.docx

Steps	Tasks	Criterion/Criteria	Value	Score
1	**Command/ Typing**	In blank document, insert/prepare sheet of labels (user-chosen), type text	3	
5	**Organization**	Re-save, print, and close labels document	2	
		TOTAL POINTS: 5		

Assessment 4: Finding Information on Creating a Picture Watermark

WS3-A4-MPEmpOpps.docx

Steps	Tasks	Criterion/Criteria	Value	Score
1	**Organization**	Open Document, use Save As	2	
2-3	**Research/ Formatting**	After using Help, insert specific image as watermark	6	
4	**Organization**	Re-save, print, and close document	2	
		TOTAL POINTS: 10		

Assessment 5: Individual Challenge (Creating a Personal Letterhead)
WS3-A5-IC-Ltrhd.docx

Steps	Tasks	Criterion/Criteria	Value	Score
1	**Typing/ Formatting**	In blank document, create letterhead containing name & contact info, a clip art image (user-chosen) positioned and sized, and font (user-chosen). May optionally create this in a header.	8	
2-3	**Organization**	Save as, print, and close document	2	
		TOTAL POINTS: 10		

Word Section 3 Marquee Challenges Grading Rubrics

Challenge 1: Formatting a Costume Document
WS3-C1-PTCostumes.docx

Steps	Tasks	Criterion/Criteria	Value	Score
1	**Organization**	Open Document, use Save As	2	
2	**Formatting**	Apply specific formatting as shown in Fig. 3.7, including: Heading style, shading, changing top margin, inserting, sizing & positioning specific image, altering paragraph alignment, other formatting (shown in Fig. 3.7, but not specified)	9	
3	**Accuracy / Organization**	Spelling and grammar check (*not required*), re-save, print, and close document	4	
		TOTAL POINTS: 15		

Challenge 2: Preparing an Announcement
WS3-C2-WENotice.docx

Steps	Tasks	Criterion/Criteria	Value	Score
1	**Typing/ Formatting**	In blank document, create document shown in Fig. 3.8, including: changing page orientation, inserting & setting background colour of specific image to transparent, using Shift + Enter, inserting user-chosen clip art image & setting background colour to transparent, inserting watermark, page border & using page color as shown in Fig. 3.8	11	
2	**Accuracy/ Organization**	Spelling and grammar check (*not required*), re-save, print, and close document	4	
		TOTAL POINTS: 15		

Word Section 4 Skills Reviews Grading Rubrics

Review 1: Formatting a First Choice Travel Document
WS4-R1-FCTZenithAdv.docx

Steps	Tasks	Criterion/Criteria	Value	Score
1	**Organization**	Open Document, use Save As	2	
2	**Formatting**	Apply theme, change theme fonts	2	
3	**Command**	Insert file name	2	
4-6	**Formatting**	Position in table, change width of several columns; Apply table style and adjust how it's applied to three tables in total	6	
7-8	**Formatting**	Apply specific style to four headings	4	
9	**Feature, Typing & Formatting**	Insert specific style of WordArt, format WordArt (size, positioning, Text Effects)	5	
10-11	**Editing/ Formatting**	Insert section break in specific position; Create newspaper columns with specific settings	4	
12-13	**Formatting, Feature & Typing**	Insert specific building block object, type text, adjust height of text box	4	
14-15	**Formatting**	Select all text in box, turn off bold, change outline	3	
16	**Formatting/ Command**	Create drop cap from first letter, change font color	3	
17	**Formatting**	Balance columns by inserting section break	2	
18-19	**Formatting**	Move insertion point, change back to one column	2	
20	**Command/ Formatting & Typing**	Insert/draw shape, change its size, position it, change shape style, type specified text	4	
21	**Organization**	Re-save, print, and close document	2	
		TOTAL POINTS: 45		

Review 2: Preparing and Formatting an Organizational Chart and Graphic
WS4-R2-MPProdDept.docx

Steps	Tasks	Criterion/Criteria	Value	Score
1	**Organization**	Open Document, use Save As	2	
2	**Feature, Formatting & Typing**	At end of document, create specific SmartArt chart and change its style, color, size, text-wrapping, and position, type text shown in Fig. 4.7	8	
3	**Feature, Formatting & Typing**	At end of document, create specific SmartArt graphic and change its style, color, size, text-wrapping, and position, type text shown in Fig. 4.8	6	
4	**Formatting**	Fine-tune both graphic images fit on one page	2	
5	**Organization**	Re-save, print, and close document	2	
		TOTAL POINTS: 20		

Review 3: Preparing, Modifying, and Formatting a Table
WS4-R3-NPCFallSch.docx

Steps	Tasks	Criterion/Criteria	Value	Score
1-2	**Command/ Typing**	In blank document, create table, type text in Fig. 4.9	5	
3	**Formatting/ Typing**	Insert new column, type text	2	
4-5	**Formatting/ Typing**	Insert new (first) row, merge cells, type & format text	4	
6	**Formatting**	Select row, bold & center text	2	
7	**Formatting**	Decrease width of cells to look like Fig. 4.10	2	
8	**Formatting**	Alter options in Table Styles Options group	2	
9	**Formatting**	Apply table style	2	
10	**Formatting**	Select first row, change font size, apply bold	2	
11	**Formatting**	Horizontally center table	2	
12-13	**Organization**	Re-save, print, and close document	2	
		TOTAL POINTS: 25		

Review 4: Saving a Document as a Web Page; Inserting a Hyperlink
WS4-R4-FCTOslo.docx, WS4-R4-FCTOslo.mht

Steps	Tasks	Criterion/Criteria	Value	Score
1	**Organization**	Open Document, use Save As	2	
2	**Formatting**	Change bottom margin	2	
3	**Formatting**	Apply Solstice theme	2	
4	**Formatting**	Apply Title style, apply Heading 2 style (8 instances)	5	
5	**Formatting/ Command**	Move insertion point, insert section break, insert/ create columns (line in-between)	4	
6-7	**Organization**	Save & print document, use Save As to save as single file web page	4	
8	**Typing**	Move insertion point, type text	2	
9	**Formatting/ Command**	Create/insert hyperlink using typed text	4	
10-11	**Feature/ Research**	Ctrl-click new hyperlink, explore website	3	
12	**Organization**	Re-save, print, and close single file webpage	2	
		TOTAL POINTS: 30		

Review 5: Merging Letters and Envelopes
**WS4-R5-PTDataSource.docx, WS4-R5-PTFabricLtrMD.docx,
WS4-R5-PTMergedFabricLtrs.docx, WS4-R5-PTMergedEnvs.docx**

Steps	Tasks	Criterion/Criteria	Value	Score
1	**Typing**	In blank document, create data source with data as shown (user chooses fields not to use)	2	
2-3	**Organization**	Save data source document, open and re-save second document	4	
4	**Accuracy**	Specify specific (Access) file as data source	2	
5-6	**Accuracy/ Typing**	Insert specific fields at specific locations, type text	4	
7	**Feature**	Merge documents to new document	2	
8	**Organization/ Finishing**	Use Save As for new document, print and close, save and close second document	4	
9	**Feature**	Create envelope, merge (Access) file to it	3	
10	**Organization / Finishing**	Use Save As for new document, print and close	2	
11	**Organization**	Close (don't save) envelope document	2	
		TOTAL POINTS: 25		

Word Section 4 Skills Assessments Grading Rubrics

Assessment 1: Formatting a Theatre Arts Division Newsletter
WS4-A1-NPCTheatreNewsltr.docx

Steps	Tasks	Criterion/Criteria	Value	Score
1	**Organization**	Open Document, use Save As	2	
2	**Command**	Move insertion point, insert second document	2	
3	**Formatting**	Apply Flow theme	2	
4	**Formatting/ Command**	Insert section break, insert/create columns	2	
5	**Formatting**	Apply style to three headings	3	
6	**Feature/ Formatting**	Position insertion point, create WordArt with specific text, format and layout WordArt (user-chosen), change size and position/wrapping of WordArt	5	
7	**Feature, Typing & Formatting**	Insert Quick Part text box, type text, change font size, apply style to text box	5	
8	**Formatting**	Move insertion point, insert continuous break	2	
9	**Organization**	Re-save, print, and close document	2	
		TOTAL POINTS: 25		

Assessment 2: Creating an Organization Chart
WS4-A2-PTDesignDept.docx

Steps	Tasks	Criterion/Criteria	Value	Score
1	**Organization**	Open Document, use Save As	2	
2	**Command/ Typing**	Move insertion point, insert/create specific SmartArt object, type text	5	
3	**Formatting**	Apply formatting and design (user-chosen), change text wrapping	3	
4	**Command/ Typing**	Move insertion point, insert/create specific SmartArt object, type text	4	
5	**Formatting/ Editing**	Apply formatting and design (user-chosen), change text wrapping, move object	2	
6	**Formatting**	Fine-tune both graphic images fit on one page	2	
7	**Organization**	Re-save, print, and close document	2	
		TOTAL POINTS: 20		

Assessment 3: Creating a Table for the Waterfront Bistro

WS4-A3-WBLunchOptions.docx

Steps	Tasks	Criterion/Criteria	Value	Score
1	**Organization**	In blank document, create table & type text (Fig. 4.11)	3	
2	**Formatting**	Apply design and layout to enhance (user-chosen)	3	
3	**Formatting**	Horizontally center table	2	
7	**Organization**	Re-save, print, and close document	2	
		TOTAL POINTS: 10		

Assessment 4: Finding Information on Flipping and Copying Objects

WS4-A4-WEStockholderMtg.docx

Steps	Tasks	Criterion/Criteria	Value	Score
1-2	**Research, Command, Typing, Formatting**	After using Help, create document shown in Fig. 4.12, including: inserting specific image, inserting and formatting a Shape, copying/ pasting and formatting a copied Shape	8	
3-4	**Organization**	Save, print, and close document	2	
		TOTAL POINTS: 10		

Assessment 5: Individual Challenge (Locating Information and Creating a Table)

WS4-A5-IC-CarRentalInfo.docx

Steps	Tasks	Criterion/Criteria	Value	Score
1-2	**Research, Command, Typing, Formatting**	After research on the Internet, create a table in new document outlining information on car rentals, modify and format table to make attractive and easy to read	8	
3-4	**Organization**	Save, print, and close document	2	
		TOTAL POINTS: 10		

Word Section 4 Marquee Challenges Grading Rubrics

Challenge 1: Formatting a Document on Orcas Island
WS4-C1-FCTOrcasIsland.docx

Steps	Tasks	Criterion/Criteria	Value	Score
1	**Organization**	Open Document, use Save As	**2**	
2	**Formatting, Command**	Apply specific formatting and use commands as shown in Fig. 4.13, including: changing theme, using Heading 2 style, applying/inserting columns, creating and formatting a drop cap, creating, formatting and positioning WordArt, inserting, formatting and positioning specific clip art image, balancing columns	**9**	
3	**Accuracy/ Organization**	Spelling and grammar check (*not required*), re-save, print, and close document	**4**	
		TOTAL POINTS: 15		

Challenge 2: Preparing a Flier for the Waterfront Bistro
WS4-C2-WBFlier.docx

Steps	Tasks	Criterion/Criteria	Value	Score
1	**Command, Typing & Formatting**	In a blank document, create document shown in Fig. 4.14, including: inserting and formatting specific image, changing font & font color, inserting artistic page border, inserting & formatting border, applying other formatting as desired (user-chosen)	**10**	
3	**Formatting, Accuracy & Organization**	Adjust Borders and Shading options if necessary, spelling and grammar check (*not required*), re-save, print, and close document	**5**	
		TOTAL POINTS: 15		

Excel Section 1 Skills Reviews Grading Rubrics

Review 1: Creating Labels, Values, and Formulas
ES1-R1-WBQtrlyIncome.xlsx

Steps	Tasks	Criterion/Criteria	Value	Score
1	**Folder/File Management**	Create folder named Excel EOS	2	
2	**Creating/ Typing**	Create worksheet, text indented in Row 8, 13, and 17	4	
3	**Formatting**	Accounting Number cell format E6:H17	1	
4	**Creating Formulas**	Create formulas E8 =e6-e7 E13 =sum(e10:e12) E15 =e8-e13 E16 =e15*22% E17 =e15-e16	5	
5	**Copying**	Copy and paste as directed from column E to F and G	3	
6 & 7	**Creating Formulas**	Use AutoSum feature in H6 for E6:G6, copy down	3	
8	**Organization**	Save file as ES1-R1-WBQtrlyIncome.xlsx in Excel EOS folder	2	
		TOTAL POINTS: 20		

Review 2: Improving the Appearance of the Worksheet; Previewing and Printing
ES1-R1-WBQtrlyIncome.xlsx

Steps	Tasks	Criterion/Criteria	Value	Score
1-3	**Modifying Worksheet**	Merge and center A through H, E5:H5 aligned right	2	
4	**Using Help**	Search for info on changing decimal places	1	
5	**Formatting**	Cells E6:H17 one decimal place	1	
6 & 7	**Printing in Backstage View**	Worksheet printed with changes	2	
8	**Printing**	Worksheet printed with cell formulas displayed	2	
9 & 10	**Organization**	Save file as ES1-R1-WBQtrlyIncome.xlsx in Excel EOS folder	2	
		TOTAL POINTS: 10		

Excel Section 1 Skills Assessments Grading Rubrics

Assessment 1: Adding Values and Formulas to a Worksheet
ES1-A1-MPTravelCosts.xlsx

Steps	Tasks	Criterion/Criteria	Value	Score
1	**Organization**	Open file from folder, rename file	2	
2 & 3	**Entering Data**	Values from data entered under Unit Cost	6	
4 & 5	**Creating Formulas**	Formulas for extended cost in column G, sum in G10	4	
6	**Formatting**	Formatting selected to improve appearance	2	
7	**Organization**	Save file as ES1-A1-MPTravelCosts.xlsx, printed copy	1	
		TOTAL POINTS: 15		

Assessment 2: Creating a New Workbook
ES1-A2-PTCostumeCont.xlsx

Steps	Tasks	Criterion/Criteria	Value	Score
1	**Organization, Entering Data & Creating Formulas**	Create new workbook using Table 1.3, formulas show projected revenue	10	
2	**Formatting**	Formatting selected to improve appearance	5	
3	**Using Features**	Cities sorted ascending	2	
4 & 5	**Organization**	Save ES1-A2-PTCostumeCont.xlsx in Excel EOS folder, print	3	
		TOTAL POINTS: 20		

Assessment 3: Creating a New Workbook
ES1-A3-WEGGProjRev.xlsx

Steps	Tasks	Criterion/Criteria	Value	Score
1 & 2	**File Management, Entering Data & Creating Formulas**	Create new workbook using information, contract price calculated formulas show projected revenue, total summed below rental and alteration fees	5	
3	**Formatting**	Formatting selected to improve appearance	2	
4 & 5	**Organization**	Save ES1-A3-WEGGProjRev.xlsx in Excel EOS folder, print	3	
		TOTAL POINTS: 10		

Assessment 4: Finding Information on Sorting
ES1-A4-WBInventory.xlsx

Steps	Tasks	Criterion/Criteria	Value	Score
1-4	**Using Help, File Management & Using Features**	Search Help for info, open file from folder, sort items ascending, rename file, print	6	
5 & 6	**Using Features**	Sort supplier name ascending, print	2	
7	**Organization**	Save ES1-A4-WBInventory.xlsx	2	
		TOTAL POINTS: 10		

Assessment 5: Creating a School Budget
ES1-A5-SchoolBudget.xlsx

Steps	Tasks	Criterion/Criteria	Value	Score
1 & 2	**Using Search Engines, Entering Data & Using Formulas**	Estimated budgetary items organized logically, totalled using sum, save file	5	
3	**Formatting**	Worksheet enhanced with formatting	3	
4 & 5	**Organization**	Print (possibly landscaped), save ES1-A5-SchoolBudget.xlsx	2	
		TOTAL POINTS: 10		

Excel Section 1 Marquee Challenges Grading Rubrics

Challenge 1: Preparing an International Student Registration Report
ES1-C1-NPCIntlRegRpt.xlsx

Steps	Tasks	Criterion/Criteria	Value	Score
1	**Entering Data**	Information from Figure 1.4 entered correctly	5	
2	**Using Formulas**	Column I contains tuition fees, totalled using SUM	3	
3	**Formatting**	Column I contains appropriate number format	2	
4	**Entering Data**	Current date row 4, name row 19	2	
5	**Using Features**	Page orientation landscaped	1	
6 & 7	**Organization**	Save ES1-C1-NPCIntlRegRpt.xlsx in Excel EOS folder, print	2	
		TOTAL POINTS: 15		

Challenge 2: Preparing a Theatre Arts Target Enrollment Report
ES1-C2-NPCTargetEnrolRpt.xlsx

Steps	Tasks	Criterion/Criteria	Value	Score
1	**Entering Data**	Information from Figure 1.5 entered correctly	5	
2 & 3	**Using Formulas**	Column titled target contains formula projecting target enrolment, totalled using SUM	3	
4 & 5	**Formatting/ Using Features**	Aligned as directed, name in row 8, date in row 9, format Target column zero decimal places, landscaped page	5	
6 & 7	**Organization**	Save ES1-C2-NPCTargetEnrolRpt.xlsx in Excel EOS folder, print	2	
		TOTAL POINTS: 15		

Excel Section 2 Skills Reviews Grading Rubrics

Review 1: Editing, Moving, Copying, and Clearing Cells; Performing a Spell Check;
Inserting and Deleting Rows
ES2-R1-WBInvToNPC.xlsx

Steps	Tasks	Criterion/Criteria	Value	Score
1	**Organization**	Open file, rename, save in Excel EOS	**3**	
2 & 3	**Editing**	15.23 in D20, no content in A8, A21 French Onion Soup	**3**	
4	**Typing**	E14--PO No., F14--TA-11-643	**2**	
5-10	**Editing/Deleting**	Rows 7, 8, 9 deleted No misspellings E7:F7 moved to E10:F10. A24 copied to A30 Rows labeled Milk and Donuts deleted Seafood Pasta added in row A after Prime Rib	**6**	
11	**Organization**	Save ES2-R1-WBInvToNPC.xlsx	**1**	
		TOTAL POINTS: 15		

Review 2: Adjusting Column Widths; Replacing Data; Moving Cells; Applying Formatting Features; Inserting a Picture

ES2-R1-WBInvToNPC.xlsx

Steps	Tasks	Criterion/Criteria	Value	Score
1-3	**Editing**	Column A width 10.00,C Autofit, D 15.00, E 7.00	**4**	
4	**Using Search and Replace**	All occurrences of 32 replaced with 36	**1**	
5	**Creating Formulas**	SUM in F33 totalling Column F	**2**	
6-12	**Formatting**	F17 and F33 Accounting Number Format F28 and F31 Comma Style A18:A27 and A29:A30 indented once 10-point Bookman Old Style bold (or other available font) in D1:D3 D1:D3 moved to F1:F3, aligned right A17:B17 merged and centered, Input cell style A28:B28.merged and centered, Input cell style Values in column C, D, and label in F16 centered	**16**	
13-18	**Modifying Worksheet**	A16:F16 top and bottom border, bold F33 top and double bottom border, bold A1:F36 outside border A5 Olive Green, Accent 3, Lighter 80% A16:F16 Olive Green, Accent 3, Lighter 60% Clarity theme applied	**8**	
19	**Inserting a Picture**	TWBLogo.jpg, first four rows, top left	**2**	
20	**Organization**	Save ES2-R1-WBInvToNPC.xlsx, print	**2**	
		TOTAL POINTS: 35		

Excel Section 2 Skills Assessments Grading Rubrics

Assessment 1: Editing Cells; Inserting Columns; Copying Formulas; Inserting Pictures; Applying Formatting Features

ES2-A1-PTMarqCost.xlsx

Steps	Tasks	Criterion/Criteria	Value	Score
1 & 2	**Organization**	Open file from folder, save in ExcelEOS folder	**1**	
3 a & b	**Editing**	Design costs, 22 New column J9,Notions New values in J10:J16	**3**	
3 c-e	**Creating Formulas**	Formulas for total cost of costume in K10 Copied down to K11:K16 Formula in L10 is K10*2 Copied down L11:L16 Formula in M0 is profit – total cost Copied down M11:M16	**6**	
3 f-h	**Formatting**	Appropriate style for numeric cells Headings aligned to improve appearance Merge and center A6 and A7	**3**	
3 l & j	**Inserting Images**	Insert PTLogo.jpg in first five rows, top left Insert appropriate sewing clip art in first five rows, top right	**4**	
3k	**Enhancing Worksheet**	Apply font, border, color, and adjust width to enhance worksheet	**5**	
4	**Formatting**	Page layout landscaped, scaled to fit on one page	**2**	
5	**Organization**	Save ES2-A1-PTMarqCost.xlsx, print.	**1**	
		TOTAL POINTS: 25		

Assessment 2: Completing and Formatting a Worksheet
ES2-A2-PTMarqCostInv.xlsx

Steps	Tasks	Criterion/Criteria	Value	Score
1 & 2	**Organization**	Open file, review, rename, save	**2**	
3	**Entering Data/ Creating Formulas**	Current date in G6 Copy costume fees to F15:F21 SUM Costume fees in F22 Formula in F24 (7X75) F25 contains $250 SUM total costume fees plus additional charges in F26 Formula in F27 (F26 *13%) Formula in F28 (SUM F26+F27 or F26:F27)	**8**	
4	**Inserting Pictures**	PTLogo.jpg inserted in A1, resized to fit in 3 top left rows	**2**	
5	**Enhancing Worksheet**	Blank rows deleted, auto adjust column widths, attractive formatting	**1**	
6	**Organization**	Save ES2-A2-PTMarqCostInv.xlsx, print	**2**	
		TOTAL POINTS: 15		

Assessment 3: Performing a Spelling Check; Adjusting Column Width; Using Find and Replace; Inserting Clip Art; Applying Formatting Features

ES2-A3-WEMBRev.xlsx

Steps	Tasks	Criterion/Criteria	Value	Score
1 & 2	**Organization**	Open file, review, rename, save	**3**	
3 a-d	**Editing/ Entering Data**	Spelled checked All data visible, autofit columns Cinema House changed to Cinema Magic A3 Date, B3 current date	**5**	
3 e & f	**Enhancing Worksheet**	Monarch butterfly image top right Appropriately formatted	**2**	
4 & 5	**Organization**	Save ES2-A3-WEMBRev.xlsx in Excel EOS folder, print portrait orientation with the width scaled to fit 1 page	**5**	
		TOTAL POINTS: 15		

Assessment 4: Finding the Select All Button

ES2-A4-WBInventory.xlsx

Steps	Tasks	Criterion/Criteria	Value	Score
1 & 2	**Using Help/ Organization**	Search Help for info, open file from folder, rename file,	3	
3 & 4	**Using Features**	Select all and apply italic formatting	5	
5	**Organization**	Save ES1-A4-WBInventory.xlsx, print	2	
		TOTAL POINTS: 10		

Assessment 5: Locating Information on Theatre Arts Programs

ES2-A5-TheatreArts.xlsx

Steps	Tasks	Criterion/Criteria	Value	Score
1 & 2	**Using Search Engines, Organization, Entering Data & Using Formulas**	Tuition and other expense items organized logically, totalled using sum, save file	5	
3	**Formatting**	Worksheet enhanced with formatting	3	
4 & 5	**Printing / Organization**	Save ES2-A5-TheatreArts.xlsx in Excel EOS folder, print	2	
		TOTAL POINTS: 15		

Excel Section 2 Marquee Challenges Grading Rubrics

Challenge 1: Creating a Direct Wages Budget Report for a Film Shoot
ES2-C1-MPLocBudg.xlsx

Steps	Tasks	Criterion/Criteria	Value	Score
1	**Entering Data**	Information and logo from Figure 2.1 entered correctly	7	
2	**Using Features**	Estimated Daily Rates linked to Daily Rate	2	
3 & 4	**Creating Formulas**	Calculate extended cost in column G SUM in G16	2	
5 & 6	**Formatting**	Apply formatting modeling Figure 2.1 Border applied to entire perimeter of border	2	
7	**Organization**	Save ES2-C1-MPLocBudg.xlsx in Excel EOS folder, print in landscaped orientation	2	
		TOTAL POINTS: 15		

Challenge 2: Creating a Room Timetable
ES2-C2-NPCRoomSch.xlsx

Steps	Tasks	Criterion/Criteria	Value	Score
1 & 2	**Entering Data, Formatting & Using Features**	Information from Figure 2.2 entered correctly, appearance enhanced with formatting features	8	
3 & 4	**Organization**	Save ES2-C2-NPCRoomSch.xlsx in Excel EOS folder, print	2	
		TOTAL POINTS: 10		

Excel Section 3 Skills Review Rubrics

Review 1: Creating Range Names; Inserting Statistical, Date, and IF Functions; Changing Page Layout Options

ES3-R1-WBQtrRev.xlsx

Steps	Tasks	Criterion/Criteria	Value	Score
1	**Organization**	Open file, rename, save in Excel EOS	3	
2	**Using Features**	Ranges named B4:B8 *Quarter1* C4:C8 *Quarter2* D4:D8 *Quarter3* E4:E8 *Quarter4* F4:F8 *TotalRev*	5	
3	**Typing**	Labels added A14 Average revenue A15 Maximum revenue A16 Minimum revenue	3	
4 & 5	**Inserting Formulas**	B14 AVE revenues Quarter 1 using range B15 MAX B16 MIN Copy to C14:F16 for Quarter 2, 3, 4, and Total Rev	7	
6-11	**Typing, Inserting Formulas & Formatting Cells**	A18 Date Created B18 Date function that is NOT dynamic, formatted to style 14-Mar-2001 A19 Next revision date Formula in B19, 350 + B18 A21 Quarterly minimum target B21 350000, formatted comma style, no decimals, and named MinTarget	10	
12-14	**Typing, Inserting Formulas & Copying**	A22 Revenue target not met by B22 IF Formula (=if(b10<mintarget,b10-mintarget) Copy formula in B22 to C22:E22	3	
15-17	**Using Features**	Page orientation landscaped Top margin 1.5 Centered horizontally Header with first/last name at left margin, date/time at right margin (one space between date & time) Footer has file name at right margin	7	
18	**Organization**	Save and print ES3-R1-WBQtrRev.xlsx	2	
		TOTAL POINTS: 40		

Review 2: Creating Charts; Drawing Shapes
ES3-R1-WBQtrRev.xlsx

Steps	Tasks	Criterion/Criteria	Value	Score
1 & 2	**Creating Charts**	2-D Cluster Column Chart on separate sheet, printed, Range A3:E8 Layout 1 Style 34 Titled Quarterly Revenue Budget Forecast	7	
3 & 4	**Creating Charts**	Pie Chart using A3:A8 and F3:F8 on separate sheet labeled Pie Chart Exploded Pie in 3-D Layout 6 Style 34 Titled Total Revenue Budget Forecast	6	
5 & 6	**Inserting Shapes, Typing & Formatting**	Up Arrow Callout shape in white space below chart 1 inch wide, 1.5 inches high, pointed toward Dining room Text inside arrow This is a 10% increase over last year Shape middle aligned	5	
7 & 8	**Organization**	Save ES3-R1-WBQtrRev.xlsx, print	2	
		TOTAL POINTS: 20		

Excel Section 3 Skills Assessments Grading Rubrics

Assessment 1: Creating Statistical and IF Functions; Using Absolute References
ES3-A1-FCTSalesComm

Steps	Tasks	Criterion/Criteria	Value	Score
1	**Organization**	Open file from folder, rename save in ExcelEOS folder	1	
2-4	**Creating Formulas, Copying & Formatting**	D4 IF formula calculating commission G4 and G5 are absolute cell references D4 copied down column D Appropriate number style format	5	
5	**Typing / Inserting Formulas**	B20 Average commission B21 Maximum B22 Minimum D20 AVE D21 MAX D22 MIN	6	
6	**Using Features**	Top margin 1.25" Left margin 1.5"	2	
7	**Organization**	Save ES3-A1-FCTSalesComm, print.	1	
		TOTAL POINTS: 15		

Assessment 2: Applying the PMT Function
ES3-A2-WELoan.xlsx

Steps	Tasks	Criterion/Criteria	Value	Score
1	**Organization**	Open file, rename, save	2	
2 & 3	**Inserting Formulas**	B7 and D7 contain PMT formula SUM in B11 and D11 reflecting total payments for each loan	6	
4	**Organization**	Save ES3-A2-WELoan.xlsx, print	2	
		TOTAL POINTS: 10		

Assessment 3: Creating Charts; Drawing Shapes
ES3-A3-NPCGrades.xlsx

Steps	Tasks	Criterion/Criteria	Value	Score
1	**Organization**	Open file, review, rename, save	3	
2 & 3	**Creating Charts**	Line chart on separate sheet labelled LineChart A+ to F for all five courses displayed Appropriate title, formatting easy to interpret Pie chart below grades, row 14 Each grade percent of 100 Percent and categories outside pie slices Appropriate title	9	
4	**Inserting Shapes**	Right-pointing block arrow points to percent value F Starting in upper left corner Text in arrow Lowest failure rate since 2008!	4	
5 & 6	**Organization**	Worksheet centered horizontally, printed, line chart printed, save ES3-A3-NPCGrades.xlsx.	4	
		TOTAL POINTS: 20		

Assessment 4: Creating Charts; Changing Page Layout; Inserting a Footer

ES3-A4-FCTEurope.xlsx

Steps	Tasks	Criterion/Criteria	Value	Score
1	**Organization**	Open file from folder, rename file	2	
2	**Typing**	New row above worksheet contains Title European Packages merged and centered	3	
3-6	**Formatting**	Row 1 height 27.00 Opulent theme A1 Title style A2:G2 Accent 1 A3:G3 Accent 2 B4:G12 Comma style, zero decimals	6	
7-9	**Creating Charts**	3D Clustered bar chart in new sheet Labelled 14NightsChart Standard and deluxe rates, all destinations, 14 nights Appropriate title Formatting enhances appearance 3D Clustered bar chart in new sheet Labelled 21NightsChart Standard and deluxe rates, all destinations, 21 nights Appropriate title Formatting enhances appearance	10	
10	**Printing**	Print 21NightsChart	1	
11 & 12	**Using Features**	Sheet 1 centered horizontally, landscaped, top margin 1.5 Custom footer, name at L margin, file name at R margin	6	
13	**Printing**	Print Sheet 1	1	
14	**Organization**	Save ES3-A4-FCTEurope.xlsx	1	
		TOTAL POINTS: 30		

Assessment 5: Finding Information on Chart Axis Options
ES3-A4-FCTEurope.xlsx

Steps	Tasks	Criterion/Criteria	Value	Score
1-3	**Using Help/ Organization**	Search Help, open file, rename, save	**4**	
4 & 5	**Modifying Data**	Value axis options Minimum value fixed 1,000 Major unit value fixed 500	**3**	
6 & 7	**Printing/ Organization**	Save ES3-A4-FCTEurope.xlsx in Excel EOS folder, print	**3**	
		TOTAL POINTS: 10		

Assessment 6: Social Networking Survey
ES3-A6-SocialNetSurvey.xlsx

Steps	Tasks	Criterion/Criteria	Value	Score
1	**Gathering Research Data**	Data in worksheet reflects interviews 10-20 people 2 questions Sites, activities	**3**	
2-5	**Creating/ Printing Charts**	Student-designed chart for data on different sites Labelled SocialNetSites Student designed chart for data on activities Labelled SocialNetAct Print both	**5**	
6	**Organization**	Save ES3-A6-SocialNetSurvey.xlsx, print sheet with source data	**2**	
		TOTAL POINTS: 10		

Excel Section 3 Marquee Challenges Grading Rubrics

Challenge 1: Creating Charts on Movie Attendance Statistics
ES3-C1-MPMovieStats.xlsx

Steps	Tasks	Criterion/Criteria	Value	Score
1	**Organization**	Open file, rename, save	3	
2	**Creating Charts**	Replicate charts in Figure 3.1 using data from file	3	
3	**Formatting**	Impact font for title and axis text Additional formatting and chart style applied to enhance appearance	5	
4 & 5	**Editing**	Bar chart, new sheet named AgeChart Doughnut char, new sheet named Income Chart	2	
6	**Organization**	Save ES3-C1-MPMovieStats.xlsx, print each chart	2	
		TOTAL POINTS: 15		

Challenge 2: Preparing an International Student Report
ES3-C2-NPCTop10.xlsx

Steps	Tasks	Criterion/Criteria	Value	Score
1	**Organization**	Open file, rename, save	3	
2	**Creating Charts**	Replicate charts in Figure 3.2 using data from file	3	
3 & 4	**Formatting**	Logo NPCLogo.jpg as illustrated Other appropriate logos related to diversity inserted Verve theme applied Formatting enhances appearance of work-sheet	5	
5	**Using Features**	Page landscaped, workbook fits on one page	2	
6	**Organization**	Save ES3-C2-NPCTop10.xlsx, print	2	
		TOTAL POINTS: 15		

Excel Section 4 Skills Reviews Grading Rubrics

Review 1: Managing and Formatting Worksheets; Using 3-D, References;
Printing Multiple Worksheets
ES4-R1-WBPayroll.xlsx

Steps	Tasks	Criterion/Criteria	Value	Score
1	**Organization**	Open file, rename, save	**4**	

2-7	**Editing**	Week 2 worksheet copied and renamed Week 3
		
		Positioned after Week 2
		
		Week 2 worksheet copied and renamed Week 4
		
		Positioned after Week 3
		
		Week 3 sheet changes
		
		     Change E9 from *0* to *5.*
		
		     Change I6 from *6* to *0.*
		
		     Change H14 from *0* to *4.*
		
		Week 4 sheet changes
		
		     Change C11 from *0* to *8.*
		
		     Change G11 from *9* to *0.*
		
		     Change I14 from *6* to *9.*
		
		Week 1-4 sheet tabs dark blue
		
		Summary tab dark red
			1	

8	**Creating Formulas**	SUM 3D reference in C6 of Summary sheet, total hours Lou Cortez all four weeks	**2**	
9	**Editing**	Drag fill C6 to Row 14	**16**	

10-12	**Using Features/ Inserting Formulas**	Week 1 sheet, merge and center C3:D3
		
		Date function in C3, November 6, 2011
		
		Merge and center C4:D4
		
		C4 formula C3 plus 3 days
		
		Repeat steps 10 & 11 for weeks 2, 3, & 4
		
		     C3 in Week2 November 13, 2011
		
		     C3 in Week3 November 20, 2011
		
		     C3 in Week4 November 27, 2011
			8	

13 & 14	**Creating Formulas**	K6 =if(j6>40,j6-40,0), formula copied through K14 K15 SUM of K6:K14 L6=(j6*b17)+(k6*b17*.5), formula copied through L14 L15 SUM of L6:L14	**2**	
15	**Editing**	Copy and paste formulas from 13 & 14 to Overtime Hours, Gross Pay in Week 2-4 sheets	**2**	

Steps	Tasks	Criterion/Criteria	Value	Score
16-18	**Creating Formulas Copying/ Pasting Formulas**	Summary sheet, D6 and E6 3D reference formulas for overtime and gross pay, Lou Cortez, all four worksheets Copy to D6:E6, Paste in D7:E14 SUM C15:E15		
19	**Formatting**	Gross Pay column, Accounting number format		
20	**Using Features**	Group all five worksheets		
21	**Organization**	Save ES4-R1-WBPayroll.xlsx		
		TOTAL POINTS: 35		

Review 2:Formatting a Table; Sorting; Filtering; and Inserting and Printing Comments
ES4-R2-WBInventory.xlsx

Steps	Tasks	Criterion/Criteria	Value	Score
1	**Organization**	Open file, rename, save in Excel EOS	2	
2	**Formatting**	A4:D45 Table Style Medium 3	2	
3 & 4	**Using Features/ Printing**	Filter items purchased in units by flats, print	2	
5-9	**Using Features**	Remove filter Sort by supplier name then item A – Z Comment in B20, A23 All comments show All comments set to print as shown on sheet	7	
10 & 11	**Organization**	Print, save ES4-R2-WBInventory.xlsx	2	
		TOTAL POINTS: 15		

Review 3: Creating a Workbook Using a Template
ES4-R3-PTStmntNov30.xlsx

Steps	Tasks	Criterion/Criteria	Value	Score
1	**Using Templates**	New workbook using sample template Billing Statement	2	
2	**Entering Data**	As shown in Figure 4.2	6	
3 & 4	**Organization**	Print, save ES4-R3-PTStmntNov30.xlsx	2	
		TOTAL POINTS: 15		

Excel Section 4 Skills Assessments Grading Rubrics

Assessment 1: Inserting, Deleting, and Renaming Worksheets; Linking Worksheets
ES4-A1-NPCInternGrades.xlsx

Steps	Tasks	Criterion/Criteria	Value	Score
1	**Organization**	Open file from folder, rename, save	**3**	
2-4	**Editing**	Delete Sheet 3 Insert new sheet before Marquee Productions named Grade Summary A3:B7 in MarqueeProductions to A3:B7 in GradeSummary keep source column widths A4:B8 in PerformanceThreads to A8:B12 in GradeSummary G3:H3 in MarqueeProductions to C3:D3 in GradeSummary keep source column widths. Link cells columns C & D GradeSummary worksheet to corresponding grades/dates in MarqueeProductions and PerformanceThreads. Copy title & subtitle in MarqueeProductions to GradeSummary. Change the font size rows 1 & 2 GradeSummary to 12-point , adjust merge and center to columns A–D. Change the Fill Color in E1:H2 to *No Fill*. Center grades in column C.	**13**	
5 & 6	**Using Features**	Group 3 worksheets, page orientation landscape	**2**	
7	**Organization**	Save ES4-A1-NPCInternGrades.xlsx, print.	**2**	
		TOTAL POINTS: 20		

Assessment 2: Formatting a Table; Filtering; Sorting
ES4-A2-PTMarqueeSch.xlsx

Steps	Tasks	Criterion/Criteria	Value	Score
1	**Organization**	Open file, rename, save	3	
2	**Formatting**	A10:H17 Table Style Light 15	2	
3-5	**Using Features/ Printing**	Filter delivery date July 9, sort A to Z Scaled to fit on one page Print with filter and sort	4	
6	**Editing**	Remove filter	1	
7	**Using Features**	Sort final delivery date oldest to newest, then sort costumes A to Z	2	
8	**Organization**	Save, print, close ES4-A2-PTMarqueeSch.xlsx	3	
		TOTAL POINTS: 15		

Assessment 3: Inserting and Printing Comments
ES4-A3-PTMarqueeSch.xlsx

Steps	Tasks	Criterion/Criteria	Value	Score
1	**Organization**	Open file, review, rename, save	2	
2-5	**Using Features**	Comment in D11 Sue is not yet done with the research. Design may not be able to start June 10 Comment in D15 These dates may need adjustment due to overlapping projects All comments showing and set to print as shown on worksheet	6	
6	**Organization**	Save, print ES4-A3-PTMarqueeSch.xlsx	2	
		TOTAL POINTS: 10		

Assessment 4: Formatting Columns and Formatting a Table; Opening an Excel 2003 Workbook and Saving as an Excel 2010 Workbook

ES4-A4-PTRentalCost.xlsx

Steps	Tasks	Criterion/Criteria	Value	Score
1	**Organization**	Open PTRentalCost.xls	2	
2 & 3	**Editing**	Column C-E headings right aligned Title Performance Threads typed in A1	2	
4-6	**Typing**	Subtitle Costume Rentals in A2 DaysRented right-aligned in F3, AutoFit column width TotalDue right-aligned in G3	4	
7-10	**Entering, Copying Formulas & Formatting**	F4 =e4-d4 formatted Comma Style no decimals Copy down row F G4 =f4*c4 formatted Accounting Number Copy down row G Column G width 12.00	7	
11-14	**Editing**	A3:G43 Table Style Light 9 Total row bottom of table Merge & center title A:G, Title style 1, Merge & center subtitle A:G, Heading 1 style to A2 Set worksheet to print on one page	7	
15	**Organization**	Convert file from 2003 to 2010 version, save, print ES4-A4-PTRentalCost.xlsx	3	
		TOTAL POINTS: 25		

Assessment 5: Finding Information on File Formats Not Supported by Excel 2010

ES4-A5-FileFormats

Steps	Tasks	Criterion/Criteria	Value	Score
1 & 2	**Using Help, Organization & Typing**	Table containing info on file format, associated software, and extension of file	5	
3-5	**Formatting**	Table style applied, easy to read, one page	3	
6 & 7	**Printing/ Organization**	Save ES4-A5-FileFormats in Excel EOS folder, print	2	
		TOTAL POINTS: 10		

Assessment 6: Smartphone Shopping
ES4-A6-Smartphones.xlsx

Steps	Tasks	Criterion/Criteria	Value	Score
1 & 2	**Using Search Engines, Organization & Typing**	Table compares 3 phones Main features on left Brand names on top Specific features of each phone in appropriate cells Last row has estimated cost	5	
3-5	**Using Comments, Formatting & Printing**	Add comment indicating recommended choice Change to landscape, print with comment showing	3	
6 & 7	**Organization**	Save ES4-A6-Smartphones.xlsx	2	
		TOTAL POINTS: 10		

Excel Section 4 Marquee Challenges Grading Rubrics

Challenge 1: Creating a Sales Invoice by Downloading a Template
ES4-C1-WBInvFCT.xlsx

Steps	Tasks	Criterion/Criteria	Value	Score
1 & 2	**Using Templates**	Download template Sales invoice (Blue Gradient design) or other suitable template	2	
3	**Entering Data**	Complete invoice using info from Figure 4.3	4	
4	**Inserting Pictures**	TWBLogo.jpg, inserted as indicated in Figure 4.3	2	
5-8	**Editing, Formatting & Typing**	Delete row between billing address and body Delete row between last line item and subtotal Format QTY column as 4.3 Type The Waterfront Bistro next to Make All Checks Payable	4	
9 & 10	**Organization**	Save ES4-C1-WBInvFCT.xlsxExcel EOS folder, print	3	
		TOTAL POINTS: 15		

Challenge 2: Importing, Formatting and Sorting a Distributor List

ES4-C2-WEDistributors.xlsx

Steps	Tasks	Criterion/Criteria	Value	Score
1-4	**Using Help, Wizards**	Open text file using wizard	**1**	
5-7	**Editing**	Widen columns as necessary Delete second address, e-mail address on both sheets Move data from one worksheet to bottom of other sheet Add column labels as shown in Figure 4.4	**5**	
8	**Inserting Pictures**	Insert WELogo.jpg Formatted with style similar to Figure 4.4	**2**	
9 & 10	**Using Features**	Custom sort as indicated in Figure 4.4 Page layout landscaped, sheet on one page	**4**	
11 & 12	**Saving Files**	Convert the worksheet, create a PDF	**2**	
13	**Organization**	ES4-C2-WEDistributors.xlsx and any other open workbooks	**1**	
		TOTAL POINTS: 15		

Integrating Programs: Word and Excel
Skills Reviews Grading Rubrics

Review 1: Copying and Pasting Data
Int1-R1-NPCExcelScores.xlsx

Steps	Tasks	Criterion/Criteria	Value	Score
1-4	**Organization**	Create a folder on storage medium Open files in Word, Excel Rename and save Excel file	2	
5-10	**Editing**	Copy nine lines from table in Word Paste into A5 in Excel worksheet Delete A5:A13 Increase width column A	4	
11	**Typing**	Average in Cell E5	1	
12-13	**Creating Formulas**	E6, AVE B6:D6 Copied down E7:E13	2	
14-16	**Formatting**	E6:E13 Cambria 12 pt, decrease decimal 4 times B6:D13, 2 numbers after decimal point B6:E13 centered	4	
17 & 18	**Organization**	Save, print, close Int1-R1-NPCExcelScores.xlsx. Close Word doc	2	
		TOTAL POINTS: 15		

Review 2: Linking an Object and Editing a Linked Object
Int1-R2-NPCWordEnroll.docx

Steps	Tasks	Criterion/Criteria	Value	Score
1-4	**Organization**	Open Word, Excel files, rename, save	2	
5	**Using Features**	Link chart to Word document TS below title	1	
6 & 7	**Formatting/ Organization**	Center chart, save, print, close Word	2	
8-10	**Organization**	Deselect chart in Excel, print	2	
11 & 12	**Typing**	Update chart making changes in A2, B4:B8	1	
13-15	**Using Features / Organization**	Open Word file, update document Print Word document, Excel chart Save Int1-R2-NPCWordEnroll.docx	2	
		TOTAL POINTS: 10		

Review 3 – Embedding an Object
Int1-R3-WERevMemo.docx

Steps	Tasks	Criterion/Criteria	Value	Score
1-3	**Organization**	Open Word document, rename, save Open Excel file	**2**	
4	**Using Features**	Embed data from A2:D8 into Word document DS below paragraph of text in memo	**2**	
5 & 6	**Organization**	Print, save Int1-R3-WERevMemo.docx Close Excel worksheet without saving	**2**	
7-9	**Editing**	Changes made to embedded worksheet in Word Date and subject modified	**2**	
10	**Organization**	Save, print, close Int1-R3-WERevMemo.docx	**2**	
		TOTAL POINTS: 10		

Access Section 1 Skills Reviews Grading Rubrics

Review 1: Adjusting Column Widths; Finding and Editing Records; Adding and Deleting Records
WEEmployees1.accdb

Steps	Tasks	Criterion/Criteria	Value	Score
1-2	**Organization**	Open database, open table	2	
3	**Formatting**	Adjust all column widths	2	
4-6	**Editing**	Change information in single fields for three records	3	
7-8	**Editing**	Delete two records	2	
9	**Editing**	Add three records as shown	4	
10	**Organization**	Close and save table	2	
		TOTAL POINTS: 15		

Review 2: Sorting; Previewing; Changing Page Orientation; Filtering; Hiding Columns; Printing
WEEmployees1.accdb

Steps	Tasks	Criterion/Criteria	Value	Score
1-2	**Organization, Accuracy**	Open database, open table, sort table	3	
3-4	**Proofing/ Finishing**	Preview & then print table	2	
5-6	**Accuracy/ Finishing**	Filter table, hide a column, print table	3	
7-8	**Organization**	Close and save table, close database	2	
		TOTAL POINTS: 10		

Access Section 1 Skills Assessments Grading Rubrics

Assessment 1: Adjusting Column Width; Finding and Editing Records; Previewing and Printing
NPCGrades1.accdb

Steps	Tasks	Criterion/Criteria	Value	Score
1-2	**Organization**	Open database, open table	**2**	
3	**Formatting**	Adjust all column widths	**2**	
4	**Typing**	Enter several grades, as shown in Step 1	**6**	
5	**Proofing/ Finishing**	Preview & then print table	**2**	
6	**Organization**	Close and save table, close database	**3**	
		TOTAL POINTS: 15		

Assessment 2: Finding, Adding, and Deleting Records; Formatting Datasheet
WBInventory1.accdb

Steps	Tasks	Criterion/Criteria	Value	Score
1-2	**Organization/ Formatting**	Open database, open table, adjust all column widths	**3**	
3	**Editing**	Locate (find) & delete three inventory items	**5**	
4	**Typing**	Add three records as shown	**4**	
5	**Formatting**	Change font size for all records	**2**	
6	**Proofing, Formatting & Finishing**	Preview table, adjust top/bottom margins, print	**3**	
6	**Organization**	Close and save table, close database	**3**	
		TOTAL POINTS: 20		

Assessment 3: Finding, Sorting, Filtering, and Deleting Records

PTCostumeInv1.accdb

Steps	Tasks	Criterion/Criteria	Value	Score
1-2	**Organization/ Formatting**	Open database, open table, adjust all column widths	4	
3	**Editing**	Locate (find) & delete three records	3	
4	**Accuracy**	Sort table	2	
5	**Proofing, Formatting & Finishing**	Preview table, adjust margins, print	3	
6	**Accuracy**	Sort table (2-level sort)	2	
7-9	**Accuracy/ Finishing**	Filter table, print filtered list, redisplay all records	3	
10-11	**Organization**	Close and save table, close database	3	
		TOTAL POINTS: 20		

Assessment 4: Finding Information on Designing a Database

AS1-A4-TableMemo.*docx*

Steps	Tasks	Criterion/Criteria	Value	Score
1-3	**Research, Feature, Typing & Formatting**	After using Help in specific way (Steps 1a-1c), use memo template (user-selected) to create memo in Word that includes: a list of all reasons that Access tables should contain one subject only	8	
4-5	**Organization**	Save, print, and close document	2	
		TOTAL POINTS: 10		

Assessment 5: Individual Challenge (Creating a Job Search Company Database)

JobSearchINfo1.accdb

Steps	Tasks	Criterion/Criteria	Value	Score
1-5	**Research, Typing & Organization**	After research on the Internet, open database, open table, input/enter at least 8 records for companies researched, adjust all column widths	6	
6	**Accuracy**	Sort table	2	
7-8	**Proofing, Formatting & Finishing**	Preview table, change font size & page layout options to minimize paper use (user-selected), print	5	
8-9	**Organization**	Close table, close database	2	
		TOTAL POINTS: 15		

Access Section 1 Marquee Challenges Grading Rubrics

Challenge 1: Updating and Printing a Catering Event Database
(WBSpecialEvents1.accdb)

Steps	Tasks	Criterion / Criteria	Value	Score
1-2	**Organization**	Open database, open table	**2**	
2	**Typing / Accuracy**	Enter/input information or make selections as shown	**5**	
3-4	**Editing**	Delete record, update data in field	**2**	
5	**Feature, Formatting & Finishing**	Create (sorted) report, change options so printout is one page, print	**4**	
6-7	**Organization**	Close table (saving changes), close database	**2**	
		TOTAL POINTS: 15		

Challenge 2: Determining Fields and Table Names for a New Database
AS1-C2-PTCostumes.docx

Steps	Tasks	Criterion/Criteria	Value	Score
1-2	**Research, Typing & Formatting**	After studying information in Table 1.5, create document in Word that includes: proposed field & table names (include primary key in each table), and information from "Additional notes"	**8**	
3-4	**Organization**	Save, print, and close document	**2**	
		TOTAL POINTS: 10		

Access Section 2 Skills Reviews Grading Rubrics

Review 1: Creating and Modifying a Table in Design View
WEEmployees2Relshp.accdb

Steps	Tasks	Criterion/Criteria	Value	Score
1	**Organization**	Open database	**2**	
2	**Feature/Typing**	Create table in Design view, enter field names & types	**4**	
3-4	**Accuracy/ Organization**	Define primary key, save table as Review	**3**	
5	**Typing**	Add two records as shown	**4**	
6-7	**Formatting/ Organization**	Adjust all column widths, re-save table	**3**	
8-9	**Accuracy, Organization & Formatting**	In Design view, change size of a field, create a validation rule (with text error message), re-save table, create input mask for date fields & format them, re-save table	**5**	
10	**Typing**	In Datasheet view, add two records	**4**	
11-12	**Proofing, Formatting & Finishing**	Use Print Preview, change to landscape, print	**3**	
13	**Organization**	Close Print Preview, close table	**2**	
		TOTAL POINTS: 30		

Review 2: Modifying, Moving, and Deleting Fields; Creating Relationships
WEEmployees2Relshp.accdb

Steps	Tasks	Criterion/Criteria	Value	Score
1	**Organization**	Open database, open Review in Design view	2	
2-3	**Accuracy**	Move two fields	2	
4	**Interactivity**	Add caption properties to five fields	5	
5-6	**Organization, Formatting & Finishing**	Re-save table, switch views, adjust all column widths, orientation and left/right margins, print	4	
7-9	**Organization/ Editing**	Open table, delete field, re-save and close table	3	
10-15	**Organization**	Add table to existing relationships, create one-to-one relationship, turn on referential integrity, save changes to relationships, generate and print (landscape) a new relationship report, save report	7	
16	**Organization**	Close relationships window, close database	2	
		TOTAL POINTS: 25		

Access Section 2 Skills Assessments Grading Rubrics

Assessment 1: Creating a Table in Design View; Creating a Lookup Field
NPCGrades2.accdb

Steps	Tasks	Criterion/Criteria	Value	Score
1-2	**Organization/ Editing**	Open database, create table with specific data types, create drop-down list	6	
3-4	**Accuracy**	Restrict properties of a field & its editing, define primary key	4	
5	**Organization**	Save table	2	
6	**Typing**	Add four records as shown	4	
7	**Formatting**	Adjust all column widths (Best Fit)	2	
8-9	**Finishing / Organization**	Print, close, and re-save table, close database	2	
		TOTAL POINTS: 20		

Assessment 2: Changing Field Size; Validating Entries; Creating an Input Mask; Formatting Dates; Formatting a Datasheet

PTCostumeInv2.accdb

Steps	Tasks	Criterion/Criteria	Value	Score
1-2	**Organization**	Open database, open table in Design view	**2**	
3-4	**Accuracy/ Formatting**	Change a field's type, change a field's size	**2**	
5-6	**Accuracy, Formatting & Interactivity**	Create validation rule & text entry for a field, create input mask for two date fields & format	**4**	
7	**Formatting**	Format date fields	**2**	
8	**Organization**	Save table, switch to Datasheet view	**2**	
9-10	**Formatting**	Adjust date column widths (Best Fit), change datasheet font size, adjust all column widths	**3**	
11-12	**Proofing/ Formatting**	Preview datasheet, change margins to fit on a page	**2**	
12-13	**Organization/ Finishing**	Save, print & close table, close database	**3**	
		TOTAL POINTS: 20		

Assessment 3: Creating a New Database

FCTExpense2.accdb

Steps	Tasks	Criterion/Criteria	Value	Score
1-3	**Research, Organization & Typing**	After reviewing Fig. 2.4, create new table and add fields, set their data types & properties	**8**	
4	**Typing**	In Datasheet view, input info from Fig. 2.4	**4**	
5-6	**Accuracy, Formatting, Interactivity & Organization**	Preview, format to print on page if possible, print, close database	**3**	
		TOTAL POINTS: 15		

Assessment 4: Creating a New Database

FCTExpense2.accdb

Steps	Tasks	Criterion/Criteria	Value	Score
1-2	**Research, Feature & Organization**	After using Help, create new database based on Events template	**6**	
3	**Typing**	In form, enter two records	**3**	
4-6	**Organization/ Accuracy**	Close form, expand Navigation pane & change view to Object Type, open table in Design view	**4**	
6-9	**Editing, Interactivity & Formatting**	Delete a field, rename a field, delete info in a field name, create caption properties for all fields, save changes, switch to Datasheet view, adjust all column widths (Best Fit)	**6**	
10	**Formatting/ Finishing**	Preview, change page orientation, print	**3**	
11-12	**Organization**	Close Print Preview, close table (save changes), close database	**3**	
		TOTAL POINTS: 25		

Assessment 5: Individual Challenge (Investigating Social Media Websites)

NewWeb20_2.accdb

Steps	Tasks	Criterion/Criteria	Value	Score
1-5	**Research, Organization & Typing**	After research on the Internet (www.go2web20.net), create database, create table in Design view with at least five fields, save table, add records	**9**	
6	**Formatting/ Finishing**	Preview, change formatting to fit on a page, print	**3**	
7-8	**Organization**	Save & close table, close database	**3**	
		TOTAL POINTS: 15		

Access Section 2 Marquee Challenges Grading Rubrics

Challenge 1: Refining Tables in Database; Creating Relationships
WEPurchases2.accdb, AS2-C1-Memo.docx

Steps	Tasks	Criterion/Criteria	Value	Score
1	**Organization**	Open database	2	
2	**Accuracy, Formatting & Interactivity**	Examine each table in Design view and modify properties of certain fields, including: length of fields, date format, input masks, and data validation	6	
3	**Formatting**	Create new field in Purchases table that includes data validation, test field	3	
4-5	**Organization, Accuracy & Finishing**	Create relationship between two tables, print relationship report	3	
6	**Formatting/ Finishing**	Format datasheets to ensure info is visible and paper minimized, print datasheets	3	
7	**Typing, Formatting, Organization & Finishing**	Create memo in Word per instructions, save, print and close, exit Word	6	
8	**Organization**	Close database	2	
		TOTAL POINTS: 25		

Challenge 2: Creating a New Database
AS1-C2-PTCostumes.docx, AS2-C2-PTCostumes.docx, AS2-C2-PTCostumes.accdb

Steps	Tasks	Criterion/Criteria	Value	Score
1-2	**Research/ Organization**	After reviewing existing document, use Save As	2	
3	**Accuracy/ Typing**	Determine properties (user-selected), type beside each field appropriately	6	
4	**Accuracy/ Typing**	Determine relationships, on new page type them out (include field names used to join)	5	
5-7	**Organization, Formatting & Typing**	Create new database, create tables and fields per Steps 3-4, populate with records (user-selected)	8	
8-9	**Organization, Accuracy & Finishing**	Create relationship between two tables, print relationship report	3	
10	**Formatting/ Finishing**	Format datasheets to ensure info is visible and paper minimized, print datasheets	4	
11-12	**Organization/ Finishing**	Re-save Word document & print it	2	
		TOTAL POINTS: 30		

Access Section 3 Skills Reviews Grading Rubrics

Review 1: Creating a Query Using the Simple Query Wizard; Sorting a Query;
Creating a Calculated Field; Extracting Records
WEEmployees3.accdb

Steps	Tasks	Criterion/Criteria	Value	Score
1	**Organization**	Open database	**2**	
2-4	**Feature/Typing**	Use Simple Query Wizard (accepting default), type specific name, view results datasheet	**3**	
4-8	**Formatting/ Organization**	In Design view sort query results, create a calculated field and name it, format a field for Currency, save & run query	**5**	
8-9	**Formatting/ Finishing**	Adjust a column width, adjust margins & print results	**3**	
10-12	**Editing/ Formatting**	Use Save As to copy query design, re-name, in Design view add criterion, save & run query	**4**	
13	**Formatting, Finishing & Organization**	Adjust margins, print query results, close query	**3**	
		TOTAL POINTS: 20		

Review 2: Creating and Modifying a Form
WEEmployees3.accdb

Steps	Tasks	Criterion/Criteria	Value	Score
1	**Command**	Create new form for Review table	**2**	
2-3	**Formatting, Editing & Organization**	Add & format specific image (logo), change text & font size for title, resize/align text box control objects, save with default name	**7**	
4	**Formatting & Finishing**	In Form view, in Print dialog, go to Setup and make changes to width of columns & what's printed, print	**4**	
5	**Organization**	Close form, save design changes if prompted	**2**	
		TOTAL POINTS: 15		

Review 3: Creating and Modifying a Report
WEEmployees3.accdb

Steps	Tasks	Criterion/Criteria	Value	Score
1	**Command**	Use Report to create new report based on a query	2	
2-4	**Formatting/ Editing**	Add & resize specific image (logo), change text & font size for title, change page orientation, move a column, decrease width of two columns, increase width of two columns, edit column names, change Report theme, delete totals where they appear	8	
5	**Formatting**	In Print Preview, change column width	3	
6-8	**Organization/ Finishing**	Save report with default name, print & close report, close database	2	
		TOTAL POINTS: 15		

Access Section 3 Skills Assessments Grading Rubrics

Assessment 1: Creating a Query in Design View; Sorting a Query; Extracting Records Using Multiple Criteria
NPCGrades3.accdb

Steps	Tasks	Criterion/Criteria	Value	Score
1	**Organization**	Open database	2	
2-4	**Command, Accuracy & Organization**	Create query in Design view to extract specific records: use all tables, create relationships through dragging & dropping, include specific fields from one table & sort, add fields from other tables, enter criteria statements, save & run query	8	
5-6	**Formatting/ Finishing**	Best Fit columns, print query in landscape	2	
7	**Organization**	Close query & save changes, close database	3	
		TOTAL POINTS: 15		

Assessment 2: Creating a Query and Report; Modifying a Report

PTCostumeInv3.accdb

Steps	Tasks	Criterion/Criteria	Value	Score
1	**Organization**	Open database	**2**	
2-8	**Command, Accuracy & Organization**	Create query in Design view using table specified: widen column, sort, save & run query, close	**7**	
9-13	**Command/ Formatting**	Create report with Report button based on query, add specific image, position & resize it, change title text & font size, adjust column widths to fit portrait, adjust other objects so report will print on a page	**8**	
14-15	**Organization/ Finishing**	Save report (default name), print & close report, close database	**3**	
		TOTAL POINTS: 20		

Assessment 3: Creating and Modifying a Form

PTCostumeInv3.accdb

Steps	Tasks	Criterion/Criteria	Value	Score
1-2	**Organization/ Command**	Open database, create form for specific table	**3**	
3-8	**Formatting/ Organization**	Change theme (user-selected), add image, position & resize it, change title & format (user-selected), decrease width of controls so will print in portrait, other formatting as required, save using default name	**8**	
9-10	**Accuracy, Formatting & Finishing**	Display & print first record (must fit on a page), close & save form, close database	**4**	
		TOTAL POINTS: 15		

Assessment 4: Finding Information on Creating a Form with a Subform
WEVendors3.accdb

Steps	Tasks	Criterion/Criteria	Value	Score
1-5	**Research, Organization & Command**	After using Help, open database, open & examine Relationships window, close window, use Form to create a form based on specific table	6	
6	**Formatting**	Modify form in Layout view (user-selected)	5	
7-9	**Accuracy, Formatting & Finishing**	Display & print first record (must fit on a page), close & save form (default name), close database	4	
		TOTAL POINTS: 15		

Assessment 5: Individual Challenge (Researching Movies on the Internet for a New Blog)
AS3-Movies.accdb

Steps	Tasks	Criterion/Criteria	Value	Score
1-3	**Research, Organization, Typing & Formatting**	After research on the Internet, and reviewing Step 3, create database, create table to store specific information (Step 3), user-selecting fields/properties	9	
4-6	**Command, Formatting, Typing & Finishing**	Create form to enter records, format (user-selected), type/add records, print first record in Form view	5	
7-8	**Command Formatting**	Create report, format (user-selected), print	4	
9	**Organization**	Close database	2	
		TOTAL POINTS: 20		

Access Section 3 Marquee Challenges Grading Rubrics

Challenge 1: Creating Queries and a Report for a Catering Events Database
WBSpecialEvents3.accdb

Steps	Tasks	Criterion/Criteria	Value	Score
1	**Organization**	Open database	**2**	
2	**Accuracy, Formatting & Finishing**	Create several queries & do formatting, including: a query showing events booked in Westview room, format (Best Fit) & print for one page, a query displaying events in June, 2011, print to Best Fit, and a query displaying all records that includes calculation (user-formatted) & a total, print Best Fit to one page	**10**	
3	**Accuracy, Formatting & Organization**	Create report based on specific query (Fig. 3.2), and: insert logo, format elements (user-selected), add totals, save with default name	**5**	
4-5	**Formatting, Finishing & Organization**	Format to fit to a page & print, close database	**3**	
		TOTAL POINTS: 20		

Challenge 2: Creating Forms and a Report for a Custom Costume Database
AS3-C2-PTCostumes.accdb

Steps	Tasks	Criterion/Criteria	Value	Score
1-2	**Organization**	Using a computer window, create copy of a database, rename & open it	**4**	
3-4	**Accuracy, Formatting, Finishing & Organization**	Create form for a table, laying it out & formatting it (user-selected), display, in Form view format & print first record, save & close form (default name)	**7**	
5	**Accuracy, Formatting & Organization**	Create report to print specific table, and: lay out & format (user-selected) use Fig. 3.3 as an example, and tools available in Report Layout Tools Arrange tab	**6**	
6-7	**Organization/ Finishing**	Save report (default name), format to minimize paper use & print, close database	**3**	
		TOTAL POINTS: 20		

Access Section 4 Skills Reviews Grading Rubrics

Review 1: Creating a Crosstab, Find Unmatched, and Find Duplicates Query
WEEmployees4.accdb

Steps	Tasks	Criterion/Criteria	Value	Score
1	**Organization**	Open database	2	
2-5	**Command, Accuracy, Formatting & Finishing**	Create crosstab query summarizing tuition payments by using TuitionRemimbursed query, by: displaying employee last names in rows & reimbursement date in columns, and summing tuition amounts, name query, add a total row to sum each column, adjust column widths, print & save	8	
6-7	**Feature, Accuracy & Finishing**	Use Find Unmatched Query Wizard to compare two tables & produce list, displaying specific fields, name, print & close query	5	
8-9	**Feature, Accuracy & Finishing**	Use Find Duplicates Query Wizard to analyze specific field in a table & produce list, displaying remaining fields, name, print & close query	5	
		TOTAL POINTS: 20		

Review 2: Adding Control Objects to a Form; Sorting a Form
WEEmployees4.accdb

Steps	Tasks	Criterlon/Criteria	Value	Score
1	**Organization**	In Layout view, open Employees form	2	
2	**Formatting**	Add & resize image at bottom of page, resize form	3	
3-4	**Editing & Formatting**	Add label control object, type text, apply italics	4	
5-6	**Organization & Accuracy**	Save form, switch to Form view, sort records	3	
7-8	**Finishing & Organization**	Display & print first record, close form	3	
		TOTAL POINTS: 15		

Review 3: Creating and Modifying a Report; Creating a Calculated Control
WEEmployees4.accdb

Steps	Tasks	Criterion/Criteria	Value	Score
1	**Command**	Create new report using EmployeeList query	**2**	
2	**Formatting, Accuracy & Editing**	Change orientation (leave room for new column), create calculated control, label it & format to Currency, adjust column widths if necessary, delete total & add line at bottom, delete logo container & page numbering object, move date & time controls, add spaces between words in column	**12**	
3-6	**Formatting, Finishing & Organization**	In Layout view, format/modify control objects if necessary, save, print & close report, close database	**6**	
		TOTAL POINTS: 20		

Access Section 4 Skills Assessments Grading Rubrics

Assessment 1: Adding a Calculated Control to a Form
PTCostumeInv4.accdb

Steps	Tasks	Criterion/Criteria	Value	Score
1-2	**Organization/ Research**	Open database, open CostumeInventory form to review layout & design	3	
3-4	**Formatting, Interactivity, Editing & Finishing**	Create calculated control, type its label & format it, edit/format other labels to improve readability, display in Form view, sort, print first record	9	
5-6	**Organization**	Save & close form, close database	3	
		TOTAL POINTS: 15		

Assessment 2: Creating and Modifying a Report; Sorting a Report
WEDistributors4.accdb

Steps	Tasks	Criterion/Criteria	Value	Score
1	**Organization**	Open database	2	
2	**Command, Formatting & Editing**	Create report and format, including: change orientation, edit title, delete two columns, edit two column headings & add space to one, align column headings, delete page-numbering control & any similar objects bottom of column, move date & time controls, insert & resize image, sort	12	
3-4	**Organization, Formatting & Finishing**	Save report (default name), delete empty / unnecessary columns, format to fit a page, print & close, close database	6	
		TOTAL POINTS: 20		

Assessment 3: Creating Mailing Labels
WEDistributors4.accdb

Steps	Tasks	Criterion/Criteria	Value	Score
1	**Organization**	Open database	2	
2	**Feature/ Formatting & Editing**	Create specific labels, change font, set up proper prototype, sort by postal code, name report	5	
3-4	**Finishing/ Organization**	Print, close report, close database	3	
		TOTAL POINTS: 10		

Assessment 4: Calculating Statistics; Creating a Crosstab Query
WBInventory4.accdb

Steps	Tasks	Criterion/Criteria	Value	Score
1	**Organization**	Open database	**2**	
2-3	**Command, Accuracy & Finishing**	In Design view, create query calculating aggregate Sum using two tables, group by one field & sum by another, type title for column, name & run query, print results datasheet, close query	**6**	
4-5	**Command, Accuracy, Formatting, Finishing & Organization**	Create crosstab query based on PurchaseItems query that summarizes purchase by inventory & purchase date: use ItemDescription & PuchaseDate for row / column headings, sum Amount, accept default name, add total row to sum columns, adjust column widths, print results datasheet, close query, close database	**12**	
		TOTAL POINTS: 20		

Assessment 5: Finding Information on Creating a Query That Asks for Input
WEEmployees4.accdb

Steps	Tasks	Criterion/Criteria	Value	Score
1-3	**Research, Accuracy, Interactivity & Organization**	After using Help, open database and create parameter query by adding table, adding four fields in order (Step 3b), and creating parameter asking for department name, save query & close it	**10**	
4-6	**Command, Finishing & Organization**	Run & test query, print results datasheet, close query, close database	**5**	
		TOTAL POINTS: 15		

Assessment 6: Individual Challenge (Researching Salary Statistics on the Internet and Creating a Blog Entry)

AS4-SalaryStats.accdb, AS4-SalaryStatsBlog.docx

Steps	Tasks	Criterion/Criteria	Value	Score
1-3	**Research, Organization, Typing & Formatting**	After research on the Internet, create database, design & create table to store specific information (Step 2-3)	8	
4	**Command, Formatting & Typing**	Design & create form to enter records, type/add records, print first record in Form view	6	
5	**Command, Accuracy & Finishing**	Design & create query to calculate three different items, print results	6	
6-8	**Command, Formatting, Finishing & Organization**	Design & create report, save, print & close report, close database	5	
9	**Organization, Typing & Finishing**	Write article in Word representing blog entry, based on data & stats, save & print it, close Word	5	
		TOTAL POINTS: 30		

Access Section 4 Marquee Challenges Grading Rubrics

Challenge 1: Summarizing Catering Event Information
WBSpecialEvents4.accdb

Steps	Tasks	Criterion/Criteria	Value	Score
1-3	**Research, Command & Accuracy**	Open database, review Fig. 4.1, create crosstab query (Step 1) based on RevByEventByQtr query	**8**	
4-7	**Command, Formatting, Finishing & Organization**	Design & create report similar to Fig. 4.1 based on same query, user-selected elements used & formatting (incorporating theme), name report same as query, print, close database	**7**	
		TOTAL POINTS: 15		

Challenge 2: Summarizing Costume Rental Revenue with Conditional Formatting
PTCostumeInv4.accdb

Steps	Tasks	Criterion/Criteria	Value	Score
1-2	**Research, Organization & Command**	Review Fig. 4.2, open database, create report based on RentalRevenue query, name report	**4**	
3	**Formatting/ Accuracy**	In Layout view, group & total report Fig. 4.2, use conditional formatting, user-selected formatting	**8**	
4-5	**Finishing & Organization**	Save, print & close report, close database	**3**	
		TOTAL POINTS: 15		

Integrating Programs: Word, Excel, and Access
Skills Reviews Grading Rubrics

Review 1: Exporting Access Data to Excel
Int2-PTCostumes.accdb, Int-R1-CostumeInventory.xlsx

Steps	Tasks	Criterion/Criteria	Value	Score
1-2	**Folder / File Management & Organization**	In Access, copy a database from one folder to another, rename & open the database	3	
3-4	**Command, Accuracy & Editing**	Export CostumeInventory table to Excel to specific folder, saving under specific name, in Excel change data in three cells	4	
5-7	**Organization/ Finishing**	Re-save workbook, print & close, close Export dialog in Access & close database	3	
		TOTAL POINTS: 10		

Review 2: Exporting Access Data to Word
Int2-WBSupplies.accdb, Int2-R2-InventoryList.rtf

Steps	Tasks	Criterion/Criteria	Value	Score
1-2	**Folder/File Management & Organization**	In Access, copy a database from one folder to another, rename & open the database	3	
3	**Command/ Accuracy**	Export InventoryList table to Word to specific folder, saving under specific name	3	
4-6	**Formatting/ Editing**	In Word auto fit table, apply table style & center table horizontally; at beginning of document press Enter & type title, change font size, apply bold, center title	6	
7-9	**Organization/ Finishing**	Re-save RTF document, print & close, close Export dialog in Access & close database	3	
		TOTAL POINTS: 15		

Review 3: Exporting an Access Report to Word

Int2-PTCostumes.accdb, Int2-R3-CostumeInventory.rtf

Steps	Tasks	Criterion/Criteria	Value	Score
1-2	**Organization/ Accuracy**	In Access, open database & export CostumeInventory report to Word, re-name document in Word	4	
3-6	**Formatting, Organization & Finishing**	In Word, change orientation to landscape & change margins to Normal, re-save RTF, print & close, exit Word, in Access close Export dialog & close database	6	
		TOTAL POINTS: 10		

Review 4: Importing Data to a New Table

Int2-PTCostumes.accdb, PTCostumeHours.xlsx

Steps	Tasks	Criterion/Criteria	Value	Score
1-2	**Organization, Command & Accuracy**	In Access open database, import into it an Excel workbook following directions in Step 2	6	
3-5	**Finishing/ Organization**	Open new table, print & close it, close database	4	
		TOTAL POINTS: 10		

Review 5: Linking Data to a New Table and Editing Linked Data

Int2-R5-FCTBookings.xlsx, Int2-FCTCommissions.accdb

Steps	Tasks	Criterion/Criteria	Value	Score
1-4	**Organization, File/Folder Management & Accuracy**	In Excel open workbook, then re-save under new name in different folder, in Access copy database to different folder & rename it, open renamed database	4	
5	**Command/ Accuracy**	In Access link Excel workbook (see details in Step 5)	5	
6-7	**Finishing/ Organization**	In Access open, print & close table, switch to Excel	3	
8-10	**Formula, Editing, Finishing & Organization**	In Excel type a formula & use fill handle to copy it, save & print file, close workbook	3	
11-13	**Organization/ Finishing**	Switch to Access, open, save, print & close table	3	
14-15	**Organization**	Close database, exit Access & exit Excel	2	
		TOTAL POINTS: 20		

PowerPoint Section 1 Skills Reviews Grading Rubrics

Review 1: Creating a Presentation for Marquee Productions
(PS1-R1-MPTeamMtg.pptx)

Steps	Tasks	Criterion/Criteria	Value	Score
1	**Folder/File Management**	Create folder	**2**	
2	**Formatting**	In blank presentation, select theme	**2**	
3-6	**Typing/ Command**	Type title & subtitle in slide 1, insert new slide, type text for slide 2, insert two more new slides & type text (all text shown in Fig. 1.4)	**7**	
7	**Command/ Typing**	Insert new slide between slides 2-3, type text as shown in Fig. 1.5	**3**	
8-11	**Formatting/ Editing**	In slide 2 change layout to Title Slide, move title and subtitle placeholders, in Slide Sorter view, move slide	**3**	
12-15	**Command/ Enhancement**	In Normal view choose Orbit transition, add sound, change duration, apply to all slides	**3**	
16-17	**Organization/ Command**	Save presentation in new folder, run full presentation	**2**	
18-20	**Command, Finishing & Organization**	View presentation as Outline in Backstage, print (all 5 slides horizontally), re-save & close presentation	**3**	
		TOTAL POINTS: 25		

PowerPoint Section 1 Skills Assessments Grading Rubrics

Assessment 1: Preparing a Presentation for Worldwide Enterprises
(PS1-A1-WEExecMtg.pptx)

Steps	Tasks	Criterion/Criteria	Value	Score
1-3	**Command, Typing & Enhancement**	Create new presentation with user-selected design, type text in Fig. 1.6, add transition, duration & sound (user-selected) to all slides, run presentation	**7**	
4-6	**Command, Finishing & Organization**	Print as handouts (5 slides horizontally), re-save & close presentation	**3**	
		TOTAL POINTS: 10		

Assessment 2: Preparing a Presentation for The Waterfront Bistro
PS1-A2-WBServices.pptx

Steps	Tasks	Criterion/Criteria	Value	Score
1-3	**Command, Typing & Enhancement**	Create new presentation with user-selected design, type text in Fig. 1.7, add transition, duration & sound (user-selected) to all slides, run presentation	7	
4-6	**Command, Finishing & Organization**	Print as handouts (5 slides horizontally), re-save & close presentation	3	
		TOTAL POINTS: 10		

Assessment 3: Finding Information on Setting Slide Show Timings
PS1-A3-MPProj.pptx

Steps	Tasks	Criterion/Criteria	Value	Score
1-2	**Feature**	After using Help, open a presentation and Save As	3	
3-5	**Command, Typing & Enhancement**	After using Help (or experimenting), set up slides to advance after 3 seconds automatically, run presentation	5	
6	**Organization**	Re-save and close presentation	2	
		TOTAL POINTS: 10		

Assessment 4: Individual Challenge (Preparing a Presentation on Cancun, Mexico)
PS1-A4-IC-Cancun.pptx

Steps	Tasks	Criterion/Criteria	Value	Score
1-3	**Research, Command & Typing**	After research on the Internet, create presentation on Cancun that includes five slides shown in Step 2, run presentation	12	
4-6	**Command, Finishing & Organization**	Print so all slides fit on a page (user-selected), save & close presentation	3	
		TOTAL POINTS: 15		

PowerPoint Section 1 Marquee Challenges Grading Rubrics

Challenge 1: Preparing a Presentation on Toronto, Ontario, Canada
PS1-C1-FCTToronto.pptx

Steps	Tasks	Criterion/Criteria	Value	Score
1	**Research, Command, Typing & Formatting**	Create presentation shown in Fig. 1.8, applying appropriate design theme & slide layouts, and sizing & moving placeholders as shown	10	
2-5	**Enhancement, Command, Finishing & Organization**	Add transition, duration & sound (user-selected) to each slide in presentation, save, print as handout so all slides fit on a page, close presentation	5	
		TOTAL POINTS: 15		

Challenge 2: Preparing a Presentation for Performance Threads
PS1-C2-PTCostume.pptx

Steps	Tasks	Criterion/Criteria	Value	Score
1	**Organization**	Open presentation, use Save As	2	
2-3	**Formatting, Editing & Enhancement**	Apply theme, add & rearrange slides, change layouts & move a placeholder (Fig. 1.9), add transition, duration & sound (user-selected) to all slides	10	
4-5	**Command, Finishing & Organization**	Re-save, print as handout so all slides fit on a page, close presentation	3	
		TOTAL POINTS: 15		

PowerPoint Section 2 Skills Reviews Grading Rubrics

Review 1: Editing and Formatting a Presentation for Marquee Productions
PS2-R1-MPAnnualMtg.pptx

Steps	Tasks	Criterion/Criteria	Value	Score
1-2	**Organization**	Open presentation, re-save	**2**	
3-6	**Formatting, Accuracy & Editing**	Apply theme, change theme colors & font, In Slides/Outline pane delete slide 5, in Slide Sorter view move slide 7 & slide 6	**5**	
7-17	**Formatting/ Editing**	In slide 4 decrease list level for last 2 bullets, in slide 6 increase indent of 3 bullets, in slide 7 copy text, in slide 3, position, press Enter, press tab & paste text and in same slide, position again, press enter & tab, and paste, in slide 7 copy text & in slide 3 position & paste, position & paste again	**8**	
18-21	**Editing/ Formatting**	In slide 1 select title text, change font, font size & bold, select subtitle text, change font, size & bold, using Format Painter apply same formatting to titles in existing slides	**4**	
22-23	**Editing**	In slide 6 change line spacing for all text, and in slide 8, change spacing before all paragraphs	**3**	
24-27	**Command/ Formatting & Command**	In slide 2, insert clip art in Fig. 2.6, change color, size & position, in slide 5 insert clip art in Fig. 2.7, change color, size & position as before, run presentation	**5**	
28-29	**Finishing/ Organization**	Print presentation as handouts (all slides on one page), re-save & close presentation	**3**	
		TOTAL POINTS: 30		

Review 2: Formatting a Presentation for Performance Threads
PS2-R2-PTPres.pptx

Steps	Tasks	Criterion/Criteria	Value	Score
1	**Organization**	Open presentation, re-save	2	
2-3	**Command/ Formatting**	Change design theme colors, in slide 1 insert image logo, change height & position to middle of slide	5	
4-5	**Formatting**	In slides 3 & 4 change line spacing for bulleted text	4	
6	**Command, Formatting, Enhancement & Typing**	In slide 2, insert SmartArt org chart, and: delete or add boxes to match Fig. 2.8, type text (using Shift+Enter), change color, apply Cartoon style, apply WordArt style fill to text	10	
7	**Command, Formatting & Accuracy**	In slide 3, insert clip art shown in Fig. 2.9, change height & color, adjust brightness, contrast & position	5	
8	**Command, Formatting, Enhancement & Typing**	In slide 5 create SmartArt Process graphic, change color, apply Cartoon style, type text	4	
9-10	**Enhancement**	In slide 2 animate org chart, and in slide 5 animate the SmartArt graphic (both user-selected)	4	
11-13	**Enhancement/ Command**	In slides 3 & 4 apply specific animation to bulleted text, run presentation	3	
14-15	**Finishing/ Organization**	Print presentation as handouts (all slides horizontal on page), re-save & close presentation	3	
		TOTAL POINTS: 40		

PowerPoint Section 2 Skills Assessments Grading Rubrics

Assessment 1: Formatting a Presentation for Niagara Peninsula College, Theatre Arts Division
PS2-A1-NPCTheatreArts.pptx

Steps	Tasks	Criterion/Criteria	Value	Score
1	**Organization**	Open presentation, re-save	**2**	
2	**Formatting**	Change design theme colors & theme font	**3**	
3-7	**Editing/ Formatting**	Move slide 7 & slide 6, in slide 2 change alignment of a paragraph, in slides 5 & 7 change line spacing in bulleted text, in slide 5 apply italics to bullets	**5**	
8	**Command/ Formatting**	In slide 1, insert logo image, change size & position	**4**	
9	**Command, Typing, Formatting & Enhancement**	In slide 3 insert SmartArt Radial graphic, type text in all circles, change SmartArt color & style (user-selected), apply other formatting as desired, position as necessary	**5**	
10	**Command, Typing, Formatting & Enhancement**	In slide 4 create SmartArt org chart & type text as shown in Fig. 2.11, apply SmartArt color & style (user-selected), apply other formatting as desired, position as necessary	**5**	
11-15	**Command, Formatting & Enhancement**	In slide 7 insert clip art related to money (user-selected), size, position & recolor to enhance slide, in slide 3 apply user-selected animation to SmartArt graphic, in slide 4 apply user-selected animation to SmartArt org chart, apply transition with sound and timing (user-selected) to all slides, run presentation	**8**	
16-17	**Finishing/ Organization**	Print presentation as handouts (four slides horizontal), re-save & close presentation	**3**	
		TOTAL POINTS: 35		

Assessment 2: Formatting a Presentation for First Choice Travel
PS2-A2-FCTVacations.pptx

Steps	Tasks	Criterion/Criteria	Value	Score
1	**Organization**	Open presentation, re-save	2	
2-3	**Formatting**	Change design theme colors & theme font	3	
4-5	**Formatting**	In slide 1 increase font size of subtitle (user-selected), in slides 2 to 6, bold, change font color, change alignment of headings	6	
6	**Command/ Formatting**	In slide 1 insert logo image, size & position (user-selected)	4	
7-9	**Formatting, Enhancement & Command**	Apply user-selected formatting to each slide to improve appearance, apply transition & sound (user-selected), run presentation	7	
10-11	**Command, Finishing & Organization**	Print as handouts (6 slides horizontally), re-save & close presentation	3	
		TOTAL POINTS: 25		

Assessment 3: Finding Information on Converting Text to a SmartArt Graphic
PS2-A3-FCTVactions.pptx

Steps	Tasks	Criterion/Criteria	Value	Score
1	**Organization**	Open presentation, use Save As	3	
2-4	**Research, Command & Enhancement**	After using Help, in slide 4 convert bulleted text to SmartArt & apply formatting to it (both user-selected)	5	
5-6	**Finishing & Organization**	Print slide 4, re-save & close presentation	2	
		TOTAL POINTS: 10		

Assessment 4: Individual Challenge (Locating Information and Preparing a Presentation)

PS2-A4-IC-PerPres.pptx

Steps	Tasks	Criterion/Criteria	Value	Score
1-2	**Research, Command & Typing**	After research on the Internet, create presentation on person chosen of at least four slides that includes: title slide and additional slides	**12**	
3-4	**Command, Formatting & Enhancement**	Insert screen capture or other image of person, apply transition & sound to each slide (both user-selected)	**4**	
5-8	**Organization, Command & Finishing**	Save & run presentation, print as handouts (six slides horizontally/page), re-save & close presentation	**4**	
		TOTAL POINTS: 20		

PowerPoint Section 2 Marquee Challenges Grading Rubrics

Challenge 1: Preparing a Presentation for Worldwide Enterprises
PS2-C1-WEDist.pptx

Steps	Tasks	Criterion/Criteria	Value	Score
1	**Research, Command, Typing & Formatting**	Create presentation in Fig. 2.12, applying design theme, different color theme & different font theme, insert clip art images & format, size & position them as shown, in slide 5 create & format SmartArt graphic	**12**	
2-3	**Organization/ Finishing**	Save, print as handout (six slides on page), close	**3**	
		TOTAL POINTS: 15		

Challenge 2: Preparing a Presentation for The Waterfront Bistro
PS2-C2-TWBInfo.pptx

Steps	Tasks	Criterion/Criteria	Value	Score
1	**Command, Formatting, Typing & Enhancement**	Create presentation shown in Fig. 2.13, and: apply theme, different theme's colors & different theme's fonts, in slides 1 & 2 insert logo image, in slide 3 create & format SmartArt org chart, in slide 4 create & format SmartArt graphic, in slide 6 insert clip art	**12**	
2-3	**Command, Finishing & Organization**	Re-save, print as handout so all slides fit on a page, close presentation	**3**	
		TOTAL POINTS: 15		

PowerPoint Section 3 Skills Reviews Grading Rubrics

Review 1: Formatting and Customizing a Biography Project Presentation
PS3-R1-MPBiography.pptx

Steps	Tasks	Criterion/Criteria	Value	Score
1	**Organization**	Open presentation, re-save	**2**	
2-12	**Editing**	In slide 4 turn on Clipboard task pane & clear contents if necessary, select & copy four names, in slide 5 position, press Enter & Tab, paste from task pane, repeat 3 times, clear Clipboard task pane & close it	**7**	
13-14	**Editing**	In slide 1 find two sets of names & replace all of them	**3**	
15-16	**Command, Typing & Formatting**	In slide 1 insert logo image, size & position, recolor to transparent, change brightness & contrast, in slide 2 insert text as WordArt, format it, change size, center on slide (all user-selected)	**7**	
17	**Command/ Formatting**	In slide 6 create table (Fig. 3.4), apply table style, change font size for all text, size & position table & columns as shown	**6**	
18-22	**Command, Typing, Formatting & Editing**	In slide 7 create arrow shapes shown in Fig. 3.5, typing text in boxes, apply shape style, change text size; in slide 1 draw Action button, name it, fill with color (user-selected), copy to slides 2 – 6; insert footer with text at bottom center; in slides 4 & 5 insert clip art (user-selected), size, position & color	**12**	
23-25	**Command, Finishing & Organization**	Run, print presentation as handouts (nine slides horizontally), re-save & close presentation	**3**	
		TOTAL POINTS: 40		

Review 2: Formatting with Slide Masters
PS3-R2-MPAnnualMtg.pptx

Steps	Tasks	Criterion/Criteria	Value	Score
1	**Organization**	Open presentation, re-save	2	
2	**Command/ Formatting**	Change design theme, change theme colors & font	3	
3-4	**Command, Accuracy & Formatting**	In Slide Master view, click top miniature and: select title text & change font size, select text styles & change font size, select second level & change font size, insert logo, recolor to complement color scheme, decrease size, position logo, close Slide Master	9	
5-6	**Enhancement/ Command**	Apply transition & sound to each slide (user-selected), run presentation	3	
7-8	**Finishing/ Organization**	Print presentation as handouts (nine slides horizontally per page), re-save & close presentation	3	
		TOTAL POINTS: 20		

Review 3: Formatting a Vacation Cruise Presentation to Run Automatically
PS3-R3-FCTCruise.pptx

Steps	Tasks	Criterion/Criteria	Value	Score
1	**Organization**	Open presentation, re-save	2	
2	**Command/ Formatting**	Insert logo image, size & position (user-selected)	4	
3	**Command/ Accuracy**	Rehearse & set timings as shown	4	
4	**Command, Enhancement & Formatting**	In slide 1 insert audio clip, display Audio Tools Playback tab, change start option, click check boxes for Hide During Show and Loop until Stopped	4	
5-6	**Command**	Set show to run continuously, run at least twice	3	
7-8	**Finishing/ Organization**	Print presentation as handouts (six slides horizontally per page), re-save & close presentation	3	
		TOTAL POINTS: 20		

PowerPoint Section 3 Skills Assessments Grading Rubrics

Assessment 1: Formatting a Presentation for Performance Threads
PS3-A1-PTCostumes.pptx

Steps	Tasks	Criterion/Criteria	Value	Score
1	**Organization**	Open presentation, use Save As	**2**	
2-4	**Command, Formatting & Typing**	In slide 1 insert logo image, size & position (user-selected); in slide 3 insert WordArt with shape, size & position user-selected; in slide 5 create shape (user-selected), copy twice, type text in shapes, format, size & position (user-selected)	**12**	
5	**Typing & Formatting**	In slide 6 type info in a table & format appropriately	**4**	
6-7	**Command**	Insert footer (all slides), run presentation	**4**	
8-9	**Finishing/ Organization**	Print presentation as handouts (nine slides horizontally/page), re-save & close presentation	**3**	
		TOTAL POINTS: 25		

Assessment 2: Formatting a Presentation for First Choice Travel
PS3-A2-FCTSouthernTours.pptx

Steps	Tasks	Criterion/Criteria	Value	Score
1	**Organization**	Open presentation, re-save	**2**	
2-3	**Command, Formatting & Typing**	In slide 2 insert WordArt with formatting, shape, size & position user-selected; in slide 6 insert WordArt with formatting, shape, size & position user-selected	**8**	
4-5	**Command**	Insert footer bottom center (all slides), rehearse & determine timings for each slide (user-selected)	**5**	
6	**Command/ Enhancement**	Insert audio MIDI clip, set to play across all slides & loop until stopped	**4**	
7-8	**Command**	Set to run continuously, run presentation twice	**3**	
9-10	**Command, Finishing & Organization**	Print as handouts (nine slides horizontally), re-save & close presentation	**3**	
		TOTAL POINTS: 25		

Assessment 3: Learning about Custom Shows
PS3-A3-FCTSouthernTours.pptx

Steps	Tasks	Criterion/Criteria	Value	Score
1	**Organization**	Open presentation, use Save As	3	
2-4	**Research/ Command**	After using Help (or experimenting) create custom show with slides 1, 7, 8 & 9, user-selected name, run presentation	5	
4-5	**Command/ Organization**	Run show, re-save & close presentation	2	
		TOTAL POINTS: 10		

Assessment 4: Individual Challenge (Locating Information and Preparing a Presentation on Social Networking Sites)
PS3-A4-IC-SocialNetwork.pptx

Steps	Tasks	Criterion/Criteria	Value	Score
1-3	**Research, Command, Typing & Enhancement**	After research on the Internet, create presentation on five social networking sites (one slide/site), that includes: info & hyperlink for each, create title slide, insert a minimum of two elements to add visual appeal & animate the objects (user-selected)	12	
4-5	**Organization/ Command**	Save & run presentation	4	
6-7	**Finishing/ Organization**	Print as handouts (six slides horizontally/ page), re-save & close presentation	4	
		TOTAL POINTS: 20		

PowerPoint Section 3 Marquee Challenges Grading Rubrics

Challenge 1: Preparing a Project Schedule Presentation for Marquee Productions
PS3-C1-MPProdSch.pptx

Steps	Tasks	Criterion/Criteria	Value	Score
1	**Command, Formatting, Typing & Editing**	Create presentation in Fig. 3.6, applying design theme, different color theme & different font theme, in Slide Master view (top miniature) change title style font & color, bold, change first level text style font size & close Slide Master, in slide 1 delete title placeholder & insert logo image, remove background color from logo, size & position as shown; in slide 2 insert shape as shown; in slide 3 create & format table as shown; in slides 4 & 5 use finances & teamwork categories to find & insert clip art; insert footer all slides (except first slide)	17	
2-3	**Organization/ Finishing**	Save, print as handout (6 slides/page), close presentation	3	
		TOTAL POINTS: 20		

Challenge 2: Preparing a Moroccan Tour Presentation for First Choice Travel
PS3-C2-FCTMorocco.pptx

Steps	Tasks	Criterion/Criteria	Value	Score
1	**Command, Formatting & Typing**	Create presentation shown in Fig. 3.7, and: apply theme; in slide 1 create WordArt as shown; in Slide Master view insert logo image to appear on slides 3 – 6, set background to transparent, size & position logo as shown; in slide 2 create Bevel shape as shown; in slides 3 & 5 insert clip art images as shown (use mountains & Morocco search terms); in slide 6 create & format table as shown	18	
2-3	**Command & Finishing**	Save, print as handout (six slides/page)	2	
		TOTAL POINTS: 20		

**Integrating Programs: Word, Excel, and PowerPoint
Skills Reviews Grading Rubrics**

Review 1: Exporting a PowerPoint Presentation to Word
Int3-R1-FCTVacations.pptx, Int3-R1-FCTVacationSpecials.docx

Steps	Tasks	Criterion/Criteria	Value	Score
1-2	**Folder/File Management & Organization**	Open Word & PowerPoint, in PowerPoint open a presentation & save to another folder	3	
3-5	**Command, Accuracy & Finishing**	In PowerPoint send data to Word as slides (see detail in Step 3), save, print & close Word Document	4	
6-9	**Editing, Accuracy & Organization**	In PowerPoint, in Slide 4, make three changes, save presentation, print Slide 4, close presentation, in Word open document and update the link	5	
10-11	**Organization / Finishing**	Print page 2, save & close document	3	
		TOTAL POINTS: 15		

Review 2: Linking and Editing an Excel Chart in a PowerPoint Slide
Int3-R2-NPCEnroll.pptx), Int2-R2-NPCEnrollChart.xlsx

Steps	Tasks	Criterion/Criteria	Value	Score
1-4	**Organization, File/Folder Management & Accuracy**	Open Excel & PowerPoint, in PowerPoint, open a presentation and re-save to another folder, make Slide 4 active	4	
5-6	**Command, Accuracy & Editing**	In Excel open a workbook & use Save As to save with different name in another folder, select chart, copy & use Paste Special to link to Slide 4 in PowerPoint	5	
7-9	**Finishing/ Organization**	In In PowerPoint increase size of chart & center it, deselect, save, print Slide 4, close presentation	4	
10-15	**Finishing, Editing, Typing & Organization**	In Excel deselect chart, save & print, from cell A7 insert a new row and type text in several cells, make cell C4 active, save, print & close workbook	5	
16-17	**Accuracy**	In PowerPoint open presentation & update link, make Slide 4 active & review changes	4	
18	**Organization, Accuracy & Finishing**	Save, print only Slide 4, close presentation	3	
		TOTAL POINTS: 25		

Review 3: Embedding and Editing a Word Table in a PowerPoint Slide

Int3-R2-NPCEnroll.pptx, NPCContacts.docx

Steps	Tasks	Criterion/Criteria	Value	Score
1-2	**Organization/ Accuracy**	Make sure Word & PowerPoint are open, in PowerPoint open a presentation, update link, make Slide 5 active	4	
3-4	**Editing, Command & Accuracy**	In Word open a document, select & copy table, in PowerPoint embed it in Slide 5 using Paste Special	5	
5-9	**Formatting, Organization, Editing & Finishing**	With table selected increase size & alter position to better fit slide, deselect table & save presentation, double-click to edit and change word, deselect table, print Slide 5	6	
10-11	**Enhancement/ Command**	Apply transition & sound to all slides (user-selected), run presentation	6	
12-13	**Organization**	Save & close presentation, exit PowerPoint, close Word document & exit Word	4	
		TOTAL POINTS: 25		

Integrating Programs: Word, Excel, Access, and PowerPoint
Skills Reviews Grading Rubrics

Review 1: Exporting Access Data to Excel
Int-PTCostumes.accdb, Int-R1-CostumeInventory.xlsx

Steps	Tasks	Criterion/Criteria	Value	Score
1-3	**Folder/File Management & Organization**	Create new folder, open Access, copy file to new folder & rename it, open database	4	
4-5	**Accuracy, Command & Typing**	Export CostumeInventory table to Excel, saving Excel file under new name, edit three cells by typing	3	
6-8	**Organization/ Finishing**	Re-save workbook, print & close, close Export dialog in Access & close database	3	
		TOTAL POINTS: 10		

Review 2: Exporting an Access Report to Word
Int-PTCostumes.accdb, Int-R2-CostumeInventory.rtf

Steps	Tasks	Criterion/Criteria	Value	Score
1-2	**Organization/ Accuracy**	Open database, export report to Word, rename it	4	
3-5	**Formatting, Organization & Finishing**	In Word, change page orientation, change margins (if necessary), re-save, print & close file, exit Word	4	
6	**Organization**	In Access, close Export dialog dialog, close database	2	
		TOTAL POINTS: 10		

Review 3: Importing Data to a New Table
Int-PTCostumes.accdb, PTCostumeHours.xlsx

Steps	Tasks	Criterion/Criteria	Value	Score
1-2	**Organization, Command & Accuracy**	In Access, open database, import into it an Excel workbook following directions in Step 2	6	
3-6	**Organization/ Finishing**	Open table, print & close, close database, exit Access	4	
		TOTAL POINTS: 10		

Review 4: Exporting a PowerPoint Presentation in Word
Int-R4-FCTVacations.pptx, Int-R4-FCTVacSpecials.docx

Steps	Tasks	Criterion/Criteria	Value	Score
1-2	**Organization & Accuracy**	Open Word & PowerPoint, in PowerPoint open a presentation, re-save & re-name in specific folder	4	
3-5	**Command, Accuracy, Organization & Finishing**	In PowerPoint, send data to Word in specific way (see Step 3), save, print & close document	6	
6-8	**Typing, Finishing & Organization**	In PowerPoint, change info on a slide, save file, print the Slide & close presentation	4	
9-10	**Organization, Accuracy & Finishing**	In Word, open document & update link, print page 2	3	
11-12	**Organization**	Re-save & close document, exit Word	3	
		TOTAL POINTS: 20		

Review 5: Linking and Editing an Excel Chart in a PowerPoint Slide
Int-R5-NPCEnroll.pptx, Int-R5-NPCEnrollChart.xlsx

Steps	Tasks	Criterion/Criteria	Value	Score
1-5	**Organization**	In PowerPoint, open presentation & re-save it, go to slide 4, open Excel, open a workbook & re-save it	4	
6	**Editing, Command & Accuracy**	Select chart, copy & link to slide 4 (use Paste Special)	4	
7-12	**Typing, Finishing & Organization**	Increase chart size & center it, deselect, save presentation, print slide 4, close presentation, switch to Excel, deselect chart, save & print worksheet	7	
13-16	**Editing, Typing, Accuracy, Finishing & Organization**	Insert row in worksheet, type text, select A4, save, print & close workbook, exit Excel	5	
17-19	**Organization, Accuracy & Finishing**	In PowerPoint, open presentation & update link, review slide 4, re-save, print slide, close presentation	5	
		TOTAL POINTS: 25		

Review 6: Embedding and Editing a Word Table in a PowerPoint Slide
Int-R6-NPCEnroll.pptx, NPCContacts.docx

Steps	Tasks	Criterion/Criteria	Value	Score
1-4	**Organization/ Accuracy**	In PowerPoint, open presentation, update link & re-save, go to slide 5, open Word & open a document	5	
5	**Editing, Command & Accuracy**	Select table, copy & embed in slide 5 (Paste Special)	4	
6-11	**Formatting, Organization, Editing & Finishing**	Increase table size & change its position, deselect, save presentation, double-click & edit some text, deselect table, print slide 5, apply animation theme to all slides (user-selected)	7	
12-14	**Command, Organization, Accuracy & Finishing**	Run presentation, save & close presentation, exit PowerPoint, close document & exit Word	4	
		TOTAL POINTS: 20		

Review 7: Linking Data to a New Table and Editing Linked Data
Int-R7-FTCBookings.xlsx, Int-FCTCommissions.accdb

Steps	Tasks	Criterion/Criteria	Value	Score
1-4	**Organization/ Accuracy**	Open Excel, open & re-save workbook, open Access, copy database to other folder, re-name database	5	
5-6	**Command, Accuracy & Finishing**	Link Excel workbook with Access database (details in Step 5), in Access open, print & close new table	6	
7-10	**Formatting, Organization, Editing & Finishing**	In Excel, type formula in C2, press Enter, use Fill Handle to copy to C13, save, print & close worksheet	5	
11-14	**Accuracy, Organization & Finishing**	In Access, open, then save, print & close table, close database, exit Access	4	
		TOTAL POINTS: 20		

Review 8: Embedding an Object
Int-R8-WERevMemo.docx, WEExcelRev.xlsx

Steps	Tasks	Criterion/Criteria	Value	Score
1-3	**Organization/ Accuracy**	Open Word, open document & re-save, in Excel, open workbook	4	
4-6	**Editing, Accuracy, Organization & Finishing**	Embed Excel data from cells a2 – d8 into Word below a paragraph, save & print document, in Excel close workbook & exit Excel	6	
7-9	**Editing, Accuracy & Typing**	Double-click worksheet in Word & edit info in six cells, deselect worksheet, type changes in memo	6	
10-11	**Organization & Finishing**	Save & print memo, close document, exit Word	4	
		TOTAL POINTS: 20		

Supplemental
Skills Assessments

Word
Supplemental Skills Assessment 1

Creating and Formatting an Advertising Flyer

1. Tammy Smith, president of the local saddle club, has asked you to create an advertising flyer to post around town in grocery stores and the Post Office. The flyer needs to be colorful and catchy so people will notice it and read it. Include the following in the flyer.
   a. The name of the club: Ash Grove Saddle Club.
   b. An introduction to the club: If You Have an Interest in Horses or Want to Learn to Ride Them, Come Join Us for Competitions, Trail Rides, Play Days, Picnics, and More!
   c. Phrases about Monthly Events:
      - **<u>Saddle Club Meetings</u>** Held on the second Tuesday of each month, 6:30 p.m. at the Saddle Club Stadium.
      - **<u>Trail Rides</u>** Sign up! Monthly locations announced. Bring a sack lunch and join the fun.
      - **<u>Play Days</u>** Events for children and adults. Every child is a winner!
   d. Contacts and phone numbers for more information:
      - Tammy Smith, President 555-7975
      - Sherry Loftis, Secretary 555-0694
      - Jonathan Wright, Events Coordinator 555-3409
      - Matt Perritt, Competition Coordinator 555-6034
2. You decide the layout and formatting of the flyer using the following guidelines:
   a. Use at least three different font colors and two different font typefaces.
   b. Include at least one graphic image or picture.
   c. For the contact information, left-align the contact name and set a right tab with dot leaders between the name and phone number so the names and numbers line up underneath each other.
3. Before posting the flyer, you would like to send it to the president for review and approval. Prepare an envelope to the president of your school in which the flyer can be sent. Attach the envelope to the flyer. Use the president's name along with the address of your school for the delivery address. Be sure to include a return address as well.
4. Print the flyer and show it to a classmate for any suggestions. Make any changes that you feel are necessary.
5. Save the document with the name **xxSaddleClubFlyer-WordSA1**, where *xx* is your initials, and print the document again if any changes were made.

Word
Supplemental Skills Assessment 1
Answer

Creating and Formatting an Advertising Flyer

In the submitted **xxSaddleClubFlyer-WordSA1.docx** (where *xx* is the student's initials), look for a colorful flyer that is both noticeable and easy to read. Suggest changes to the student if the flyer looks too cluttered or if the text is too small to read from a short distance. The layout and formatting of the flyer will be different for each student, although the content will be basically the same. Specifically, the flyer should include the following "sets" of words:

1. Ash Grove Saddle Club
2. If You Have an Interest in Horses or Want to Learn to Ride Them, Come Join Us for Competitions, Trail Rides, Play Days, Picnics, and More!
3. **Saddle Club Meetings** Held on the second Tuesday of each month, 6:30 p.m. at the Saddle Club Stadium.
4. **Trail Rides** Sign Up! Monthly locations announced. Bring a sack lunch and join the fun.
5. **Play Days** Events for children and adults. Every child is a winner!
6. For more information contact:
   - Tammy Smith, President 555-7975
   - Sherry Loftis, Secretary 555-0694
   - Jonathan Wright, Events Coordinator 555-3409
   - Matt Perritt, Competition Coordinator 555-6034

The flyer should include at least three different font colors and two different font typefaces and a graphic image or picture. The contact information should be lined up with the names on the left and the phone numbers on the right with dot leaders between them. The students have been asked to show their flyers to a classmate so they get ideas from each other and get a chance to experience feedback for their work.

Students are to prepare an envelope to the president of your school that includes the president's name and your school's address as the delivery address. A return address should be included as well.

Word
Supplemental Skills Assessment 1
Model Answer

Creating and Formatting an Advertising Flyer

Ash Grove Saddle Club

If You Have an Interest in Horses or Want to Learn to Ride
Them, Come Join Us for Competitions, Trail Rides, Play Days,
Picnics, and More!

- ✓ <u>Saddle Club Meetings</u> Second Tuesday of each month, 6:30 p.m. at the Saddle Club Stadium.

- ✓ <u>Trail Rides</u> Sign up! Monthly locations announced. Bring a sack lunch and join the fun.

- ✓ <u>Play Days</u> Events for children and adults. Every child is a winner!

For more information contact:

Tammy Smith, President 555-7975
Sherry Loftis, Secretary 555-0694
Jonathan Wright, Events Coordinator 555-3409
Matt Perritt, Competition Coordinator...............................555-6034

Student Name
123 Oak Street
Indianapolis, IN 46203

Tammy Smith
8877 Eastland Drive
Indianapolis, IN 46201

xxSaddleClubFlyer-WordSA1.docx

Word
Supplemental Skills Assessment 1
Grading Rubric

Creating and Formatting an Advertising Flyer

Steps	Tasks	Criterion/Criteria	Value	Score
1	**Typing/ Accuracy**	Create flyer that includes the following information: name of club, introduction to the club, phrases about monthly events; contacts and phone numbers	**10**	
2	**Formatting**	Use at least three different font colors and two different font typefaces; add at least one graphic image or picture; left-align contact name and set a right tab with dot leaders between the name and phone number	**10**	
3	**Typing/ Accuracy**	Create envelope that contains a return address and a delivery address that includes president's name along with the school's address; attach envelope to the flyer	**6**	
4	**Printing**	Print flyer and show to classmate	**2**	
5	**Organization**	Save document with the name **xxSaddleClubFlyer-WordSA1**, where xx is student initials; print the document again	**2**	
		TOTAL POINTS: 30		

Word
Supplemental Skills Assessment 2

Creating and Formatting an Events Newsletter

1. Create a newsletter about current events for a school, church, or other organization that contains the following:
   a. Include at least four topics and provide enough material for a one-page newsletter.
   b. Include a title for the newsletter and subtitles for each topic.
   Hint: Students might enjoy creating a holiday newsletter for this assignment.
2. Format the newsletter as follows:
   a. Center the title of the newsletter across the top of the page.
   b. Add a border and apply light shading to the title.
   c. Set the body of the newsletter in two columns with a line between the columns.
   d. Use a sans serif font of your choice for the titles and subtitles.
   e. Use a serif font of your choice for the body paragraphs of the newsletter.
   f. Bold and enlarge the title of the newsletter. Italicize the subtitles.
   g. Create a footer that includes your name and the page number.
   h. Include a drop cap, text box, or draw a shape to enhance the appearance of the newsletter.
3. Format the document in any other way you see fit.
4. Spell check your document.
5. Save the document with the name **xxEventsNewsletter-WordSA2**, where *xx* is your initials, and print the document.

Word
Supplemental Skills Assessment 2
Answer

Creating and Formatting an Events Newsletter

In the submitted file **xxEventsNewsletter-WordSA2.docx,** where *xx* corresponds with the student's initials, the student will create a one-page, two-column newsletter with a line between the columns. The title should be centered across the top with a border and light shading applied. Look for correct spelling and formatting. A serif font should be used for the body of the newsletter and sans serif fonts should be used for the titles. The title should be enlarged and bolded while the subtitles should be italicized. A drop cap, text box, or shape should be included somewhere throughout the newsletter. The content will vary for each student, but each should contain at least four topics within the newsletter. The newsletter should include a footer containing the student's name and the page number.

Student work will vary based on the subject selected for the activity. A student may wish to use graphics in the newsletter to experiment with text wrapping.

Word
Supplemental Skills Assessment 2
Model Answer

Creating and Formatting an Events Newsletter

Tallulah Springs High Newsletter

It's a Wonderful Life!

The Tallulah High Drama club will be performing its version of *It's a Wonderful Life* on December 10th, 2005. The play begins at 7:00 p.m. in the auditorium. Students are allowed to bring guests. Admission is free.

Our Fabulous Track Team

Congratulations to the Tallulah High track team for finishing first in District Competition! Brian Christopher deserves special mention for setting a new district record. A special edition of the newsletter will be published next week with all the details. Way to go Tigers and way to go Brian!

Math Team Meeting

The Math team will meet Tuesday at 1:00 p.m. to discuss strategies for its upcoming Math Bowl. All students who are participating in the bowl are required to attend. See Mrs. Pringle in room 347 for a letter that will excuse you from your 6th period class.

Debate Team Now Forming

A new Debate team will begin practice for the upcoming year. If you are interested in becoming a part of this fun activity, please contact Mr. Eric Roberts in room 348. Students must be in good standing to participate.

Cheerleading Tryouts

Varsity cheerleading tryouts were held last week. The new members of the squad are:

- Lori Beth Alvarez
- Sandra Gloss
- Susan Chan
- Jackie Lee
- Carolyn Waldegerma
- Autumn Fields
- Eslie Goodman

Congratulations to the new members! ☺

Need Help?

Tallulah High students don't need to struggle with homework. Free tutoring is available for all students. Tutoring hours are from 3:20 p.m. to 5:00 p.m., Monday through Friday. Not only is the tutoring free, transportation will also be provided. Stop by the guidance office to pick up an application. A parent's signature is required.

Student Name   Page 1

xxEventsNewsletter-WordSA2.docx

Word
Supplemental Skills Assessment 2
Grading Rubric

Creating and Formatting an Events Newsletter

Steps	Tasks	Criterion/Criteria	Value	Score
1-2	**Typing/Accuracy**	Create a one-page newsletter about current events for a school, church, or other organization that includes at least four topics; add title for the newsletter and subtitles for each topic	**13**	
2	**Formatting**	Center, bold, and enlarge title of newsletter across the top of page; add a border and apply light shading to the title; set body of newsletter in two columns with a line between the columns; use an appropriate sans serif font for titles and subtitles; use appropriate serif font for the body paragraphs of newsletter; italicize subtitles; create a footer that includes name and page number; include drop cap, text box, or draw a shape to enhance appearance of newsletter	**15**	
5	**Organization**	Save document with the name **xxEventsNewsletter-WordSA2**, where xx is student initials; print the document again	**2**	
		TOTAL POINTS: 30		

Excel
Supplemental Skills Assessment 1

Insurance Report

1. A friend has made several visits to doctors in the past month because of a serious illness and has asked you to calculate what will be owed after the insurance has been paid. The insurance company usually takes about a month to process a claim and your friend is hoping you can help figure the amount right away so he or she can plan ahead.
2. Create a worksheet to include the following information from the visits to the doctor:

Date of Visit	Doctor	Cost of Visit
2/4/2010	Goodman	$113.00
2/5/2010	Goodman	$145.00
2/11/2010	Loman	$120.00
2/12/2010	Goodman	$110.00
2/15/2010	Loman	$140.00
2/18/2010	Loman	$175.00
2/19/2010	Loman	$135.00
2/22/2010	Walker	$215.00
2/25/2010	Walker	$235.00
2/27/2010	Loman	$120.00
2/28/2010	Goodman	$105.00

4. Your friend has a co-payment of $25.00 and the insurance will pay 80% of the remaining cost. Create a formula for each visit that will calculate the amount your friend will have to pay.
5. The insurance company is supposed to respond within 30 days of billing. The doctor's office has said that they will bill within 3 days of the visit. Add a column that will indicate the date the insurance company will respond for each visit.
6. Use a built-in function to calculate the highest cost of visit. In addition, use a built-in function to calculate the total amount that your friend will have to pay. Label these areas appropriately.
7. Add a title to the worksheet that is centered over the columns.
8. Format the worksheet to your choosing and include your name in a footer.
9. Format the worksheet so that it appears horizontally and vertically centered on the page when it is printed.
10. Save the file giving it the name **xxInsuranceReport-ExcelSA1**, replacing *xx* with your initials. Print the worksheet.

Excel
Supplemental Skills Assessment 1
Answer

Insurance Report

In file **xxInsuranceReport-ExcelSA1.xlsx**, where *xx* corresponds to the student's initials, the student will be creating a worksheet for a friend to calculate what will be owed after the insurance company has paid on several visits to doctors in a month. The students will format their worksheets. Look for the following items in each worksheet:

1. Information from the visits including the date of the visit, the doctor's name, and the cost of the visit.
2. A formula that calculates the amount owed after a $25 co-payment and then 80% coverage.
3. The MAX and SUM functions being used to calculate the highest cost of visit and the total amount owed.
4. A formula that calculates the date the insurance company should respond for each visit, which will be 33 days after the visit.
5. A title that is merged and centered over the columns.
6. The worksheet that is horizontally and vertically centered.
7. A footer including the student's name.

The following shows the data that should be entered or calculated in the worksheet:

Date of Visit	Doctor	Cost of Visit	Amount Owed	Insurance Responds
2/4/2010	Goodman	$113.00	$42.60	3/9/2010
2/5/2010	Goodman	$145.00	$49.00	3/10/2010
2/11/2010	Loman	$120.00	$44.00	3/16/2010
2/12/2010	Goodman	$110.00	$42.00	3/17/2010
2/15/2010	Loman	$140.00	$48.00	3/20/2010
2/18/2010	Loman	$175.00	$55.00	3/23/2010
2/19/2010	Loman	$135.00	$47.00	3/24/2010
2/22/2010	Walker	$215.00	$63.00	3/27/2010
2/25/2010	Walker	$235.00	$67.00	3/30/2010
2/27/2010	Loman	$120.00	$44.00	4/1/2010
2/28/2010	Goodman	$105.00	$41.00	4/2/2010

Excel
Supplemental Skills Assessment 1
Model Answer

Insurance Report

Insurance Records				
Date of Visit	Doctor	Cost of Visit	Amount Owed	Insurance Responds
2/4/2010	Goodman	$113.00	$42.60	3/9/2010
2/5/2010	Goodman	$145.00	$49.00	3/10/2010
2/11/2010	Loman	$120.00	$44.00	3/16/2010
2/12/2010	Goodman	$110.00	$42.00	3/17/2010
2/15/2010	Loman	$140.00	$48.00	3/20/2010
2/18/2010	Loman	$175.00	$55.00	3/23/2010
2/19/2010	Loman	$135.00	$47.00	3/24/2010
2/22/2010	Walker	$215.00	$63.00	3/27/2010
2/25/2010	Walker	$235.00	$67.00	3/30/2010
2/27/2010	Loman	$120.00	$44.00	4/1/2010
2/28/2010	Goodman	$105.00	$41.00	4/2/2010
Highest Cost of Visit		$235.00		
Total Amount Owed			$542.60	

Student Name

xxInsuranceReport-ExcelSA1.xlsx

Excel
Supplemental Skills Assessment 1
Grading Rubric

Insurance Report

Steps	Tasks	Criterion/Criteria	Value	Score
2	**Typing/ Accuracy**	Create worksheet that includes the date of visit, the doctor's name, and the cost of visit	**10**	
3	**Formulas**	Create formula that calculates the amount owed after a $25 co-payment and then 80% coverage (Formula : **=CostofVisit-(CostofVisit-25)*.80**)	**4**	
4	**Formulas**	Create formula in a new column that calculates the date the insurance company should respond for each visit, which will be 33 days after the visit (Formula: **=DateofVisit+33**); label appropriately	**3**	
5	**Functions**	Use built-in function to calculate highest cost of visit (MAX function); use built-in function to calculate total amount that friend will have to pay (SUM function); label appropriately	**6**	
6-8	**Formatting**	Add title to worksheet that is centered over columns; add student name in footer; format worksheet to appear horizontally and vertically centered on page	**5**	
9	**Organization**	Save file with the name **xxInsuranceReport-ExcelSA1**, where xx is student initials; print the file	**2**	
		TOTAL POINTS: 30		

Excel
Supplemental Skills Assessment 2

Stock Shares Analysis

1. You have saved $1,500 and you are considering investing your money by buying shares of stock. You are interested in purchasing stock from companies that you personally support. Go online and find the following information about stock prices from five companies with which you do business:
   a. Stock price from one year ago
   b. Today's stock price

2. Now enter this data into an Excel worksheet. Be sure to include the title *Stock Shares Analysis* and include your name as a subtitle. Enter the information for each company in different rows. Enter the name of the company in the first column, the stock price from one year ago in the second column, and today's stock price in the third column. Enter the investment amount in the row below the companies. Label the amount appropriately in a separate cell.

3. Calculate the percent of growth (or decline) from last year to this year for each company by entering the appropriate formula in the fourth column of information. The percent of growth is calculated by subtracting last year's price from today's price and dividing the result by last year's price. (If the result is a negative number, there was a decline rather than growth.)

4. Calculate how many shares you can purchase with your savings (investment amount) based on today's price for each company. Enter the formula for this information in the fifth column. Add a comment in this column indicating how the shares were calculated. In other words, explain the formula.

5. In the sixth column, enter a formula that will display "Increased" if the value of the shares increased or "Declined" if the value of the stock declined from last year to this year.

6. Identify all columns appropriately.

7. Create a line chart that shows the growth or decline from last year to this year. Be sure to include a title, labels, and a legend.

8. Sort the companies and their data in alphabetical order.

9. Save the worksheet as **xxStock-ExcelSA2**, replacing *xx* with your initials, and print the worksheet.

10. You are curious to see how many shares you could purchase from any one company if you saved an extra $500. Increase the savings amount to $2,000 and print the worksheet again. Close the worksheet without saving the changes.

Excel
Supplemental Skills Assessment 2
Answer

Stock Shares Analysis

Each student will research stock prices from different companies, but the layout of the spreadsheet (file name **xxStock-ExcelSA2.xlsx**, with *xx* corresponding to the student's initials) should be basically the same and each should contain the same types of formulas. Each should contain the following information:

1. The title *Stock Shares Analysis* and the student's name as the subtitle.
2. Savings of $1,500.
3. The following information for five different companies:
   a. The name of the company
   b. Stock price from one year ago
   c. Today's stock price
   d. The percent of growth (or decline) from last year to this year
      The percent of growth is calculated by subtracting last year's price from today's price and dividing the result by last year's price. (If the result is a negative number, there was a decline rather than growth.)
   e. "Increased" or "Declined," depending on the growth or decline of the stock from last year to this year. The increase or decline is determined by using the IF function.
   f. The number of shares that can be purchased with the savings based on today's price for each company.
4. A comment should be added to the *Shares Purchased* column indicating how the shares were calculated.
5. A line chart that shows the growth or decline from last year to this year for each company. A title, labels, and a legend should be included.
6. The student should have two printouts. The first will show the original data (see **xxStock-ExcelSA2_Step9.pdf**). In the second printout the student should have changed the savings to $2,000, which will then change the amounts of shares that can be purchased (see **xxStock-ExcelSA2_Step10.pdf**).

Excel
Supplemental Skills Assessment 2
Model Answer

Stock Shares Analysis

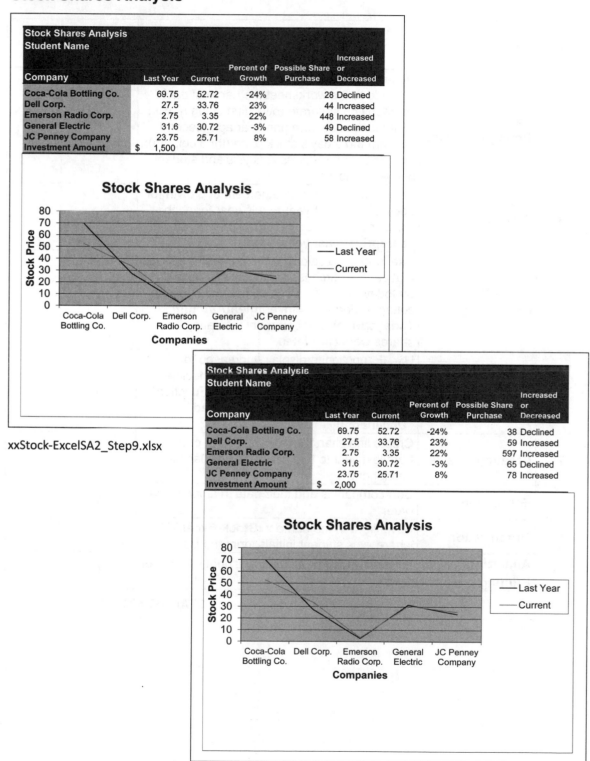

Stock Shares Analysis
Student Name

Company	Last Year	Current	Percent of Growth	Possible Share Purchase	Increased or Decreased
Coca-Cola Bottling Co.	69.75	52.72	-24%	28	Declined
Dell Corp.	27.5	33.76	23%	44	Increased
Emerson Radio Corp.	2.75	3.35	22%	448	Increased
General Electric	31.6	30.72	-3%	49	Declined
JC Penney Company	23.75	25.71	8%	58	Increased
Investment Amount	$ 1,500				

xxStock-ExcelSA2_Step9.xlsx

Stock Shares Analysis
Student Name

Company	Last Year	Current	Percent of Growth	Possible Share Purchase	Increased or Decreased
Coca-Cola Bottling Co.	69.75	52.72	-24%	38	Declined
Dell Corp.	27.5	33.76	23%	59	Increased
Emerson Radio Corp.	2.75	3.35	22%	597	Increased
General Electric	31.6	30.72	-3%	65	Declined
JC Penney Company	23.75	25.71	8%	78	Increased
Investment Amount	$ 2,000				

xxStock-ExcelSA2_Step10.xlsx

Excel
Supplemental Skills Assessment 2
Grading Rubric

Stock Shares Analysis

Steps	Tasks	Criterion/Criteria	Value	Score
1-2	**Researching/ Typing/Accuracy**	Research stock prices from five companies and add to the worksheet the name of each company on separate rows (first column) with their stock price from one year ago (second column)and today's stock price (third column); include the title *Shares Analysis* and student name as subtitle	7	
3	**Formulas**	Use formula to calculate percent of growth (or decline) from last year to this year for each company (Formula: **=(Todaysprice-Last yearsprice)/Last yearsprice**)	3	
4	**Formulas/ Formatting**	Use formula to calculate the number of shares that can be purchased with savings based on today's price for each company (fifth column) (Formula: **=InvestmentAmount/ Todaysprice**); add comment indicating how shares were calculated	4	
5	**Functions**	Use IF function to display "Increased" or "Declined" depending on growth or decline of stock from last year to this year (Function: **=IF(PercentofGrowth>0, "Increased", "Declined")**)	4	
7	**Creating Charts**	Create line chart that shows growth or decline from last year to this year; add title, labels, and legend	6	
8	**Formatting**	Sort companies and their data in alphabetical order	2	
9	**Organization**	Save file with the name **xxStock-ExcelSA2**, where xx is student initials; print the file	2	
10	**Analyzing/ Printing**	Increase investment to $2000; print worksheet again	2	
		TOTAL POINTS: 30		

Access
Supplemental Skills Assessment 1

Pre-Owned Car Business

1. You have been asked by the owner of a pre-owned car dealership to set up a way to track the cars in his inventory. He often needs to search his records for specific makes and models or cars made in certain years. He also wants to be able to generate reports based on his sales and reports on which sales representatives are doing the most business.

2. Create a new Access database and set up table named *Sales Reps* using this information:

Rep Number	Last Name	First Name	Address	City	State	ZIP	Phone
1	Perry	Jim	3453 E. State	Jacksonville	FL	32231	904-555-4353
2	Bauer	Evan	5347 W. Grand	Jacksonville	FL	32232	904-555-3423
3	Dickens	Billy	2351 S. Ferguson	Jacksonville	FL	32232	904-555-5632

3. Create a table named *Inventory* with the data shown below, using these guidelines:
   a. Set up an autonumber to use for a primary key.
   b. Use a drop-down list to enter the condition. Possible conditions are Excellent, Good, Fair, and Poor.
   c. Use a drop-down list for the sale representative. The drop-down list should reference the Sales Reps table for choices.

Make	Model	Year	Description	Condition	Cost	Selling Price	Date Arrived	Date Sold	Sales Rep
Pontiac	Grand Am	2005	4-Door, Red	Excellent	$8,000	$9,990	5/5/10	6/1/10	Perry
Lincoln	Town Car	2001	2-Door, White	Good	$5,500	$5,995	4/15/10	4/20/10	Dickens
Chevrolet	Cavalier	2005	4-Door, Blue	Excellent	$7,000		5/15/10		
Toyota	Corolla	2001	4-Door, Black	Fair	$4,000		5/1/10		
Ford	Tempo	2002	2-Door, Red	Poor	$2,000		5/5/10		
Chevrolet	Lumina	2005	2-Door, White	Excellent	$8,500		5/12/10		
Ford	Focus	2003	5 Speed, Black	Good	$6,500	$7,000	4/20/10	4/30/10	Perry
Ford	Escort	2000	2-Door, White	Excellent	$5,500		5/3/10		
Plymouth	Neon	2001	4-Door, Blue	Good	$6,500		5/1/10		

4. Create a form to enter a4nd edit inventory information. You decide on the design of the form.

5. Enter the following record into the Inventory table using the new form:

Make	Model	Year	Description	Condition	Cost	Selling Price	Date Arrived	Date Sold	Sales Rep
Ford	Taurus LX	2003	Wagon, Gray	Excellent	$8,200		5/20/10		

6. The Chevrolet Lumina was sold on 5/20/10 by Bauer for $9,300. Update the record using the form.

7. Create the followin0g reports using whatever method you prefer. Format the reports so that information is easy to find, give each report an applicable title, and include the date and your name on the report. ***Hint: You may need to create a query to obtain the desired information, and then base the report on the query.***
   a. All vehicles available for sale, sorted by cost in descending order.
   b. All vehicles sold, grouped by Sales Rep.
   c. All vehicles made by Ford.

8. Print the reports.

Access
Supplemental Skills Assessment 1
Answer

Pre-Owned Car Business

The student will create a database for the owner of a pre-owned car dealership to set up a way to track the cars in his inventory and to generate reports based on his sales and reports on which sales representatives are doing the most business. Verify that the student has created lookup lists for the *Condition* and *Sales Rep* fields in the Inventory table. A new record for a Ford Taurus LX and its associated information should have been added to the Inventory table. The form (see **InventoryForm-AccessSA1_Step4.pdf**) should be formatted with a title. The database solution can be found in the **PreOwnedCars-AccessSA1** database.

The reports solutions can be found in the For Sale report (see **InvntoryforSales-AccessSA1_Step7a.pdf**), the By Sales Rep report (see **InventorySoldBySalesRep-AccessSA1_Step7b.pdf and InventorySoldBySalesRep-AccessSA1_Step7b_alternateformat.pdf**), and the Ford Inventory report (see **FordInventory-AccessSA1_Step7c.pdf**).

Access
Supplemental Skills Assessment 1
Model Answer

Pre-Owned Car Business

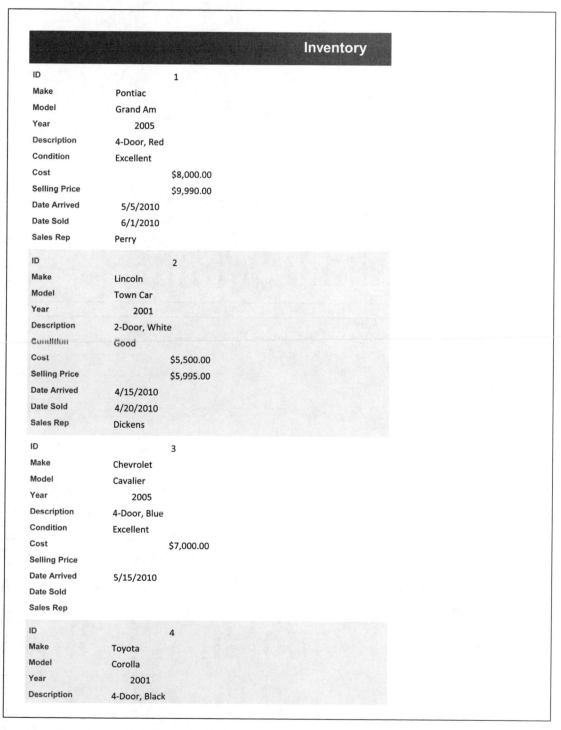

	Inventory
ID	1
Make	Pontiac
Model	Grand Am
Year	2005
Description	4-Door, Red
Condition	Excellent
Cost	$8,000.00
Selling Price	$9,990.00
Date Arrived	5/5/2010
Date Sold	6/1/2010
Sales Rep	Perry

ID	2
Make	Lincoln
Model	Town Car
Year	2001
Description	2-Door, White
Condition	Good
Cost	$5,500.00
Selling Price	$5,995.00
Date Arrived	4/15/2010
Date Sold	4/20/2010
Sales Rep	Dickens

ID	3
Make	Chevrolet
Model	Cavalier
Year	2005
Description	4-Door, Blue
Condition	Excellent
Cost	$7,000.00
Selling Price	
Date Arrived	5/15/2010
Date Sold	
Sales Rep	

ID	4
Make	Toyota
Model	Corolla
Year	2001
Description	4-Door, Black

InventoryForm-AccessSA1_Step 4 (1 of 3)

InventoryForm-AccessSA1_Step 4 (2 of 3)

Condition	Fair
Cost	$4,000.00
Selling Price	
Date Arrived	5/1/2010
Date Sold	
Sales Rep	

ID	5
Make	Ford
Model	Tempo
Year	2002
Description	2-Door, Red
Condition	Poor
Cost	$2,000.00
Selling Price	
Date Arrived	5/5/2010
Date Sold	
Sales Rep	

ID	6
Make	Chevrolet
Model	Lumina
Year	2005
Description	2-Door, White
Condition	Excellent
Cost	$8,500.00
Selling Price	$9,300.00
Date Arrived	5/12/2010
Date Sold	5/20/2010
Sales Rep	Bauer

ID	7
Make	Ford
Model	Focus
Year	2003
Description	5 Speed, Black
Condition	Good
Cost	$6,500.00
Selling Price	$7,000.00
Date Arrived	4/20/2010
Date Sold	4/30/2010
Sales Rep	Perry

InventoryForm-AccessSA1_Step 4 (3 of 3)

ID	8
Make	Ford
Model	Escort
Year	2000
Description	2-Door, White
Condition	Excellent
Cost	$5,500.00
Selling Price	
Date Arrived	5/3/2010
Date Sold	
Sales Rep	

ID	9
Make	Plymouth
Model	Neon
Year	2001
Description	4-Door, Blue
Condition	Good
Cost	$6,500.00
Selling Price	
Date Arrived	5/1/2010
Date Sold	
Sales Rep	

ID	10
Make	Ford
Model	Taurus LX
Year	2003
Description	Wagon, Gray
Condition	Excellent
Cost	$8,200.00
Selling Price	
Date Arrived	5/20/2010
Date Sold	
Sales Rep	

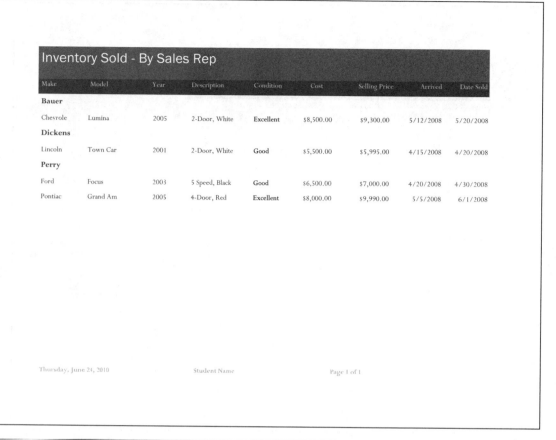

Inventory Sold - By Sales Rep

Make	Model	Year	Description	Condition	Cost	Selling Price	Arrived	Date Sold
Bauer								
Chevrole	Lumina	2005	2-Door, White	Excellent	$8,500.00	$9,300.00	5/12/2008	5/20/2008
Dickens								
Lincoln	Town Car	2001	2-Door, White	Good	$5,500.00	$5,995.00	4/15/2008	4/20/2008
Perry								
Ford	Focus	2003	5 Speed, Black	Good	$6,500.00	$7,000.00	4/20/2008	4/30/2008
Pontiac	Grand Am	2005	4-Door, Red	Excellent	$8,000.00	$9,990.00	5/5/2008	6/1/2008

Thursday, June 24, 2010   Student Name   Page 1 of 1

InventoryForm-AccessSA1_Step 7b

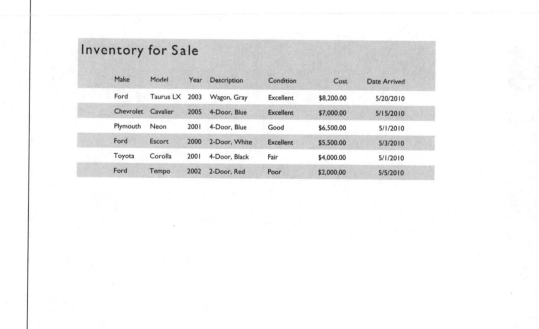

Inventory for Sale

Make	Model	Year	Description	Condition	Cost	Date Arrived
Ford	Taurus LX	2003	Wagon, Gray	Excellent	$8,200.00	5/20/2010
Chevrolet	Cavalier	2005	4-Door, Blue	Excellent	$7,000.00	5/15/2010
Plymouth	Neon	2001	4-Door, Blue	Good	$6,500.00	5/1/2010
Ford	Escort	2000	2-Door, White	Excellent	$5,500.00	5/3/2010
Toyota	Corolla	2001	4-Door, Black	Fair	$4,000.00	5/1/2010
Ford	Tempo	2002	2-Door, Red	Poor	$2,000.00	5/5/2010

Tuesday, June 29, 2010   Report by Student Name   Page 1 of 1

InventoryForm-AccessSA1_Step 7a

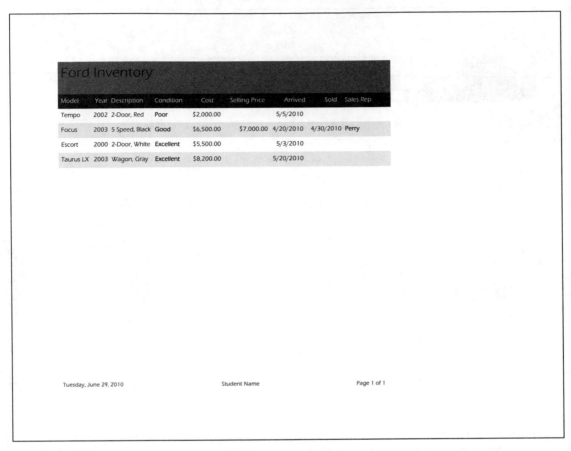

Ford Inventory

Model	Year	Description	Condition	Cost	Selling Price	Arrived	Sold	Sales Rep
Tempo	2002	2-Door, Red	Poor	$2,000.00		5/5/2010		
Focus	2003	5 Speed, Black	Good	$6,500.00	$7,000.00	4/20/2010	4/30/2010	Perry
Escort	2000	2-Door, White	Excellent	$5,500.00		5/3/2010		
Taurus LX	2003	Wagon, Gray	Excellent	$8,200.00		5/20/2010		

Tuesday, June 29, 2010   Student Name   Page 1 of 1

InventoryForm-AccessSA1_Step 7c

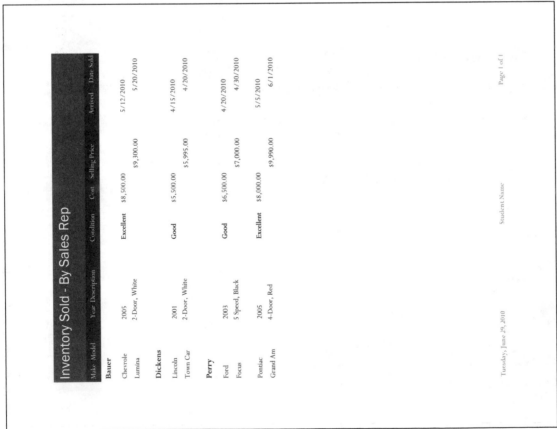

Inventory Sold - By Sales Rep

Make-Model	Year	Description	Condition	Cost	Selling Price	Arrived	Date Sold
Bauer							
Chevrole	2005		Excellent	$8,500.00		5/12/2010	
Lumina		2-Door, White			$9,300.00		5/20/2010
Dickens							
Lincoln	2001		Good	$5,500.00		4/15/2010	
Town Car		2-Door, White			$5,995.00		4/20/2010
Perry							
Ford	2003		Good	$6,500.00		4/20/2010	
Focus		5 Speed, Black			$7,000.00		4/30/2010
Pontiac	2005		Excellent	$8,000.00		5/5/2010	
Grand Am		4-Door, Red			$9,990.00		6/1/2010

Tuesday, June 29, 2010   Student Name   Page 1 of 1

InventoryForm-AccessSA1_Step 7b_alternateformat

Access
Supplemental Skills Assessment 1
Grading Rubric

Pre-Owned Car Business

Steps	Tasks	Criterion/Criteria	Value	Score
2	**Creating Databases/Tables**	Create a new database; create a table named *Sales Reps*; use appropriate data types and field sizes for the information in the table	5	
3	**Creating Tables**	Create a table named *Inventory*; use appropriate data types and fields sizes for the information in the table; set up an autonumber to use for a primary key; use drop-down list to enter conditions for the *Condition* field; use drop-down list for the Sales Rep field	10	
4	**Creating Forms**	Create form based on *Inventory* table; format appropriately	2	
5-6	**Maintaining Databases**	Add new record pertaining to the Ford Taurus LX to *Inventory* table; delete record pertaining to Chevrolet Lumina from the *Inventory* table	2	
7	**Creating Reports**	Create and format appropriately the following reports; include an applicable title, the date, and student name on each of the reports • Vehicles available for sales; sorted by cost in descending order • Vehicles sold, grouped by Sales Rep • Vehicles made by Ford	10	
8	**Printing Reports**	Print three reports created in Step #7	1	
		TOTAL POINTS: 30		

Access
Supplemental Skills Assessment 2

Practice with Queries

1. Open the **WEEmployees4.accdb** database file (located in the AccessS4 subfolder on the CD that accompanies the textbook). Create, save, and print the following queries:

Query Name	Display Fields	Include Records	Sorted By
Employees by Department	First_Name Last_Name Annual_Salary Department	All	Department Ascending
Employees with the Dental Plan	Employee_No First_Name Last_Name	Where Dental Plan is True	None
Salaries over $50,000	Employee_No First_Name Last_Name Annual_Salary Department	Where Annual Salary is over $50,000	Annual Salary Descending

2. Modify the Employees by Department query by calculating the total salaries for each department. Save the modified query as *Total Salaries by Department*.

3. Create a report based on the Employees by Department query. You choose the layout and formatting of the report. Save the report as *Employees by Department* and print it.

4. Create a report that displays the employees' names (in alphabetical order by last name), current salary, and projected salary for next year. The projected salary is based on a 3% increase of the current year salary. Save the report as *Projected Salaries for 20xx* where *xx* represents next year. Print the report.

Access
Supplemental Skills Assessment 2
Answer

Practice with Queries

1. The student will create three queries that all require the use of more than one table. The second query requires a field that will not be displayed to be used in determining which records to include.

2. The records in the Salaries over $50,000 query should be displayed in descending order according to amount.

3. The Employees by Department query will be modified to display the total annual salaries grouped by department. This new query will be saved as *Total Salaries by Department*.

4. The student will also create a report based on the Employees by Department query. The records should be displayed in descending order according to department. The student will choose the layout and formatting of the report.

5. The student will create a report containing the following fields: employees' names (in alphabetical order by last name), current salaries, and projected salaries. The projected salaries field is a new field that is based on a 3% increase of the current annual salary. A possible calculation would be: (=[Annual Salary]*.03+[Annual Salary]).

Access
Supplemental Skills Assessment 2
Model Answer

Practice with Queries

Employees by Department   6/25/2012

First_Name	Last_Name	Annual_Salary	Department
Carl	Zakowski	$44,387.00	European Distribution
Hanh	Postma	$69,725.00	European Distribution
Valerie	Fitsouris	$44,694.00	European Distribution
Terry	Yiu	$42,238.00	European Distribution
Donald	McKnight	$42,126.00	European Distribution
George	Featherstone	$38,175.00	European Distribution
Leo	Couture	$43,659.00	European Distribution
Vanessa	Comeaux	$38,175.00	North American Distribution
Lyle	Besterd	$45,651.00	North American Distribution
Angela	Doxtator	$45,558.00	North American Distribution
Jorge	Biliski	$44,892.00	North American Distribution
Sam	Vestering	$69,725.00	North American Distribution
Pat	Hildebrand	$40,175.00	North American Distribution
Pat	Hildebrand	$40,175.00	North American Distribution
Norm	Liszniewski	$43,695.00	North American Distribution
Jane	Charlton	$38,175.00	Overseas Distribution
Edward	Thurston	$42,248.00	Overseas Distribution
Thom	Hicks	$42,824.00	Overseas Distribution
Balfor	Jhawar	$44,771.00	Overseas Distribution
Mike	Fitchett	$42,857.00	Overseas Distribution
Roman	Deptulski	$69,725.00	Overseas Distribution
Guy	Lafreniere	$45,395.00	Overseas Distribution

Page 1

EmployeesbyDepartment-AccessSA2_Step1

Employees with Dental Plan   6/25/2012

Employee_No	First_Name	Last_Name
1000	Sam	Vestering
1005	Roman	Deptulski
1015	Lyle	Besterd
1020	Angela	Doxtator
1025	Jorge	Biliski
1040	Guy	Lafreniere
1055	Edward	Thurston
1065	Norm	Liszniewski
1075	Mike	Fitchett
1100	George	Featherstone
1105	Vanessa	Comeaux
1110	Jane	Charlton

Page 1

EmployeeswithDentalPlan-AccessSA2_Step1

Salaries Over 50000   6/25/2012

Employee_No	First_Name	Last_Name	Annual_Salary	Department
1010	Hanh	Postma	$69,725.00	European Distribution
1005	Roman	Deptulski	$69,725.00	Overseas Distribution
1000	Sam	Vestering	$69,725.00	North American Distribution

Page 1

SalariesOver50000-AccessSA2_Step1

Total Salaries by Department

6/25/2012

Total Annual Salaries	Department
$325,004.00	European Distribution
$368,046.00	North American Distribution
$325,995.00	Overseas Distribution

TotalSalariesbyDepartment-AccessSA2_Step2

Employees by Department

First_Name	Last_Name	Annual_Salary	Department
Carl	Zakowski	$44,387.00	European Distribution
Hanh	Postma	$69,725.00	European Distribution
Valerie	Fitsouris	$44,694.00	European Distribution
Terry	Yiu	$42,238.00	European Distribution
Donald	McKnight	$42,126.00	European Distribution
George	Featherstone	$38,175.00	European Distribution
Leo	Couture	$43,659.00	European Distribution
Vanessa	Comeaux	$38,175.00	North American Distribution
Lyle	Besterd	$45,651.00	North American Distribution
Angela	Doxtator	$45,558.00	North American Distribution
Jorge	Biliski	$44,892.00	North American Distribution
Sam	Vestering	$69,725.00	North American Distribution
Pat	Hildebrand	$40,175.00	North American Distribution
Pat	Hildebrand	$40,175.00	North American Distribution
Norm	Liszniewski	$43,695.00	North American Distribution
Jane	Charlton	$38,175.00	Overseas Distribution
Edward	Thurston	$42,248.00	Overseas Distribution
Thom	Hicks	$42,824.00	Overseas Distribution
Balfor	Jhawar	$44,771.00	Overseas Distribution
Mike	Fitchett	$42,857.00	Overseas Distribution
Roman	Deptulski	$69,725.00	Overseas Distribution
Guy	Lafreniere	$45,395.00	Overseas Distribution

EmployeesbyDepartment-AccessSA2_Step3

Projected Salaries for 20XX

Last_Name	First_Name	Annual_Salary	Projected_Annual_Salary
Besterd	Lyle	$45,651.00	$47,020.53
Biliski	Jorge	$44,892.00	$46,238.76
Charlton	Jane	$38,175.00	$39,320.25
Comeaux	Vanessa	$38,175.00	$39,320.25
Couture	Leo	$43,659.00	$44,968.77
Deptulski	Roman	$69,725.00	$71,816.75
Doxtator	Angela	$45,558.00	$46,924.74
Featherstone	George	$38,175.00	$39,320.25
Fitchett	Mike	$42,857.00	$44,142.71
Fitsouris	Valerie	$44,694.00	$46,034.82
Hicks	Thom	$42,824.00	$44,108.72
Hildebrand	Pat	$40,175.00	$41,380.25
Hildebrand	Pat	$40,175.00	$41,380.25
Jhawar	Balfor	$44,771.00	$46,114.13
Lafreniere	Guy	$45,395.00	$46,756.85
Liszniewski	Norm	$43,695.00	$45,005.85
McKnight	Donald	$42,126.00	$43,389.78
Postma	Hanh	$69,725.00	$71,816.75
Thurston	Edward	$42,248.00	$43,515.44

ProjectedSalariesfor20XX-AccessSA2_Step4 (1 of 2)

Last_Name	First_Name	Annual_Salary	Projected_Annual_Salary
Vestering	Sam	$69,725.00	$71,816.75
Yiu	Terry	$42,238.00	$43,505.14
Zakowski	Carl	$44,387.00	$45,718.61

ProjectedSalariesfor20XX-AccessSA2_Step4 (2 of 2)

Access
Supplemental Skills Assessment 2
Grading Rubric

Practice with Queries

Steps	Tasks	Criterion/Criteria	Value	Score
1	**Creating Queries**	Open **WEEmployees4.accdb** database file and create the following queries: • **Employees by Department** query – Display First_Name, Last_Name, Annual_Salary, and Department fields; display all records; sort *Department* field in ascending order • **Employees with the Dental Plan** query – Display Employee_No, First_Name, and Last_Name fields; include records where Dental Plan is True • **Salaries over $50,000** query – Display Employee_No, First_Name, Last_Name, Annual_Salary, and Department fields; include records where Annual Salary is over $50,000; sort *Annual Salary* field in descending order	9	
2	**Formulas in Queries**	Modify *Employees by Department* query by calculating the total salaries for each department; save modified query as *Total Salaries by Department;* (Use the Aggregate function SUM; grouped by *Department)*	5	
3	**Creating Reports**	Create report named *Employees by Department,* based on the *Employees by Department* query; format appropriately; print the report	6	
4	**Creating Reports**	Create report named *Projected Salaries for 20xx,* where xx represents next year; display employees' names (in alphabetical order by last name), current salary, and projected salary for next year (new field); (Project Salary formula: **=[Annual Salary]*.03+[Annual Salary]**); format appropriately; print report	10	
		TOTAL POINTS: 30		

PowerPoint
Supplemental Skills Assessment 1

Fund-Raising Event

1. Create a PowerPoint presentation for a fund-raising event that will be held at the local mall for publicity.

    a. You decide on the cause.

    b. You decide on the fund-raising event.

    c. Include at least four slides detailing the event, including the following information:

        – Introduce the event and the cause.

        – Detail how the money will be used.

        – State the date/time/place of event.

        – State who to contact for further questions.

    d. Include at least one graphic image or picture per slide.

    e. Include two levels of text indent (use List Level buttons) for at least one slide.

    f. Select a design template and an animation scheme.

2. Run the presentation. Save it with the name **xxFundRaiser-PPSA1**, where *xx* is your initials, and print the slide handouts at six slides per page.

PowerPoint
Supplemental Skills Assessment 1
Answer

Fund-Raising Event

The student will create a PowerPoint presentation (file name **xxFundRaiser-PPSA1.pptx**, where *xx* corresponds with the student's initials) for a fund-raising event that will be held at the local mall for publicity. The student will decide on the cause being supported as well as the event for the fund-raiser. The student will also select a design template and animation scheme. Look for the following to be included in the presentation:

1. At least four slides detailing the event, including the following information:

    a. Introduce the event and the cause.

    b. How the money will be used.

    c. Date/time/place of event.

    d. Who to contact for further questions.

2. At least one graphic image or picture per slide.

3. Two levels of text indent for at least one slide.

Also look for continuity among the design template, the graphic images, and the theme of the cause and the event. Students should also present the material in a clear and organized manner with no spelling or grammar errors.

PowerPoint
Supplemental Skills Assessment 1
Model Answer

Fund-Raising Event

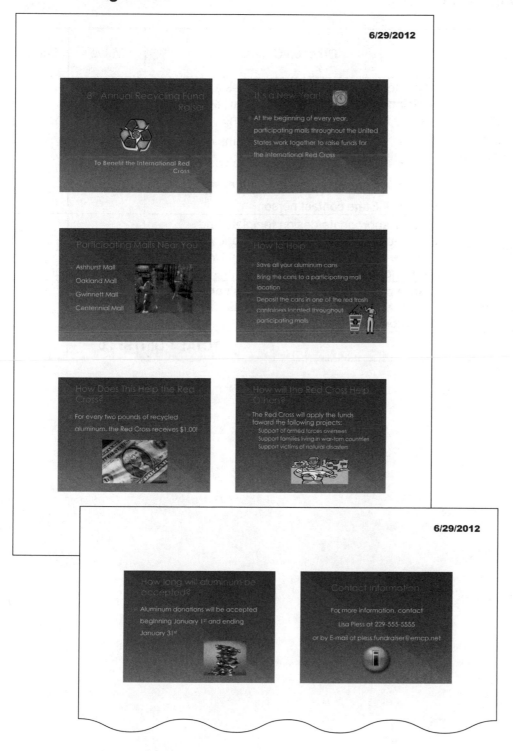

xxFundRaiser-PPSA1.pdf

PowerPoint
Supplemental Skills Assessment 1
Grading Rubric

Fund-Raising Event

Steps	Tasks	Criterion/Criteria	Value	Score
1	**Creating Presentations**	Create presentation that promotes a fund-raising event held at the local mall; add four slides that will include the following information: • Introduce the event and the cause • Detail how money will be used • State date/time/place of event • State contact person	10	
1	**Formatting**	Apply appropriate design template and animation scheme; add at least one graphic image or picture per slide; include two levels of text indent for at least one slide	8	
2	**Organization**	Save presentation as **xxFundRaiser-PPSA1. pptx**, where **xx** is student's initials; print slide handouts at six slides per page	2	
		TOTAL POINTS: 20		

PowerPoint
Supplemental Skills Assessment 2

Social Club Meeting

1. Create a PowerPoint presentation for a social club meeting. You decide on what type of club as well as the actual content of the slides. This will be the first meeting of the year and should contain the following on at least five different slides:

   a. Welcome everyone to the meeting.

   b. Summarize the events of last year.

   c. List the monies spent during the past year and how they were spent.

   d. Ask for goals for the upcoming year.

   e. Ask for actions to be taken before the next meeting.

2. Format the presentation as you wish, including the following items:

   a. Include at least two graphic images or pictures.

   b. Select a design template and transition effects.

   c. Add sound or video to one slide.

   d. Include WordArt.

   e. Include at least one action button or hyperlink.

   f. Include an appropriate header or footer.

3. Set the show to transition automatically after an appropriate amount of time.

4. Set the show to run continuously so that when the final slide has displayed, the show will begin again.

5. Run the presentation. Save it with the name **xxClubMeeting-PPSA2**, where *xx* is your initials, and print the slide handouts at six slides per page.

PowerPoint
Supplemental Skills Assessment 2
Answer

Social Club Meeting

The student will create a PowerPoint presentation for a social club's first meeting of the year (file name **xxClubMeeting-PPSA2.pptx**, with *xx* corresponding to student's initials). The student will decide on what type of club as well as the actual content of the slides. The following should be included on at least five different slides:

- Welcome everyone to the meeting.

- Summarize the events of last year.

- List the monies spent during the past year and how they were spent.

- Ask for goals for the upcoming year.

- Ask for actions to be taken before the next meeting.

The student will choose the formatting but should include the following items:

- At least two graphic images or pictures

- A design template and transition effects

- Sound or video on one slide

- Word Art

- At least one action button or hyperlink

- A header or footer

The show should run continuously in a loop and transition automatically after an appropriate amount of time.

Also look for continuity among the design template, the graphic images, the sound effect, and the content of the presentation. Students should also present the material in a clear and organized manner with no spelling or grammar errors.

Have each student present his or her slide show to the class. Since each student will select the material, the presentations will all look different.

PowerPoint
Supplemental Skills Assessment 2
Model Answer

Social Club Meeting

6/29/2012

Glenview Puzzle Club

Where people come to put things back together!

WELCOME TO
THE
2010 SEASON

What We Did in 2009

- Donated 350 puzzles for children's charities
- Took 1st place in district competition
- Took 2nd place in state competition
- Increased membership by 3%
- Had an 85% attendance average at monthly meetings

2009 Expenditures

Expense	Price
Puzzles for Children's Charities	$720.36
District Competition Expenses	400.00
State Competition Expenses	600.00
Supplies (mounting materials, frames, etc...)	200.00
Promotional Brochures	500.00
Monthly meeting expenditures	049.04
Total	$3,770.00

We Hope to Do in 2010

- Increase the number of puzzles donated to children's charities to 500.
- Repeat our win at district competition
- Take 1st place at state competition
- Take 1st, 2nd, or 3rd place at the national level
- Increase membership by 5%
- Increase average attendance to 90%

Before We Meet Again...

- Volunteers are needed to create and print 2010 promotional brochures
- Candidates are needed for new officer elections
- A vote needs to be taken on a possible increase in monthly dues

1

xxClubMeeting-PPSA2.pptx

PowerPoint
Supplemental Skills Assessment 2
Grading Rubric

Social Club Meeting

Steps	Tasks	Criterion/Criteria	Value	Score
1	**Creating Presentations**	Create presentation for a social club's first meeting of the year; add five slides that will include the following information: • Welcome everyone to the meeting • Summarize the events of the last year • List monies spent during the past year and how they were spent • Ask for goals for upcoming year • Ask for actions to be taken before next meeting	10	
2	**Formatting Presentations**	Include at least two graphic images or pictures; select a design template and transition effects; add sound or video to one slide; include WordArt; add at least one action button or hyperlink; add an appropriate header or footer	15	
3-4	**Formatting Presentations**	Set show to run continuously in a loop and transition automatically after an appropriate amount of time	4	
5	**Organization**	Save presentation as **xxClubMeeting-PPSA2.pptx**, where xx is student's initials; print slide handouts at six slides per page	1	
		TOTAL POINTS: 30		

Supplemental
Marquee Challenges

Word Section 1
Supplemental Marquee Challenge

Preparing a Memo

1. Using a template, prepare a memo to your instructor describing at least five new features that you learned about in the first section of Word. Match the look of **Features-WordS1SMC.pdf**, but write the memo using your own words.
2. Insert the current date. Also provide a descriptive subject line.
3. The memo should include at least three paragraphs.
4. Create a folder named *WordSection1*. Save the memo as **Features-WordS1SMC.docx** in the newly created folder and print it.

Word Section 1
Supplemental Marquee Challenge
Model Answer

Preparing a Memo

Memorandum

To: Instructor's Name

From: Student's Name

Date: Current Date

Re: Features in Word Section 1

A variety of features were covered in Word Section 1. The paragraph that follows includes only a few of the features that I learned in this section.

To help ensure that proper spelling and punctuation is maintained in a document, the Spelling and Grammar feature can be used. Although this feature is a wonderful tool, it should not totally replace proofreading the document. It is possible that some words may be spelled correctly but used incorrectly in the sentence. When there is a need for a synonym, antonym, or related words while composing at the keyboard, the Thesaurus can be helpful. Printing provides a hard copy of the document. Before printing a document, it is highly recommended that a print preview take place. When a document is previewed prior to printing, there is an opportunity to ensure proper formatting. Ultimately, previewing can help eliminate wasted paper.

Keep in mind that the features mentioned above are only a few of the many features that were learned in Word Section 1. There were many more discussed with great explanations.

1

Features-WordS1SMC.docx

Word Section 1
Supplemental Marquee Challenge
Grading Rubric

Preparing a Memo

Steps	Tasks	Criterion/Criteria	Value	Score
1	**Formatting**	Use memo template	2	
1-3	**Typing/Accuracy**	Type memo describing at least five new features learned in Word Section 1; insert date to update automatically; provide descriptive subject line	14	
5	**Organization**	Save memo as **Features-WordS1SMC.docx** in newly created folder named *WordSection1*	4	
		TOTAL POINTS: 20		

Word Section 2
Supplemental Marquee Challenge

Creating a Commencement Program

1. Create the commencement program as shown in **Program-WordS2SMC.pdf**.
2. Use your school's name and the appropriate year in which the next graduation ceremony will take place at your college.
3. Apply the Title style to the first two lines of the program. Then center the information.
4. Apply the Quote style to the date, time, and venue. Center the information and remove the paragraph spacing between the lines.
5. Save the document as **Program-WordS2SMC.docx**.
6. Print and then close **Program-WordS2SMC.docx**.

Word Section 2
Supplemental Marquee Challenge
Model Answer

Creating a Commencement Program

YOUR SCHOOL'S NAME
COMMENCEMENT PROGRAM FOR 20XX

Saturday, May xx, 20xx
10:00 a.m.
The Center

Processional .... Tyler Jackson

Welcome .... Andrea Pearson

Student Speaker .... Devin Jeters

Presentation of the 20xx Graduating Class .... Allison Kerr

Conferring of Diplomas .... President Joe Wright

Award Presentation .... Suzanne Richards
- Phi Theta Kappa Award .... Olivia Evans
- Alumni Foundation Award .... George Roberts
- The Pamela Gorden Award .... Kelly Lewis

Excellence in Education Award .... Elizabeth Anderson

Recessional .... Tyler Jackson

Program-WordS2MSC.docx

Word Section 2
Supplemental Marquee Challenge
Grading Rubric

Creating a Commencement Program

Steps	Tasks	Criterion/Criteria	Value	Score
1-2	**Typing/ Accuracy**	Create commencement program as shown in **Program-WordS2SMC.pdf**	10	
3-4	**Formatting**	Apply Title style to first two lines of the program; center the information; apply Quote style to the date, time, and venue; center information and remove paragraph spacing between the lines	8	
5-6	**Organization**	Save document as **Program-WordS2SMC. docx**; print the document	2	
		TOTAL POINTS: 20		

Word Section 3
Supplemental Marquee Challenge

Creating a Golf Etiquette Report

1. Create the introduction of the golf report as shown in **GolfReport-WordS3SMC.pdf**.
2. Apply the Sideline cover page. Remove all unused placeholders.
3. Choose a graphic similar to the one shown on the cover page.
4. Insert the Mod header to begin on page 2.
5. The left margin should be set to 1.5 inches.
6. Apply the Metro theme to the report.
7. In the body of the report, apply the Light Green shading to the side headings.
8. Add the Draft 1 watermark to the report.
9. Save the document as **GolfReport-WordS3SMC.docx**.
10. Print and then close **GolfReport-WordS3SMC.docx**.

Word Section 3
Supplemental Marquee Challenge
Model Answer

Creating a Golf Etiquette Report

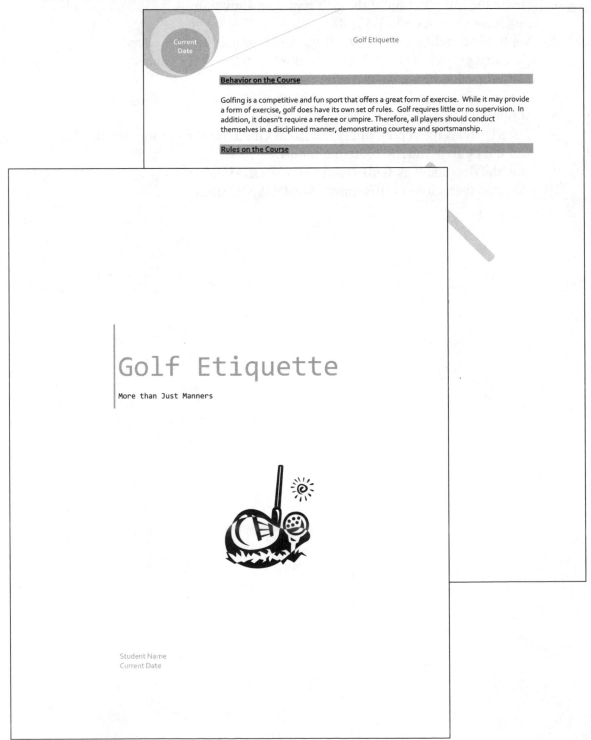

GolfReport-WordS3SMC.docx

Word Section 3
Supplemental Marquee Challenge
Grading Rubric

Creating a Golf Etiquette Report

Steps	Tasks	Criterion/Criteria	Value	Score
1	**Typing/ Accuracy**	Create introduction as shown in **GolfReport-WordS3SMC.pdf**	8	
2-8	**Formatting**	Apply the Sideline cover page; remove unused placeholders; choose similar golf graphic; insert the Mod header to appear on page 2; set left margin at 1.5 inches; apply the Metro theme; apply the Light Green shading to the side headings; add the Draft 1 watermark	10	
5-6	**Organization**	Save document as **GolfReport-WordS3SMC. docx**; print the document	2	
		TOTAL POINTS: 20		

Word Section 4
Supplemental Marquee Challenge

Creating a Mineral Newsletter

1. Create the newsletter as shown in **Minerals-WordS4SMC.pdf**.
2. Apply the font Cambria 12 to the body of the newsletter.
3. Use the Diamond basic shape in the title.
4. The drop cap should drop only two lines in the paragraph.
5. In the *Amethyst* section, hyperlink the word *quartz* to http://geology.about.com/library/bl/images/blquartz.htm.
6. Apply Light List table style to the table.
7. Save the newsletter as **Minerals-WordS4SMC.docx** and print it.
8. Save the newsletter again as a Web Page.

Word Section 4
Supplemental Marquee Challenge
Model Answer

Creating a Mineral Newsletter

In the very thin shell of the Earth's crust are found many minerals. Because of their purity, scarcity, or social value, some minerals are called gems.

Amethyst
Amethyst is the purple variety of the mineral quartz. Amethyst owes its color to the presence of iron atoms in the crystal matrix, which otherwise consists of silicon and oxygen in the proportion SiO_2.

Diamond
Diamond is the hardest mineral, number 10 in the Mohs scale of mineral hardness. This 4-millimeter specimen shows several faces of diamond's natural crystal form, which is an octahedron—imagine two pyramids joined base to base so their tips point opposite directions. The flat triangles on the diamond correspond to the faces of the octahedron. Crystallographers call them (111) faces, and they are the hardest part of the diamond. Diamond crystals usually have rounded, grooved edges as can be seen next to the flat faces.

Opal
Opal is a delicate mineral, hydrated silica or amorphous quartz. The mineral includes a fairly large amount of water molecules, and opals should not be left in direct sunlight or high temperatures.

Ruby
Ruby is just a special name for gemmy red corundum. Every other color of gem-quality corundum is called sapphire. This ruby pebble, a rock-shop specimen from India, measures about 3 centimeters in length and displays the clean hexagonal cross-section of corundum crystals. The flat face on this side is a parting plane, a break that results from a crystal weakness, in this case a plane of twinning.

The following table displays examples of minerals and where they can be found.

Mineral	Can be found in:
Amethyst	Colorado/California
Diamond	Africa
Opal	Australia
Ruby	Sri Lanka

Minerals-WordS4SMC.docx

Word Section 4
Supplemental Marquee Challenge
Grading Rubric

Creating a Mineral Newsletter

Steps	Tasks	Criterion/Criteria	Value	Score
1	**Typing/ Accuracy**	Create newsletter as shown in **Minerals-WordS4SMC.pdf**	**10**	
3-6	**Formatting**	Apply Cambia 12 pt font to the body of the newsletter; use Diamond basic shape in the title; Apply drop cap two lines in the paragraph; hyperlink the word *quartz* to http://geology.about. com/libraray/bl/images/blquartz.htm	**7**	
7-8	**Organization**	Save document as **Minerals-WordS4SMC.docx** and print it; Save the document again as a Web Page	**3**	
		TOTAL POINTS: 20		

Excel Section 1
Supplemental Marquee Challenge

Preparing an Inventory Worksheet

1. You work at the local clothing store, Yourlastname Tops and Bottoms. Prepare and format the Inventory worksheet as shown in **TopsandBottoms-ExcelS1SMC.pdf**.
2. Use appropriate formulas and functions to calculate the following items in the worksheet:
   - Total list price of each item
   - Retail price of each item
   - Total retail price of each item
   - Totals for number of items in stock, total list price, and total retail price
3. Use the Help menu to learn how to format the appropriate cells to Currency and Percent.
4. Save the worksheet as **TopsandBottoms-ExcelS1SMC.xlsx**.
5. Print and close **TopsandBottoms-ExcelS1SMC.xlsx**.

Excel Section 1
Supplemental Marquee Challenge
Model Answer

Preparing an Inventory Worksheet

YOURLASTNAME TOPS AND BOTTOMS
Inventory

Item	Number in Stock	List Price	Total List Price	Percent of Markup	Retail Price	Total Retail Price
Junior Jeans	125	$ 32.89	$ 4,111.25	15%	$ 37.82	$ 4,727.94
Men's Dress Slacks	225	29.99	6,747.75	32%	39.59	8,907.03
Women's Blouses	75	17.50	1,312.50	17%	20.48	1,535.63
T-shirts	288	11.50	3,312.00	12%	12.88	3,709.44
Children's Sweaters	168	15.00	2,520.00	8%	16.20	2,721.60
Total	881		$ 18,003.50			$ 21,601.63

TopsandBottoms-ExcelS1SMC.xlsx

Excel Section 1
Supplemental Marquee Challenge
Grading Rubric

Preparing an Inventory Worksheet

Steps	Tasks	Criterion/Criteria	Value	Score
1	**Formatting**	Prepare worksheet as shown in **TopsandBottoms-ExcelS1SMC.pdf**	6	
2	**Formulas/ Functions**	Total List Price = Number in Stock * List Price Retail Price = List Price*% of Markup + List Price Total Retail Price = Number in Stock * Retail Price Use SUM function to calculate totals for number of items in stock, total list price, and total retail price	10	
3	**Formatting**	Format appropriate cells to Currency and Percent	2	
4-5	**Organization**	Save worksheet as **TopsandBottoms-ExcelS1SMC.xlsx** and print it	2	
		TOTAL POINTS: 20		

Excel Section 2
Supplemental Marquee Challenge

Preparing an Employee Wages Worksheet

1. You are the accountant for YOURLASTNAME Print Shop. Prepare and format the Employee Wages worksheet as shown in **EmployeeWages-ExcelS2SMC_Step8.pdf**.
2. Use a formula to calculate weekly pay.
3. Use a built-in function to calculate the total hours per week and weekly pay.
4. Apply the Grid theme to the worksheet.
5. Apply the Title cell style to cells A1:D2.
6. Change the row height of rows 1 and 2 to 45.00 (60 pixels).
7. Insert a clip art image similar to the one shown on the worksheet.
8. Save the worksheet as **EmployeeWages-ExcelS2SMC.xlsx**.
9. Print **EmployeeWages-ExcelS2SMC.xlsx**.
10. Insert below Clerk 3 a new position that includes the following information:

Position	Clerk 4
Pay Rate	8.50
Hours per Week	20

    Copy the formulas to complete the remaining information for the new position (if necessary).
11. Print and close **EmployeeWages-ExcelS2SMC.xlsx**.

Excel Section 2
Supplemental Marquee Challenge
Model Answer

Preparing an Employee Wages Worksheet

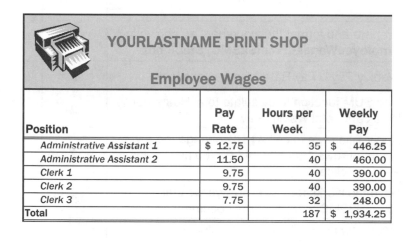

Position	Pay Rate	Hours per Week	Weekly Pay
Administrative Assistant 1	$ 12.75	35	$ 446.25
Administrative Assistant 2	11.50	40	460.00
Clerk 1	9.75	40	390.00
Clerk 2	9.75	40	390.00
Clerk 3	7.75	32	248.00
Total		187	$ 1,934.25

EmployeeWages-ExcelS2SMC_Step8.xlsx

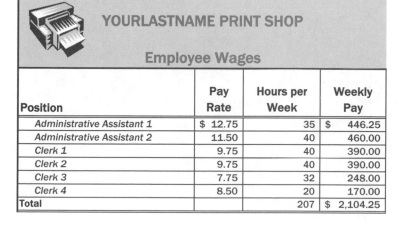

Position	Pay Rate	Hours per Week	Weekly Pay
Administrative Assistant 1	$ 12.75	35	$ 446.25
Administrative Assistant 2	11.50	40	460.00
Clerk 1	9.75	40	390.00
Clerk 2	9.75	40	390.00
Clerk 3	7.75	32	248.00
Clerk 4	8.50	20	170.00
Total		207	$ 2,104.25

EmployeeWages-ExcelS2SMC_Step11.xlsx

Excel Section 2
Supplemental Marquee Challenge
Grading Rubric

Preparing an Employee Wages Worksheet

Steps	Tasks	Criterion/Criteria	Value	Score
1	**Creating/ Formatting**	Prepare and format the worksheet as shown in **EmployeeWages-ExcelS2SMC_Step8.pdf**	7	
2	**Formulas**	Weekly Pay = Pay Rate * Hours per Week	2	
3	**Functions**	Use SUM function to calculate total Hours per Week and total Weekly Pay	2	
4-7	**Formatting**	Apply Title style to cell A1:D2; change the row height of rows 1 and 2 to 45.00 (60 pixels); insert a similar clipart	3	
8-9	**Organization**	Save the worksheet as **EmployeeWages-ExcelS2SMC.xlsx**; print the document	2	
10	**Editing**	Insert row below Clerk 3 that includes the following information: Position – Clerk 4 Pay Rate – 8.50 Hours per Week 20 Copy formula to new row	3	
11	**Printing**	Print the worksheet **EmployeeWages-ExcelS2SMC.xlsx**	1	
		TOTAL POINTS: 20		

Excel Section 3
Supplemental Marquee Challenge

Managing Data for a Loan Company

1. You work for YOURLASTNAME Lending Hands, which specializes in loaning money to first-time home buyers. Prepare and format the worksheet as shown in **LendingHands-ExcelS3SMC.pdf**.
2. Using formulas and functions to calculate the following items in the worksheet:
   - Down payment (percentage (subject to change) of home price)
   - Loan amount
   - Monthly payment
   - Average price for each type of home
3. If there are more than 15 homes available for each type of home, an ad is to be placed in the local newspaper. Use the IF function to determine whether or not a new ad is to be placed in the newspaper.
4. Prepare and format the 3-D column chart by comparing the price of each type of home as shown. Apply Chart Style 8.
5. Format the worksheet to landscape orientation and center it vertically and horizontally on the page.
6. Insert a footer at the center that includes the current date.
7. Save the worksheet as **LendingHands-ExcelS3SMC.xlsx**.
8. Print and close **LendingHand-ExcelS3SMC.xlsx**.

Excel Section 3
Supplemental Marquee Challenge
Model Answer

Managing Data for a Loan Company

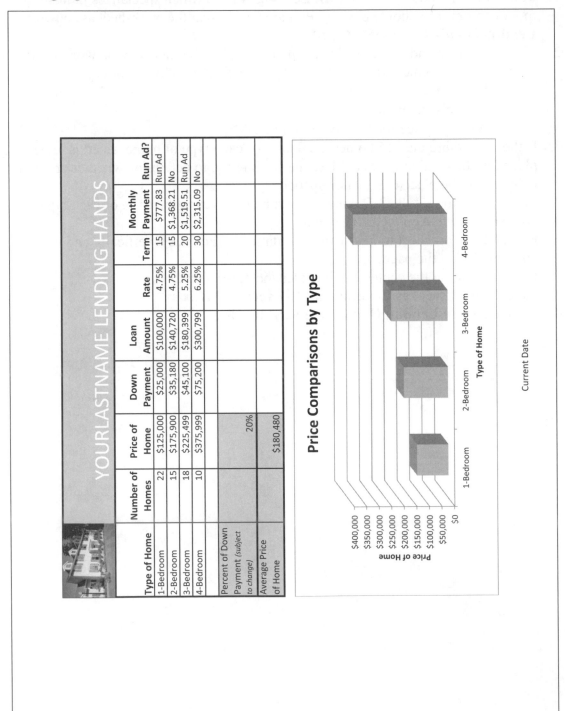

YOURLASTNAME LENDING HANDS

Type of Home	Number of Homes	Price of Home	Down Payment	Loan Amount	Rate	Term	Monthly Payment	Run Ad?
1-Bedroom	22	$125,000	$25,000	$100,000	4.75%	15	$777.83	Run Ad
2-Bedroom	15	$175,900	$35,180	$140,720	4.75%	15	$1,368.21	No
3-Bedroom	18	$225,499	$45,100	$180,399	5.25%	20	$1,519.51	Run Ad
4-Bedroom	10	$375,999	$75,200	$300,799	6.25%	30	$2,315.09	No
Percent of Down Payment *(subject to change)*		20%						
Average Price of Home		$180,480						

Price Comparisons by Type

Current Date

LendingHand-ExcelS3SMC.xlsx

Excel Section 3
Supplemental Marquee Challenge
Grading Rubric

Managing Data for a Loan Company

Steps	Tasks	Criterion/Criteria	Value	Score
1	**Creating/ Formatting**	Prepare and format the worksheet as shown in **LendingHands-ExcelS3SMC.pdf**	5	
2-3	**Formulas/ Functions**	Down Payment = Price of Home *% of Down Payment (absolute cell reference) Loan Amount= Price of Home – Down payment Use PMT function to calculate Monthly Payment USE AVERAGE function to calculate average price Use IF function to determine ad in newspaper	5	
4	**Creating/ Formatting**	Prepare and format 3-D column chart by comparing the price of each type of home as shown ; apply chart style 8; add X and Y axis titles and main chart title	5	
5	**Formatting**	Format worksheet to landscape orientation and center it vertically and horizontally on page	3	
6	**Formatting**	Insert a footer at the center that includes the current date	1	
7-8	**Organization**	Save worksheet as **LendingHands-ExcelS3SMC.xlsx** and print it	1	
		TOTAL POINTS: 20		

Excel Section 4
Supplemental Marquee Challenge

Using 3-D Cell References to Calculate First Quarter Sales

1. Prepare the worksheets as shown below. All sheets should appear the same with exception of the actual sales in each sheet.

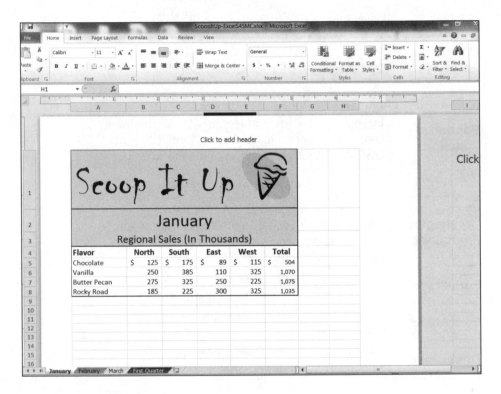

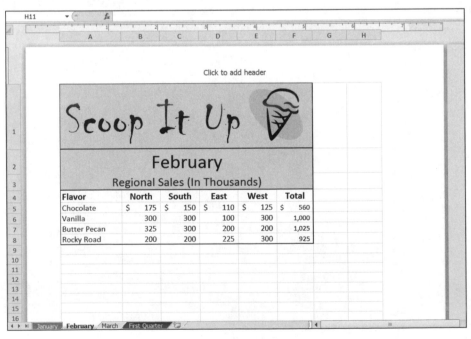

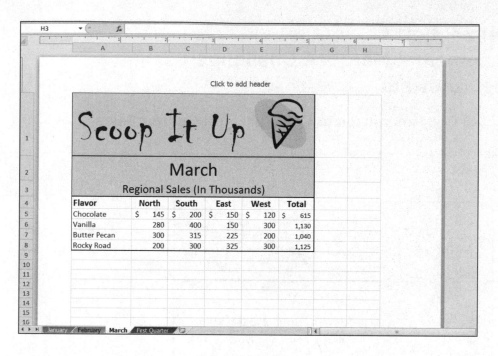

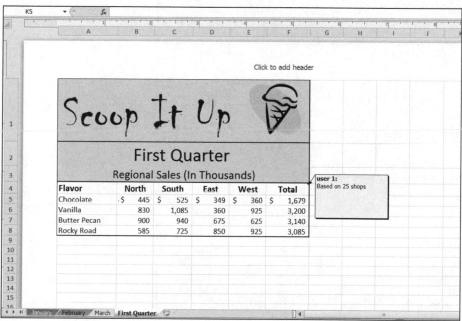

2. Name and color the sheet tabs appropriately.
3. In the First Quarter sheet, use the 3-D cell reference formulas to calculate the total sales for each of the regions and for each flavor of ice cream.
4. In the First Quarter sheet, add the comment *Based on 25 shops* to the cell that contains the Total label. Set the comment to display on the sheet when it is printed.
5. Format the First Quarter sheet to print in landscape orientation and vertically and horizontally centered.
6. Save the worksheet as **ScoopItUp-ExcelS4SMC.xlsx**.
7. Print the entire workbook **ScoopItUp-ExcelS4SMC.xlsx**.

Excel Section 4
Supplemental Marquee Challenge
Model Answers

Using 3-D Cell References to Calculate First Quarter Sales

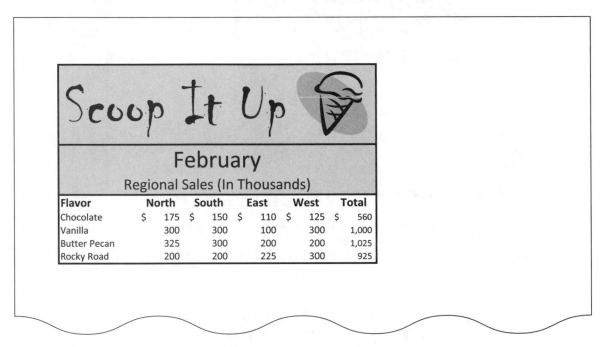

ScoopItUp-ExcelS4SMC.xlsx

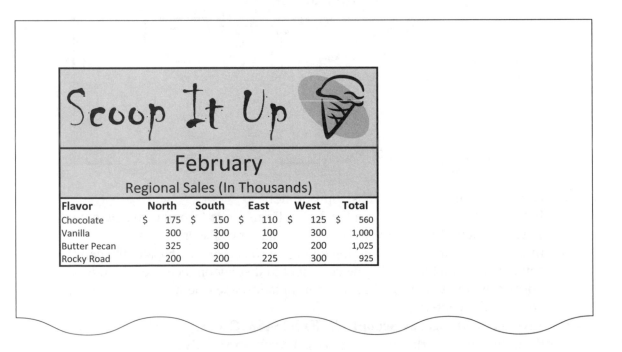

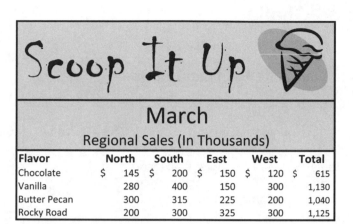

March

Regional Sales (In Thousands)

Flavor	North	South	East	West	Total
Chocolate	$ 145	$ 200	$ 150	$ 120	$ 615
Vanilla	280	400	150	300	1,130
Butter Pecan	300	315	225	200	1,040
Rocky Road	200	300	325	300	1,125

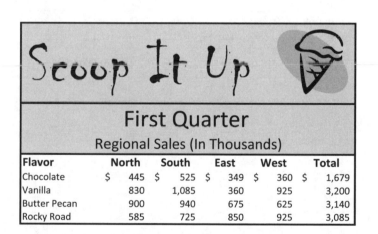

First Quarter

Regional Sales (In Thousands)

Flavor	North	South	East	West	Total
Chocolate	$ 445	$ 525	$ 349	$ 360	$ 1,679
Vanilla	830	1,085	360	925	3,200
Butter Pecan	900	940	675	625	3,140
Rocky Road	585	725	850	925	3,085

Excel Section 4
Supplemental Marquee Challenge
Grading Rubric

Using 3-D Cell References to Calculate First Quarter Sales

Steps	Tasks	Criterion/Criteria	Value	Score
1-2	**Creating/ Formatting**	On all sheets - merge and center title; insert graphic; bold column titles; format currency and comma styles; name and color sheet tabs appropriately	10	
3	**Functions**	Insert 3-D cell reference formulas to calculate the total sales for each of the regions and for each flavor of ice cream	4	
4	**Formatting**	Add comment *Based on 25 shops* to the Total label cell; set comment to display on the sheet when printed	2	
5	**Formatting**	Format the First Quarter sheet to print in landscape orientation and vertically and horizontally centered	2	
6-7	**Organization**	Save workbook as **ScoopItUp-ExcelS4SMC.xlsx** and print the entire workbook	2	
		TOTAL POINTS: 20		

Access Section 1
Supplemental Marquee Challenge

Maintaining Data in a Database

1. You have been asked to maintain the JustShoes database for your local shoe store, Just Shoes.
2. Open the **JustShoes-AccessS1SMC.accdb** database and enable the content. (File is available in the DataFile folder in the Instructor Resources CD.)
3. A new pair of black Nike running shoes just arrived. They are size 8 and priced at 79.99. Add the information to the Shoe Inventory form.
4. A customer has entered the store and wants to know what type of Nike or Adidas shoes are available. Use the appropriate feature to provide the customer with an answer. Sort the records in alphabetical order by brand. Print out the results.
5. Display all of the records (if necessary).
6. Move the *Price* field so that it appears to the right of the *Size* field.
7. A customer purchased the green pair of size 10 Puma walking shoes, priced at $48.99. Make the necessary adjustments to the table.
8. Hide the *ID* column.
9. Print the results.
10. Save and close **JustShoes-AccessS1SMC.accdb**.

Access Section 1
Supplemental Marquee Challenge
Model Answer

Maintaining Data in a Database

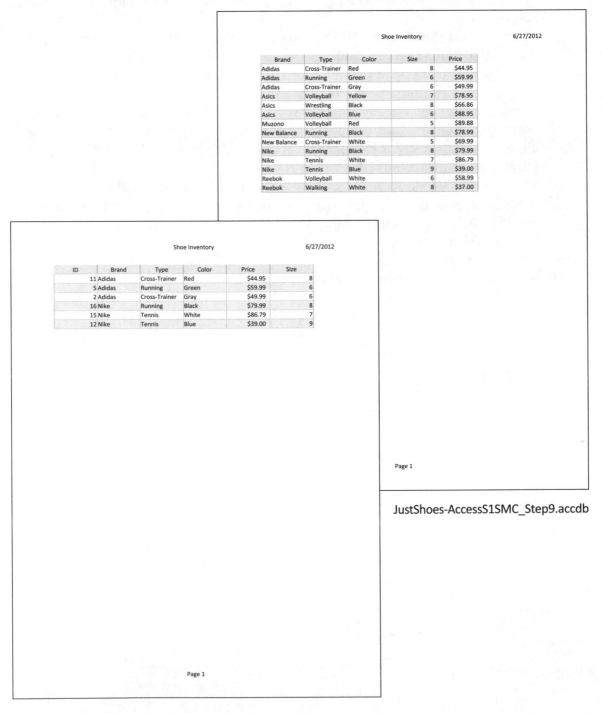

Shoe Inventory — 6/27/2012

Brand	Type	Color	Size	Price
Adidas	Cross-Trainer	Red	8	$44.95
Adidas	Running	Green	6	$59.99
Adidas	Cross-Trainer	Gray	6	$49.99
Asics	Volleyball	Yellow	7	$78.95
Asics	Wrestling	Black	8	$66.86
Asics	Volleyball	Blue	6	$88.95
Muzono	Volleyball	Red	5	$89.88
New Balance	Running	Black	8	$78.99
New Balance	Cross-Trainer	White	5	$69.99
Nike	Running	Black	8	$79.99
Nike	Tennis	White	7	$86.79
Nike	Tennis	Blue	9	$39.00
Reebok	Volleyball	White	6	$58.99
Reebok	Walking	White	8	$37.00

Page 1

JustShoes-AccessS1SMC_Step9.accdb

Shoe Inventory — 6/27/2012

ID	Brand	Type	Color	Price	Size
11	Adidas	Cross-Trainer	Red	$44.95	8
5	Adidas	Running	Green	$59.99	6
2	Adidas	Cross-Trainer	Gray	$49.99	6
16	Nike	Running	Black	$79.99	8
15	Nike	Tennis	White	$86.79	7
12	Nike	Tennis	Blue	$39.00	9

Page 1

JustShoes-AccessS1SMC_Step4.accdb

Access Section 1
Supplemental Marquee Challenge
Grading Rubric

Maintaining Data in a Database

Steps	Tasks	Criterion/Criteria	Value	Score
3	**Adding Record**	Add new record to Shoe Inventory Form: Brand, Nike; Type, Running; Color, Black; Size, 8; and Price, 79.99	5	
4	**Filtering/ Sorting**	Apply filter to show Nike or Adidas shoes; sort in ascending order; print results	6	
5	**Formatting**	Remove filter; display all records	2	
6	**Formatting**	Move *Price* field so that it appears to the right of the *Size* field	2	
7	**Deleting Record**	Delete record: Brand, Puma; Type, Walking; Color, Green; Size, 10; Price, 48.99	2	
8-9	**Formatting/ Printing**	Hide *ID* column; print results	2	
9-10	**Organization**	Save and close **JustShoes-AccessS1SMC. accdb**	1	
		TOTAL POINTS: 20		

Access Section 2
Supplemental Marquee Challenge

Creating Tables and Relationships in a Database

1. You have been hired by the Tri-State Dental Group to create a database for its office.
2. Consider the following information.

Dentist Information:	Patient Information:
• Dentist ID (example 100, 101, etc.) • First Name • Last Name • Specialty: Dentures, Capping, Filling, Plastic Sealants, Children, Seniors • Dental Hygienists: Jordan Allen, Lindsey Erikson, Kate Bentley, Danielle Anderson, and Elizabeth Karey It is important to keep track of the dentists' schedules as well. The dentists are either considered full-time or part-time.	• Patient ID (example 100, 101, etc.) • Dentist ID • First Name • Last Name • Street Address • City, State, and ZIP • Phone Number • Health Insurance (Yes/No) • Date of Last Visit • Next Scheduled Visit • Fee Charged

3. Create a database named **Tri-StateDentalGroup-AccessS2SMC.accdb**.
4. Use the information above to create two tables. Name the tables appropriately. The tables should be designed so that information can be taken from both of them to create queries, forms, and reports. *Hint: A relationship will need to be created.*
5. When adding fields to the table, determine the appropriate field names, data types, and field sizes. Use input masks, data validation, lookup lists, etc., to restrict data and to ensure consistency, accuracy, and reliability between and within the tables.
6. Print a relationship report.
7. Save and close **Tri-StateDentalGroup-AccessS2SMC.accdb**.

Access Section 2
Supplemental Marquee Challenge
Model Answer

Creating Tables and Relationships in a Database

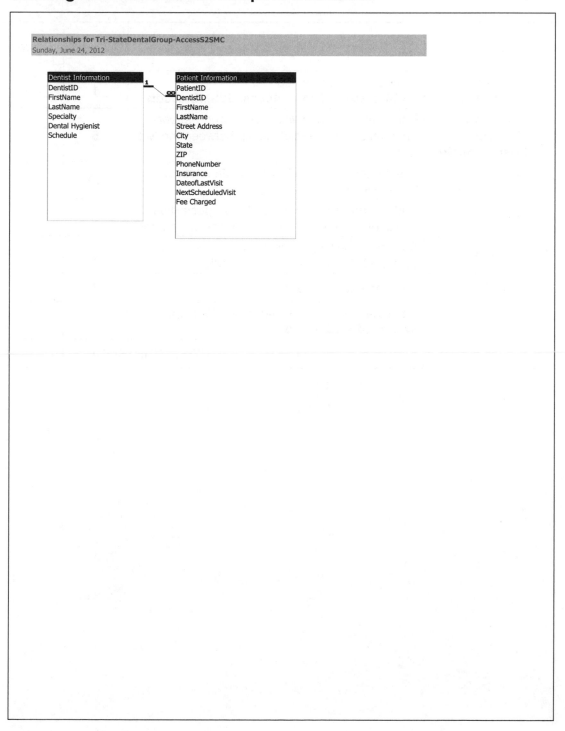

Relationships-AccessS2SMC_Step6

Access Section 2
Supplemental Marquee Challenge
Grading Rubric

Creating Tables and Relationships in a Database

Steps	Tasks	Criterion/Criteria	Value	Score
3	**Creating Database**	Create database named **Tri-StateDentalGroup-AccessS2SMC.accdb**	1	
4	**Creating Tables/ Relationships**	Name tables *Dentist Information* and *Patient Information*; create relationship between the two tables	5	
4	**Creating/ Formatting**	Assign appropriate field names, data types, and fields sizes to both tables	10	
5	**Formatting**	Add lookup wizard to the dentists' specialities and schedules and the dental hygienists' names	6	
5	**Formatting**	Add input mask to Phone Number, Date of Last Visit, and Next Scheduled Visit fields	6	
6	**Printing**	Print the relationship report	1	
7	**Organization**	Save the database **Tri-StateDentalGroup-AccessS2SMC.accdb**	1	
		TOTAL POINTS: 30		

Access Section 3
Supplemental Marquee Challenge

Creating Queries, Forms, and Reports for Tri-State Dental Group

1. You have been asked by the Tri-State Dental Group to create queries, forms, and reports from their database.
2. Open **Tri-StateDentalGroup-AccessS2SMC.accdb** and enable the content. Save the file as **Tri-StateDentalGroup-AccessS3SMC**.
3. Create a query that displays patients whose next scheduled visits are before 11/1/11. The results should display the patients' first and last names, the dates of the visits, and the last name of their dentists. Sort the query results by patients' last names. Name the query *Next Visit*.
4. Patients who have insurance are responsible for paying the deductible amount. Letters are sent to these patients indicating the deductible amount owed to Tri-State Dental Group. Create a query that lists the patient's first and last names, address, city, state, ZIP, fee charged, and the deductible amount. All deductibles are 10% of the fee charged. Format all fields appropriately. ***Note: It is assumed that all patients who have insurance have the same type of insurance and the same deductible.*** Save the query as **Deductibles**. Print the results in landscape orientation.
5. Create an attractive form that includes the patients who have insurance. Include all of the fields in the Patient Information table except the insurance field. ***Hint: A query may be necessary.*** You determine the layout, style, and form design. Include an appropriate title. Add and position the current date below the title. Name the form **Patients Covered by Insurance**.
6. Modify the Next Visit query by removing the criteria. Save the new query as **Upcoming Visits**. Then create an attractive report based on the new query. You determine the layout, style, and report design. Add the logo image **Tri-State.jpg** to the top of the report and resize, if necessary. Remove the page number (if necessary). Format the report appropriately. Save the report as *Patients' Upcoming Visits*. Print the report in landscape orientation.

Access Section 3
Supplemental Marquee Challenge
Model Answer

Creating Queries, Forms, and Reports for Tri-State Dental Group

	Next Visit		6/27/2012

Patient First Name	Patient Last Name	Next Scheduled Visit	Dentist Last Name
Laura	King	9/8/2011	Garrison
Kurt	Lovelace	7/21/2011	Schutt
Candace	Lowes	8/15/2011	Peterson
David	Miller	10/22/2011	Evans
Tara	White	10/15/2011	Schutt

NextVisit_Step3

	Deductibles		6/27/2012

FirstName	LastName	Street Address	City	State	Zip	Fee Charged	Deductible Amount
Alex	Allen	120 Eastland Estates	Newburgh	IN	47653	$75.00	$7.50
Candace	Lowes	P.O. Box 89	Evansville	IN	47715	$55.00	$5.50
Corey	Alexander	9000 Carrington Drive	Evansville	IN	47711	$225.00	$22.50
Jonathan	Kemmerer	10 Oak Street	Mt. Vernon	IL	62864	$135.00	$13.50
Jacob	Peeks	1985 Allen Lane	Evansville	IN	47710	$75.00	$7.50
Tammy	Forrester	P.O. Box 3005	Newburgh	IN	47653	$335.00	$33.50
Tara	White	200 Bentley Drive	Henderson	KY	42420	$85.00	$8.50
David	Miller	42 South Main	Evansville	IN	47714	$115.00	$11.50
Laura	King	555 Landon Court	Henderson	KY	42419	$225.00	$22.50
Kurt	Lovelace	9220 E. Deer Lane	Newburgh	IN	47653	$125.00	$12.50

Page 1

Deductibles_Step4

Patients Covered by Insurance

Thursday, August 09, 2012

PatientID	500
DentistID	100
FirstName	Alex
LastName	Allen
Street Address	120 Eastland Estates
City	Newburgh
State	IN
Zip	47653
PhoneNumber	(812) 853-4564
DateofLastVisit	6/16/2010
NextScheduledVisit	12/16/2011
Fee Charged	$75.00

PatientID	502
DentistID	104
FirstName	Corey
LastName	Alexander
Street Address	9000 Carrington Drive
City	Evansville
State	IN
Zip	47711
PhoneNumber	(812) 457-6545
DateofLastVisit	4/5/2010

NextScheduledVisit	11/14/2011
Fee Charged	$225.00

PatientID	503
DentistID	108
FirstName	Jonathan
LastName	Kemmerer
Street Address	10 Oak Street
City	Mt. Vernon
State	IL
Zip	62864
PhoneNumber	(812) 882-1236
DateofLastVisit	5/15/2010
NextScheduledVisit	12/8/2011
Fee Charged	$135.00

PatientID	506
DentistID	103
FirstName	Tara
LastName	White
Street Address	200 Bentley Drive
City	Henderson
State	KY
Zip	42420
PhoneNumber	(270) 558-5454
DateofLastVisit	2/16/2010

NextScheduledVisit	7/21/2011
Fee Charged	$125.00

NextScheduledVisit	10/15/2011
Fee Charged	$85.00
PatientID	507
DentistID	107
FirstName	David
LastName	Miller
Street Address	42 South Main
City	Evansville
State	IN
Zip	47714
PhoneNumber	(812) 429-6661
DateofLastVisit	1/21/2010
NextScheduledVisit	10/22/2011
Fee Charged	$115.00
PatientID	509
DentistID	103
FirstName	Kurt
LastName	Lovelace
Street Address	9220 E. Deer Lane
City	Newburgh
State	IN
Zip	47653
PhoneNumber	(812) 858-6456
DateofLastVisit	4/12/2010

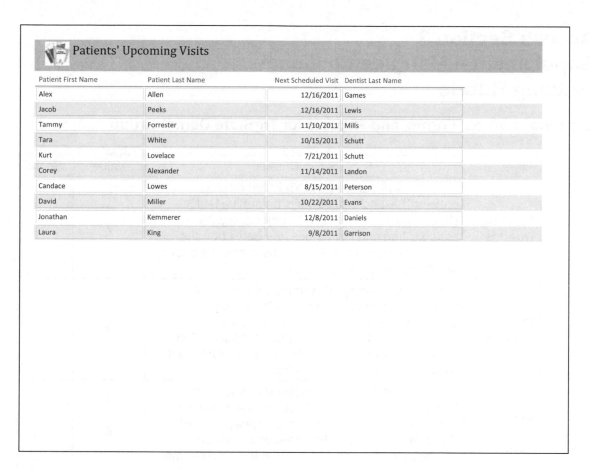

Patients' Upcoming Visits

Patient First Name	Patient Last Name	Next Scheduled Visit	Dentist Last Name
Alex	Allen	12/16/2011	Games
Jacob	Peeks	12/16/2011	Lewis
Tammy	Forrester	11/10/2011	Mills
Tara	White	10/15/2011	Schutt
Kurt	Lovelace	7/21/2011	Schutt
Corey	Alexander	11/14/2011	Landon
Candace	Lowes	8/15/2011	Peterson
David	Miller	10/22/2011	Evans
Jonathan	Kemmerer	12/8/2011	Daniels
Laura	King	9/8/2011	Garrison

Patients'UpcomingVisits_Step6

Access Section 3
Supplemental Marquee Challenge
Grading Rubric

Creating Queries, Forms, and Reports for Tri-State Dental Group

Steps	Tasks	Criterion/Criteria	Value	Score
3	**Creating Queries**	Create query named **Next Visit** that displays patients' next scheduled visits before 11/1/11 (Criterion should be# <11/1/10#); display the patients' first and last names, the dates of visits, and the last names of their dentists; sort the query results by patients' last names	7	
4	**Creating Queries**	Create query named **Deductibles** that displays patient's first and last names, address, city, state, ZIP, fee charged, and the deductible amount (Calculation: **Deductible Amount: [Fee Charged]*.10**); format fields appropriately; format results in landscape orientation	7	
5	**Creating Queries/ Forms**	Create query that includes patients who have insurance; include all fields except the insurance field; create a form, based on the query, named **Patients Covered by Insurance;** include an appropriate title; add and position the current date below the title	8	
6	**Updating Queries/ Creating Reports**	Modify *Next Visit* query by removing criteria; save new query as **Upcoming Visits**; create attractive report based on new query; add logo **Tri-State. jpg** to top of report and resize (if necessary); remove page number (if necessary); save report as *Patients' Upcoming Visits;* print report in landscape orientation	8	
		TOTAL POINTS: 30		

Access Section 4
Supplemental Marquee Challenge

Summarizing, Querying, and Displaying Information for FitnessNFun

1. You have been asked by the FitnessNFun health club to summarize and query data in their database. In addition, you will edit forms and create calculations in a report.

2. Open **FitnessNFun-AccessS4SMC.accdb** and enable the content.

3. The manager would like to see the total, average, highest, and lowest salaries for each of the trainers by expertise. Create a new query named *Trainers' Salaries* that provides this information to the manager. ***Hint: Use aggregate functions.***

4. A letter will be sent to all members encouraging them to attend the 10th Annual Fitness Fair. To avoid sending duplicate letters, it is necessary to determine whether or not members have been entered more than one time. Use the appropriate query to find records (members) that have been entered more than once. The results should show all of the information relating to the members. Save the query as *Fitness Fair*.

5. It is the manager's desire that every member be assigned a trainer. Use the appropriate query to determine whether or not all members have been assigned a trainer. Name the query *Missing Trainers*.

6. Add the label containing the text *After adding a new member, please sort the list.* to the Member Information form. Position the label at the bottom of the form below the *Trainer ID* field. Then sort the list in alphabetical order by members' last names. Save the form.

7. Open the Trainer Information report. The *Trainer ID* field is no longer needed; delete it. Within each expertise group, sort the trainers' last names in alphabetical order. In addition, all of the trainers will be given a 3% bonus. Add a field named *Annual Salary with Bonus* that shows the total amount the trainer will receive after the bonus. Position the field to the right of *Annual Salary*. Format the new field appropriately. Save the report again.

Access Section 4
Supplemental Marquee Challenge
Model Answer

Summarizing, Querying, and Displaying Information for FitnessNFun

Trainers' Salaries   8/9/2012

Expertise	Total Annual Salary	Average Annual Salary	Highest Annual Salary	Loweset Annual Salary
Aerobic	$54,850.00	$27,425.00	$27,850.00	$27,000.00
Swimming	$59,000.00	$29,500.00	$30,500.00	$28,500.00
Tennis	$94,450.00	$31,483.33	$32,500.00	$30,200.00
Weights	$83,500.00	$27,833.33	$31,000.00	$23,000.00

Page 1

Trainers'Salaries_Step3

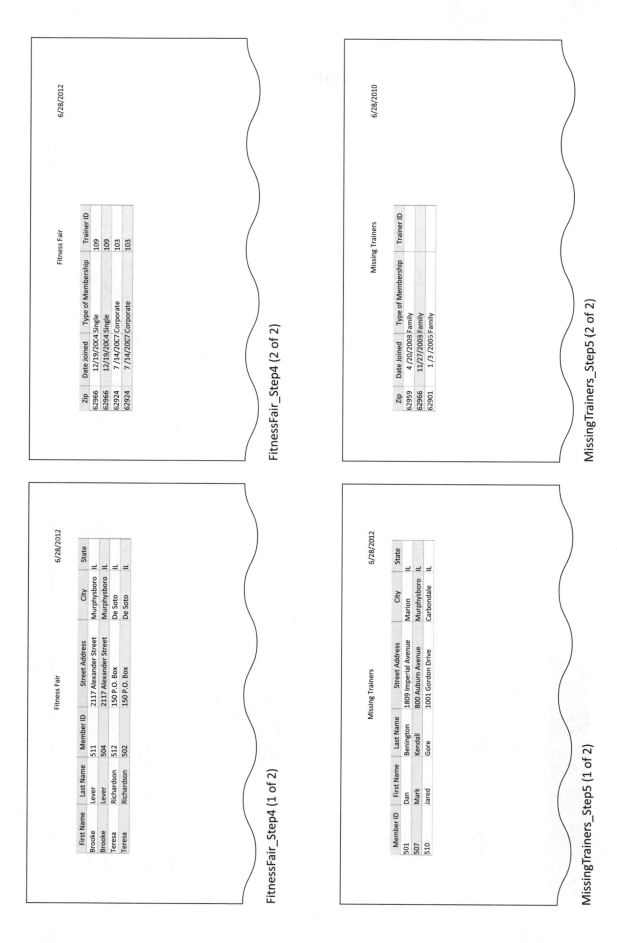

Fitness Fair   6/28/2012

First Name	Last Name	Member ID	Street Address	City	State
Brooke	Lever	511	2117 Alexander Street	Murphysboro	IL
Brooke	Lever	504	2117 Alexander Street	Murphysboro	IL
Teresa	Richardson	512	150 P.O. Box	De Soto	IL
Teresa	Richardson	502	150 P.O. Box	De Soto	IL

FitnessFair_Step4 (1 of 2)

Fitness Fair   6/28/2012

Zip	Date Joined	Type of Membership	Trainer ID
62966	12/19/2004	Single	109
62966	12/19/2004	Single	109
62924	7/14/2007	Corporate	103
62924	7/14/2007	Corporate	103

FitnessFair_Step4 (2 of 2)

Missing Trainers   5/28/2012

Member ID	First Name	Last Name	Street Address	City	State
501	Dan	Benington	1809 Imperial Avenue	Marion	IL
507	Mark	Kendall	800 Auburn Avenue	Murphysboro	IL
510	Jared	Gore	1001 Gordon Drive	Carbondale	IL

MissingTrainers_Step5 (1 of 2)

Missing Trainers   6/28/2010

Zip	Date Joined	Type of Membership	Trainer ID
62959	4/20/2003	Family	
62966	11/27/2003	Family	
62901	1/3/2005	Family	

MissingTrainers_Step5 (2 of 2)

Member Information

Member ID: 501
First Name: Dan
Last Name: Benington
Street Address: 1809 Imperial Avenue
City: Marion
State: IL
Zip: 62959
Date Joined: 4/20/2008
Type of Membership: Family
Trainer ID:

After adding a new member, please sort the list.

Member ID: 505
First Name: Kate
Last Name: Clark
Street Address: 100 N. 3rd Street
City: Marion
State: IL
Zip: 62959
Date Joined: 9/8/2005
Type of Membership: Corporate
Trainer ID: 102

After adding a new member, please sort the list.

Member ID: 510
First Name: Jared
Last Name: Gore

Street Address: 1001 Gordon Drive
City: Carbondale
State: IL
Zip: 62901
Date Joined: 1/3/2006
Type of Membership: Family
Trainer ID:

After adding a new member, please sort the list.

Member ID: 503
First Name: Nick
Last Name: Hardesty
Street Address: 200 S Grand Avenue
City: Carbondale
State: IL
Zip: 62901
Date Joined: 8/20/2006
Type of Membership: Single
Trainer ID: 107

After adding a new member, please sort the list.

Member ID: 500
First Name: Jessica
Last Name: Jackson
Street Address: 190 East 4th Street
City: Carbondale
State: IL
Zip: 62901
Date Joined: 2/18/2008
Type of Membership: Single

Trainer ID: 101

After adding a new member, please sort the list.

Member ID: 507
First Name: Mark
Last Name: Kendall
Street Address: 800 Auburn Avenue
City: Murphysboro
State: IL
Zip: 62966
Date Joined: 11/27/2008
Type of Membership: Family
Trainer ID:

After adding a new member, please sort the list.

Member ID: 511
First Name: Brooke
Last Name: Lever
Street Address: 2117 Alexander Street
City: Murphysboro
State: IL
Zip: 62966
Date Joined: 12/19/2004
Type of Membership: Single
Trainer ID: 109

After adding a new member, please sort the list.

Member ID: 504
First Name: Brooke

Last Name: Lever
Street Address: 2117 Alexander Street
City: Murphysboro
State: IL
Zip: 62966
Date Joined: 12/19/2004
Type of Membership: Single
Trainer ID: 109

After adding a new member, please sort the list.

Member ID: 506
First Name: Jacob
Last Name: Lewis
Street Address: 9494 Panther Creek Drive
City: De Soto
State: IL
Zip: 62924
Date Joined: 6/1/2004
Type of Membership: Single
Trainer ID: 103

After adding a new member, please sort the list.

Member ID: 512
First Name: Teresa
Last Name: Richardson
Street Address: 150 P.O. Box
City: De Soto
State: IL
Zip: 62924
Date Joined: 7/14/2007

Type of Membership:	Corporate
Trainer ID:	103

After adding a new member, please sort the list.

Member ID:	502
First Name:	Teresa
Last Name:	Richardson
Street Address:	150 P.O. Box
City:	De Soto
State:	IL
Zip:	62924
Date Joined:	7 /14/2007
Type of Membership:	Corporate
Trainer ID:	103

After adding a new member, please sort the list.

Member ID:	508
First Name:	Amy
Last Name:	Sanders
Street Address:	407 S. Carrell Street
City:	Marion
State:	IL
Zip:	62959
Date Joined:	3 /5 /2007
Type of Membership:	Single
Trainer ID:	100

After adding a new member, please sort the list.

Member ID:	509

First Name:	Tim
Last Name:	White
Street Address:	118 Washington Street
City:	Marion
State:	IL
Zip:	62959
Date Joined:	8 /8 /2007
Type of Membership:	Corporate
Trainer ID:	105

After adding a new member, please sort the list.

Trainer Information

Expertise	First Name	Last Name	Annual Salary	Annual Salary with Bonus
Aerobic				
	Cierra	Williams	$27,000.00	$27,810.00
	Vicki	Likert	$27,850.00	$28,685.50
Swimming				
	Landon	Nelson	$28,500.00	$29,355.00
	Stephanie	Garrett	$30,500.00	$31,415.00
Tennis				
	Alison	Johnson	$32,500.00	$33,475.00
	Felicia	Reed	$31,750.00	$32,702.50
	Megan	George	$30,200.00	$31,106.00
Weights				
	Clayton	Parrish	$31,000.00	$31,930.00
	David	Denton	$23,000.00	$23,690.00
	Andrew	Patterson	$29,500.00	$30,385.00

Monday, June 28, 2010

TrainerInformation_Step7

Access Section 4
Supplemental Marquee Challenge
Grading Rubric

Summarizing, Querying, and Displaying Information for FitnessNFun

Steps	Tasks	Criterion/Criteria	Value	Score
3	**Creating Queries**	Create query named *Trainer's Salary* to include the aggregate functions SUM, AVERAGE, MAX, and MIN to display the total, average, highest, and lowest salaries for each of the trainer by expertise	5	
4	**Creating Queries**	Create query named *Fitness Fair* to find records (members) that have been entered more than once	5	
5	**Creating Queries**	Create query named *Missing Trainers* to determine whether or not all members have been assigned a trainer	5	
6	**Modifying Forms**	Edit *Member Information* form: add label containing the text *After adding a new member, please sort the list.;* position label at the bottom of form below the *Trainer ID* field; sort the list in alphabetical order by members' last names; save the form	5	
7	**Modifying Reports**	Edit *Trainer Information* report: delete *Trainer ID* field; sort trainers' last name in alphabetical order; add field to the right of *Annual Salary* field named *Salary with Bonus* that will calculate 3% bonus =**[Annual Salary]*.03+[Annual Salary];** format new field to Currency	10	
		TOTAL POINTS: 30		

PowerPoint Section 1
Supplemental Marquee Challenge

Promoting Accounting on Your Campus

1. You have been hired as a recruiter for your college. You will create the presentation as shown in **Accounting-PPS1SMC.pdf** to be used as you promote the Accounting degree on your campus.
2. Apply the appropriate design theme and slide layouts. Size, move, and remove placeholders, if necessary.
3. Add transitions to each of the slides.
4. Add an appropriate sound to at least one of the slides.
5. Move the *Internships* slide so that it appears after the *Financial Aid* slide.
6. Print the presentation with all of the slides on one page.
7. Save the presentation as **Accounting-PPS1SMC.pptx**.

PowerPoint Section 1
Supplemental Marquee Challenge
Model Answer

Promoting Accounting on Your Campus

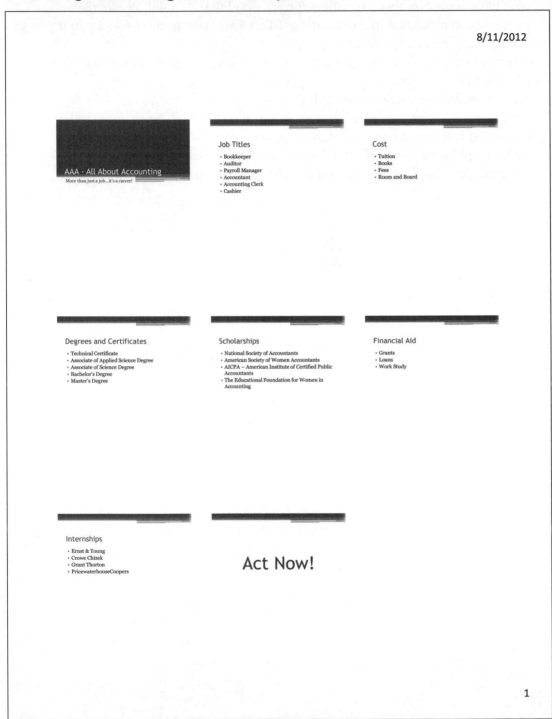

Accounting-PPS1SMC.pptx

PowerPoint Section 1
Supplemental Marquee Challenge
Grading Rubric

Promoting Accounting on Your Campus

Steps	Tasks	Criterion/Criteria	Value	Score
1	**Creating Presentations**	Create presentation as shown in **Accounting-PPS1SMC.pdf**	10	
2	**Formatting**	Apply slide layouts appropriately; apply Urban design theme	4	
3	**Formatting**	Add transitions to each slide	4	
4	**Formatting**	Add appropriate sound to at least one of the slides	2	
5	**Organization**	Move the Internships slide so that it appears after the Financial Aid slide	2	
6	**Printing**	Print presentation with all of slides on one page	2	
7	**Organization**	Save presentation as **Accounting-PPS1SMC.pptx**	1	
		TOTAL POINTS: 25		

PowerPoint Section 2
Supplemental Marquee Challenge

Promoting FitnessNFun Health Club

1. You are having a grand opening at your local health club, FitnessNFun. Create the presentation as shown in **FitnessNFun.pdf** to be used at a city-wide health fair. Save it as **FitnessNFun-PPS2SMC.pptx**.
2. Choose and apply a design theme, theme color, and theme font of your choice. Make necessary adjustments.
3. Insert similar images on the slide shown, or you may choose and insert appropriate images to other slides.
4. Apply custom animation to at least three slides.
5. Save the presentation again and print it as a handout with six slides per page.

PowerPoint Section 2
Supplemental Marquee Challenge
Model Answer

Promoting FitnessNFun Health Club

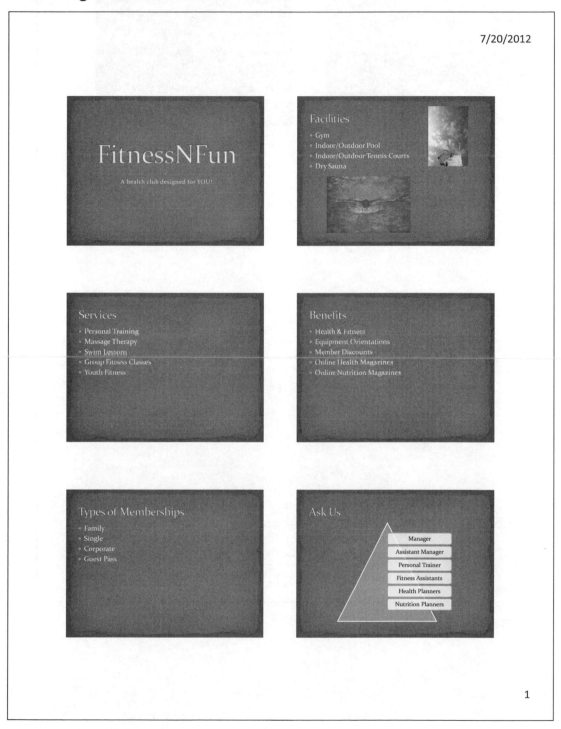

FitnessNFun-PPS2SMC.pptx (1 of 2)

2

FitnessNFun-PPS2SMC.pptx (2 of 2)

PowerPoint Section 2
Supplemental Marquee Challenge
Grading Rubric

Promoting FitnessNFun Health Club

Steps	Tasks	Criterion/Criteria	Value	Score
1	**Creating Presentations**	Create presentation named **FitnessNFun.pdf**	8	
2	**Formatting**	Apply an appropriate design theme, theme color, and theme font	5	
3	**Formatting**	Apply SmartArt Diagram on the *Ask Us* slide; insert at least two other appropriate images	10	
4	**Formatting**	Add custom animations to at least three slides	6	
5	**Organization**	Save the presentation as **FitnessNFun-PPS2SMC.pptx**	1	
		TOTAL POINTS: 30		

PowerPoint Section 3
Supplemental Marquee Challenge

Marketing Your Coffee Shop

1. You plan to market your newly opened coffee shop, Café Shop and More. You've decided that one way to market the coffee shop is to create a presentation that can be placed at a kiosk in your local mall. Create the presentation as shown in **CafeShopandMore-PPS3SMC.pdf** and save it as **CafeShopandMore-PPS3SMC.pptx**.
2. The buttons on Slides 2 and 7 are action buttons hyperlinked to the related slides.
3. On Slide 6, a text box was used to insert the asterisk notation.
4. Add an appropriate sound or video to at least one slide.
5. Save the presentation again, and print it as a handout with six slides per page.

PowerPoint Section 3
Supplemental Marquee Challenge
Model Answer

Marketing Your Coffee Shop

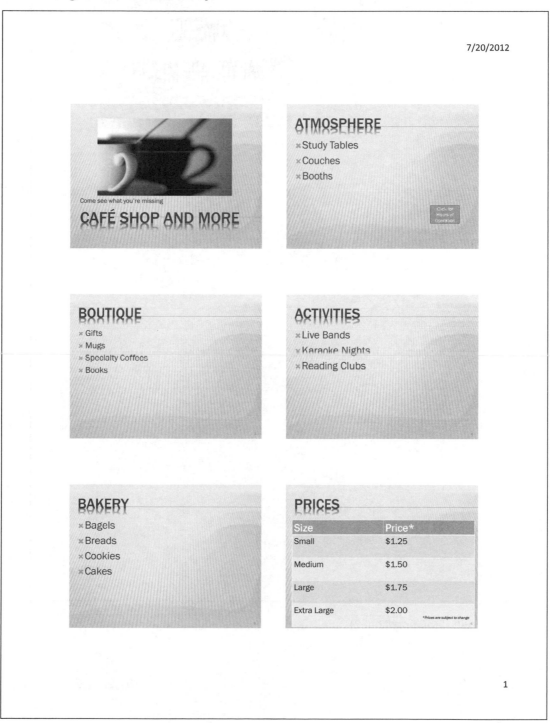

CafeShopandMore-PPS3SMC.pptx (1 of 2)

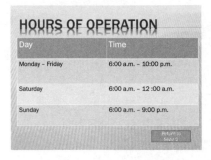

2

CafeShopandMore-PPS3SMC.pptx (2 of 2)

PowerPoint Section 3
Supplemental Marquee Challenge
Grading Rubric

Marketing Your Coffee Shop

Steps	Tasks	Criterion/Criteria	Value	Score
1	**Creating Presentations/ Formatting**	Create presentation as shown in **CafeShopandMore-PPS3SMC.pdf**; use WordArt on last slide; add page numbers to lower right corner of all slides except the title slide (footer); set presentation to run automatically at a kiosk	15	
2	**Formatting**	Add action buttons on Slides 2 and 7 that are hyperlinked to related slides	6	
3	**Formatting**	On slide 6, add text box that includes the asterisk notation	4	
4	**Formatting**	Add an appropriate sound or video to at least one slide	2	
5	**Organization**	Save presentation as **CafeShopandMore-PPS3SMC.pptx**; print it as a handout with six slides per page	3	
		TOTAL POINTS: 30		